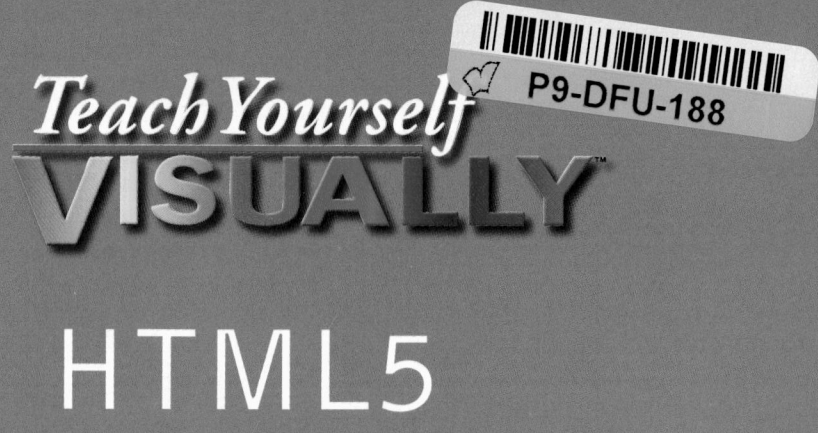

Teach Yourself VISUALLY™

HTML5

Visual™

by Mike Wooldridge

WILEY

John Wiley & Sons, Inc.

Teach Yourself VISUALLY™ HTML5

Published by
John Wiley & Sons, Inc.
10475 Crosspoint Boulevard
Indianapolis, IN 46256

www.wiley.com

Published simultaneously in Canada

Wiley also publishes its books in a variety of electronic formats and by print-on-demand. Some content that appears in standard print versions of this book may not be available in other formats. For more information about Wiley products, visit us at www.wiley.com.

Library of Congress Control Number: The Library of Congress number is available from the Library of Congress.

ISBN: 978-1-118-06332-3

Manufactured in the United States of America

10 9 8 7 6 5 4 3 2 1

Trademark Acknowledgments

Contact Us

For general information on our other products and services please contact our Customer Care Department within the U.S. at 877-762-2974, outside the U.S. at 317-572-3993 or fax 317-572-4002.

For technical support please visit www.wiley.com/techsupport.

WILEY   Sales | Contact Wiley at (877) 762-2974 or fax (317) 572-4002.

Credits

Acquisitions Editor
Aaron Black

Project Editor
Terri Edwards

Technical Editor
Namir Shammas

Copy Editor
Scott Tullis

Editorial Director
Robyn Siesky

Business Manager
Amy Knies

Senior Marketing Manager
Sandy Smith

Vice President and Executive Group Publisher
Richard Swadley

Vice President and Executive Publisher
Barry Pruett

Project Coordinator
Patrick Redmond

Graphics and Production Specialists
Andrea Hornberger
Jennifer Mayberry
Heather Pope

Quality Control Technician
Dwight Ramsey

Proofreader
Betty Kish

Indexer
BIM Indexing & Proofreading Services

Vertical Websites Project Manager
Laura Moss-Hollister

Vertical Websites Assistant Project Manager
Jenny Swisher

Vertical Websites Associate Producer
Shawn Patrick

Screen Artist
Ana Carrillo

About the Author

Mike Wooldridge is a Web developer based in the San Francisco Bay Area. He's written dozens of books for the Visual series. You can access more information about HTML5 and the example files used in this book at his website: www.wooldridge.net/html5

Author's Acknowledgments

Mike thanks Brianna Stuart for her help in preparing the book manuscript. He thanks Terri Edwards for her project management, Scott Tullis for his copy editing, and Namir Shammas for his technical editing. This book is dedicated to Mike's eleven-year-old son who helps Mike teach Web classes.

How to Use This Book

Who This Book Is For

This book is for the reader who has never used this particular technology or software application. It is also for readers who want to expand their knowledge.

The Conventions in This Book

① Steps

This book uses a step-by-step format to guide you easily through each task. **Numbered steps** are actions you must do; **bulleted steps** clarify a point, step, or optional feature; and **indented steps** give you the result.

② Notes

Notes give additional information — special conditions that may occur during an operation, a situation that you want to avoid, or a cross-reference to a related area of the book.

③ Icons and Buttons

Icons and buttons show you exactly what you need to click to perform a step.

④ Tips

Tips offer additional information, including warnings and shortcuts.

⑤ Bold

Bold type shows command names or options that you must click or text or numbers you must type.

⑥ Italics

Italic type introduces and defines a new term.

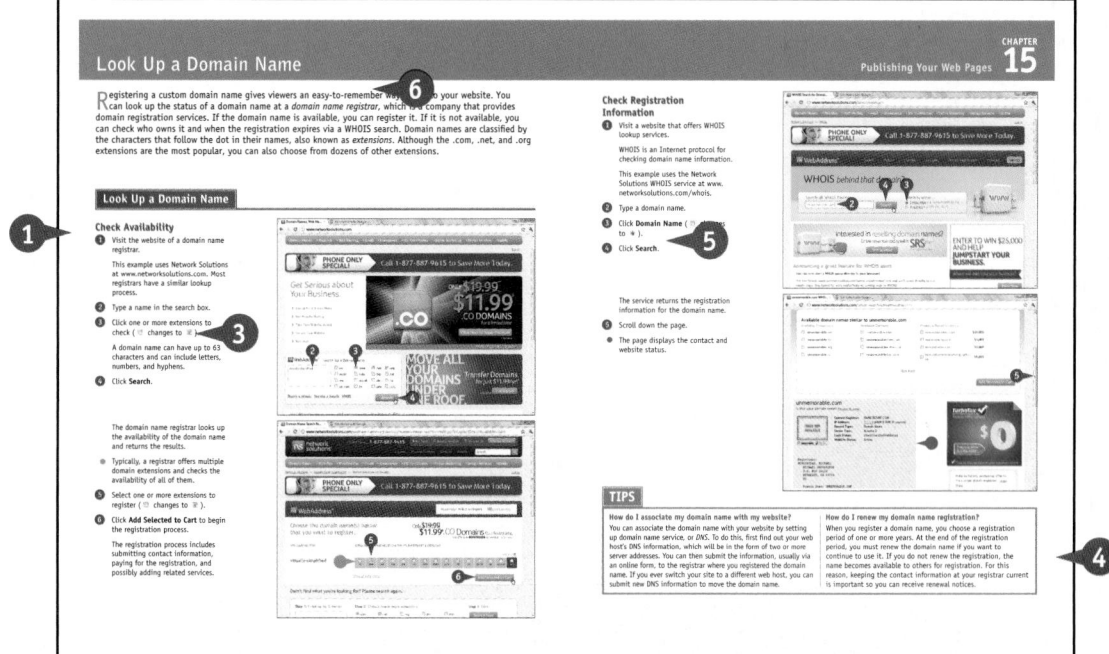

Table of Contents

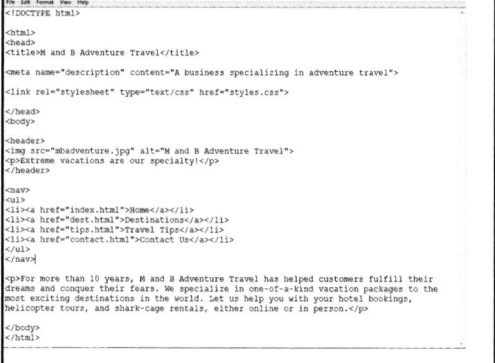

Chapter 4 Adding CSS Styles

Table of Contents

Chapter 5   Styling Text

Chapter 6   Adding Images

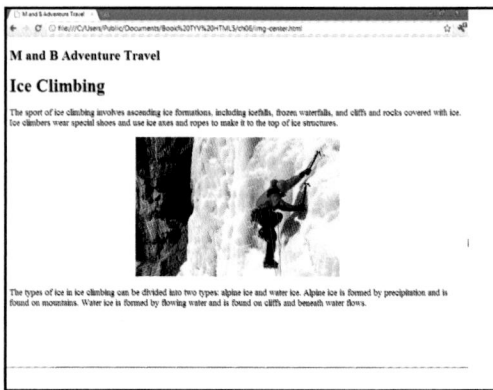

Chapter 7 — Adding Links

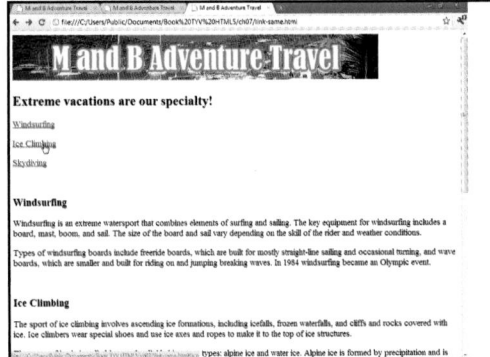

Chapter 8 — Working with Tables

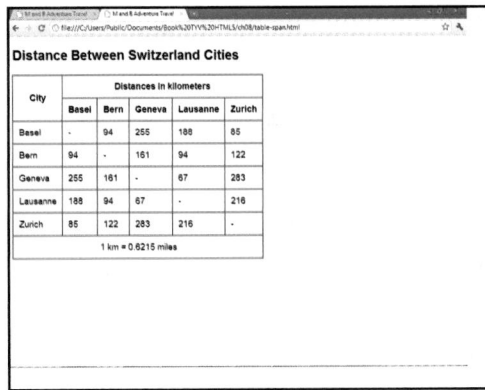

Table of Contents

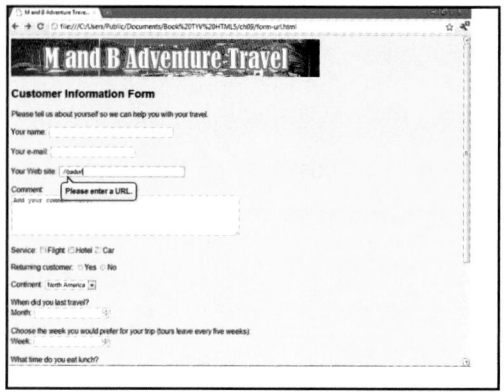

Chapter 10   Controlling Page Layout

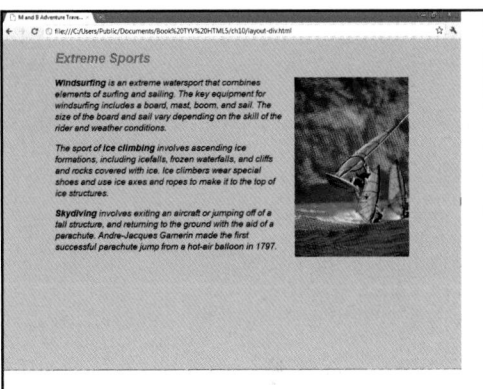

Chapter 11   Adding Semantic Tags

Table of Contents

Chapter 12   Working with JavaScript

```
<!DOCTYPE html>
<html>
<head>
<title>JavaScript</title>

<script type="text/javascript" src="browser.js"

<script type="text/javascript">
function change() {
document.getElementById("tochange").innerHTML =
document.getElementById("new").value;
}
</script>

</head>
<body>
```

Chapter 13   Adding Canvases

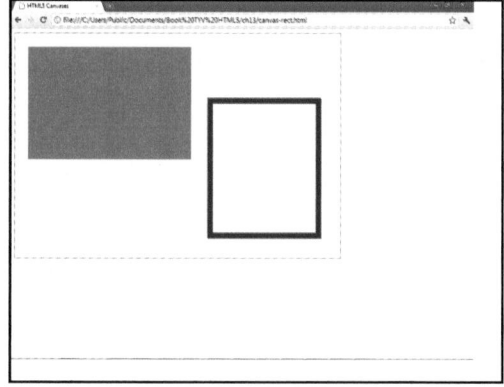

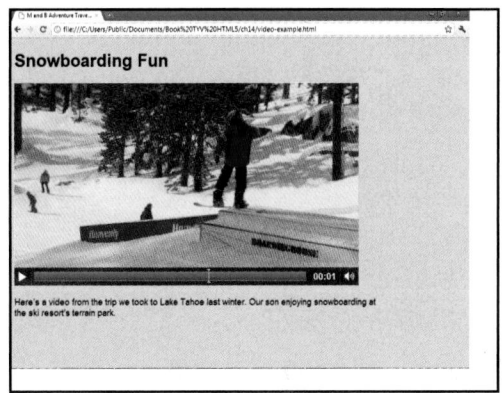

Getting Started with HTML5 and Web Pages

Are you interested in building your own web pages? This chapter introduces you to HTML5, the newest version of the language used to create web pages. It also explains the basics behind HTML editors and web browsers, which you use to design and view your web content. With a web browser, you can view HTML code for any page on the web and save the HTML to your computer. This can serve as a starting point for creating your pages.

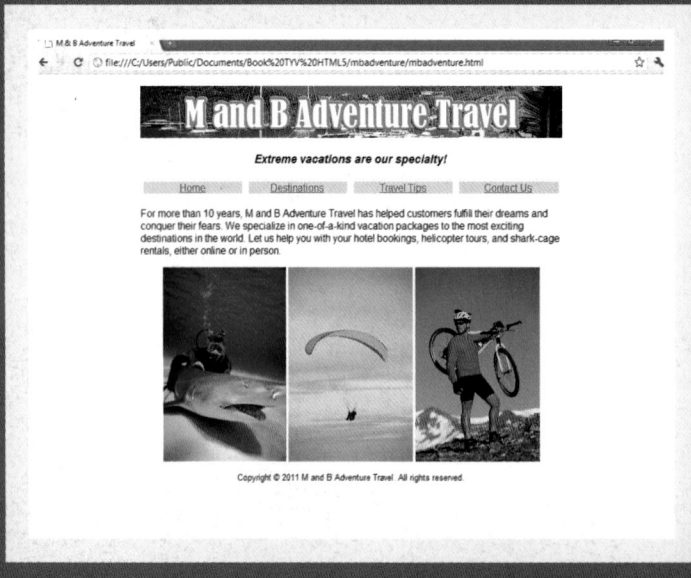

Internet Basics

The Internet is a worldwide collection of interconnected computer networks that enables businesses, organizations, governments, and individuals to communicate in a variety of ways. One of the most popular ways users communicate on the Internet is by publishing and interacting with web pages. You can create web pages from scratch using HTML. You can also use the Internet to send and receive e-mail, chat with other users, and transfer files between computers.

The Internet began as a military research project in the late 1960s. In 2010, the number of Internet users around the globe topped 2 billion.

Types of Connections

Users connect to the Internet through a variety of methods. A relatively inexpensive but slow way to connect is with dial-up service, which involves using a modem and a phone line. Faster ways to connect include *DSL* (Digital Subscriber Line), cable modem, satellite, and fiber-optic access. Networks include special wireless transmitters that allow computers, mobile phones, and other devices to access the Internet wirelessly. Connection speeds can play an important part in a user's Internet experience because slower connections result in slower file transfers and web page viewing. Companies that help you connect to the Internet are known as *Internet service providers*, or ISPs.

Internet Devices

People have traditionally connected to the Internet through desktop computers. In recent years, more and more users access it through wireless devices such as laptops, mobile phones, and, most recently, tablets such as the iPad. Screen sizes on these devices can vary widely, which can make designing web pages that look good and work well on all screens a challenge. A graphically rich website that looks beautiful on a large desktop monitor might be difficult to use on a mobile phone. Writing correct HTML can help make your online content accessible to everyone no matter what device they view it with.

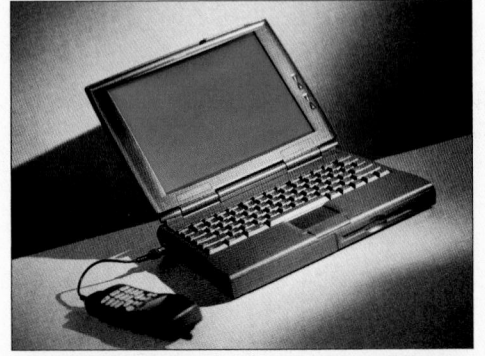

Communication Standards

The Internet infrastructure relies on a variety of standards that dictate how computers and networks talk to each other. For example, *Transmission Control Protocol/Internet Protocol*, or TCP/IP, is a set of rules that controls how Internet messages flow between computers. *Hypertext Transfer Protocol*, or HTTP, is a set of rules that determines how browsers should request web pages and how server computers should deliver them. Having agreed-upon protocols allows seamless communication among the many different types of computers that connect to the Internet.

The World Wide Web

The World Wide Web is a giant collection of documents, or pages, stored on computers around the globe. Commonly called *the web*, this collection of pages represents a wealth of text, images, audio, and video available to anyone with a computer and an Internet connection. Web pages are stored on *servers*, which are Internet-connected computers running software that allows them to serve up information to other computers. When you place a text file, image, or other document in a special web directory on a server, that information is available for other web users to view. Chapter 15 talks about how to transfer information to a web server.

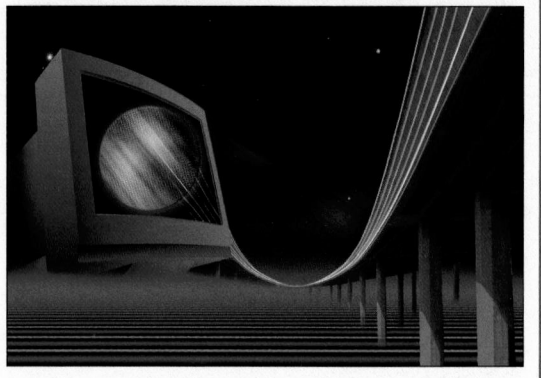

URLs and Links

Every page on the web has a unique address called a URL, which is short for *Uniform Resource Locator*. A URL looks like this:

http://www.example.com/index.html

If you know a page's URL, you can type it into a web browser to view that page over the Internet. You can also view pages by way of hyperlinks, or *links*, which are clickable words or images on web pages. Every link on a web page is associated with a URL that connects it to another page, media file, or other resource on the Internet. Users can jump from one web page to another by clicking links. Chapter 7 discusses how to create links with HTML.

Browsers

A web browser is software that enables you to view and interact with web pages. When you type a URL or click a link in a web browser, the browser retrieves the appropriate page from a server on the Internet and displays that page. Microsoft Internet Explorer, Mozilla Firefox, Google Chrome, and Apple Safari are the four most popular browsers in use today. Each program has evolved through a number of versions, with newer versions supporting more recent web features. As you build your pages using HTML code, remember that different browsers may display your pages slightly differently depending on the version.

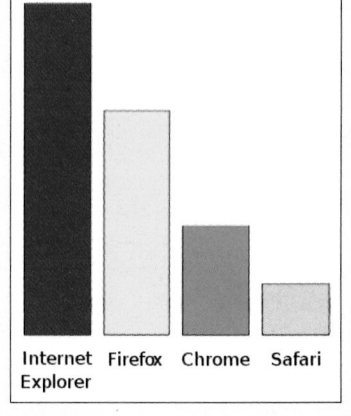

Introducing HTML5

You can build web pages using HTML, which is short for *Hypertext Markup Language*, and HTML5 is the latest version of the language. HTML documents are made up of text content and special codes known as *tags* that tell web browsers how to display the content. HTML documents are identified by their .html or .htm file extensions. You can edit the code in an HTML document by opening the document in a text editor.

For the most part, HTML is platform independent, which means you can view web pages on any computer operating system, including Windows, Mac, and Linux.

HTML Tags

HTML consists of text interspersed with special instructions known as *tags*. Surrounded by brackets, < >, HTML tags tell a browser how to organize and present text, images, and other web page content. Many tags are written using an opening tag and a closing tag that surround content that appears on the page. When writing HTML tags, you can use upper- or lowercase letters. To make the coding easier to read and understand, you can add extra white space, which web browsers ignore. For details, see the section "Understanding HTML5 Syntax."

```
Untitled - Notepad
File  Edit  Format  View  Help
<nav>
   <ul>
      <li>Home</li>
      <li>Destinations</li>
      <li>Travel Tips</li>
      <li>Contact Us</li>
   </ul>
</nav>
```

Rendering HTML

When a browser displays a web page, it retrieves the HTML file for that page from a server, parses the HTML tags to determine how the content should be formatted, and renders the page. The HTML tags tell the browser what images, video, audio, and other content need to be downloaded and integrated into the page. The HTML may also tell the browser to download style sheets and interactive scripts to further enhance the page. To view the HTML underlying a web page, see the section "View HTML5 Code in a Browser."

HTML Standards

The *World Wide Web Consortium*, or W3C, is the primary group guiding the evolution of the HTML language. The W3C is made up of hundreds of companies and organizations including web industry leaders such as Microsoft, Apple, and Google. The standards developed by the W3C give developers of web servers and browsers a set of common guidelines with which to develop their products. You can visit the W3C's website at www. w3.org. The HTML5 standard was originally developed by a separate organization called the Web Hypertext Application Technology Working Group (WHATWG). In 2007, the W3C adopted WHATWG's version as the starting point for its version of HTML5.

HTML Versions

The most recent version of HTML is HTML5. As this book is being written, the HTML5 specification is still under development, but many popular web browsers already support much of the HTML5 functionality. Version 5 includes rules for using more than 100 different HTML tags, most of which are covered in this book. HTML5 improves on previous versions by including new tags for defining common types of page content, better support for audio and video, and drawing capability with the new `<canvas>` tag. HTML5 succeeds HTML 4.01, which was released in 1999.

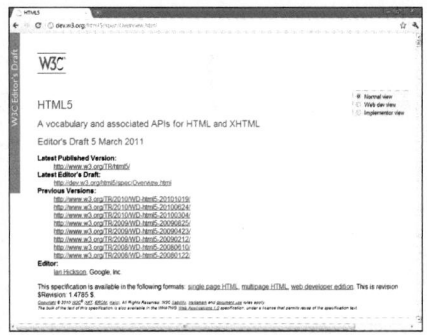

Browser Support

The development of a new HTML5 standard and the appearance of new features in web browsers are both gradual processes. As the specification of new HTML5 features became more complete, browsers began to support the features. Current versions of Google Chrome, Microsoft Internet Explorer, Mozilla Firefox, and Apple Safari support most of the HTML5 features described in this book. Google Chrome, which is used in the book examples, currently provides the widest HTML5 support of the four browsers.

XHTML

XHTML, or *Extensible Hypertext Markup Language*, is an alternative version of HTML that conforms to the stricter standards of XML, or *Extensible Markup Language*. XHTML is tag based and uses many of the same tags as HTML. However, in XHTML, all tags must be closed, tag names and attributes must be coded in lowercase, and attribute values for tags must be surrounded by quotes. For a time, the W3C group was developing a new XHTML 2.0 standard to take the place of HTML 4.01. In 2009, the group switched course to focus instead on HTML5. For more about XHTML, visit the W3C site at www.w3.org.

Explore Web Browsers

A web browser is software that can retrieve HTML documents from the web, parse the HTML instructions, and display the resulting web pages. In addition to retrieving the HTML, the browser takes care of downloading all the associated images, style sheets, scripts, and other information needed for the page to appear and function properly.

You can also use a browser to display HTML documents you save locally on your computer. When coding your HTML, you can use a web browser to test your work.

Finding a Browser

Most computer operating systems come with a web browser already installed. Internet-connected mobile phones and tablets also come with web browsers. Microsoft Windows 7 computers include the Internet Explorer browser, whereas Apple Mac computers include the Safari browser. Google Chrome and Mozilla Firefox are other web browsers that have become increasingly popular in recent years. Chrome, which currently includes excellent HTML5 support, is used in the examples in this book. You can learn more about Chrome and download it for free at www.google.com/chrome. For more information about web browsers, see www.wooldridge.net/html5.

Browser Discrepancies

There are many web browsers in use today, and numerous versions of each. Although most of them interpret HTML essentially the same way, differences in interpretation mean that not all of them display web pages in exactly the same manner. These differences are especially apparent with new HTML5 features. The current versions of Google Chrome, Microsoft Internet Explorer, Mozilla Firefox, and Apple Safari support most but not all of the HTML5 features discussed in this book. Given the fact that some HTML5 features are still under development, it will be some time before all of the major browsers support the complete standard. As always, you can avoid surprises by writing clean, well-formed HTML code and testing your pages in different browsers and on different devices as you work.

Explore HTML Editors

Because HTML documents are plain-text documents, you can use any text-editing program to code HTML5 and create a web page. All computer operating systems come with some sort of text editor installed. You can also use a variety of web-specific coding environments that write your HTML5 code, validate it, and upload it to a web server. Higher-end editing tools help you write style sheets, scripts, and other types of code in addition to HTML5.

Simple Text Editors

Simple text editors, also called plain-text editors, are easy to find. Microsoft Windows 7 comes with Notepad, whereas Apple Mac computers come with TextEdit. Simple text editors offer no-frills word processing and are often the best choice when you are learning to write HTML5. This book uses the Notepad editor in its examples. For more about text editors, visit www.wooldridge.net/html5.

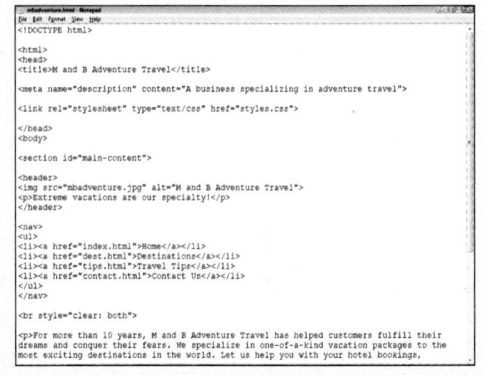

HTML Editors

HTML editors, such as Adobe Dreamweaver and Microsoft Expression, are dedicated programs for writing HTML5 code and managing web pages. These programs can shield you from having to write HTML5 code by offering a graphical environment for building web pages as well as a text-based environment. Most HTML editors also color your tags for easier viewing, validate your code, and help you upload finished pages to a server.

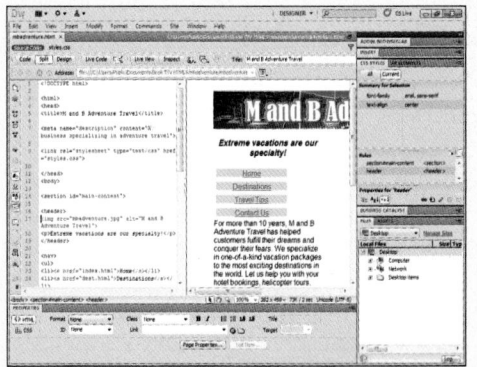

Word Processing Programs

You can also use word processing programs, such as Microsoft Word, to write HTML5. In Word, you can select Web Page as the file type when you save a document, and the program automatically adds the appropriate tags and saves the document as a text file. However, commercial word processors tend to store lots of extra information with your code, which can make it a challenge to edit the files in other editors. It is generally better to use a text editor for working with HTML5 if you are going to be directly editing the code.

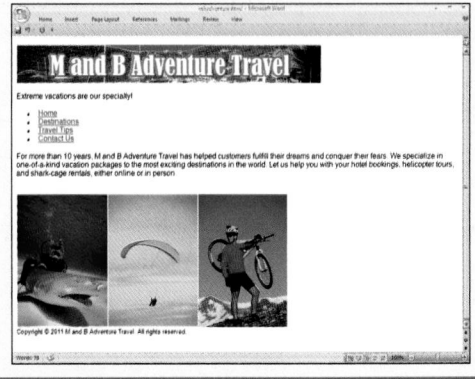

Understanding HTML5 Syntax

HTML5 is a language for describing web page content. HTML5 rules, or *syntax*, govern the way in which code is written and how web browsers interpret it. HTML5 with incorrect syntax can result in words, images, and other elements on your web page showing up in unexpected places or not at all. It can also result in your pages appearing differently in different web browsers. Learning the correct way to write your code can save you time and confusion later and ensure that web users see your pages as you intended them to be seen.

Writing HTML5

In HTML5, as in all versions of HTML, tags determine how page content is organized and formatted. Tags consist of words or abbreviations surrounded by angle brackets, < >. This HTML5 code creates a paragraph in your page:

`<p>Hello, world!</p>`

Tags can be written using upper- or lowercase letters. The following are all legal versions of the line break tag:

`<BR> <br> <Br>`

You can type tag names in uppercase to distinguish the code from other text. Lowercase tag names is the convention used in this book. Because web browsers read the tags as instructions rather than page content, the bracketed information does not appear in the browser window when the page is rendered.

Tag Structure

Certain structural HTML5 tags identify different parts of your document. For example, the `<body>` and `</body>` tags surround the main body content that appears in the browser window. The `<head>` and `</head>` tags surround accessory information, including references to style sheets and metadata, that does not appear directly in the browser window. The `<html>` and `</html>` tags appear at the very beginning and very end of the document, respectively. Many tags, such as the paragraph tags `<p>` and `</p>`, are written using an opening tag and a closing tag, whereas others, such as the image tag (`<img>`), stand alone. Closing tags must always include a slash (/) before the tag name.

```
example.html - Notepad
File  Edit  Format  View  Help
<!DOCTYPE html>

<html>
<head>
<title>M and B Adventure Travel</title>

<link rel="stylesheet" type="text/css" href="styles.css">

</head>
<body>
```

Text Styling

One of the key changes in HTML5 is the removal of many style-related instructions from HTML tags. In HTML5, tags are meant to tell a browser what text on a page *means* rather than how it *looks*. For example, an `<h1>` tag defines text as an important heading but does not specify what color or font it is, or how it is aligned on a page. When using HTML5, you provide style instructions for your text by including Cascading Style Sheets, or CSS. CSS works in concert with HTML to specify colors, alignment information, and other details about how content looks on the page. CSS is introduced in Chapter 4.

```
styles.css - Notepad
File  Edit  Format  View  Help
body {
  padding: 10px 50px 10px 50px;
  font-family: arial, sans-serif
}
section#main-content {
  width: 680px;
  margin-left: auto;
  margin-right: auto
}
header {
  text-align: center
}
header p {
  font-style: italic;
  font-weight: bold;
  font-size: 18px
}
nav ul {
  list-style-type: none;
  padding: 0;
  text-align: center }
nav li {
```

Other Tags

Among the central features of web pages are the hyperlinks that enable you to navigate from one page to another and one site to another. The `<a>`, or anchor, tag lets you define text or other page elements as clickable hyperlinks. Links are covered in Chapter 7. You can organize page content into rows and columns using table tags, which include `<table>`, `<tr>`, `<td>`, and others. Tables are covered in Chapter 8.

City	Temperature (°C)	
	Low	High
Auckland	16.4	23.8
Wellington	13.4	20.3
Christchurch	12.2	22.5
Queenstown	10.7	22.5

Attributes and Values

Each HTML5 tag has specific attributes that you can assign to it to customize its behavior. Most attributes work by setting a numeric or descriptive value. For example, you can apply a CSS style to a paragraph on your page by using the `style` attribute. The code for creating a paragraph colored red looks like this:

```
<p style="color: red">My colorful text.</p>
```

Some attributes are required for an HTML tag to function properly. The `<img>` tag requires a `src` attribute so that the browser can insert the correct image file on the page:

```
<img src="myphoto.jpg">
```

Attributes always go inside the opening HTML5 tag, and enclosing attribute values in quotation marks is good form.

M and B Adventure Travel

Ice Climbing

Entities

You can add special characters to a page, such as a copyright symbol or a fraction, by using special codes called *entities*. Entities represent characters not readily available on the keyboard. All entities are preceded by an ampersand (&) and followed by a semicolon (;). For example, the following code adds a copyright symbol to your page:

```
&copy;
```

Entities are also useful for displaying characters that have special meaning in HTML5. For example, to create a less-than symbol on your web page, you use the following code:

```
&lt;
```

You cannot use a plain less-than symbol (<) because in HTML5 it is used to start a tag. For more about entities and special characters, see Chapter 3.

Avoiding Syntax Errors

To avoid errors in your pages, always take the time to proofread your code. Most HTML editors have features that highlight bad syntax. Make sure your tags have brackets, your closing tags include a slash, and your attribute values are surrounded by quotation marks. Multiple HTML5 tags should be properly nested, meaning your closing tags should be in the reverse order of the opening tags. For example:

```
<p style="color: red"><b>My red, bold text.</b></p>
```

To help make your HTML5 readable, consider adding new lines to your code instead of running everything together on one long line. Doing so does not affect how your page appears because web browsers ignore extra white space. Testing your web pages in multiple web browsers can also be a good way to discover syntax errors because browsers can vary in their leniency to certain types of errors.

New Features in HTML5

HTML5 rolls out many new features that web designers have been requesting for years. New tags in HTML5 enable designers to more accurately describe the content on an average web page. HTML5 tags also add native support for video and audio — content that has become integral to the typical online experience. The newest versions of web browsers are beginning to support these new HTML5 features, and this book covers these features in detail.

Semantic Tags

HTML5 introduces a host of new tags that help you define the *semantics*, or meaning, of your web page content. The tags include `<nav>` for defining sections that include site navigation, `<heading>` for defining the titles and tag lines at the beginning of your pages, and `<footer>` for defining the copyright information and boilerplate text at the end. These tags make your pages easier to understand by search engines, enabling them to generate more useful search results. The tags also help web browsers determine what parts of your pages are the most important; if there is limited room on the screen, web browsers will know what content to feature more prominently.

```
<nav class="horiz">
<ul>
<li><a href="index.html">Home</a></li>
<li><a href="adventures.html">Adventures</a></li>
<li><a href="blog.html">Blog</a></li>
<li><a href="contact.html">Contact Us</a></li>
</ul>
</nav>

<aside class="right-side">
<h1>Related Photos</h1>
<img src="bungee.jpg"><br>
<img src="bungee2.jpg">
</aside>

<article class="sport-feature">
```

Richer Multimedia

HTML5 offers a new `<video>` tag for embedding video clips into your pages and an `<audio>` tag for integrating sound. In the past, developers used the nonstandard `<embed>` tag and the generic `<object>` tag for adding multimedia. The `<embed>` and `<object>` tags passed the duties for playing the video or sound to third-party plugins. Web browsers that support the new `<video>` and `<audio>` tags include native support for certain video and audio files, which means the browsers play the content directly. With the tags, web developers can create custom player controls, style the media with CSS, and more. The new multimedia tags are covered in Chapter 14.

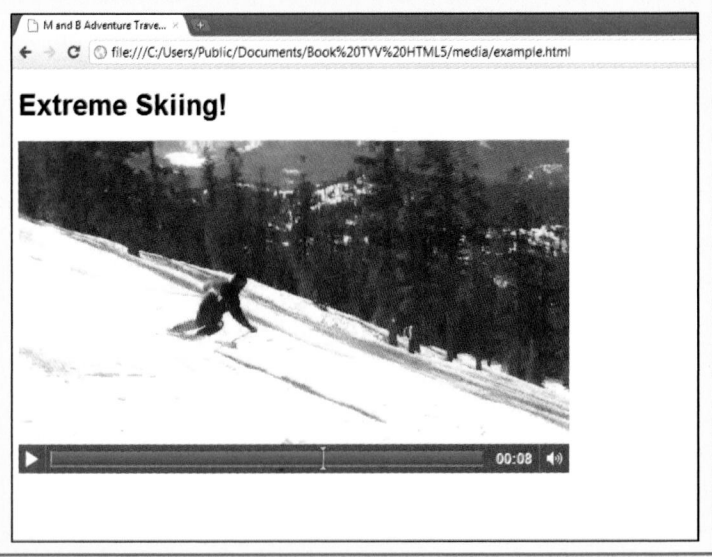

Drawing on Canvases

A new <canvas> tag enables you to define a rectangular area on your page on which you can draw. You can use scripting commands to create shapes, draw straight and curved lines, apply color gradients, and even add images or parts of images within the area. In the past, designers needed to create such visual content in a separate image editor or drawing program and then embed the result as an image. With HTML5, you can create drawings using the <canvas> tag and JavaScript. The drawings can change depending on the data that a user submits or actions performed on the page. The <canvas> tag is covered in Chapter 13.

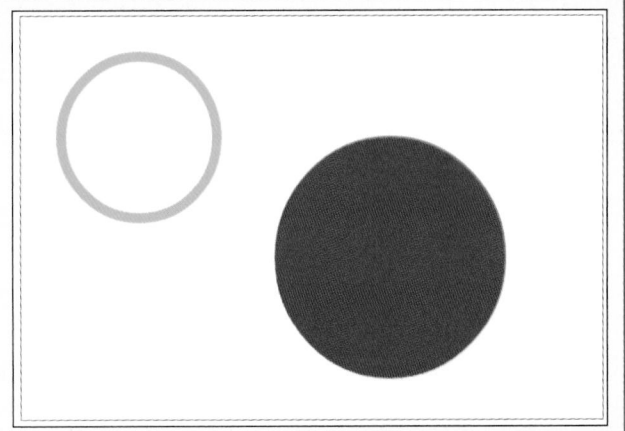

Fancier Forms

HTML5 adds a number of new input elements for web forms. For example, you can create text fields that accept only e-mail addresses or web URLs. If a user submits a form with invalid data entered into such fields, you can highlight the form field using CSS styles. Some web browsers also pop up alert text when you submit wrong data. New time elements in HTML5 display menus for setting a date, month, week, or time in a form. There is also a new slider element that allows users to select a value from within a range of numbers by clicking and dragging a control. These new features mean that developers can provide rich functionality in their web forms with simple HTML5 tags. Previously, developers have had to resort to using complicated, custom scripts to provide such features.

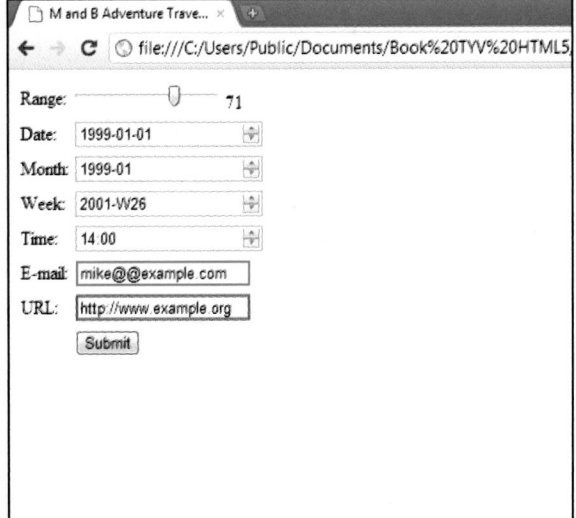

Moving Styles to CSS

In addition to adding new features, the standards groups that designed HTML5 have also taken some features away. Most of these deprecated features are tags and attributes that previously enabled you to apply formatting to content on your page. For example, in HTML 4.01 you could use the following align attribute with your <p> tag to define a paragraph's alignment:

`<p align="right">My old aligned paragraph.</p>` (Invalid in HTML5!)

This align attribute has been removed from HTML5. Instead, you can use Cascading Style Sheets, or CSS, to define alignment rules. You can then apply those rules, as CSS classes, in your HTML code:

`<p class="align-right">My new aligned paragraph.</p>` (Valid in HTML5)

Moving style-related commands out of HTML and into CSS reduces repetition in your code and makes it easier to maintain a consistent look and feel across a website. CSS styles are introduced in Chapter 4.

View HTML5 Code in a Browser

Y ou can view the HTML5 code for any web page that you have loaded into your web browser. Viewing HTML5 from different websites is a good way to learn how to write your own code and can spawn new ideas for your own pages. You can also save a web page locally for use as a template or to study later.

In Microsoft Windows 7, Google Chrome opens the HTML5 code in a separate browser tab with the tags highlighted in color. To view an HTML5 page that you have saved locally, see Chapter 2.

View HTML5 Code in a Browser

View the Source Code

1 Open a web page in your browser window.

2 Click 🔧.

3 Click **Tools**.

4 Click **View source**.

Note: Other web browsers have the View Source command under a View menu. See your browser's documentation for more information.

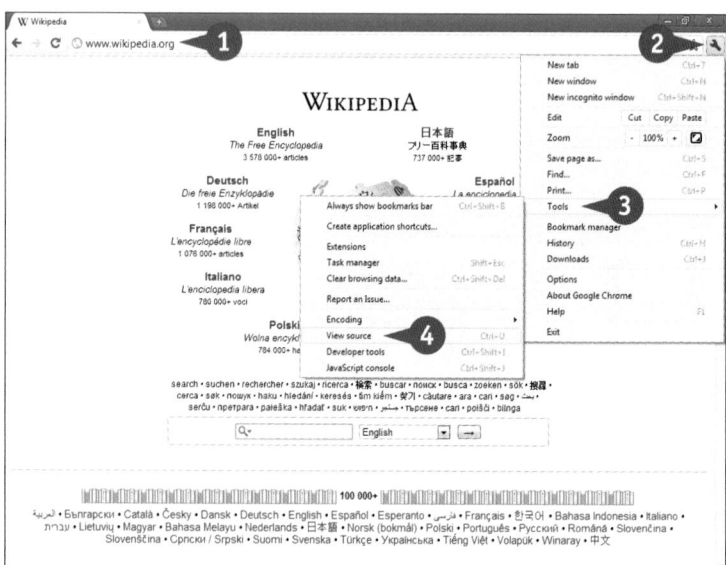

A new browser tab appears, displaying the HTML source code for the page.

5 Click the **Close** button (×) when finished.

The tab closes.

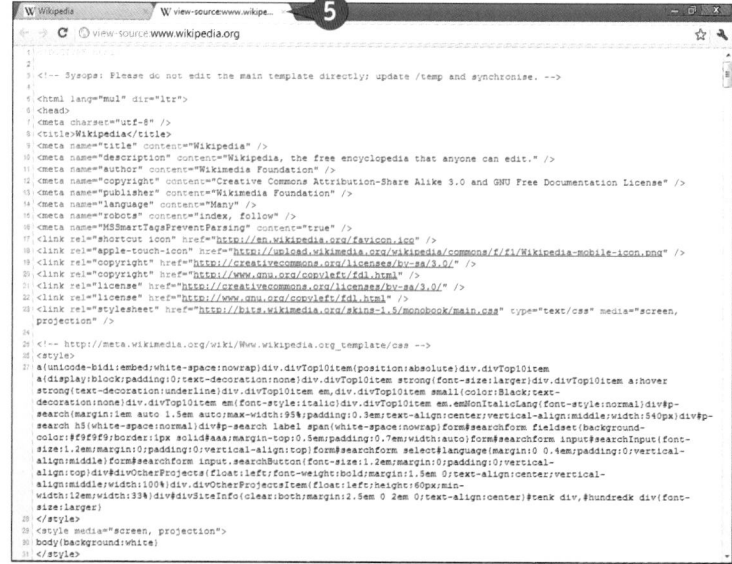

Save the Source Code

1. Click ✎.
2. Click **Save page as**.

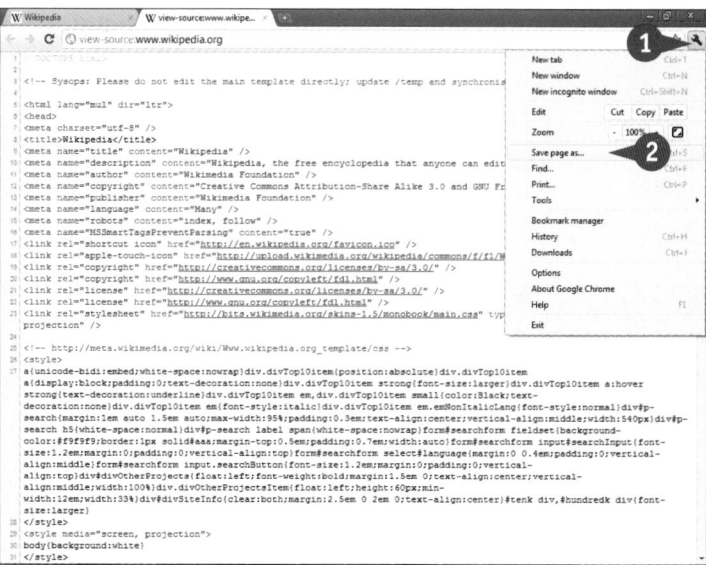

The Save As dialog box appears.

3. Click here to navigate to the folder where you want to store the page.

4. Type a name for the page.

   HTML pages should have a .html file extension.

5. Click **Save**.

Chrome saves the page.

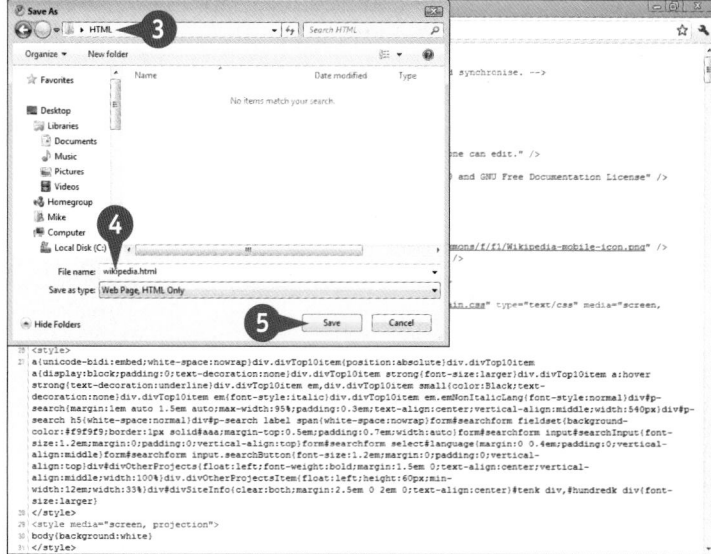

TIPS

Will the HTML5 documents that I save to my computer work when I open them in a browser?
Possibly. It depends on how the HTML5 is coded. In addition to the HTML5 instructions, you may have to download images, style sheets, scripts, and other external content separately and then edit the HTML5 so that the page references them correctly. For more about referencing other content from your document, see Chapter 7.

How else can I save a web page in my browser?
In Chrome, you can click ✎ and then **Save page as**. Under the Save as type menu, the browser gives you two ways to save your page. **Web Page, HTML Only** is the default type and saves a single HTML page. **Web Page, Complete** saves the HTML and external content to a separate folder on your computer.

Creating Your First HTML5 Web Page

Are you ready to begin creating a web page? This chapter shows you how to get started with a basic HTML5 document.

HTML5 includes a number of basic structural tags that appear in almost every page. Becoming familiar with these tags is a good first step to learning how to create your pages.

This chapter also teaches you how to save an HTML5 document in a text editor and open the document in a web browser, so you can see the results of your work.

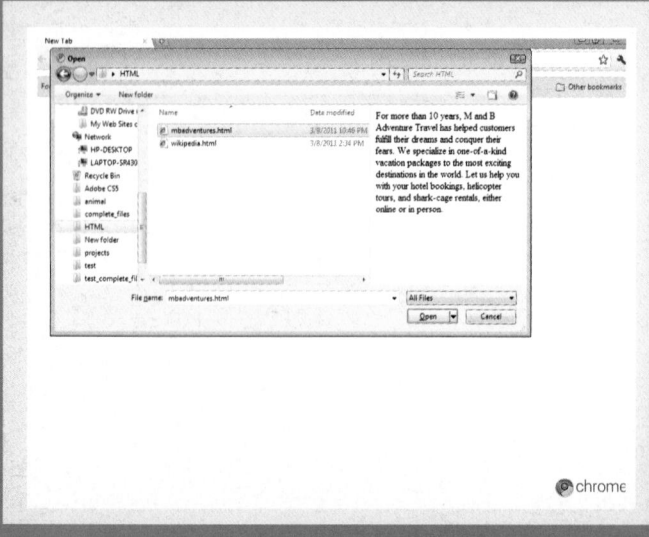

Understanding HTML5 Document Structure

Although web pages can differ widely in terms of content and layout, most pages have certain HTML tags that give them the same basic structure. These tags tell a web browser where the HTML for a page begins and ends; where to find metadata, references to style sheets and scripts, and other important elements; what content appears in the browser window; and how different sections of the page, such as headers, footers, and navigational areas, are arranged. Understanding this structure helps you correctly organize the content in your HTML5 pages.

DOCTYPE Declaration

The DOCTYPE declaration at the beginning of your page specifies that the document is written in HTML. In HTML5, the DOCTYPE declaration is required. In past versions of HTML, the DOCTYPE declared what types of HTML tags a browser can expect to see in your document. This is no longer the case.

HTML Tags

The <html> and </html> tags at the beginning and end of a text document identify it as HTML code. When a browser encounters these tags, it knows that anything within the two tags defines a web page. In HTML5 these tags are required.

Document Head

You use the head of an HTML document to add descriptive and accessory information to your web page. The document head tags, <head> and </head>, immediately follow the opening <html> tag and are required in HTML5. The document head contains information that does not appear in the browser window, including title information, metadata, and references to scripts and style sheets. For more about scripts, see Chapter 12. For more about style sheets, see Chapter 4.

Document Title

The <title> and </title> tags define a page title and appear inside the document head. You can add a title to your HTML5 document to help people and search engines identify your web page. For example, if you are building a web page for a business, you might want to include the company's name and specialization in the title. Most web browsers display the title in the browser window's title bar.

Metadata

Metadata means "data about data." On a web page, metadata can include author information, the type of editor used to create the page, a description of the content, relevant keywords, and copyright information. Search engines often use metadata when trying to categorize a page. You place metadata inside the document head. Metadata is optional in an HTML5 document.

Body

The visible content that makes up your web page, including paragraphs, lists, tables, images, canvases, and video, lives in the body of your HTML document.

```
example.html - Notepad
File  Edit  Format  View  Help
<!DOCTYPE html>

<html>
<head>
<title>M and B Adventure Travel</title>

<meta name="description" content="A business specializing in adventure travel">

<link rel="stylesheet" type="text/css" href="styles.css">

</head>
<body>

<header>
<img src="mbadventure.jpg" alt="M and B Adventure Travel">
<p>Extreme vacations are our specialty!</p>
</header>

<nav>
<ul>
<li><a href="index.html">Home</a></li>
<li><a href="dest.html">Destinations</a></li>
<li><a href="tips.html">Travel Tips</a></li>
<li><a href="contact.html">Contact Us</a></li>
</ul>
</nav>

<p>For more than 10 years, M and B Adventure Travel has helped customers fulfill their
dreams and conquer their fears. We specialize in one-of-a-kind vacation packages to the
most exciting destinations in the world. Let us help you with your hotel bookings,
helicopter tours, and shark-cage rentals, either online or in person.</p>

</body>
</html>
```

The body of the document is identified by the <body> and </body> tags. The body of a document comes after the head of a document and is required in HTML5. Most of the HTML tags covered in this book belong inside the body of the document and determine how its content is formatted. To learn how to begin adding content to the page body, see Chapter 3.

Semantic Tags

New in HTML5 are various *semantic* tags that enable you to describe the meaning of different parts of your web page. These tags include the <header> tag for defining header content, <nav> tag for defining navigation, and <footer> tag for defining footer content. In previous versions of HTML, section markup was limited to tags such as <div>, which defined a section of HTML but did not tell you what the meaning of the section was.

Start an HTML5 Document

You can start an HTML5 document using a text editor, HTML editor, or word processing program. You use sets of HTML tags to define the basic structure of your page.

The <html> and <head> tags are required elements that appear at the beginning of all HTML documents. Although not required, the <title> also appears in almost all HTML documents. To save time, you can create a text file that includes these tags and use the file as a template each time you want to create a web page.

Start an HTML5 Document

1 Open an editor or word processing program.

Note: The examples in this book use Windows Notepad. See Chapter 1 to learn more about editors.

2 Type <!DOCTYPE html>.

This tag declares the document as HTML.

3 Press **Enter**.

4 Type <html>.

5 Press **Enter**.

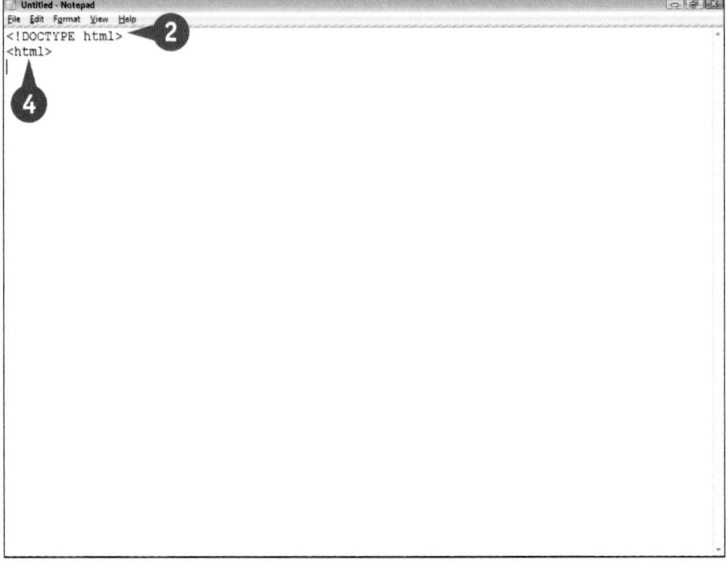

6 Type <head>.

This tag defines where the title, metadata, and other descriptive information appear.

Note: For more about adding metadata to a web page, see the section "Add Metadata."

7 Press **Enter**.

8 Type `<title>`.

9 Type title text for your page.

Title text describes the contents of the page and appears in the title bar of the web browser.

10 Type `</title>`.

11 Press Enter.

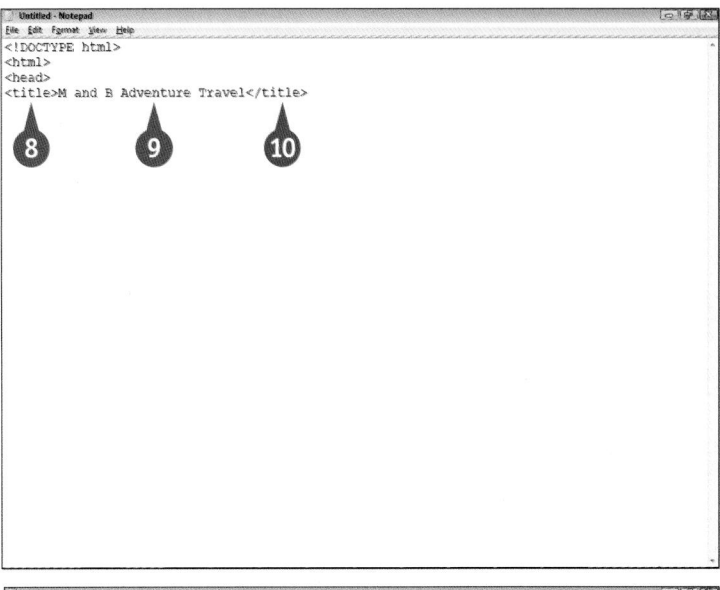

12 Type `</head>`.

This tag completes the document head information for the page.

13 Press Enter.

Note: You do not need to press Enter each time you start a new tag or add a closing tag. However, placing tags on their own lines can help make your code more readable.

Note: Browsers ignore extra white space in the code when rendering web pages.

TIPS

Which should I add first to my HTML5 document, the tags or the page content?
It is usually easier to start your HTML5 document by typing the basic structural tags, which include the `<html>`, `<head>`, and `<body>` tags. These tags appear in all HTML5 documents, and typing them first helps ensure they have valid syntax and are in the correct order. After you add the basic structural tags, you can add the body content and additional tags to format that content.

Does it matter if I type my HTML5 tag and attribute names in uppercase, lowercase, or mixed case?
No. The HTML5 standard allows for different cases in your HTML text. However, formatting your HTML5 tags consistently is good form. Some people type tags in all uppercase letters to make it easier to distinguish HTML code from the page content. Other people type tags in all lowercase to be consistent with similar but stricter coding languages such as XML. Tag names are written in all lowercase in this book.

continued ▶ **21**

You can use the body tags, `<body>` and `</body>`, to define the content in your web page. Page content can include lines of text, bulleted and numbered lists, tables, forms, canvas areas, and more. Content added between the body tags appears in the viewing area of a web browser.

You can apply CSS styles to the body to change the background color and other overall characteristics of the page. See Chapter 5 for details.

Start an HTML5 Document (continued)

14 Type `<body>`.

This tag marks the beginning of the actual content of your web page.

15 Press **Enter**.

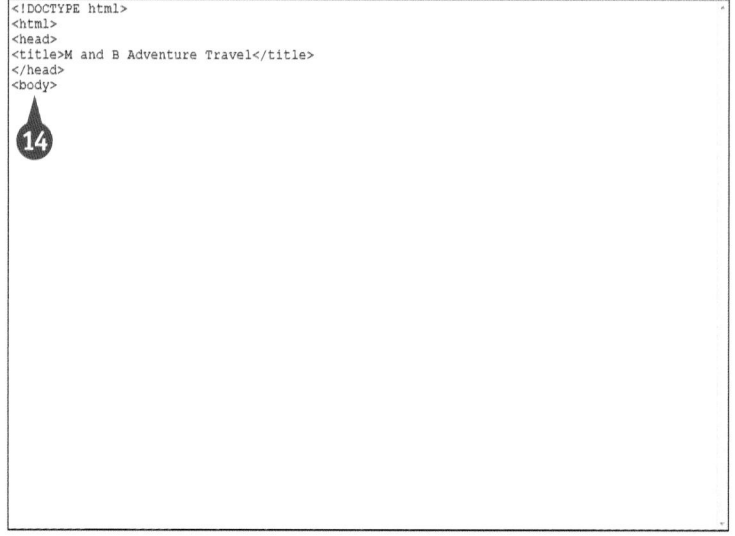

16 Type the body text you want to appear on the page.

Body text is the content that appears in the browser window. For practice, you can type a simple paragraph for the body text.

17 Press **Enter**.

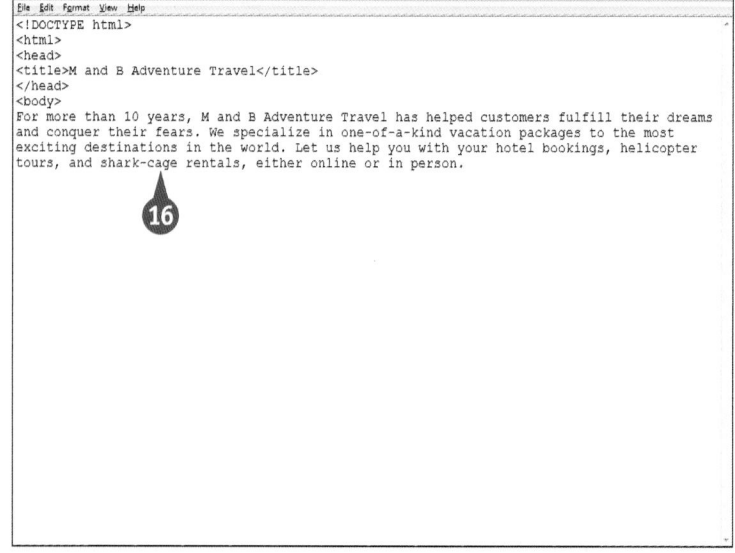

18 Type `</body>`.

This tag closes the body portion of the page.

19 Press **Enter**.

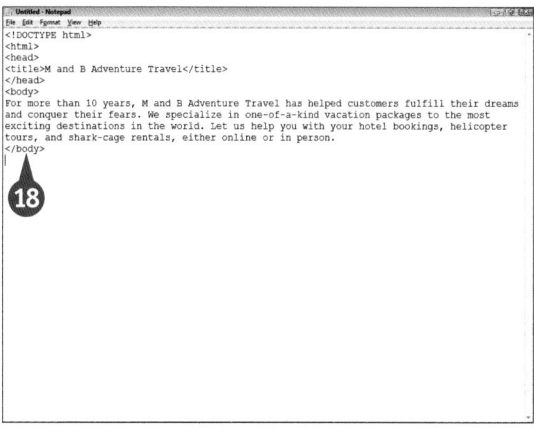

20 Type `</html>`.

This tag ends the HTML code of your document.

You can save your document and view the page in a web browser.

Note: To learn how to save a file, see the section "Save an HTML5 Document." To learn how to view the results of your HTML coding, see the section "View an HTML5 Page."

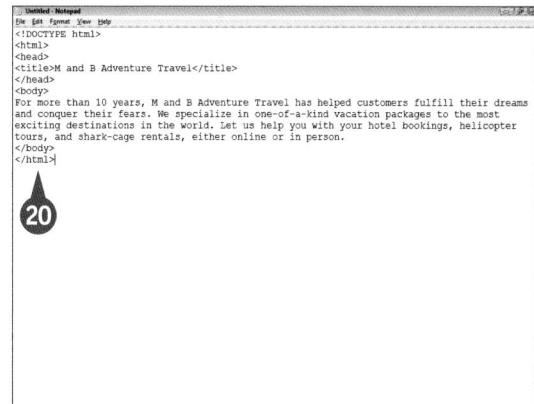

TIP

How can I open an HTML5 document from the Notepad text editor?

You can open an HTML5 document for editing from inside Notepad:

1 In Notepad, click **File**.

2 Click **Open**.

The Open dialog box appears.

3 Navigate to the folder that contains the HTML file.

4 Click ▼ and select **All Files**.

Any HTML files in that folder appear.

5 Click the HTML5 file. Such files usually have a .html or .htm extension.

6 Click **Open**.

Notepad opens the HTML document.

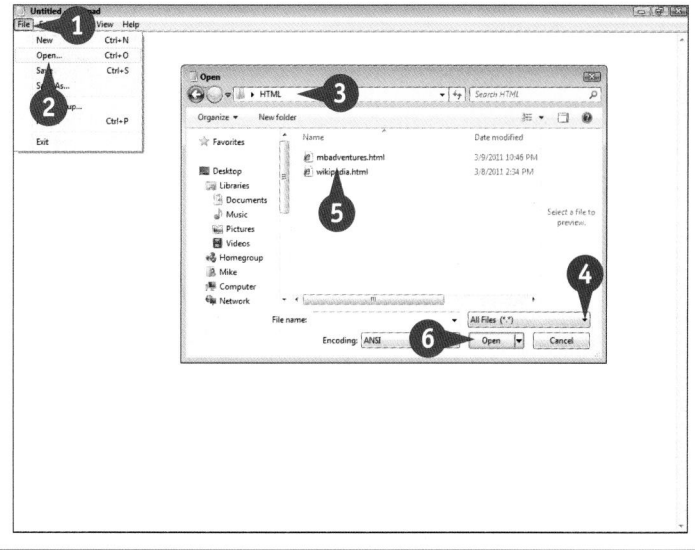

Save an HTML5 Document

You can save your web page as an HTML file so that users can view it in a web browser. When saving a web page, you can use either the .html or .htm file extension.

When naming a web page, it is best not to use spaces and to keep the characters limited to letters, numbers, hyphens (-), and underscores (_). If you are creating a home page for a website, the page is commonly named index.html or default.htm.

Save an HTML5 Document

1 Click **File**.

Note: Your text editor may have a different command name for saving files. See your program's documentation for more information.

2 Click **Save**.

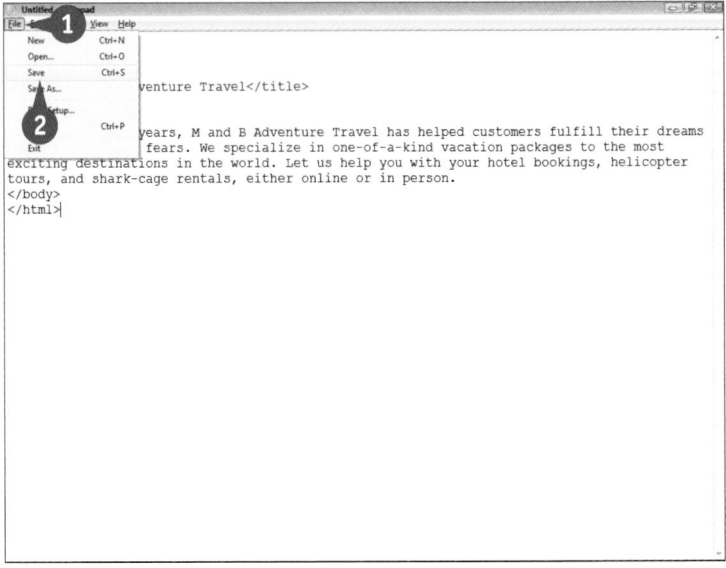

The Save As dialog box appears.

3 Click here to navigate to the folder or drive where you want to store the file.

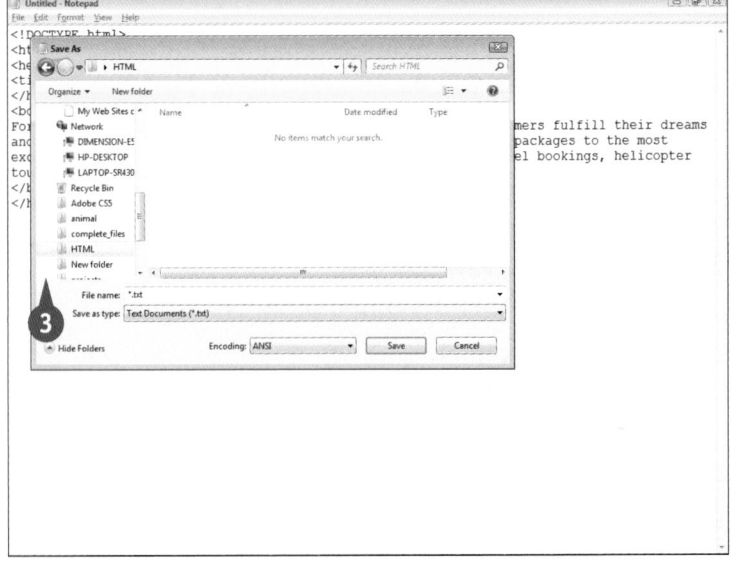

④ Type a name for the file, followed by **.html** or **.htm**.

⑤ Click **Save**.

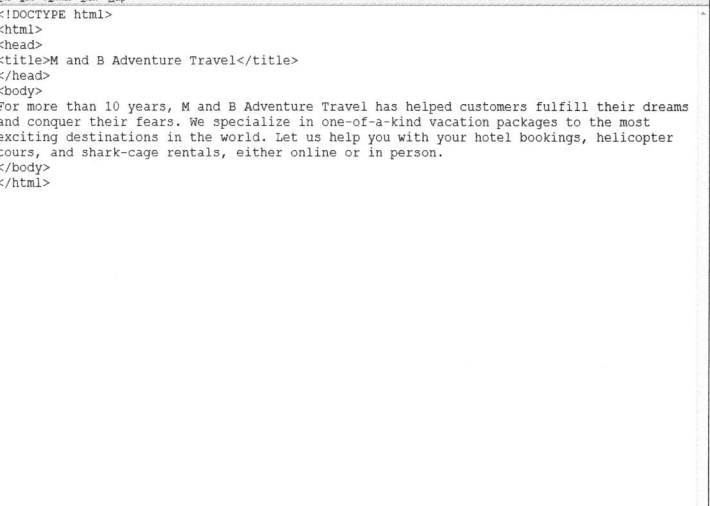

The editor saves the file.

Note: To open the file in a browser for viewing, see "View an HTML5 Page."

TIPS

What is the difference between the .html and .htm extensions?

The shorter .htm extension is left over from the early, pre-Windows days, when filenames could have only three-character file extensions. Some Windows-based programs still default to the .htm extension. Today's computers can handle longer filenames and extensions, so the three-character limit is no longer an issue. Although web browsers and servers can read either extension, you probably want to opt for .html because it is more universally used.

What makes a good filename for a web page?

When naming a file, you should keep the name simple so that you can easily remember it and locate it again later. In addition, because you need to type filenames when creating hyperlinks, it is best to use a name that relates to the pages you are designing. For example, if you are creating a page that lists contact information for your company, the filename for that page might be contact.html. Filenames that contain words relevant to a page can help search engines correctly recognize your page. Search engines read filenames when processing web pages and can take those names into account when categorizing the pages.

View an HTML5 Page

After you create and save an HTML5 document, you can view it in your web browser. Your web browser can view HTML5 pages that you have saved on your computer as well as pages on the Internet. Opening an HTML5 page that you are simultaneously editing in a text editor is a useful way to determine if the page appears correctly as you add content and tags. When you open a page from your computer in a browser, the file-system path leading to the page appears in the browser address field.

View an HTML5 Page

1 Open your web browser.

This example uses the Google Chrome browser.

2 Press **Ctrl** + **O**.

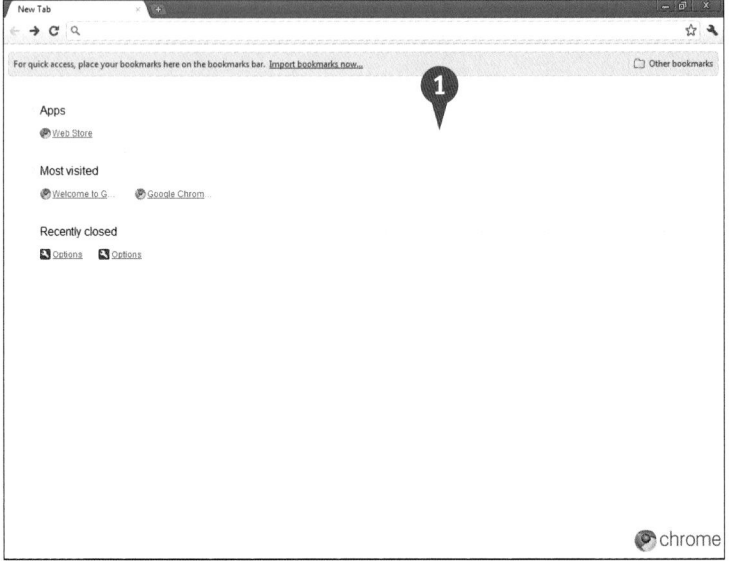

The Open dialog box appears.

3 Click here to navigate to the folder or drive in which your HTML5 document is stored.

4 Click the filename.

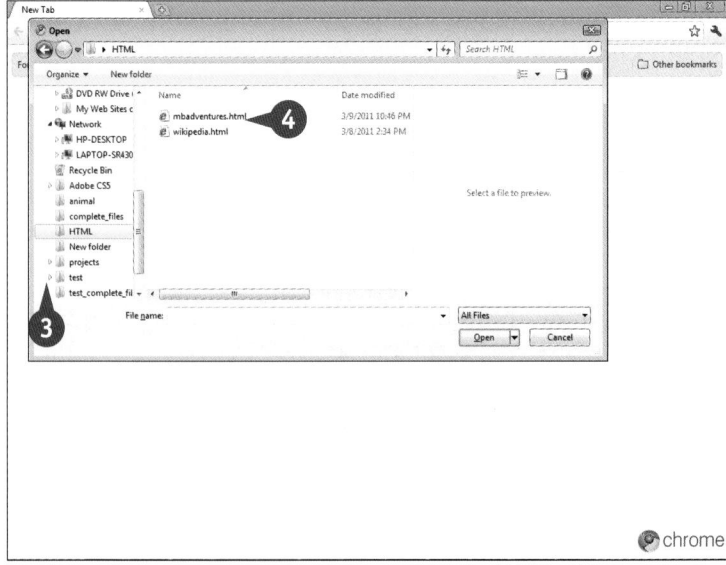

● In the dialog box, a preview of the page appears.

⑤ Click **Open**.

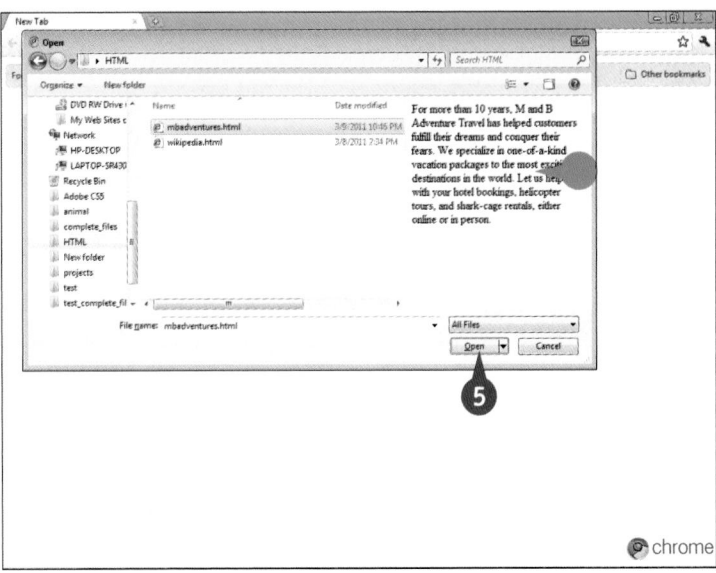

The web browser displays the page.

● The title information appears here.

● The body information appears here.

● The location of the HTML file appears here.

Note: You cannot see metadata in the browser window.

● If you make changes to the HTML of the page that appears in the browser, you can click ⟳ to refresh the page and view the changes.

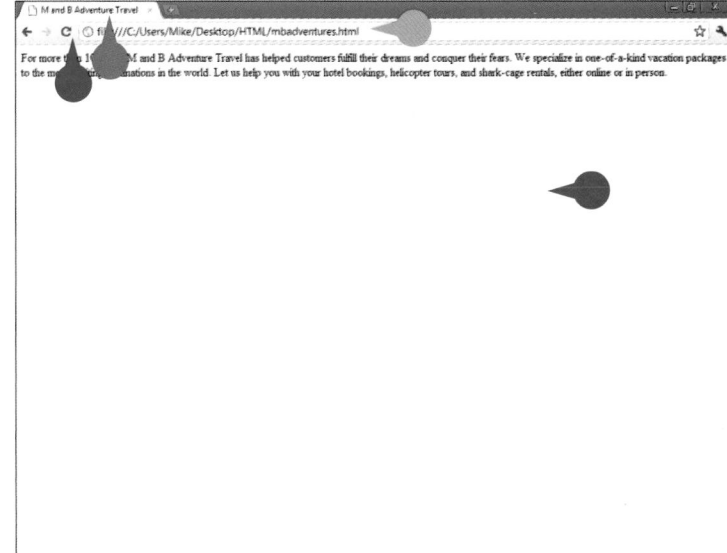

TIPS

Does it matter what browser I use to view the pages I build?
No. All popular web browsers are set up to view HTML5 pages that you have saved on your computer, also known as *offline pages*. You may need to follow a slightly different set of steps to open an offline HTML5 document in a browser other than Google Chrome, such as Internet Explorer or Apple Safari. Be sure to consult your browser's documentation for more information.

What happens if I cannot view my page?
If you do not see any content for your page, you need to double-check your HTML5 code for errors. Make sure your document uses correctly paired start and end tags, and proofread your HTML5 code to make sure everything is correct. Also make sure you named your page with an .html or .htm extension.

Add Metadata

You can add metadata to your page to include extra descriptive information that does not appear in the browser window. Metadata can include a page description, author and copyright information, keywords, and more. What you insert in metadata tags can help search engines categorize your page.

You define metadata in the document header using the `<meta>` tag. The `<meta>` tag includes a `name` attribute that determines what type of metadata you are adding with the tag. You add metadata to the document header of your HTML5 page, inside the `<head>` and `</head>` tags.

Add Metadata

Add an Author Name

① Click between the `<head>` and `</head>` tags and press `Enter` to start a new line.

In this example, the metadata appears below the `<title>` tags.

② Type `<meta name= "author"` followed by a space.

③ Type `content="My Name">`, replacing *My Name* with your name.

④ Press `Enter`.

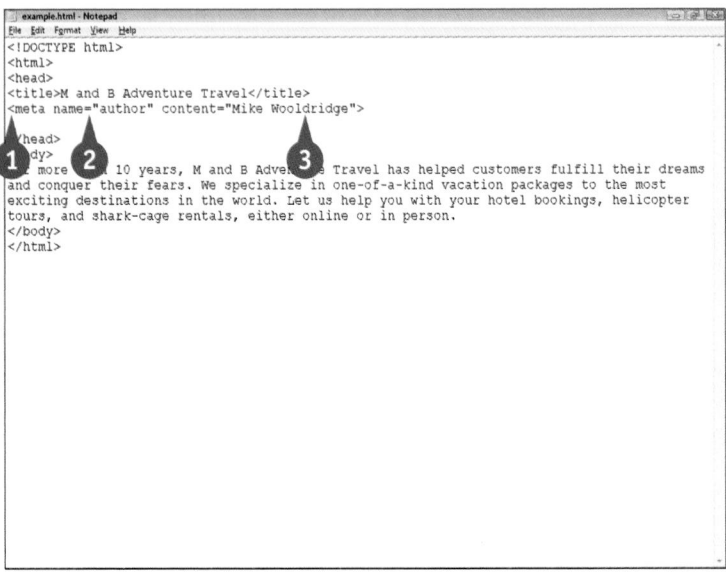

Add a Page Description

⑤ Type `<meta name= "description"` and a blank space.

⑥ Type `content="Page Description">`, replacing *Page Description* with your own page description.

⑦ Press `Enter`.

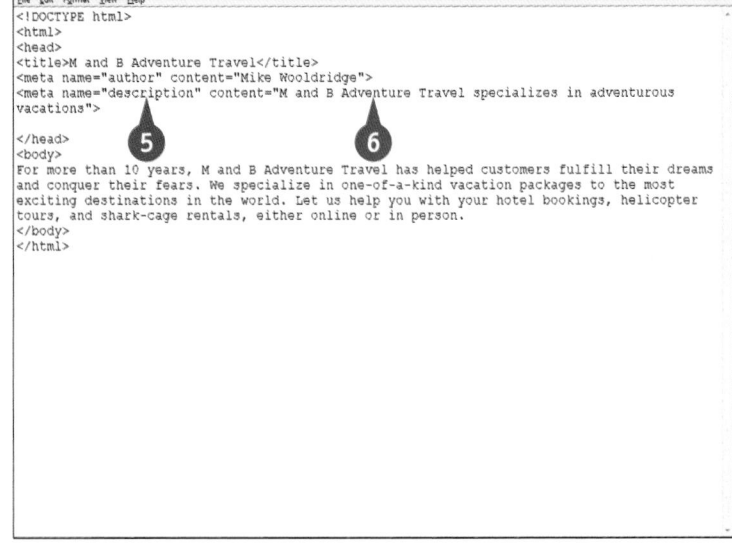

Specify Keywords

8 Type `<meta name="keywords"` and a space.

9 Type `content="My Keywords">`, replacing *My Keywords* with a keyword.

For multiple keywords, use a comma followed by a space to separate the keywords.

10 Press **Enter**.

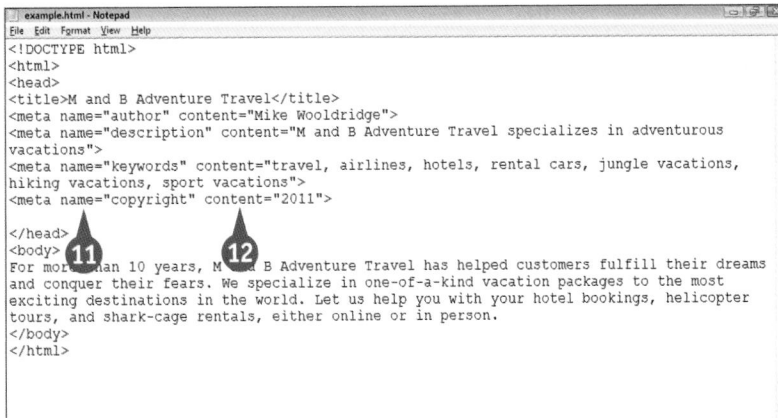

Add a Copyright

11 Type `<meta name="copyright"` and a space.

12 Type `content="2011">`, replacing *2011* with your own numbers or copyright information.

13 Press **Enter**.

The metadata is now a part of the HTML document.

TIPS

How do I add the name of the program I used to design my page to the metadata information?

To specify an authoring program, type `<meta name="generator" content="Program Name">`. Substitute the name of your program for the text *Program Name*.

Who can view my metadata?

The only way users can see your metadata information is if they view the HTML code for the page. In Google Chrome, to view the HTML code of a page in your browser window, click 🔧, **View**, and then **View source**. This opens a text window displaying the HTML used to create the page. Any metadata assigned to the document appears at the top, inside the `<head>` and `</head>` tags.

Adding and Modifying Text

Are you ready to begin building your web page by adding text? You can add text by typing words into your HTML document and then surrounding the words with tags. You can create simple paragraphs with <p> tags and a hierarchy of different headings with a variety of heading tags. You can create lists using <ol> or <ul> tags in combination with the <li> tag. This chapter shows you how to do all of this and more, including how to add special characters to your page by typing alphanumeric codes.

```
dl.html - Notepad
File  Edit  Format  View  Help
<!DOCTYPE html>
<html>
<head>
<title>M and B Adventure Travel</title>
</head>
<body>

<h1>What's in a Bag?</h1>

<dl>
<dt>Backpack</dt>
        <dd>A bag for carrying hiking supplies and lunch</dd>
<dt>Fannypack</dt>
        <dd>A bag for carrying a passport, wallet, and camera</dd>
<dt>Suitcase</dt>
        <dd>A bag for carrying clothes and toiletries</dd>
<dt>Briefcase</dt>
        <dd>A bag for carrying business documents, files, and pens</dd>
</dl>

</body>
</html>
```

Create a New Paragraph

You can use paragraph tags to start new paragraphs in an HTML document. In a word processing program, you press **Enter** or **Return** to separate blocks of text. Web browsers do not read these line breaks. Instead, you must insert a <p> tag in your HTML any time you want to start a new paragraph in your web page.

Paragraphs are left-aligned by default, but you can specify a different alignment using CSS. See Chapters 4 and 5 to learn more about CSS and text alignment. Paragraph text is normal-sized and unstyled by default. To add bold or italic styling, or to change the text to small print, see the other sections in this chapter.

Create a New Paragraph

1 Type <p> to start a new paragraph.

2 Type your text.

3 Type </p> at the end of the paragraph.

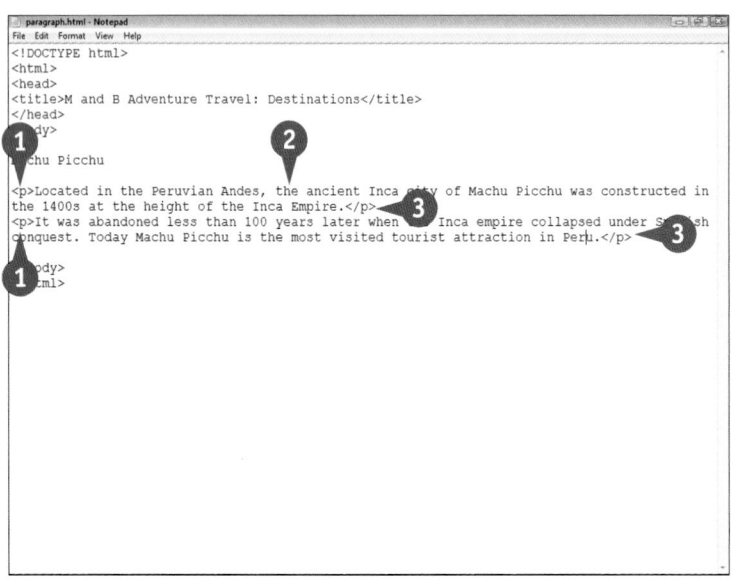

When displayed in a Web browser, the text appears as a paragraph with extra space before and after it.

Note: To create a paragraph that is set off from other paragraphs on a page, see the section "Add a Block Quote."

Add a Line Break

You can use the line break tag, `<br>`, to control where your text breaks. Web browsers normally wrap text automatically; a line of text that reaches the right side of the browser window breaks and continues on the next line. You can insert a line break to instruct the browser to break the text at a specific place and go to a new line.

You can also use the `<br>` tag to add blank lines between paragraphs. This is useful if you want to add extra space above or below a block of text or a heading. By inserting multiple `<br>` tags consecutively, you can increase the amount of space.

Add a Line Break

1 Type `<br>` in front of the line of text that you want to appear as a new line.

2 Type additional `<br>` tags for each line of text where you want a line break.

Note: You do not need a closing tag for the `<br>` tag.

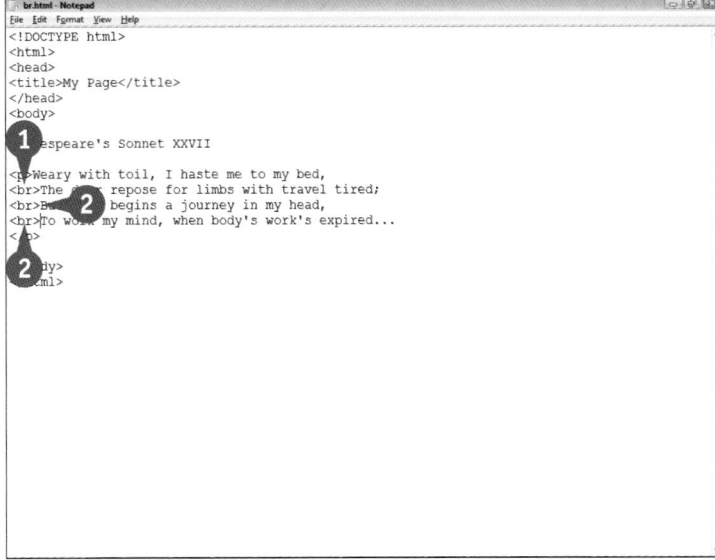

● When a web browser displays the page, each instance of the tag creates a new text line.

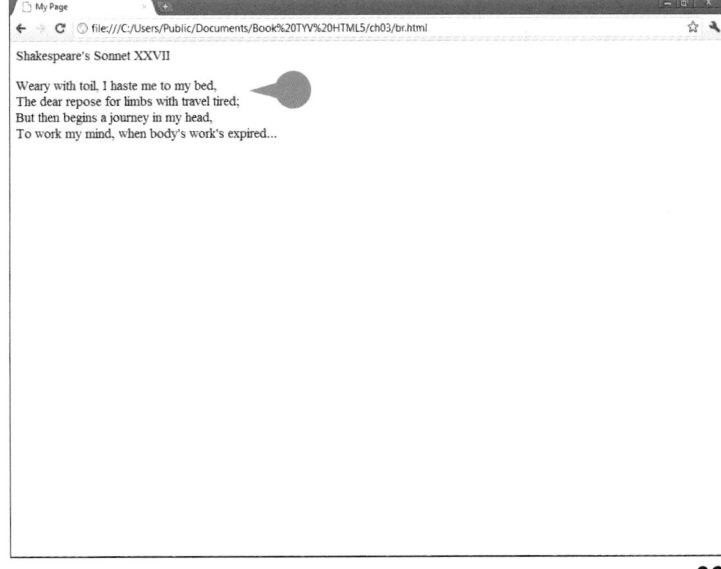

Add a Line Break Opportunity

You can use the `<wbr>` tag to specify where a browser may add a line break if needed. You can use this tag for long words that might present problems if they were to appear near the end of a line and cause awkward spacing. The `<wbr>` tag differs from the `<br>` tag in that it results in a new line only if the flow of text requires it. The `<wbr>` tag is new in HTML5.

Add a Line Break Opportunity

① Type `<wbr>` in your text where you want to specify that a line break should occur if needed.

② You can type additional `<wbr>` in tags to specify other line break opportunities.

Note: You do not need a closing tag for the `<wbr>` tag.

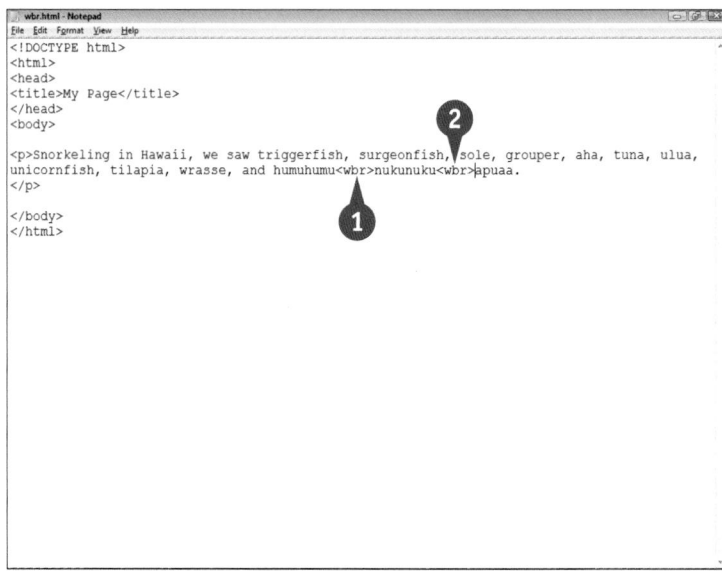

● If the `<wbr>` occurs at the end of a line, the web browser applies a line break.

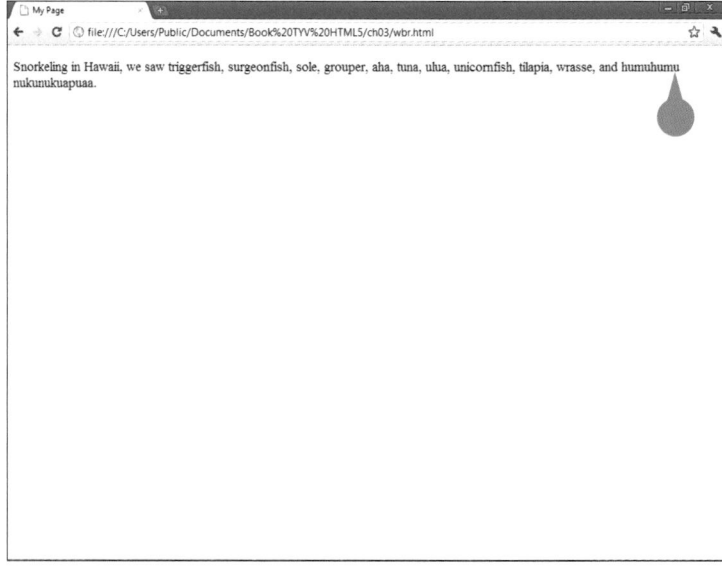

Add a Horizontal Rule

You can add a dividing line, or horizontal rule, across your page to separate blocks of information. Horizontal rules can be useful for separating topics on a page or for setting off diagrams from the flow of text.

By default, most browsers display a horizontal rule as a thin gray line. Horizontal rules must occupy a line by themselves and cannot appear within a paragraph.

Add a Horizontal Rule

① Type <hr> where you want to insert a horizontal rule.

Note: You do not need a closing tag for the <hr> tag.

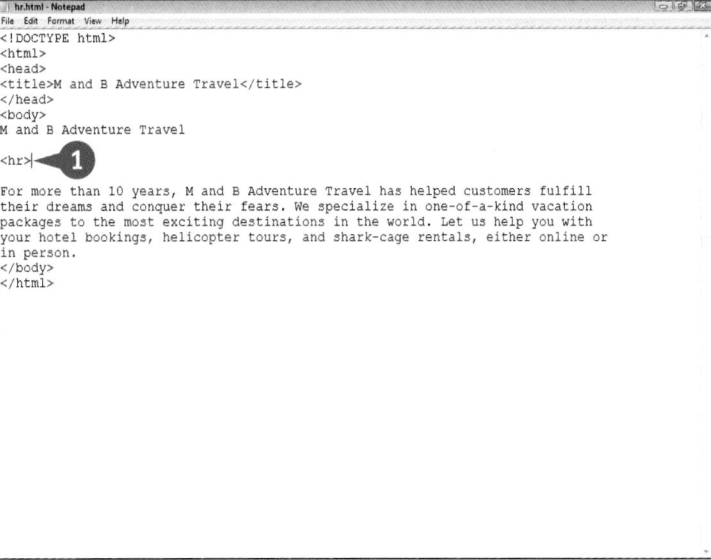

● The browser displays the line across the page.

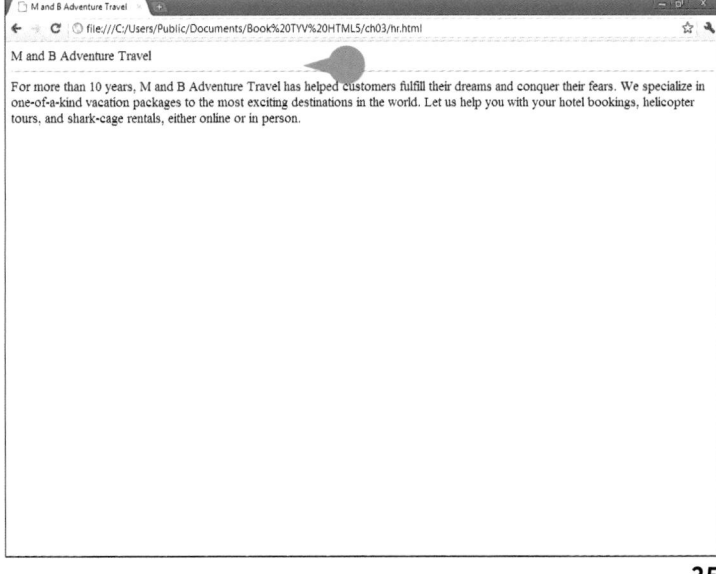

Insert a Blank Space

You can insert blank spaces within a line of text to indent your text. You can also use blank spaces to help position an element on a line, such as a graphic or photo. The HTML code for adding such spaces is , which stands for *nonbreaking space*. Using such code is necessary for adding extra space because web browsers ignore any extra space in your HTML code. For details about other special HTML codes, see the "Insert Special Characters" section. Adding a nonbreaking space is an alternative to inserting a line break tag, <br>, which adds space between lines of text. You can also add space around elements on your page with CSS styles. See Chapter 4 for an introduction to CSS.

Insert a Blank Space

① Type   in the line where you want to add a blank space.

To add multiple spaces, type the code multiple times.

The code stands for *nonbreaking space*. Web browsers do not create a line break where you insert these characters. For more about special characters, see "Insert Special Characters."

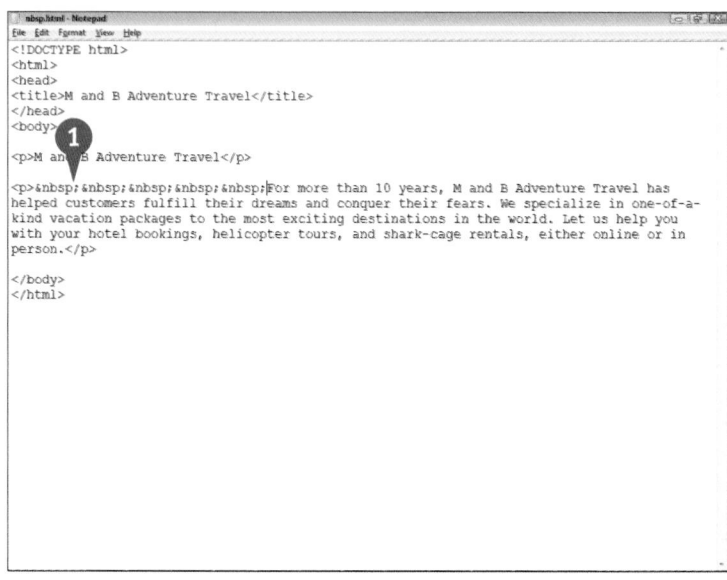

The browser displays blank spaces in the line.

● In this example, the blank spaces indent a paragraph.

Note: You can also indent a paragraph using the text-indent CSS declaration. See Chapter 5 for details.

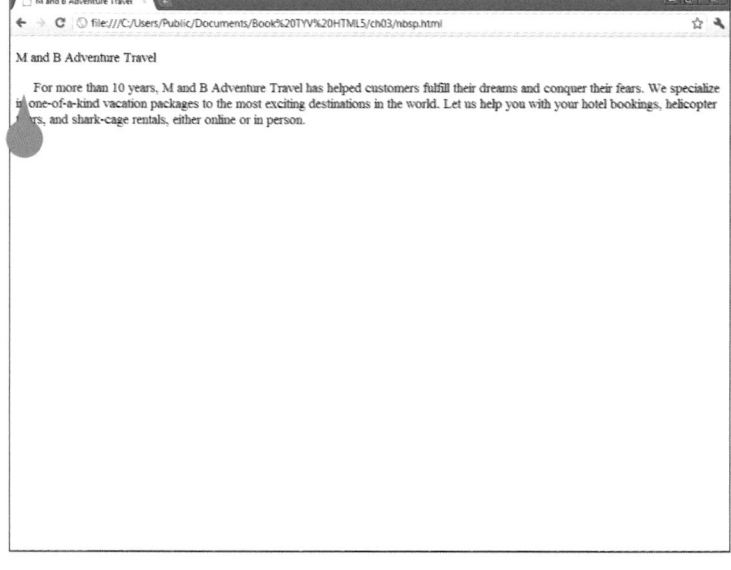

Make Text Bold

You can add bold formatting to your text to emphasize keywords and set them off from other text in a passage. For example, you might make a company name bold in a paragraph or add bold formatting to important terms in a list of items. You add bold text to a page by surrounding the text with <b> and </b> tags. In most browsers, the <strong> tag has the same effect as the <b> tag.

Make Text Bold

① Type <b> in front of the text you want to make bold.

② Type </b> at the end of the text.

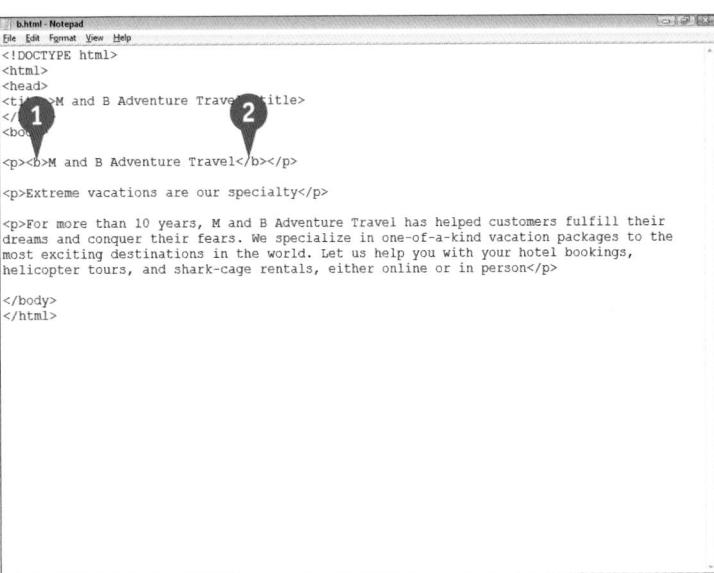

● When displayed in a Web browser, the text appears as bold.

Note: To create bold text using the font-style property in CSS, see Chapter 5.

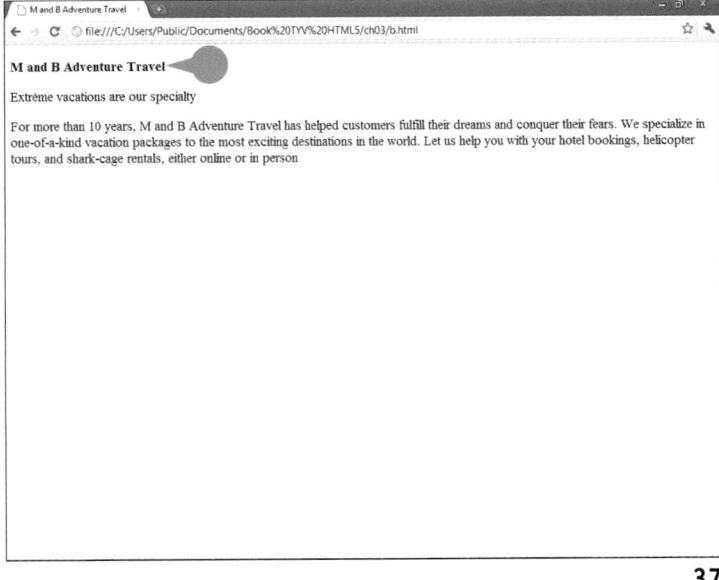

Italicize Text

You can italicize your text to give it more emphasis or set it off from other text in a passage. Common uses for italicized text include highlighting a new term, setting apart the title of a literary work, or marking text as having a different voice. You add italicized text to a page by surrounding the text with `<i>` and `</i>` tags. In most browsers, the `<em>` tag has the same effect as the `<i>` tag.

Italicize Text

1 Type `<i>` in front of the text you want to italicize.

2 Type `</i>` at the end of the text.

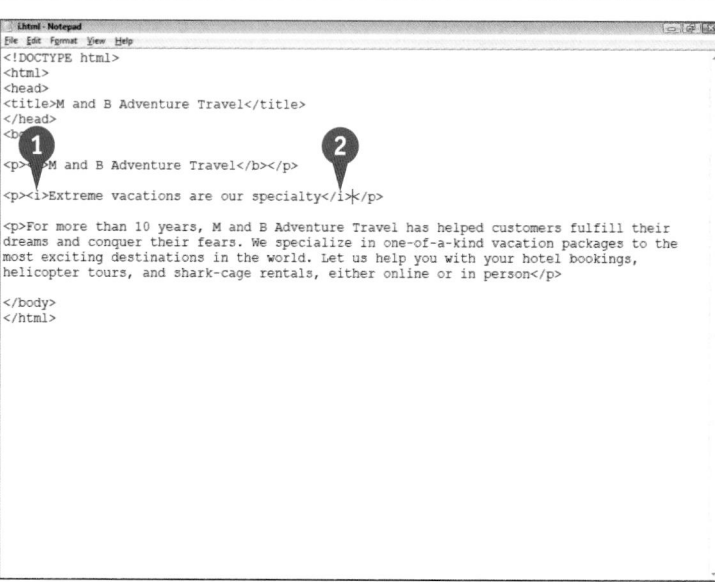

● When displayed in a Web browser, the text appears in italics.

Note: To italicize text using the `font-style` property in CSS, see Chapter 5.

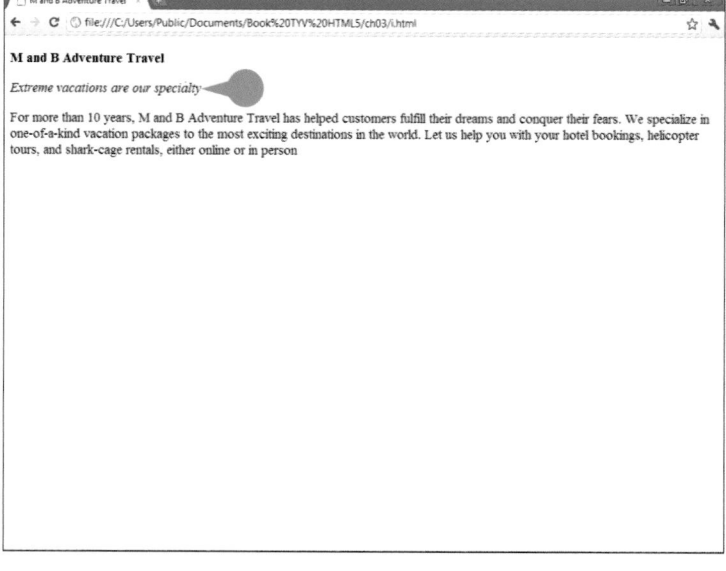

Insert Preformatted Text

You can use the preformatted tags, `<pre>` and `</pre>`, to display all the line breaks and spaces you enter in your HTML code for a passage of text. Web browsers ignore hard returns, line breaks, and extra spaces between words unless you surround the content with preformatted tags. If you type a paragraph with spacing just the way you want it, you can assign the preformatted tags to keep the spacing in place. Preformatted text is also useful for displaying computer code on a web page because the exact spacing of such code can be important.

Insert Preformatted Text

1 Type `<pre>` above the text you want to keep intact.

2 Type `</pre>` below the text.

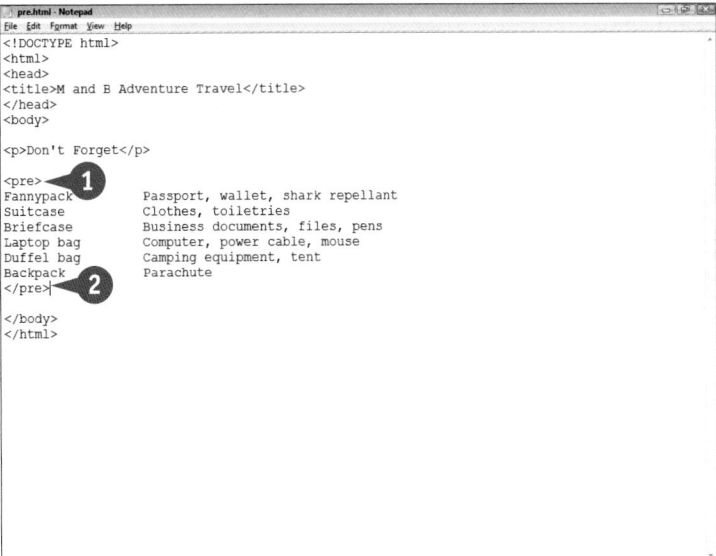

● When displayed in a Web browser, the text retains all your original line breaks and spacing.

Browsers display preformatted text in a monospace font by default. All characters in a monospace font have equal width. This can help you align words within the text into columns.

Insert a Heading

You can use headings to help clarify information on a page, organize text, and create visual structure. You can choose from six heading levels for a document, ranging from heading level 1 (<h1>), the largest, to heading level 6 (<h6>), the smallest. Browsers display headings as bold text on a web page with space above and below, similar to paragraphs. On a basic web page with text content, you typically use an <h1> tag as the main title, the <h2> tag for subtitles, and so on. You can customize the size, font, color, alignment, and other attributes of your headings using CSS styles. See Chapter 5 for details.

Insert a Heading

① Type <h?> in front of the text you want to turn into a heading, replacing ? with the heading level number you want to assign.

You can set a heading level from 1 to 6.

② Type </h?> at the end of the heading text, replacing ? with the corresponding heading level you assign.

③ Type additional heading tags for any other text that you want to emphasize on the page.

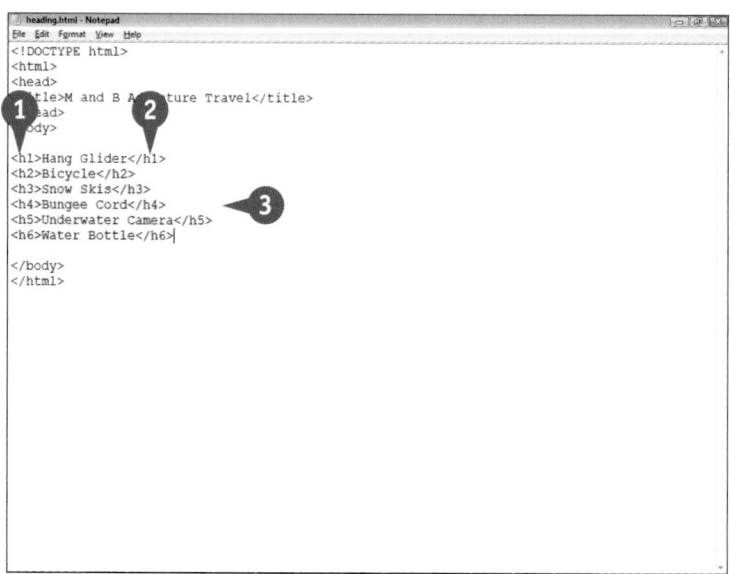

● The heading appears in bold text in the web browser.

This figure shows an example of each heading size in descending order.

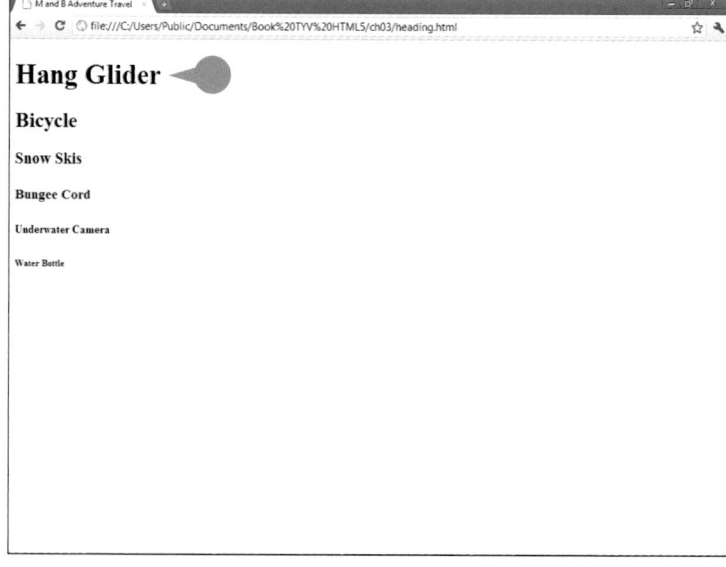

Add a Block Quote

You can use block quotes to set off a passage of text from the rest of the document. In the browser, the `<blockquote>` tag typically adds an equal amount of extra space on both sides of the text. Block quotes are commonly used with quoted text or excerpts from other sources. Another way to add space around blocks of text is with CSS styles. You can also change color, font size, and other characteristics of your blocks of text with CSS. See Chapter 5 for details.

Add a Block Quote

① Type `<blockquote>` in front of the text you want to turn into a block quote.

② Type `</blockquote>` at the end of the text.

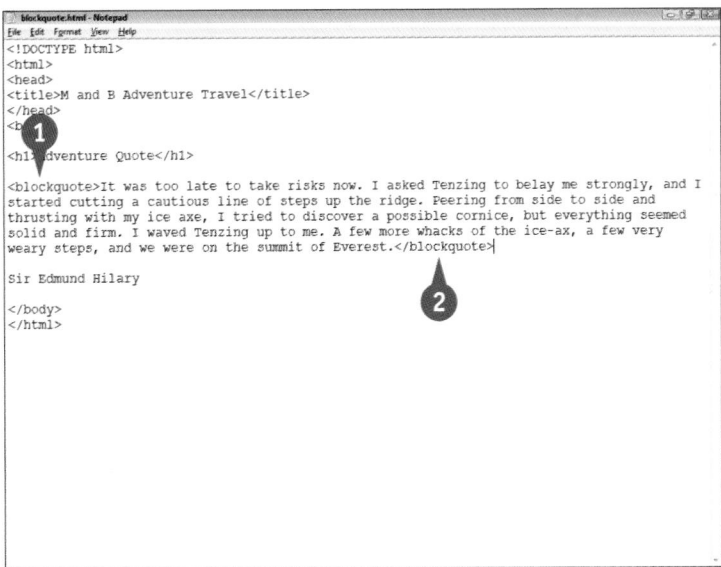

● The web browser displays the block quote as inset text on the document page.

Note: You can mark text within a passage as quoted using the `<q>` and `</q>` tags. The web browser adds quotation marks to the surrounded text.

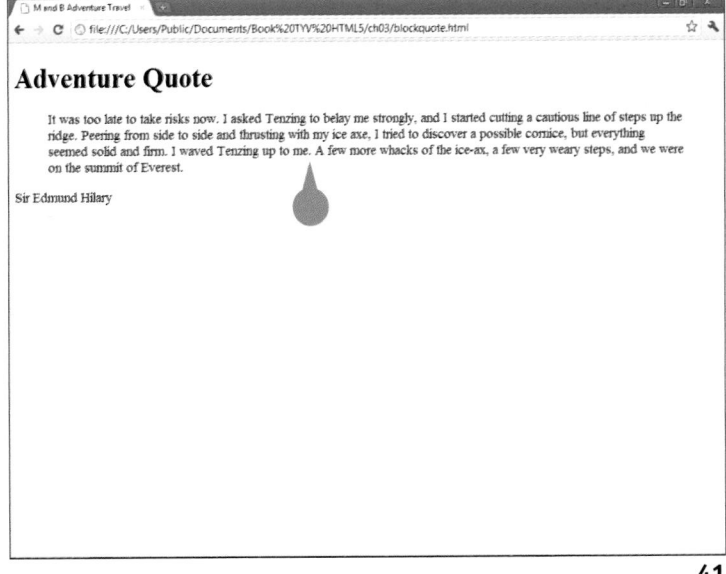

Add Small Print

You can add small print to your page by surrounding text with `<small>` and `</small>` tags. Small print typically includes disclaimers, legal restrictions, copyright information, and other subordinate comments. Not surprisingly, web browsers display this type of text in a smaller sized font.

Small print is often put in the footer of a page. For details about marking a section of your page as a footer using the `<footer>` tag, see Chapter 11.

Add Small Print

1 Type `<small>` in front of the text you want to mark as small text.

2 Type `</small>` at the end of the text.

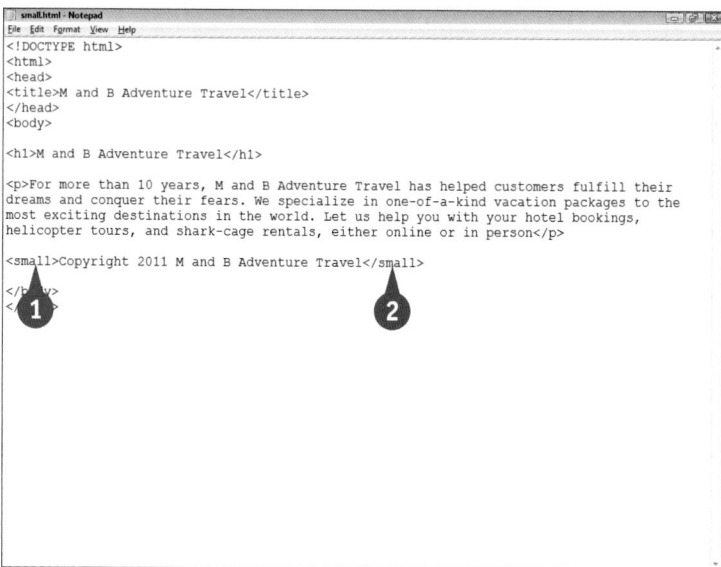

● The web browser displays the text smaller than the regular text on the page.

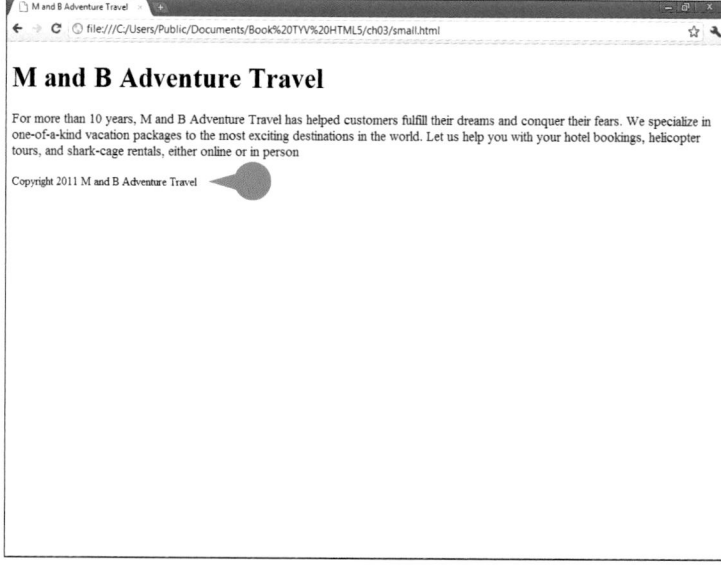

Insert a Comment

You can use comments to write notes to yourself within your HTML code. Comments do not appear when a browser displays a web page. For example, you might leave a comment about a future editing task or leave a note to other web developers viewing your HTML source code. Comments can also be useful for highlighting important sections of HTML code, such as where the header, footer, or navigation section on a page starts and ends. In HTML5, you can also define such sections with semantic tags. See Chapter 11 for details.

You can also place comments around HTML code to turn that code off. The browser does not interpret HTML tags inside comments.

Insert a Comment

1 Type < ! -- where you want to place a comment.

2 Type the comment text.

3 Type -->.

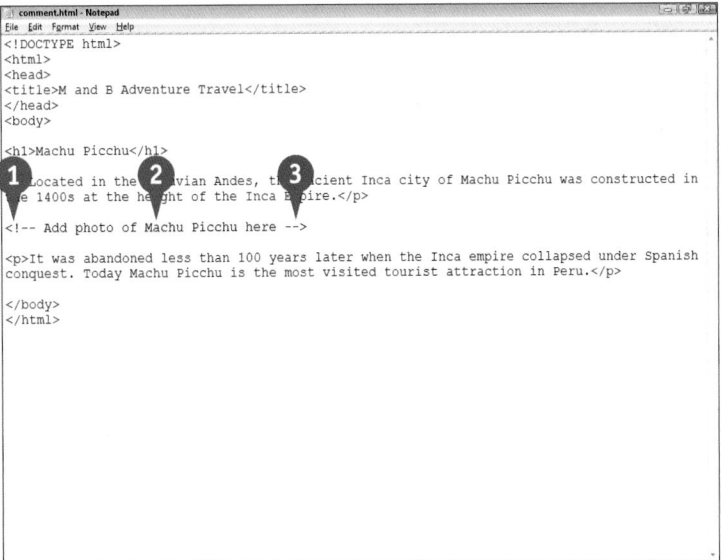

● The comment does not appear on the page when viewed in a web browser.

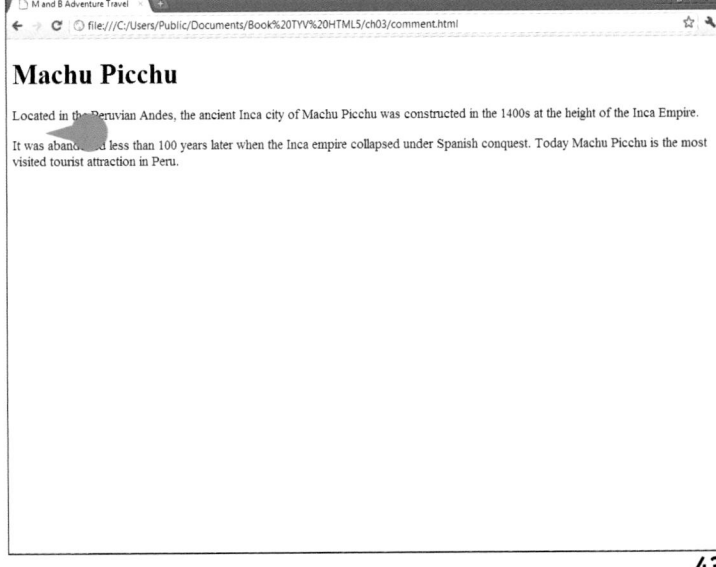

Create a Numbered List

You can use numbered lists on your web page to display all kinds of ordered lists. For example, you can use numbered lists to show steps or prioritize items. You create a numbered list by inserting <ol> and </ol> tags around <li> and </li> tags. The <li> tags specify the list items. You can change the style of the numbers in your list using the type attribute. This enables you to order content using letters or Roman numerals.

Create a Numbered List

Place Text in a Numbered List

1 Type <ol> above the text you want to turn into a numbered list.

2 Type <li> in front of each item in the list.

3 Type </li> after each list item.

4 Type </ol> after the list text.

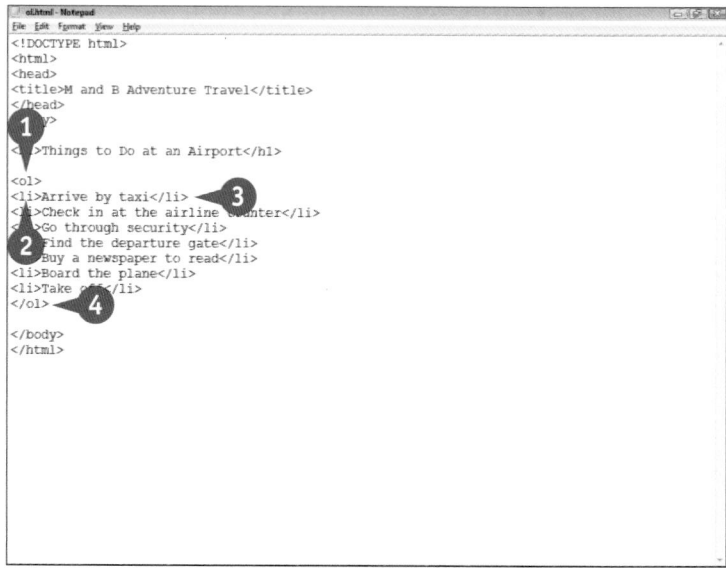

● The text appears as a numbered list on the web page.

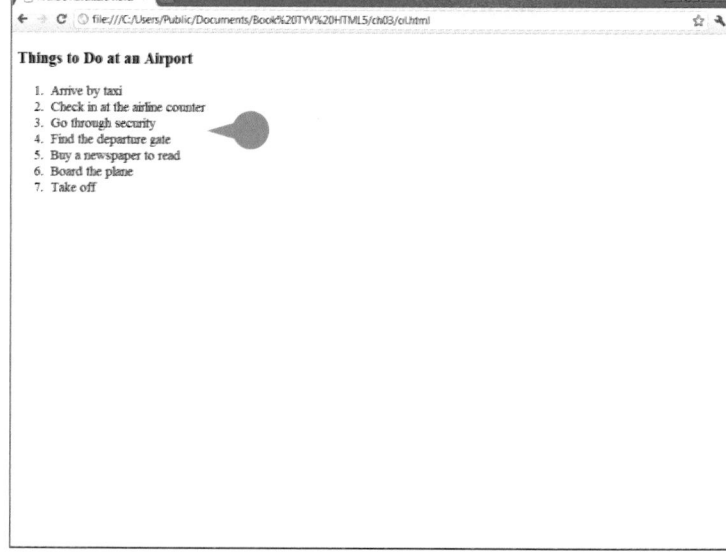

Set a Number Style

1 Type `type="?"` within the `<ol>` tag, replacing *?* with a number style code:

A: A, B, C

a: a, b, c

I: I, II, III

i: i, ii, iii

1: 1, 2, 3

The numbered list appears in the style you selected.

● In this example, the list uses letters rather than numbers.

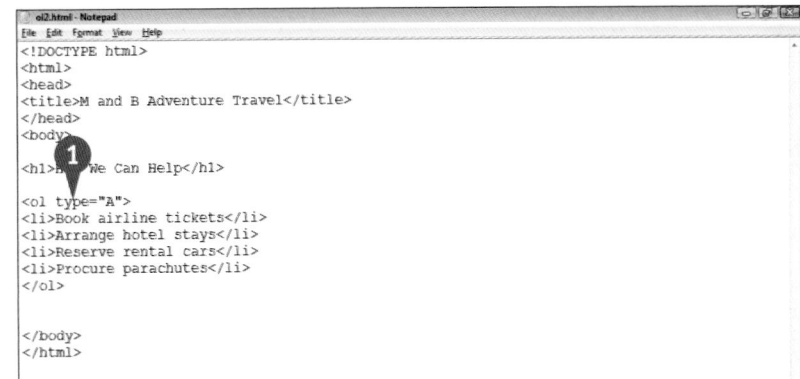

```
ol2.html - Notepad
File  Edit  Format  View  Help
<!DOCTYPE html>
<html>
<head>
<title>M and B Adventure Travel</title>
</head>
<body>

<h1>How We Can Help</h1>

<ol type="A">
<li>Book airline tickets</li>
<li>Arrange hotel stays</li>
<li>Reserve rental cars</li>
<li>Procure parachutes</li>
</ol>

</body>
</html>
```

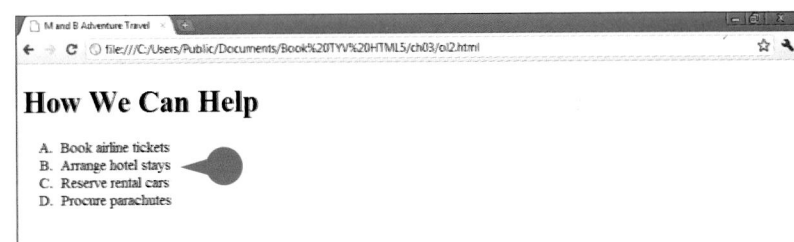

M and B Adventure Travel

← → C ⓘ file:///C:/Users/Public/Documents/Book%20TYV%20HTML5/ch03/ol2.html

How We Can Help

A. Book airline tickets
B. Arrange hotel stays
C. Reserve rental cars
D. Procure parachutes

TIPS

How do I add another item to my numbered list?
Simply insert the text where you want it to appear in the list and add the `<li>` and `</li>` tags before and after the text. The web browser displays the new list order the next time you view the page, rearranging numbers where necessary.

How do I start my numbered list with different numbering from the default numbering?
By default, a web browser reads your numbered list coding and starts with the number 1. To start with a different number, you must add a `start` attribute to the `<ol>` tag. For example, if the numbering is to start at 5, the coding would read `<ol start="5">`.

Create a Bulleted List

You can add a bulleted list to your document to set a list of items apart from the rest of the page of text. You can use a bulleted list, also called an unordered list, when you do not need to show the items in a particular order. You create a bulleted list by inserting `<ul>` and `</ul>` tags around `<li>` and `</li>` tags. The `<li>` tags specify the list items.

By default in most browsers, bullets appear as solid circles. You can use a CSS style to display another bullet style such as a square or an open circle. For details, see Chapter 5.

Create a Bulleted List

1 Type `<ul>` above the text you want to turn into a bulleted list.

2 Type `type="?"` within the `<ul>` tag, replacing ? with a bullet style code, for example `circle`, `disc`, or `square`.

3 Type `<li>` in front of each item in the list.

4 Type `</li>` after each list item.

5 Type `</ul>` after the list text.

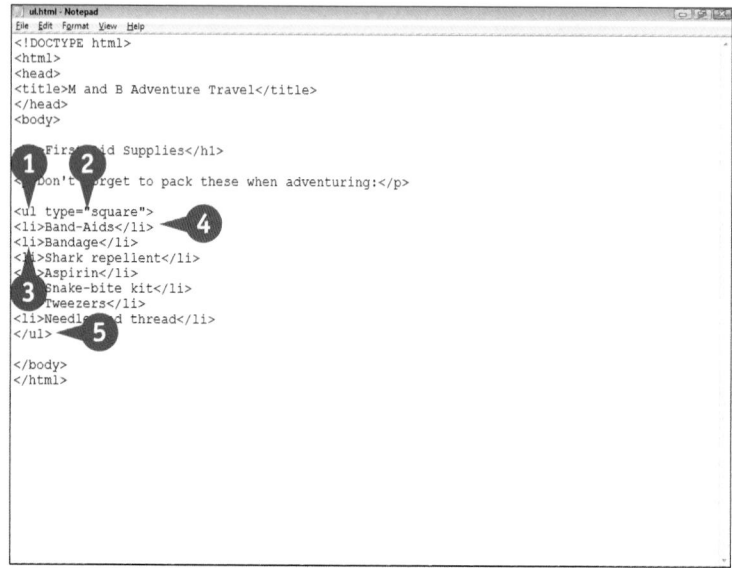

● The text appears as a bulleted list on the web page.

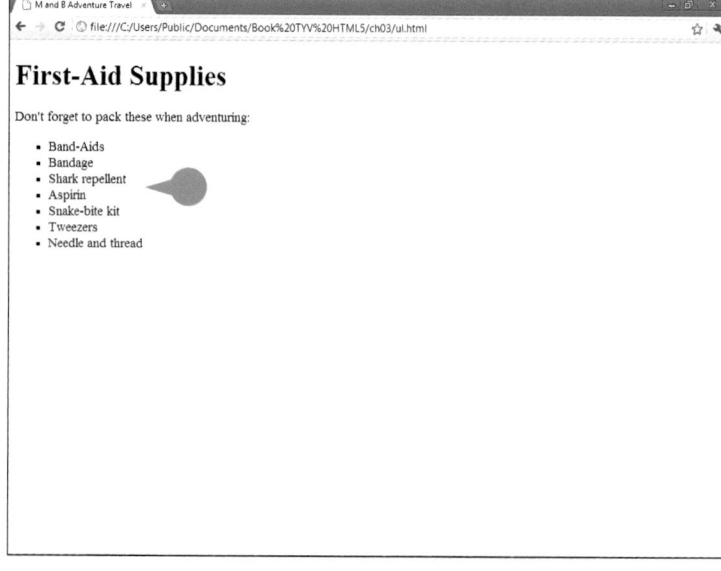

Create a Nested List

Y ou can use a nested list to add a list within a list to your web page. Nested lists enable you to display listed text at different levels within the list hierarchy, such as when you are displaying products arranged in categories and subcategories. Web browsers use indentation to show where list items exist in the hierarchy. You can use both numbered and bulleted lists within an existing list. To create plain numbered and bulleted lists, see the earlier sections in this chapter.

Create a Nested List

1 Click where you want to insert a nested list, or add a new line within the existing list and type `<ol>` for a numbered list or `<ul>` for an unordered list.

Note: To create a numbered list, see the section "Create a Numbered List." To create a bulleted list, see the section "Create a Bulleted List."

2 Type the new list text, including the `<li>` and `</li>` tags, using the same technique you used to create the original list.

3 Type `</ol>` or `</ul>` at the end of the nested list.

- The text appears as a nested list on the web page.

  Browsers usually set off nested lists with different bullet styles. In this example, a nested list gets an open circle.

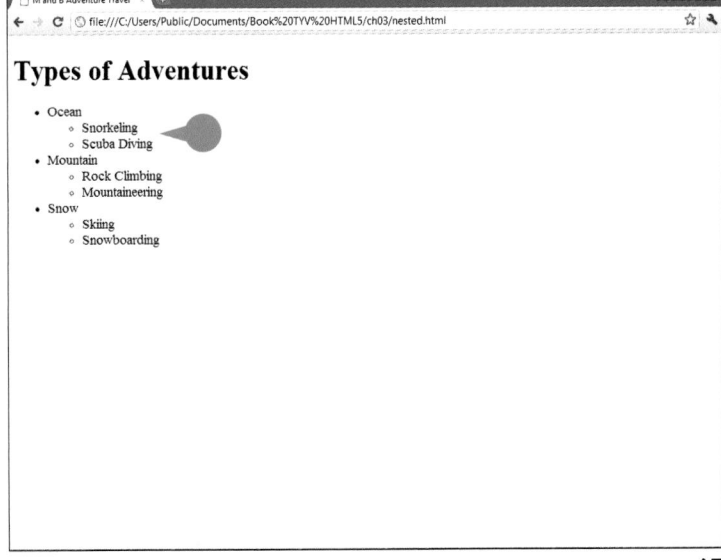

Create a Definition List

You can use a definition list in your document to define content in the format of a glossary or dictionary. Typically, items in a definition list come in pairs, with the first element being the term to be defined and the second being the definition. You use the `<dl>` tag to delimit your definition list, the `<dt>` tag to define your terms, and the `<dd>` tag to add your definitions. When displayed, definitions are typically indented relative to the terms.

Create a Definition List

1 Type `<dl>` above the text you want to set as a definition list.

2 Type `<dt>` in front of each term and `</dt>` after each term.

3 Type `<dd>` in front of each definition and `</dd>` after each definition.

4 Type `</dl>` after the definition list text.

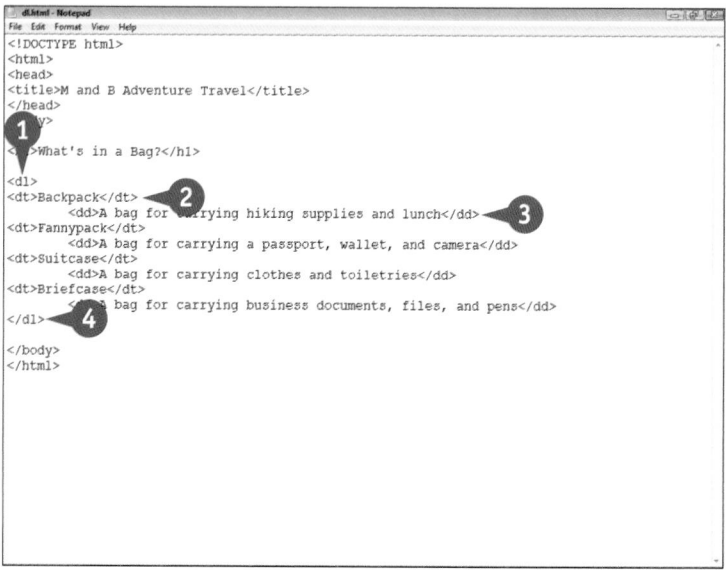

● The text appears as a definition list on the web page.

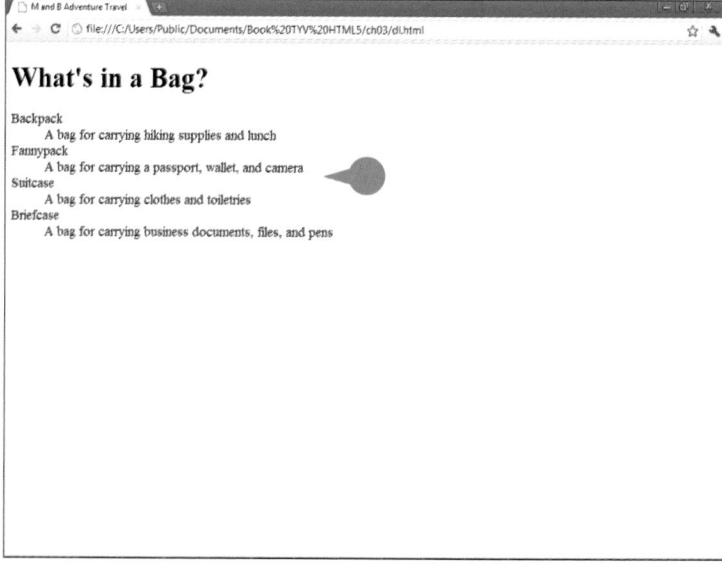

Define an Abbreviation

You can mark text as being an abbreviation in your content using the <abbr> tag. You can then spell out the abbreviation using a `title` attribute within the <abbr> tag. This can be helpful for an abbreviation whose meaning is not obvious to viewers. In most browsers, positioning your cursor over text defined as an abbreviation shows any associated title text as a popup. Search engines can also read the abbreviation information to better categorize your page.

Define an Abbreviation

① Type <abbr> before the text you want to define as an abbreviation.

② Type </abbr> after the text.

③ Within the <abbr> tag, type `title="?"`, replacing ? with the expansion of the abbreviation.

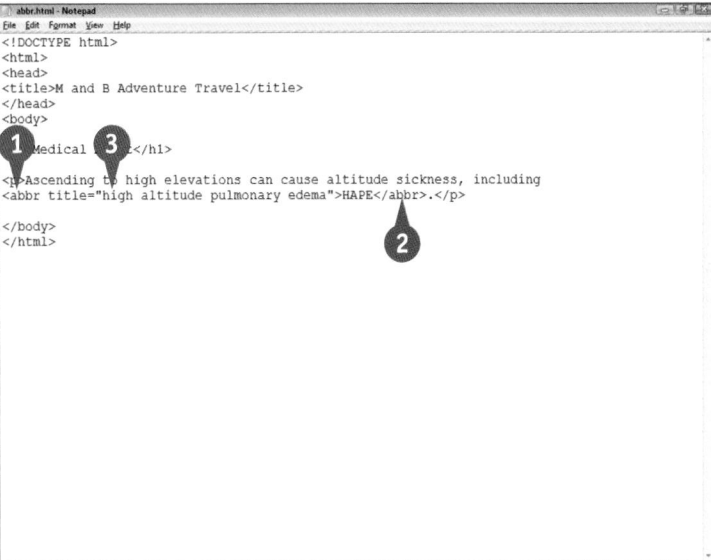

● In a web browser, when you position the cursor over the abbreviated text, a popup appears, showing the title content.

Add a Date and Time

You can use the `<time>` tag to mark text in your document as a date and time. You can specify the exact time value with the `datetime` attribute. The `<time>` tag can be used to mark event start and end times, birthdates, holidays, or other time-related content. Adding the tag allows scripts and search engines to programmatically retrieve the exact time or date associated with the content from your page. The `<time>` tag is new to HTML5.

Add a Date and Time

1. Type content on your page that includes a date and time.

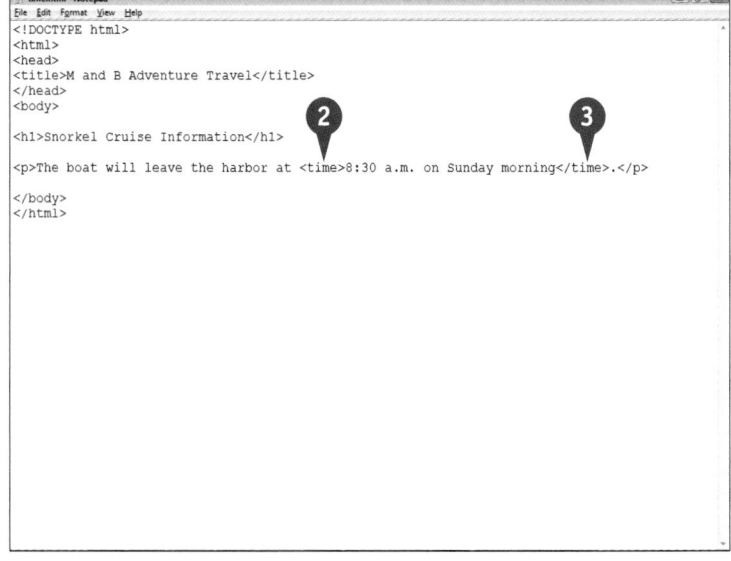

2. Type `<time>` at the beginning of the time text.

3. Type `</time>` at the end of the time text.

Note: This is the simplest way to mark text on your page as a time, without additional attributes.

④ Click in the `<time>` tag and type `datetime="YYYY-MM-DD"`, replacing *YYYY* with the year, *MM* with the month, and *DD* with the day.

⑤ After the date, type a `T` and then the time as `HH:MM:SS`, replacing *HH* with the hour, *MM* with the minutes, and *SS* with the seconds.

● A web browser displays the time without any extra formatting. However, scripts in your page can access the `datetime` value.

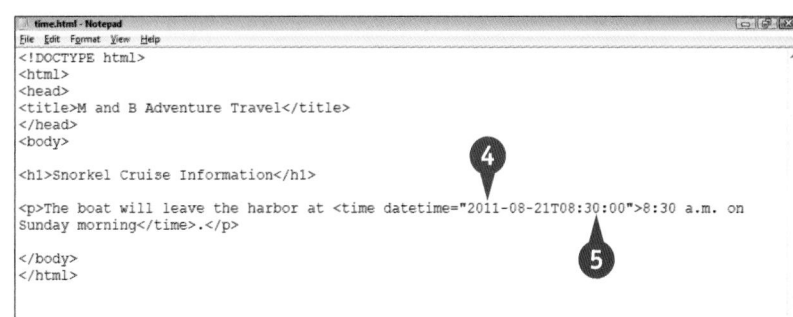

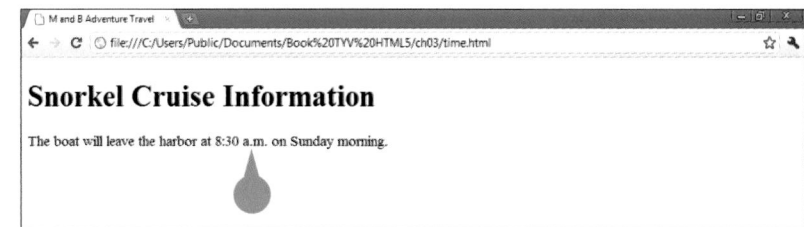

TIPS

Is a time required in the datetime attribute?
No. If you want, you can leave out the hours, minutes, and seconds as well as the preceding "T" and the HTML is valid. The `datetime` value must, at a minimum, include a year, month, and day.

How do I specify the publication date of my web page?
You can mark a date on your page as the time that your page was created by adding a `pubdate` attribute to the date's `<time>` tag:

```
This page was created <time
datetime="2011-03-15" pubdate>March 15,
2011</time>.
```

The `pubdate` attribute stands alone and does not require a value.

Insert Special Characters

You can use HTML code to insert special characters into your web page text. Special characters are characters that do not usually appear on your keyboard.

The codes used to insert special characters are called *entities*. Entities consist of number or name codes preceded by an ampersand and ending with a semicolon, such as `&frac12;` for the fraction ½ or `&para;` for a paragraph symbol.

Insert Special Characters

1 Click where you want to insert a special character.

2 Type the number or name code for the character, with an ampersand (`&`) before the code and a semicolon (`;`) following the code.

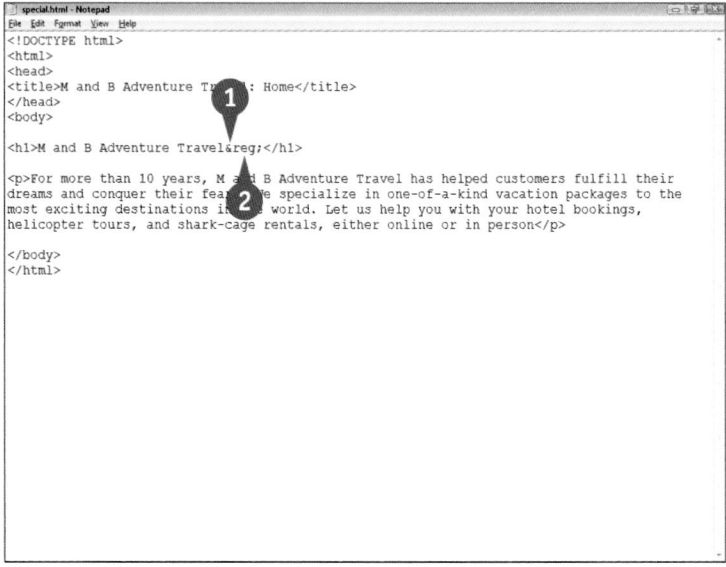

● The Web browser displays the designated character in the text.

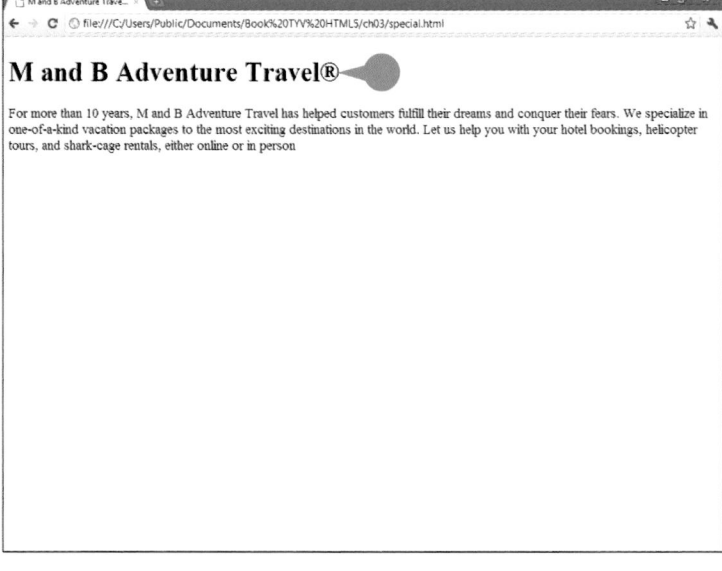

Special Characters

To properly insert many special characters into your web page text, you need to know their entity codes. The following table lists the common special characters you can insert. For a more detailed list, see www.wooldridge.net/html5. For more on inserting these special characters, see the section "Insert Special Characters."

Description	Special Character	Code	Description	Special Character	Code
Copyright	©	&copy;	small o, slash	ø	&oslash;
Registered trademark	®	&reg;	em dash	—	&mdash;
Trademark	™	&trade;	en dash	–	&ndash;
paragraph mark	¶	&para;	micro	µ	&micro;
nonbreaking space			macron	¯	&macr;
quotation mark	"	&quot;	superscript one	¹	&sup1;
left angle quote	«	&laquo;	superscript two	²	&sup2;
right angle quote	»	&raquo;	superscript three	³	&sup3;
ampersand	&	&amp;	one-half fraction	½	&frac12;
inverted exclamation	¡	&iexcl;	one-fourth fraction	¼	&frac14;
inverted question mark	¿	&iquest;	three-fourths fraction	¾	&frac34;
broken vertical bar	¦	&brvbar;	degree	°	&deg;
section	§	&sect;	multiply	×	&times;
not	¬	&not;	division	÷	&divide;
acute accent	´	&acute;	plus-or-minus	±	&plusmn;
cedilla	¸	&cedil;	less-than	<	&lt;
bullet	•	&bull;	greater-than	>	&gt;
capital N, tilde	Ñ	&NTilde;	dagger	†	&dagger;
small n, tilde	ñ	&ntilde;	double dagger	‡	&Dagger;
capital A, tilde	Ã	&Atilde;	cent	¢	&cent;
small a, tilde	ã	&atilde;	pound sterling	£	&pound;
capital A, grave accent	À	&Agrave;	euro	€	&euro;
small a, grave accent	à	&agrave;	yen	¥	&yen;
capital O, slash	Ø	&Oslash;	general currency	¤	&curren;

Adding CSS Styles

HTML5 code is for defining the meaning of your web page content. To define how your page looks — for example, the size of the text, the background colors, and the spacing around images — you need to use Cascading Style Sheets, or CSS. This chapter gives you the basics about defining CSS styles and assigning them to your HTML tags. Getting a solid foundation with CSS is important in HTML5 because many style features that were available in previous versions of HTML now must be done using CSS.

```
page-with-styles.html - Notepad
File  Edit  Format  View  Help
<!DOCTYPE html>
<html>
<head>
<title>M and B Adventure Travel</title>

<style>
body { color: black;
       background: white }
h2   { color: red }
p    { font-size: 10px;
       text-align: center }
</style>

</head>
<body>

<header>
<h1>M and B Adventure Travel</h1>
<h2>Extreme vacations are our specialty</h2>
</header>

<nav>
<a href="index.html">Home</a>
<a href="dest.html">Destinations</a>
<a href="tips.html">Travel Tips</a>
<a href="contact.html">Contact Us</a>
</nav>

<section>
<p>For more than 10 years, M and B Adventure Travel has helped customers fulfill their
dreams and conquer their fears. We specialize in one-of-a-kind vacation packages to the
most exciting destinations in the world. Let us help you with your hotel bookings,
helicopter tours, and shark-cage rentals, either online or in person</p>
</section>
```

Understanding Style Sheets

HTML5 enables you to define many different types of content on a web page, including headings, paragraphs, lists, images, input fields, canvases, and multimedia. To specify how this content looks, you need to add Cascading Style Sheets, or CSS. CSS lets you specify colors, font families, backgrounds, margin widths, alignment, and much, much more. You can define CSS rules inside your HTML document or in a separate file. Like HTML documents, CSS documents are simple text files. By relegating formatting controls to a separate CSS document, you can free your HTML documents of repetitive coding and concentrate on the content that makes up your pages.

Separating Styling from HTML

A central tenet of HTML5 is that HTML tags specify what your content *means*. For example, you define the most important heading on a page with an `<h1>` tag. Telling a web browser how that heading is *presented* is done separately with CSS. With CSS, you can specify that your heading be bright red, 36 pixels tall, and aligned to the right side of the page. Separating styling from your HTML is convenient for browsers that do not render web pages visually. For example, speech-based browsers that read page content aloud for the sight impaired can ignore the CSS and just interpret the HTML.

Defining Style Sheets

A CSS style sheet is typically a text file separate from your HTML document. A style sheet holds formatting codes that control the appearance of your web page. You can use style sheets to change the look of any web page element, such as paragraphs, lists, backgrounds, and more. Any time you want to apply the formatting from an external style sheet to an HTML document, you attach the style sheet to the page using a `<link>` tag. Style sheet files have a .css file extension. Style sheets can also be internal, residing within your HTML code between `<style>` and `</style>` tags.

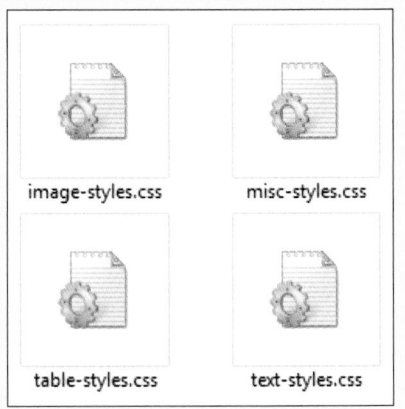

image-styles.css   misc-styles.css

table-styles.css   text-styles.css

Controlling Multiple Pages

You can link every page in your website to a single style sheet. Any changes you make to the style sheet rules are reflected in every HTML document linking to the sheet. By storing all the formatting information in one place, you can easily update the appearance of your site's pages all at once. This can be a real timesaver if your site consists of lots of pages.

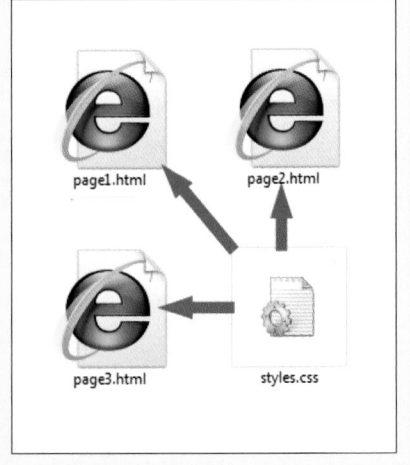

page1.html   page2.html

page3.html   styles.css

Style Sheet Syntax

Style sheets are made up of rules, and each rule has two distinct parts: a selector and a declaration. The selector specifies the element to which you want to apply a style rule, and the declaration specifies the formatting for the selector:

```
h2 {color: red}
```

In the above example, the selector is h2 and {color: red} is the declaration (●). When applied to a page, this rule makes all level 2 headings appear in red.

```
<!DOCTYPE html>
<html>
<head>
<title>M and B Adventure Travel</title>

<style>
body { color: black;
       background: white }
h2   { color: red }
p    { font-size: 10px;
       text-align: center }
</style>

</head>
<body>
```

Style Sheet Declarations

A declaration consists of one or more property-value pairs such as font-size: 12px or position: absolute. Each property and value is separated by a colon; multiple property-value pairs in a declaration are separated by semicolons. Putting each property-value pair on a separate line when writing your rules is good form. Similar to HTML, you can add extra spaces and line breaks to your style sheet code to make your code more readable.

Style Classes

If you want to apply formatting to only a particular instance of a tag, you can define a CSS *class* for that tag:

```
p.huge {font-size: 60px}
```

The above code defines a "huge" class that can be applied to HTML paragraphs. You can apply the class using the class attribute inside a paragraph tag:

```
<p class="huge">Enormous text.</p>
```

In this example, only paragraphs that have the huge class applied to them will have the font-size rule applied.

Inheritance

Tags you add inside other tags inherit the outer tag's formatting, unless you specify otherwise. For example, if you define a style for the <body> tag (●), any heading or paragraph tags you nest within the <body> tag inherit the same formatting (●). HTML inheritance makes it easy to keep the formatting consistent as you add new items within an element.

```
<!DOCTYPE html>
<html>
<head>
<title>M and B Adventure Travel</title>
<style>
body { color: black; font-family: arial }
</style>
</head>
<body>

<h1>M and B Adventure Travel</h1>

<p>For more than 10 years, M and B Adventure Travel has helped customers fulfill their
dreams and conquer their fears. We specialize in one-of-a-kind vacation packages to the
most exciting destinations in the world. Let us help you with your hotel bookings,
helicopter tours, and shark-cage rentals, either online or in person</p>

</body>
</html>
```

Create an Internal Style Sheet

You can create an internal style sheet that resides within the `<head>` tag of your HTML5 document. The styles of an internal style sheet are delineated by `<style>` and `</style>` tags and apply only to the HTML in that document. Internal style sheets are handy if your website consists of a single page because you can change both style rules and HTML in the same file. If you want to apply the same styles to multiple web pages, consider putting the styles in an external style sheet. See the section "Create an External Style Sheet" for details.

Create an Internal Style Sheet

① Within the `<head>` and `</head>` tags, add a new line and type `<style type="text/css">`.

② Add a new line and type the element tag for which you want to create a style rule.

In this example, a new style rule is created for the `h1` element.

You can add extra spaces for legibility.

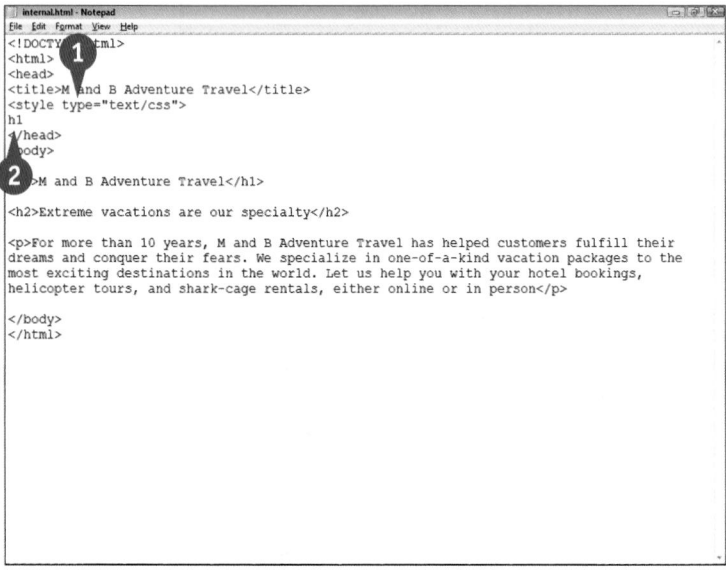

③ Type `{`.

④ Type the properties and values for the rule.

If you intend to add more than one property-value pair to a declaration, be sure to separate the pairs with semicolons.

⑤ Type `}` to end the rule.

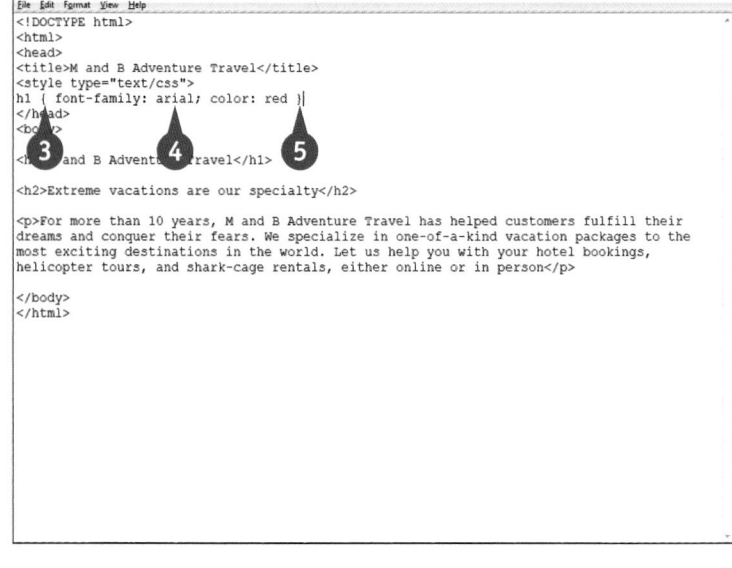

6 Repeat steps **2** to **5** to continue adding style rules to your internal style sheet.

Note: To learn more about writing style rules, see Chapters 5 and 10.

```
internal.html - Notepad
File  Edit  Format  View  Help
<!DOCTYPE html>
<html>
<head>
<title>M and B Adventure Travel</title>
<style type="text/css">
h1 { font-family: arial; color: red }
h2 { font-family: arial; font-style: italic }
p { font-size: 12px }
</head>
<body>

<h1>M and B Adventure Travel</h1>

<h2>Extreme vacations are our specialty</h2>

<p>For more than 10 years, M and B Adventure Travel has helped customers fulfill their
dreams and conquer their fears. We specialize in one-of-a-kind vacation packages to the
most exciting destinations in the world. Let us help you with your hotel bookings,
helicopter tours, and shark-cage rentals, either online or in person</p>

</body>
</html>
```
6

7 Add a new line and type `</style>`.

You can save your page and test it in a browser to see the style sheet results.

Note: To learn more about viewing HTML5 documents in a browser, see Chapter 2.

```
internal.html - Notepad
File  Edit  Format  View  Help
<!DOCTYPE html>
<html>
<head>
<title>M and B Adventure Travel</title>
<style type="text/css">
h1 { font-family: arial; color: red }
h2 { font-family: arial; font-style: italic }
p { font-size: 12px }
</style>
</head>
<body>

<h1>M and B Adventure Travel</h1>

<h2>Extreme vacations are our specialty</h2>

<p>For more than 10 years, M and B Adventure Travel has helped customers fulfill their
dreams and conquer their fears. We specialize in one-of-a-kind vacation packages to the
most exciting destinations in the world. Let us help you with your hotel bookings,
helicopter tours, and shark-cage rentals, either online or in person</p>

</body>
</html>
```
7

TIPS

What does the type attribute of the <style> tag mean?
The `type` attribute defines the styling language used inside the `<style>` tag. The value `text/css` specifies that the code is CSS. The `text/css` value is also the default, which means if you do not include the attribute, any CSS code inside the `<style>` tag will still be recognized and work correctly.

Can I link another web page to my internal style sheet?
No. A page cannot access another page's internal style sheet. If you want multiple web pages to take advantage of a set of style rules, you must define those rules in an external style sheet and link the pages to the sheet. An internal style sheet is useful only if you want to apply those styles to a single HTML document. See the section "Create an External Style Sheet" to learn more.

Create an External Style Sheet

You can use an external style sheet to define formatting and layout instructions and then apply those instructions to your HTML5 documents. Style sheets can include rules for customizing text, tables, form elements, and more. You can save the style sheet as a text file and assign the .css file extension to identify the file as a Cascading Style Sheet. For easy access, you can save the file in the same folder as your HTML5 files. If you have multiple style sheets and want to keep them separate, you can save them in a subdirectory.

For more on style sheets and how they work, see the section "Understanding Style Sheets."

Create an External Style Sheet

① Create a new document in your text editor.

Note: To create and save HTML documents, see Chapter 2.

② To create a style rule, type the element tag for which you want to define formatting properties.

This example creates a style rule for level 1 headings.

③ Type a space.

④ Type {.

⑤ Type one or more property-value pairs.

Separate each property and value with a colon. Separate multiple pairs with semicolons. You can add extra spaces for legibility.

In this example, the rule includes setting a font and a font color.

Note: To learn more about writing style rules, see Chapters 5 and 10.

⑥ Type } to end the rule.

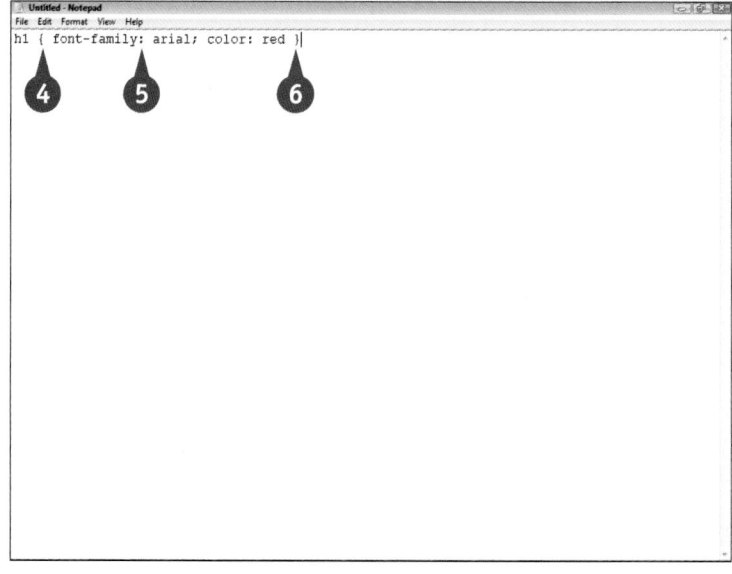

7 Repeat steps **2** to **6** to continue adding rules to your style sheet.

8 Click **File**.

9 Click **Save**.

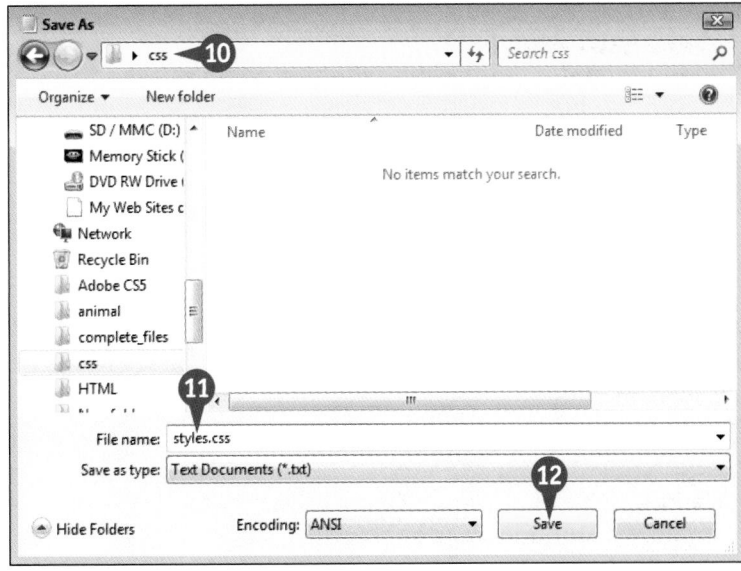

The Save As dialog box appears.

10 Navigate to the folder that contains your HTML pages.

11 Type a unique file name for your style sheet and a **.css** extension.

12 Click **Save**.

Your text editor saves the new style sheet.

Note: To learn how to apply a style sheet to an HTML5 document, see the section "Link to a Style Sheet."

TIPS

How do I add comments to my styles?

You can add comments to your style sheets to describe and identify your style rules. Style sheet comments begin with /* and end with */. For example, you might add a comment explaining the rationale for applying a style rule:

```
h3 {color: #ff0000} /* Highlight level-3
headings with red */
```

Web browsers do not interpret comment information in style sheets. Note that CSS comments are different from HTML comments. See Chapter 3 for details about HTML comments.

Can I override the normal styles of an HTML tag with CSS?

Yes. You may use CSS to change how HTML tags normally appear, even making some tags behave like others. For example, you can change the style of a heading tag so that it looks just like regular paragraph text, or vice versa. See Chapter 5 for some of the many types of styles you can apply to tags with CSS.

Link to a Style Sheet

You can link to an external style sheet to assign a set of formatting rules to your HTML5 document. You use the `<link>` tag to specify the filename and location of the style sheet. You can link multiple documents to the same style sheet to give all the pages in your site a consistent look and feel. You can also assign multiple style sheets to a single document by adding more than one `<link>` tag. To learn how to create a style sheet, see the section "Create an External Style Sheet."

Link to a Style Sheet

① Open the HTML5 document you want to link to a style sheet.

② Click within the `<head>` and `</head>` tags and add a new line.

③ Type `<link rel="stylesheet" type="text/css".`

This specifies that the linked content is a style sheet defined with CSS.

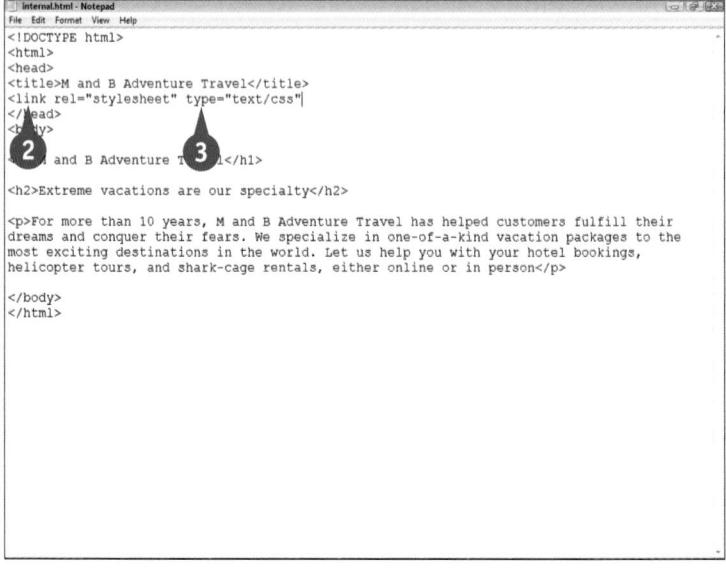

④ Type a blank space and `href="?">`, replacing *?* with the name of the style sheet file.

If the style sheet is located in a subdirectory, precede the filename with the subdirectory name and a slash, for example `css/styles.css`.

The style sheet is now linked with the page.

You can test your page in a browser to see the style sheet results.

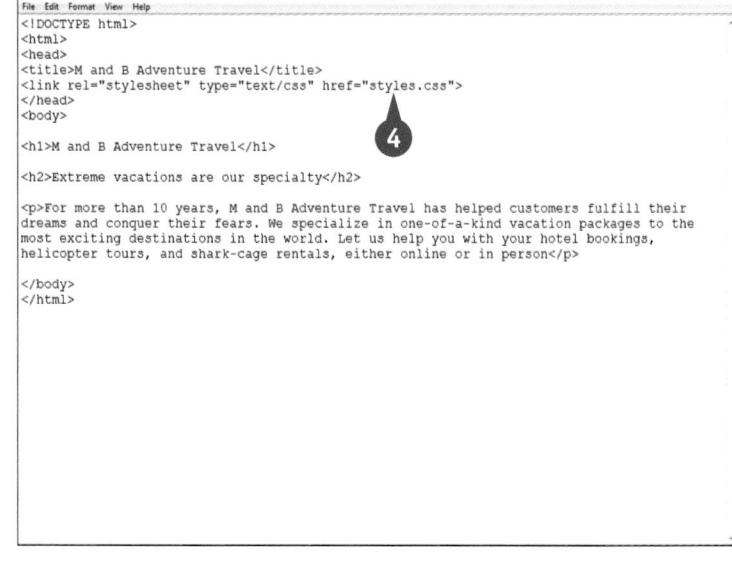

Apply a Style Locally

You can apply a style to a single instance of a tag in your document using an HTML attribute. The `style` attribute enables you to apply a style rule to a tag without having to define the rule separately in an internal or external style sheet.

A style applied locally overrides any styles found on external or internal style sheets for the same tag. Applying styles locally works best for one-time changes or for quickly testing a style on content. You should use internal or external style sheets for styles you plan to apply more than once.

Apply a Style Locally

1. Click in the tag for the element you want to change and type `style="?"`, replacing `?` with the properties and values you want to assign.

   Separate multiple property-value pairs with semicolons.

Note: To learn more about writing style rules, see Chapters 5 and 10.

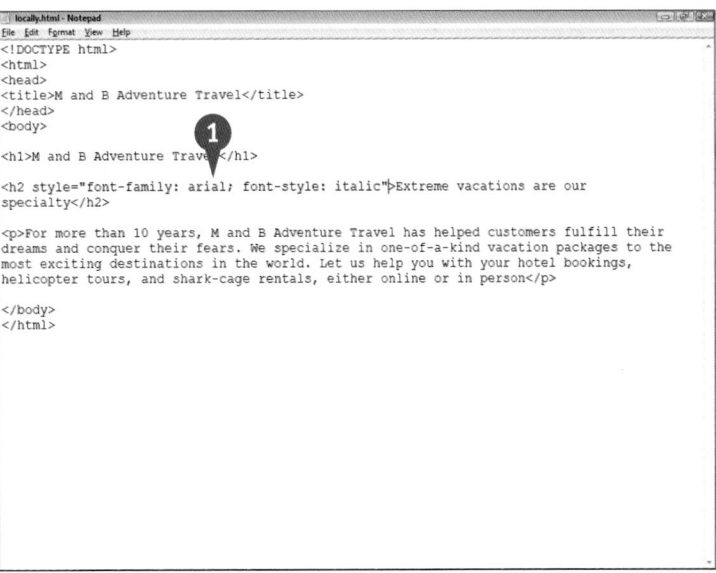

2. Open the HTML5 document in a web browser.

Note: To learn about viewing an HTML5 document in a web browser, see Chapter 2.

● The web browser applies the style to the tag content.

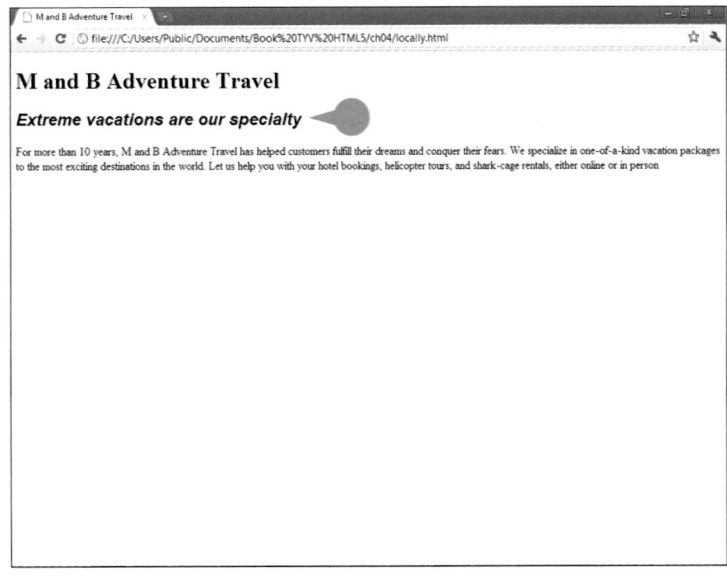

Apply a Style to a Tag

You can create a CSS rule that applies styles to an HTML tag. For example, if you want all the paragraphs on your page to have text in the Arial font face with a size of 14 points, you can create a CSS declaration with those style properties and use p as the selector. Any text surrounded by <p> tags will have that formatting. Similarly, you can apply styles to customize the color and boldness of your <h2> tags or the alignment of your images with the <img> tag.

You can define styles for your HTML tags in an internal or external style sheet. To learn more about creating style sheets, see the sections "Create an Internal Style Sheet" and "Create an External Style Sheet."

Apply a Style to a Tag

Define the Styles

1 In your external or internal style sheet, type the tag for which you want to create a class.

Note: For more about creating internal and external style sheets, see the previous sections in this chapter.

2 Type {.

3 Type one or more property-value pairs for the class.

Separate multiple pairs with semicolons.

In this example, a color style and a font style are applied to a level 1 heading.

Note: To learn more about formatting text with style rules, see Chapters 5 and 10.

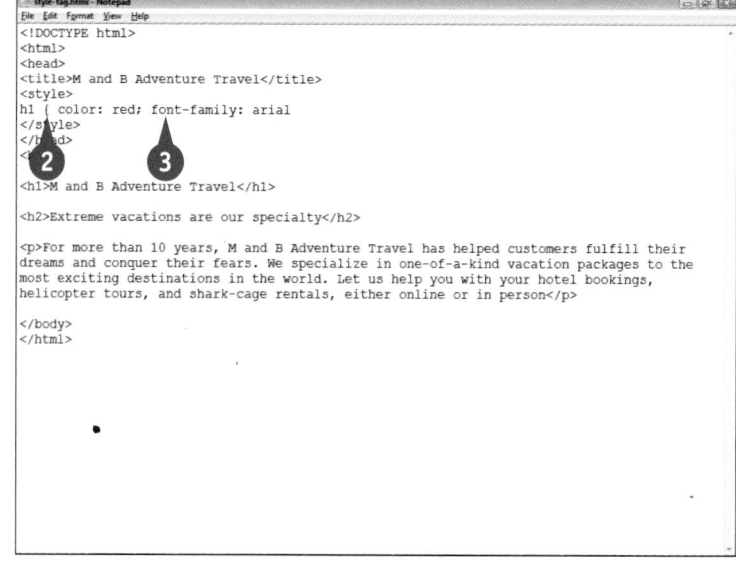

4 Type } to end the style rule.

The tag now has styles associated with it.

If you are editing an external style sheet, save the sheet.

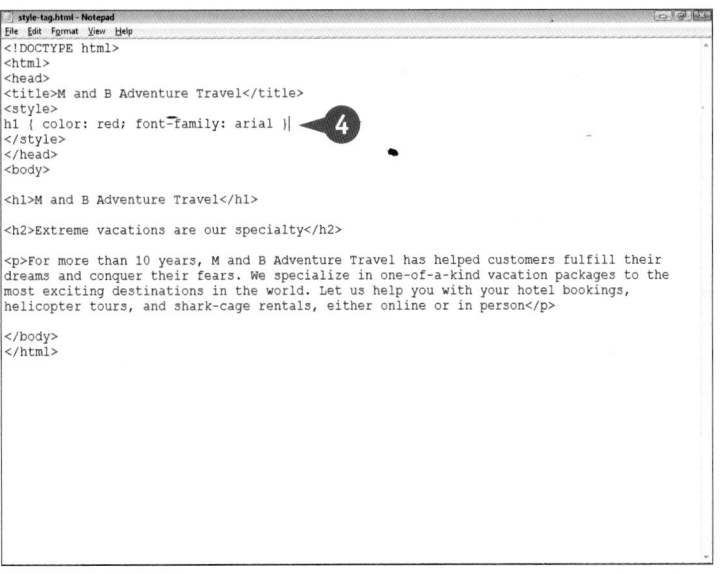

View the Styled Tag

1 In your web browser, open the page.

● The web browser applies the styles to the tag content.

How can I apply one or more styles to multiple tags at once?

You can separate a list of selectors by commas to apply the same set of styles to all of them:

```
h1, h2, h3 {color: red;
font-size: 36px}
```

The style rule above turns all three types of headings on your page red and sizes them to 36 pixels. Writing style rules this way saves you time and makes your code more compact.

How do I apply one or more styles to all HTML tags at once?

You can use the universal selector (*) to apply styles to every HTML tag in your document:

```
* {padding: 0}
```

The style rule above removes the padding from all the elements on your page. Note that you can override such a rule by writing additional rules for specific tags. Adding the following to your style sheet applies padding to h3 headings while, due to the previous rule, all other elements still have no padding:

```
h3 {padding: 10px}
```

Apply a Style Using a Class

You can create a CSS class to apply a style rule to specific instances of HTML tags in a page. For example, if you want the introductory paragraphs formatted differently from all the other paragraphs, you can create a class specifically for the introductory paragraphs. After you create the class and assign it using the `class` attribute, the browser applies the formatting to all the affected paragraphs.

You can set up a class in an internal or external style sheet. To learn more about creating style sheets, see the sections "Create an Internal Style Sheet" and "Create an External Style Sheet."

Apply a Style Using a Class

Define a Class

① In your external or internal style sheet, type the tag for which you want to create a class.

② Type a period.

③ Type a name for the class.

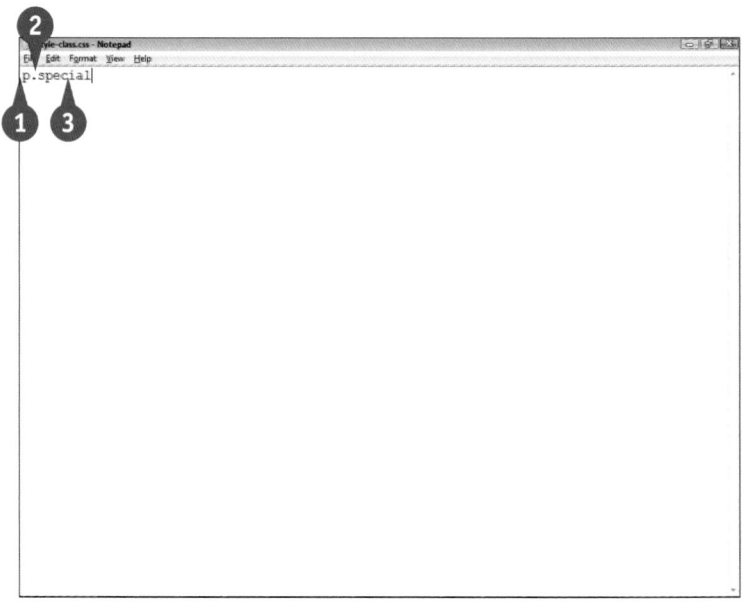

④ Type {.

⑤ Type one or more property-value pairs for the class.

Separate multiple pairs with semicolons.

⑥ Type } to end the style rule.

Your class is now defined.

In this example, a color style and a font weight are applied the paragraph tags.

Note: To learn more about formatting text with style rules, see Chapters 5 and 10.

If you are editing an external style sheet, save the sheet.

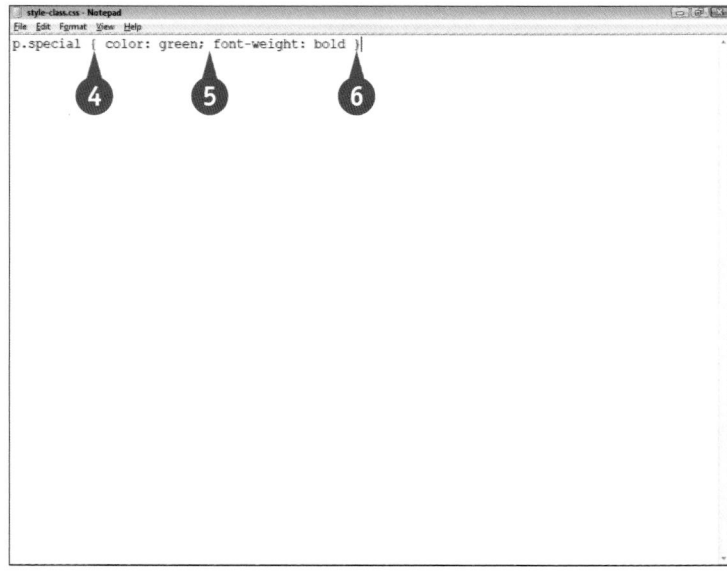

Assign a Class

1 Open the HTML5 document and click in the tag to which you want to assign a class.

2 Type `class="?"`, replacing *?* with the class name.

3 Save the HTML5 document.

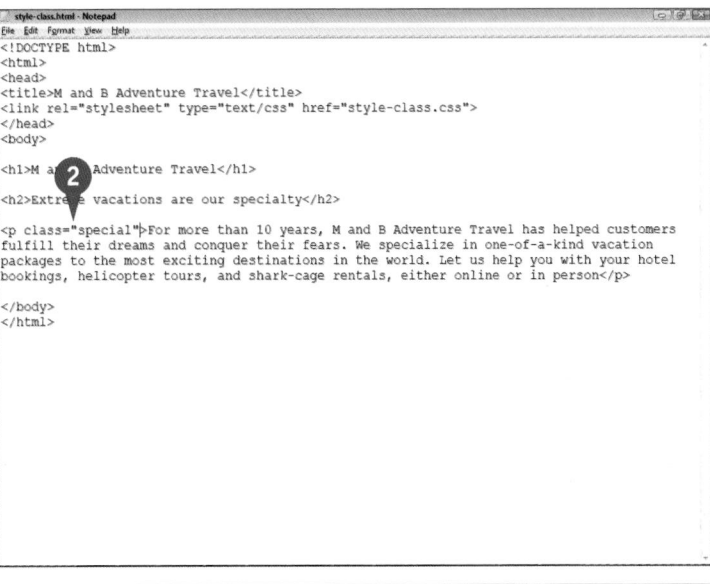

4 Open the HTML5 document in a web browser.

Note: To learn about viewing an HTML5 document in a web browser, see Chapter 2.

● The web browser applies the styles associated with the class to the tag content.

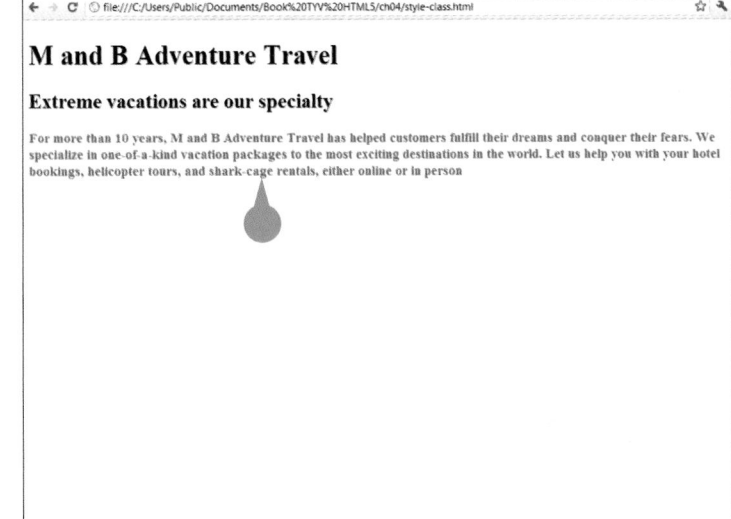

What is a generic class?

You can use a generic class to format more than one type of tag. For example, you might use a generic class to format both paragraphs and level 3 headings in a document. When defining a generic class, simply type a period followed by the class name and then your declaration. For example:

`.myclass {color: blue}`

Do not type an HTML tag before the period. The following HTML examples apply the class to different tags:

`<p class="myclass">`
`<h3 class="myclass">`

Can I assign multiple classes to a tag?

Yes, you can assign multiple classes to a tag to add more than one set of styles to that tag. You separate the class names with spaces. For example:

`<p class="huge fancy">This is a`
`standout sentence.</p>`

The paragraph above would have the styles associated with both the `huge` class and the `fancy` class applied to it.

Apply a Style Using an ID

You can apply an id attribute to an HTML tag on your page to give it a unique identifier. You can then apply styles to that HTML tag using a special CSS selector for that tag. Using the id attribute to apply styles is an alternative to using the class attribute. See "Apply a Style Using a Class" for more about applying CSS classes.

You can set your ID rules in an internal or external style sheet. To learn more about creating style sheets, see the sections "Create an Internal Style Sheet" and "Create an External Style Sheet."

Apply a Style Using an ID

Set Up the ID

① Inside the HTML tag to which you want to set an ID, type id="?", replacing ? with a unique identifier.

The identifier must begin with a letter and may be followed with letters, numbers, hyphens (-), underscores (_), and colons (:).

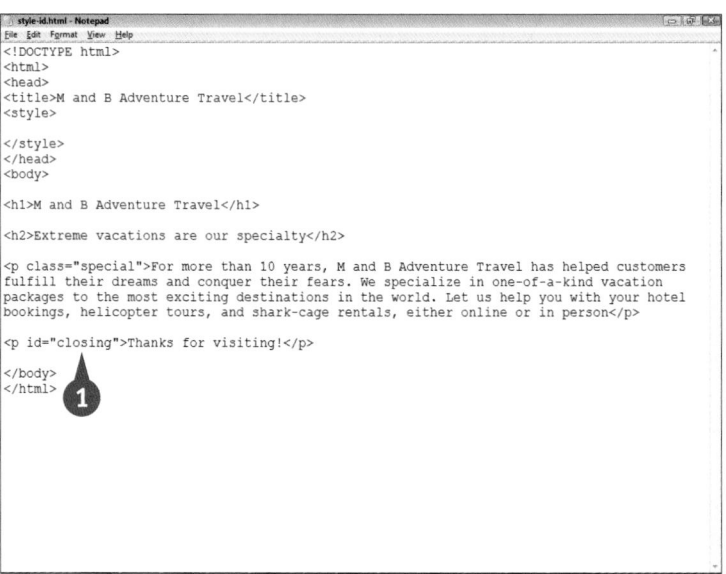

Assign a Style

① In your style sheet, type the name of the HTML tag.

② Type #?, replacing ? with the identifier you assigned to the tag.

In this example, styles are applied using an internal style sheet.

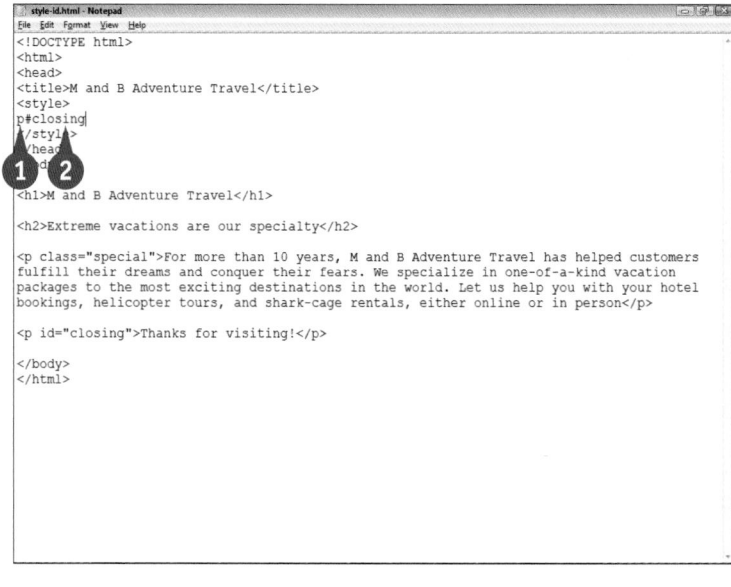

3 Type {.

4 Type the property-value pairs for the ID style, separating multiple pairs with semicolons.

In this example, closing paragraph text is centered and uppercased.

Note: To learn more about writing style rules, see Chapters 5 and 10.

5 Type }.

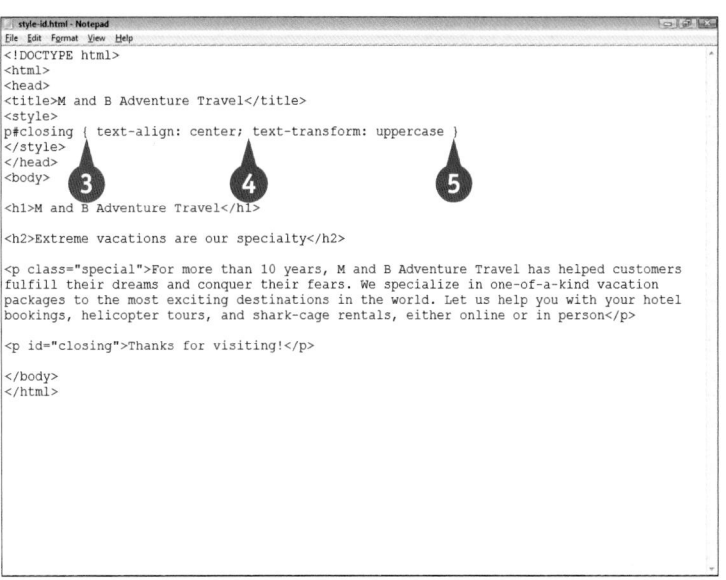

View the Style

1 In your web browser, open the page.

● The web browser applies the styles to the tag content.

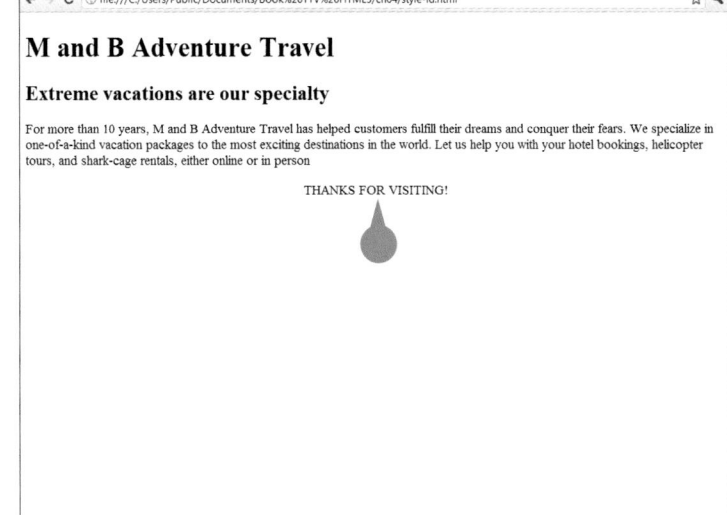

TIP

Can I apply the same ID identifier to multiple HTML tags?

By definition, such an identifier should be assigned to only one tag on your page. For example, if you assign a `page-title` identifier to an `<h1>` tag at the top of your page using the `id` attribute, you should not assign the `page-title` identifier to any other instances of the `<h1>` tag, or to any other tags, on the page.

However, if you do assign that identifier to multiple tags on a page, most browsers do not complain and apply any associated styles to all of the tags.

To follow the official CSS specification, if you want to define a style and apply it to multiple tags on a page, you should create a class. See "Apply a Style Using a Class" for details.

Link to Media-specific Style Sheets

You can link to several style sheets in your HTML document and specify that different styles sheets be applied for different media using the `media` attribute. For example, one style sheet could be applied when the document is displayed on a computer screen, another style sheet could be applied when the document is printed, and yet another could be applied for viewing on a mobile phone or other handheld device.

Link to Media-specific Style Sheets

Create Media-specific Links

1 Create a separate external style sheet for each type of media that you want to support.

Note: For details about creating external style sheets, see "Create an External Style Sheet."

2 Link to each of the style sheets in your document using the `<link>` tag.

Note: For details about linking to style sheets, see "Link to a Style Sheet."

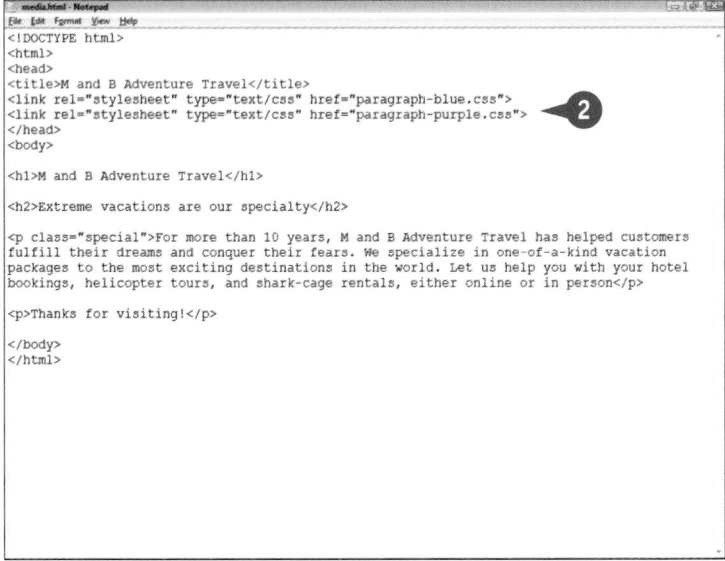

3 Within the `<link>` tag for one of the style sheets, type `media="?"`, replacing *?* with a valid media type.

This example specifies screen media for displaying styles specific to traditional computer monitors. For details about the available media types, see the tip below.

To specify that the style sheet be applied to all media types, you can set the value to `all`.

4 Within the `<link>` tag for another style sheet, type `media="?"`, replacing *?* with a valid media type.

This example specifies print media for displaying styles specific to printed pages.

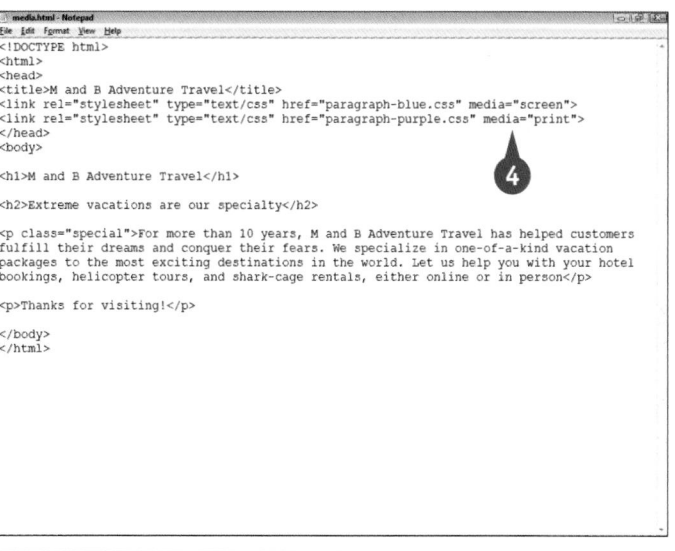

View the Media-specific Styles

1 View your HTML document on a specific type of media.

● The style sheet for that media is applied to the page.

In this example, the web page was printed from a web browser and displays print-specific styles.

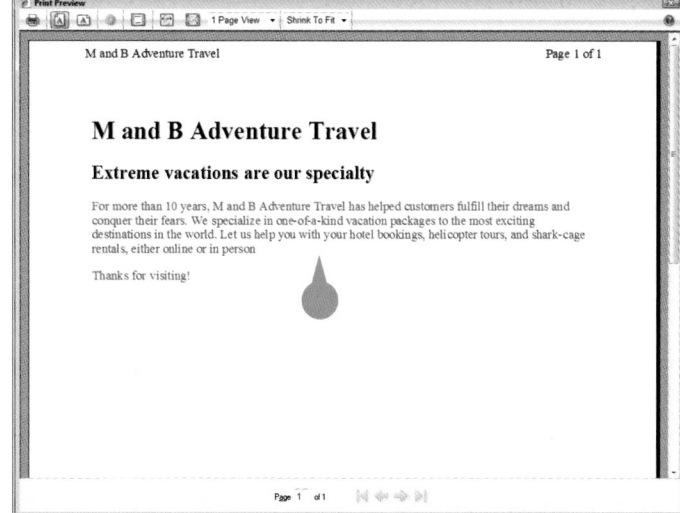

What are the different media types available?

all	For all devices	projection	For projected presentations
braille	For braille tactile feedback devices	screen	For color computer screens
embossed	For paged braille printers	speech	For speech synthesizers
handheld	For handheld devices such as mobile phones	tty	For teletypes, terminals, and other media that use a fixed-pitch character grid
print	For printed pages and for documents viewed in print preview mode	tv	For televisions

Note that some advanced mobile phones such as the iPhone and Android phones as well as the iPad do not respect the handheld media type. See "Link to Style Sheets for iPads, iPhones, and Android Phones" for details.

Link to Style Sheets for iPads, iPhones, and Android Phones

Creating styles specifically for iPad tablets, iPhones, and phones based on the Android operating system requires specialized coding. You cannot simply specify the `handheld` media type when you link to your CSS as described in "Link to Media-specific Style Sheets."

The iPad, iPhone, and Android OS web browser ignore `handheld` links and instead behave more like browsers on traditional computers — they load style sheets specific to the `screen` media type. However, you can create style sheets specific to browsers on these devices by checking the maximum width of the device screen.

Link to Style Sheets for iPads, iPhones, and Android Phones

Link to an iPad-specific Style Sheet

1 Create an external style sheet with rules specific to the iPad.

Note: For details about creating external style sheets, see "Create an External Style Sheet."

2 Link to the style sheet in your document using the `<link>` tag.

Note: For details about linking to style sheets, see "Link to a Style Sheet."

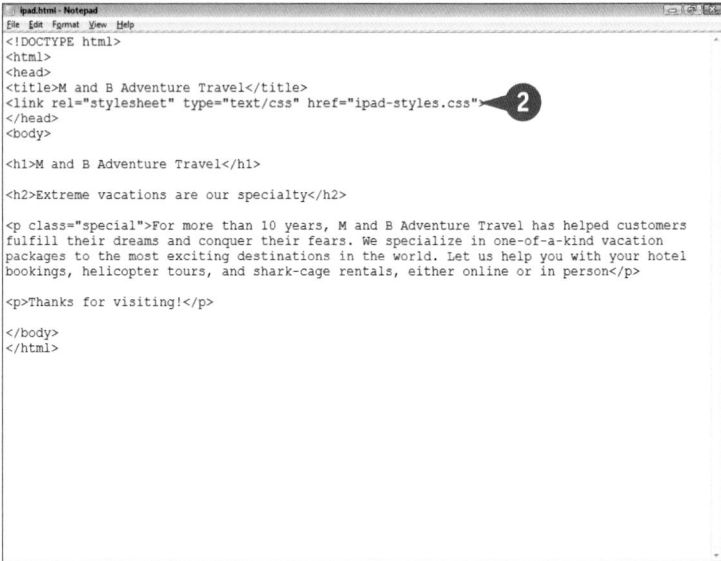

3 Within the `<link>` tag for one of the style sheets, type `media="?"`, replacing *?* with `only screen and (max-device-width: 1024px)`.

The current iPad screen has a width of 1024 pixels on its longer side.

When the page is opened on an iPad, the styles are applied.

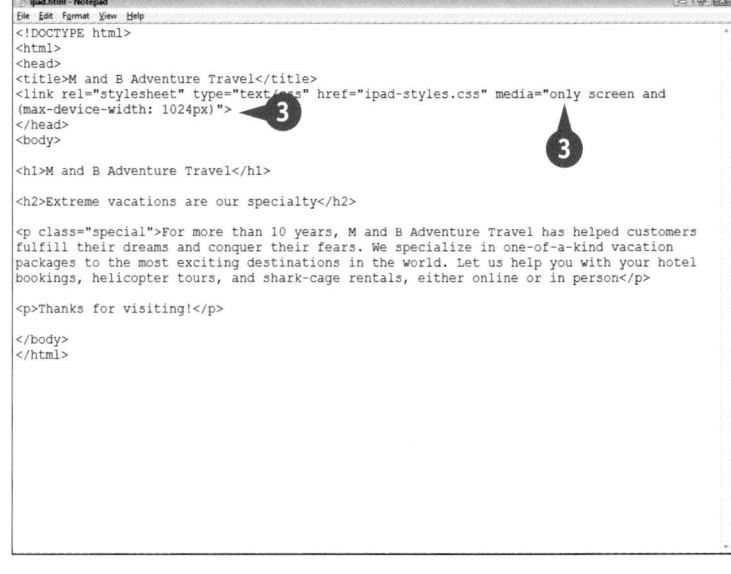

Link to an iPhone- and Android-specific Style Sheet

1 Create a style sheet with rules specific to the iPhone and Android phones.

2 Link to the style sheet in your document using the <link> tag.

Note: For details about linking to style sheets, see "Link to a Style Sheet."

```
iphone.html - Notepad
File  Edit  Format  View  Help
<!DOCTYPE html>
<html>
<head>
<title>M and B Adventure Travel</title>
<link rel="stylesheet" type="text/css" href="iphone-styles.css">        2
</head>
<body>

<h1>M and B Adventure Travel</h1>

<h2>Extreme vacations are our specialty</h2>

<p class="special">For more than 10 years, M and B Adventure Travel has helped customers
fulfill their dreams and conquer their fears. We specialize in one-of-a-kind vacation
packages to the most exciting destinations in the world. Let us help you with your hotel
bookings, helicopter tours, and shark-cage rentals, either online or in person</p>

<p>Thanks for visiting!</p>

</body>
</html>
```

3 Within the <link> tag for one of the style sheets, type `media="?"`, replacing *?* with `only screen and (max-device-width: 480px)`.

The current iPhone and Android phone screens have a width of 480 pixels on their longer sides.

When the page is opened on an iPhone or Android phone, the styles are applied.

```
iphone.html - Notepad
File  Edit  Format  View  Help
<!DOCTYPE html>
<html>
<head>
<title>M and B Adventure Travel</title>
<link rel="stylesheet" type="text/css" href="iphone-styles.css" media="only screen and
(max-device-width: 480px)">        3
</head>
<body>

<h1>M and B Adventure Travel</h1>

<h2>Extreme vacations are our specialty</h2>

<p class="special">For more than 10 years, M and B Adventure Travel has helped customers
fulfill their dreams and conquer their fears. We specialize in one-of-a-kind vacation
packages to the most exciting destinations in the world. Let us help you with your hotel
bookings, helicopter tours, and shark-cage rentals, either online or in person</p>

<p>Thanks for visiting!</p>

</body>
</html>
```

TIPS

What should I keep in mind when optimizing a page for mobile devices such as the iPhone?

Key things to consider are that you are designing for a smaller screen, navigation by touch, and slower download speeds. You should consider increasing the font size to make text more legible and links easier to tap; turning off the display of larger images to reduce the page download time; and disabling CSS float styles to convert multicolumn layouts into single-column layouts, which can be easier to view on smaller screens. Details on how to make such style changes are covered in later parts of this book.

Is there a way to make a CSS rule specific to a media type?

Yes. The steps above describe loading an entire external style sheet based on the media type. To limit a specific CSS rule to a media type, you can use the `@media` directive and surround the rule with an additional set of brackets:

`@media only screen and (max-device-width: 480px) { p.bigger {font-size: 16px;} }`

The CSS code above sets the font size for paragraphs displayed on iPhones.

Define Styles for Nested Tags

You can set up style rules for your page based on how tags are nested inside other tags. For example, you can specify that a style rule be applied to a heading tag, but only when that heading is nested inside a certain type of section tag. You create such a style rule by specifying a sequence of tags or tag classes in the selector. The nested order of tags on your page must match the sequence of the tags in the selector for the style to be applied. Defining style rules this way enables you to efficiently apply styles to precise sections of your page.

Define Styles for Nested Tags

Define the Style

1 Type the name of the outer tag or tag class.

Note: For details about creating CSS classes, see "Apply a Style Using a Class."

2 Type a space.

3 Type the name of the inner tag or tag class.

In this example, the selector is made up of an outer tag class, `section.first`, and an inner tag, h2.

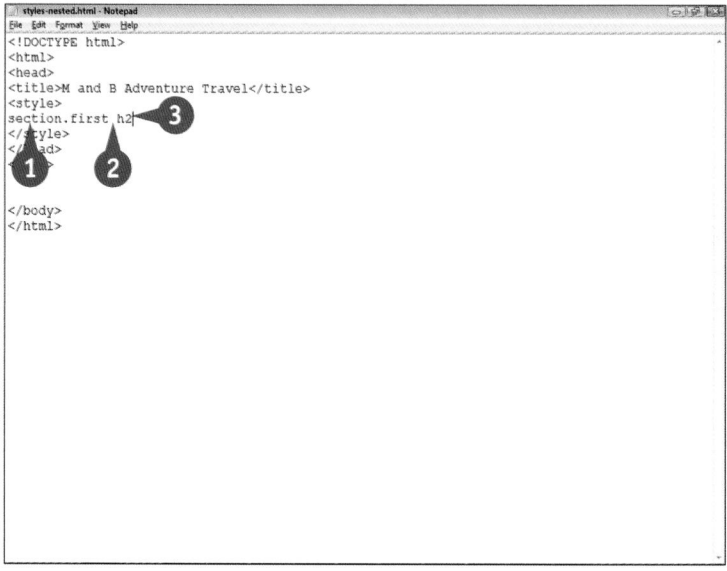

4 Type {.

5 Type the property-value pairs for the style, separating multiple pairs with semicolons.

6 Type }.

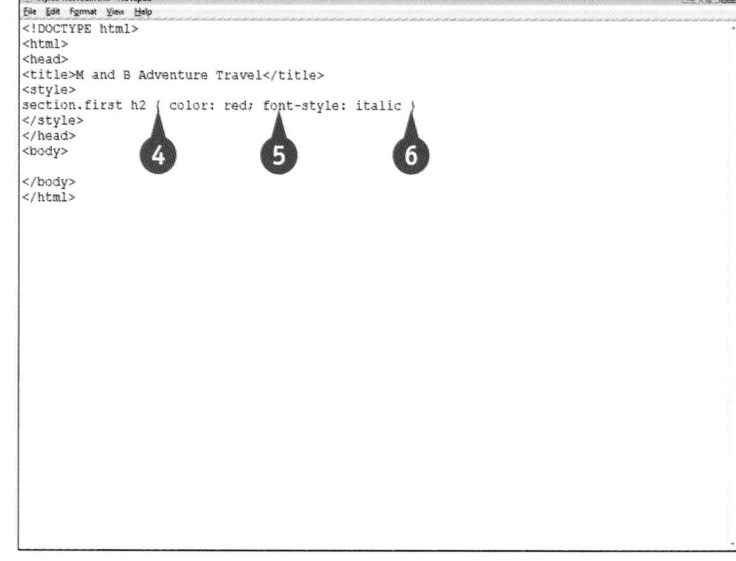

Apply the Style

7 Type the outer tag. Add a `class` attribute if one was defined in the style.

8 Within the outer tag, type your inner tag. Add a `class` attribute if one was defined.

9 Type the content.

10 Type a closing inner tag.

11 Type a closing outer tag.

12 You can add other page content.

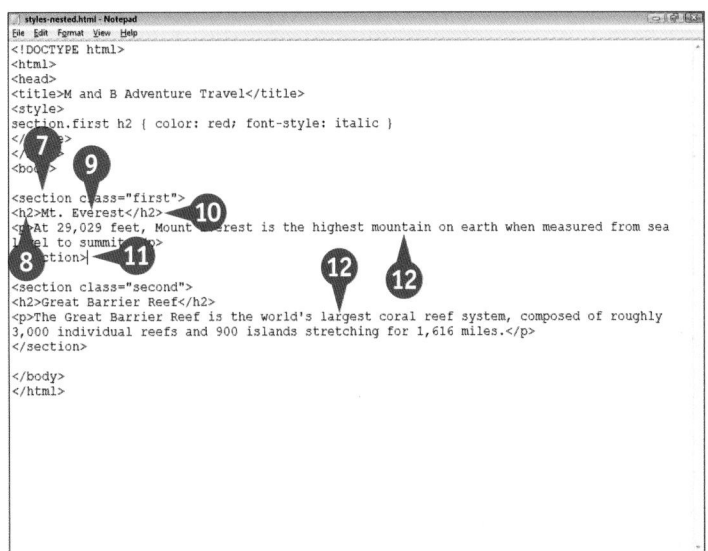

View the Styled Content

The web browser applies the styles to nested tags.

● In this example, the style is applied only to the `<h2>` content within the `<section>` tag with the `first` class.

● The style is not applied to the other `<h2>` content on the page.

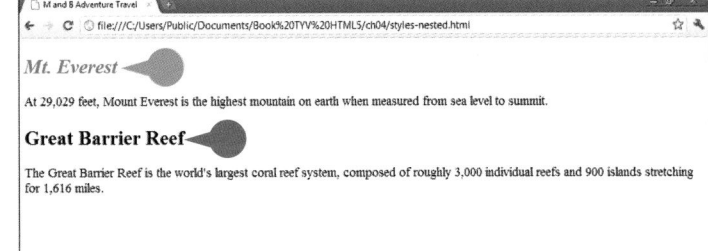

TIPS

What is the terminology to describe the nested relationship of tags on a page?

We can use family-tree terminology. The outer tags are known as *ancestors* and the inner tags are known as *descendants*. In the example above, the `<h1>` tag must be a descendant of the `<section>` tag for the style to be applied.

Tags directly next to each other in the hierarchy can be given more specific classification. The outer tag is a *parent* and the next tag immediately on the inside is a *child*.

How do I specify a parent-child relationship in my CSS rule?

You can specify that a style rule be applied only to the immediate descendant, or child, of a tag using a greater-than symbol (>) in the selector. The following applies a rule to a `<p>` tag that is directly inside of an `<article>` tag:

`article > p {font-size: 16px; color: green}`

This rule would apply to the following:

`<article><p>Hello, HTML5!</p></article>`

The rule *would not* apply to the following:

`<article><section><p>Hello, HTML5!</p>`
`</section></article>`

Styling Text

Ready to add some pizzazz to the words and paragraphs on your web page? This chapter shows you how to apply formatting to your HTML5 text using style sheet rules. You can emphasize words on your page by making the words capitalized or a different size. By adding color, either to the words themselves or as a background, you can make elements on your page stand out or match your website's theme. You can also use style sheet rules to change the alignment and spacing of the text on your page.

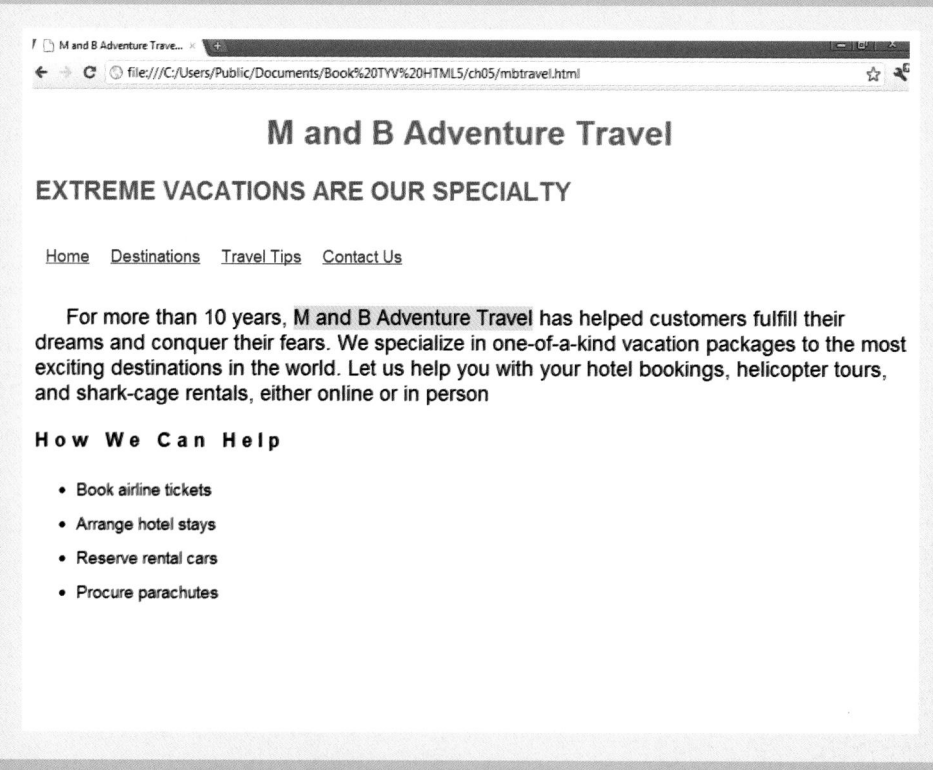

Change the Font Size

You can use the `font-size` property to change the font size for a document's text. By changing font size, you can emphasize or de-emphasize different sections of text on your page. Instead of going through your document and changing each instance of a tag, you can use the style sheet rule to change the font size for all uses of the tag in your document. The `font-size` property accepts a variety of measurement units with the most common being points (`pt`) and pixels (`px`).

Change the Font Size

① Click inside the tag declaration and type `font-size:` and a space.

Note: To learn more about writing style sheets and rules, see Chapter 4.

② Type a font size in points (`pt`), pixels (`px`), millimeters (`mm`), centimeters (`cm`), inches (`in`), picas (`pc`), x-height (`ex`), or em space (`em`).

You can also type a descriptive (`xx-small`, `x-small`, `small`, `medium`, `large`, `x-large`, or `xx-large`) font size.

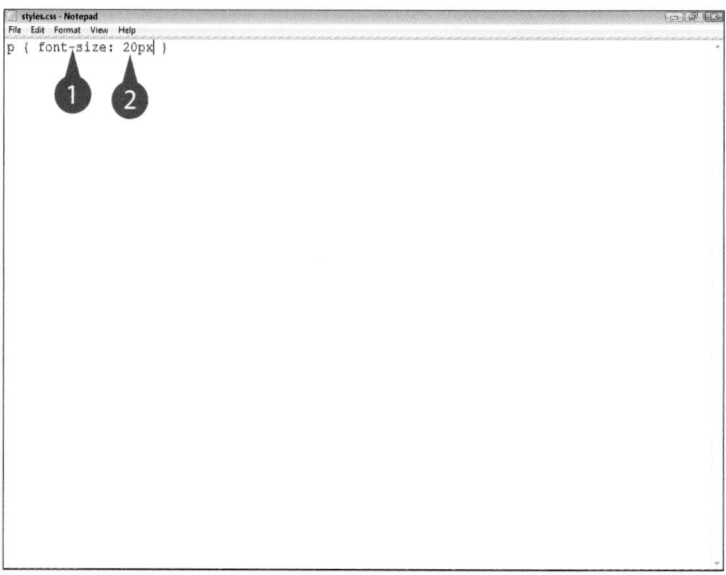

The web browser assigns the font size to the paragraph text.

● In this example, the font size is assigned to the paragraph text.

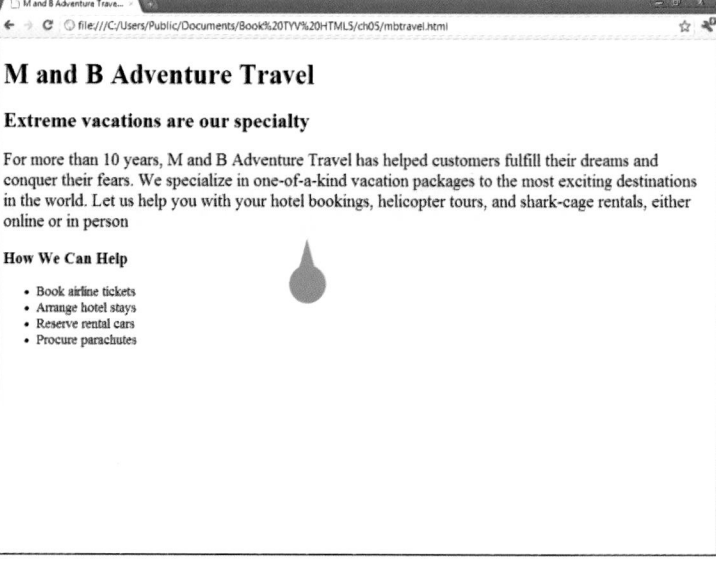

Indent Text

#4

You can indent the first line in a paragraph using the `text-indent` property in a style rule. This can give the paragraphs on your page a more traditional look and feel. You can set the indentation as a specific measurement value or as a percentage of the overall text block width. You can create an outdent, also known as a hanging indent, by setting the `text-indent` property to a negative number.

Indent Text

① Click inside the tag declaration and type `text-indent: ?`, replacing `?` with the amount of space you want to indent, measured in pixels (`px`).

Note: To learn more about writing style sheets and rules, see Chapter 4.

You can also set a size measurement in millimeters (`mm`), centimeters (`cm`), inches (`in`), points (`pt`), picas (`pc`), x-height (`ex`), or em space (`em`).

You can also set an indent size as a percentage of the text block width, such as `20%`.

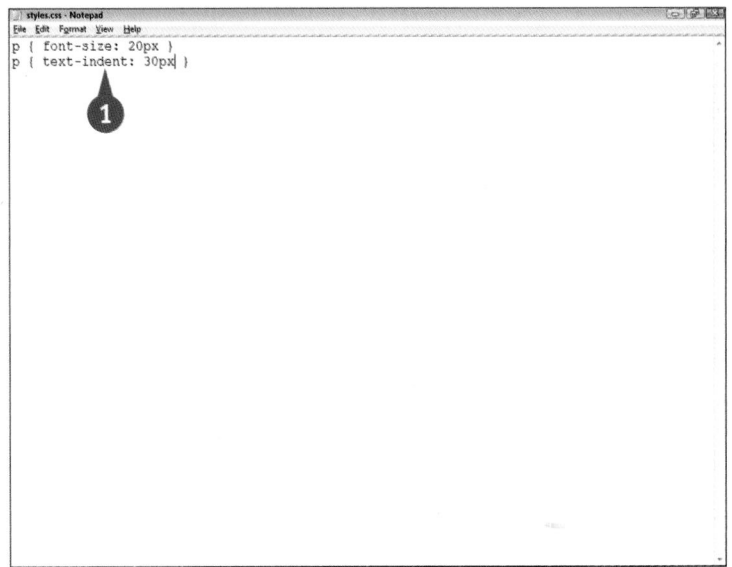

The web browser indents the first line of all the text to which the tag is applied.

● In this example, the content in the `<p>` tags is indented.

Note: To indent entire sections of text with margins, see Chapter 10.

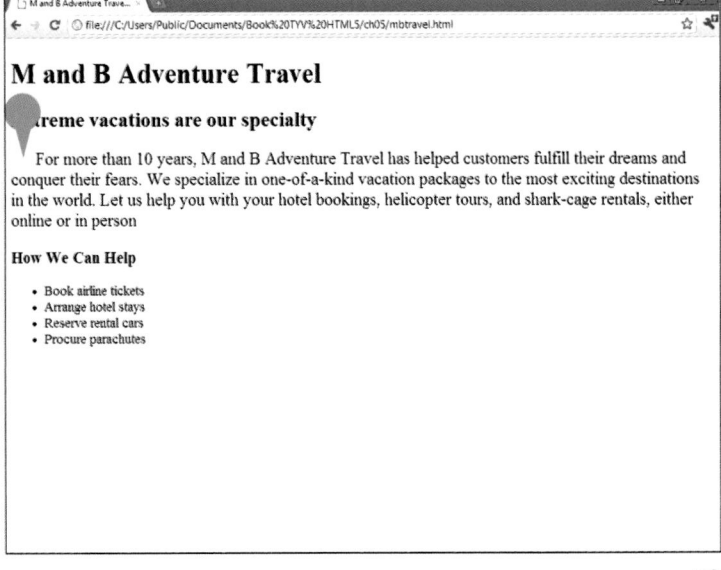

Change the Color of Text

You can use the `color` property to change the color of text in your web page. You can specify a recognized color name, a hexadecimal color value, or an RGB value. You can change the text color to make it match the theme of your website. You can use color to emphasize important content, such as alert text or error messages. You can also use the `color` property to change other web page elements, such as tables, borders, and horizontal rules.

Change the Color of Text

Use a Color Name

1 Click inside the tag declaration and type `color:` followed by a space.

Note: To learn more about writing style sheets and rules, see Chapter 4.

2 Type a color name for the color you want to assign.

Note: Some common, supported color names are listed in the tip on the next page.

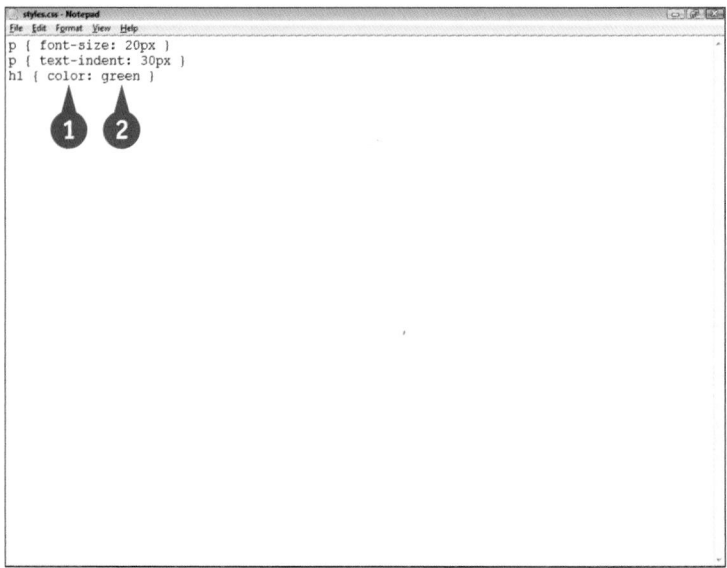

The web browser uses the assigned color for the text to which the tag is applied.

● In this example, color is assigned to the `<h1>` tag.

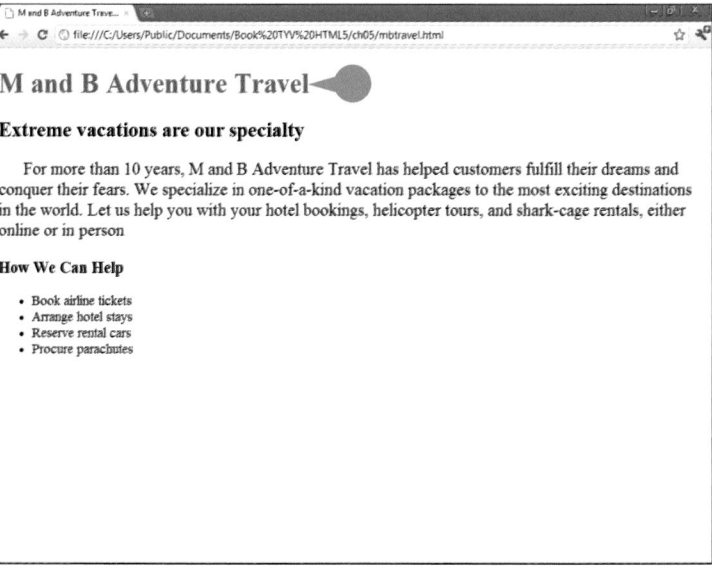

Use a Hexadecimal Code

1 Click inside the tag declaration and type `color:` followed by a space.

2 Type a hexadecimal value for the color you want to assign.

Note: Hexadecimals codes can be used to generate millions of different colors. For more information, visit: www.wooldridge.net/html5

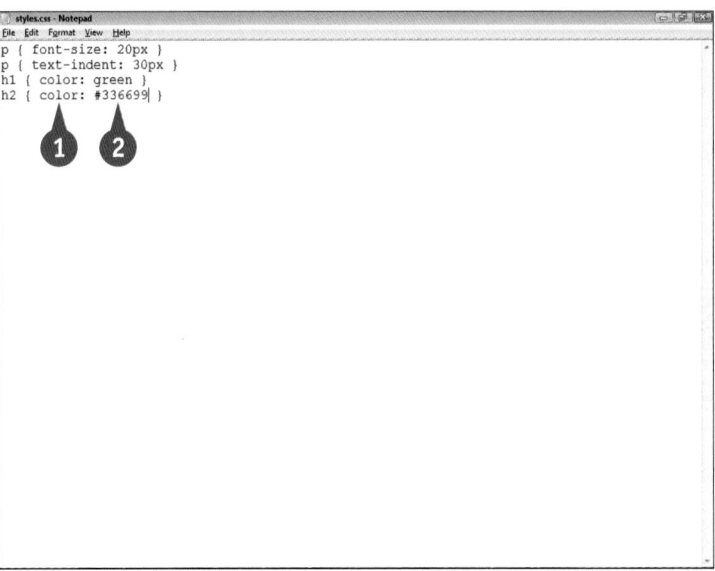

The web browser uses the assigned color for the text to which the tag is applied.

● In this example, color is assigned to the `<h2>` tag.

What colors can I set for my web page text?

You can set color using six-digit hexadecimal values preceded by a number sign (#), as shown in the following table. In a hexadecimal code, the three pairs of digits or letters after the # control the amount of red, green, and blue in the color, respectively. Browsers can also understand the color names listed below. For more information about web colors, see: www.wooldridge.net/html5

Color	Hexadecimal Value	Color	Hexadecimal Value
Aqua	#00FFFF	Navy	#000080
Black	#000000	Olive	#808000
Blue	#0000FF	Purple	#800080
Fuchsia	#FF00FF	Red	#FF0000
Gray	#808080	Silver	#C0C0C0
Green	#008000	Teal	#008080
Lime	#00FF00	White	#FFFFFF
Maroon	#800000	Yellow	#FFFF00

To change the font for your HTML text, you can use the `font-family` property. You can specify a font by name. Because not all fonts are available on all computers, you can designate a second or third font choice. That way, if the computer does not have the first choice installed, the browser tries to display the next choice instead.

For best results, assign multiple font choices and be sure to include a common font, such as Arial, Verdana, Courier, or Times New Roman.

Change the Font

1 Click inside the tag declaration and type `font-family:`.

Note: To learn more about writing style sheets and rules, see Chapter 4.

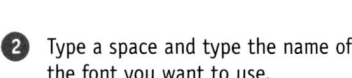

```
styles.css - Notepad
File  Edit  Format  View  Help
p { font-size: 20px }
p { text-indent: 30px }
h1 { color: green }
h2 { color: #336699 }
body { font-family: }
```

1

2 Type a space and type the name of the font you want to use.

```
styles.css - Notepad
File  Edit  Format  View  Help
p { font-size: 20px }
p { text-indent: 30px }
h1 { color: green }
h2 { color: #336699 }
body { font-family: arial }
```

2

3 To designate a second font choice, type a comma, a space, and the second font name.

If the font name includes a space, surround the name in quotes.

You can repeat step **3** to assign additional fonts.

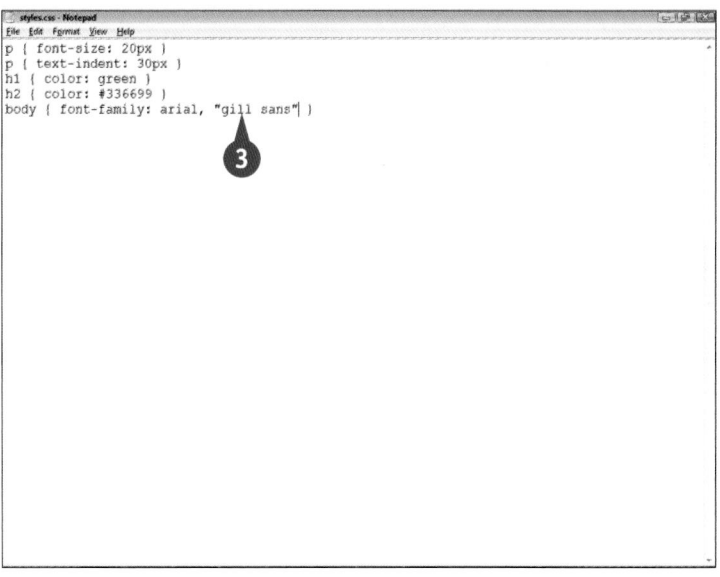

The web browser uses the assigned font for any text to which the tag is applied.

In this example, the style rule is applied to the `<body>` tag, so all the body text is affected.

Can I apply multiple style settings to my fonts at the same time?
Yes. You can write a style rule that combines several font settings at the same time using the `font` property. For example, you can designate the font, font size, and font style for a particular tag instead of writing three different rules for the tag. Your combined rule might look like this:

`p {font: italic 18pt "Times New Roman", Arial}`

Some browsers may require you to type the properties in a particular order, such as font style before font size.

What are serifs?
Serifs are the small decorations that appear at the ends of some letters. Fonts can be classified by whether or not they include serifs. Common serifed fonts include Times New Roman, Georgia, and Palatino. Popular non-serifed, or *sans serif*, fonts include Arial, Verdana, and Helvetica. Sans serif fonts can be easier to read at smaller sizes on web pages.

Change Text Alignment

You can control the horizontal positioning of blocks of text in your page using the `text-align` property. You can use this technique to align paragraphs, headings, tables, and other elements. You can align text to the left or right, center the text, or create justified text. By default, most browsers align text to the left. Aligning text to the middle is helpful when placing titles on your page with heading tags.

Change Text Alignment

① Click inside the tag declaration and type `text-align:` and a space.

② Type an alignment (`left`, `center`, `right`, or `justify`).

Note: To learn more about writing style sheets and rules, see Chapter 4.

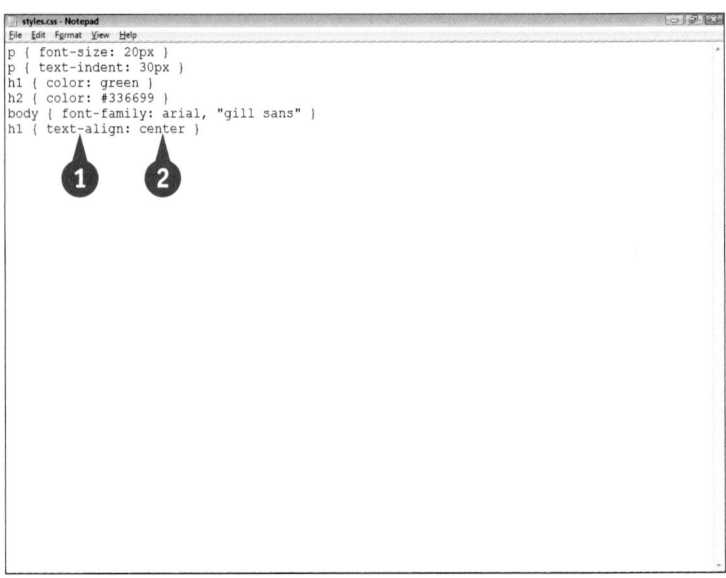

The web browser assigns the alignment to the content.

● In this example, the `<h1>` content is centered.

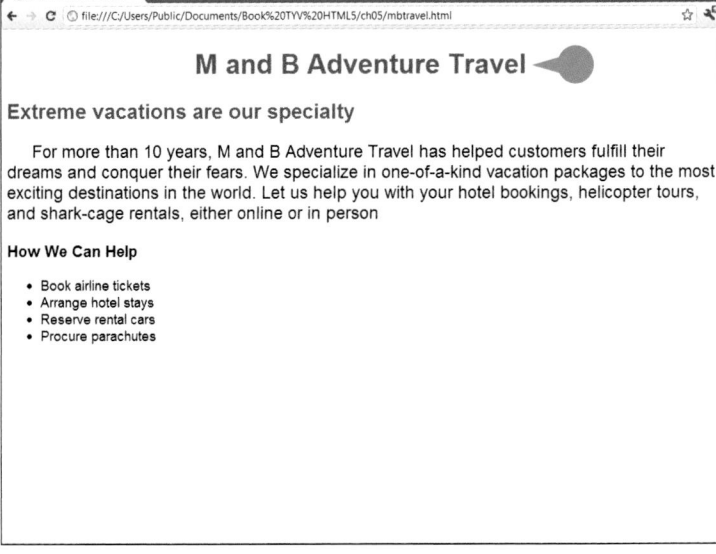

Change the Text Case

Y ou can use the `text-transform` property to change the text case for a tag. For example, you may want all `<h2>` text to appear in all capital letters. The property controls how the browser displays the text regardless of how it was typed.

You can choose from four case values: `capitalize`, `uppercase`, `lowercase`, and `none`. Use the `capitalize` value if you want the first character of each word to appear capitalized. Use the `none` value to leave text as is. The `none` value cancels any case values the text may have inherited from surrounding HTML tags.

Change the Text Case

1 Click inside the tag declaration and type `text-transform:` and a space.

2 Type a text case value (`capitalize`, `uppercase`, `lowercase`, or `none`).

Note: To learn more about writing style sheets and rules, see Chapter 4.

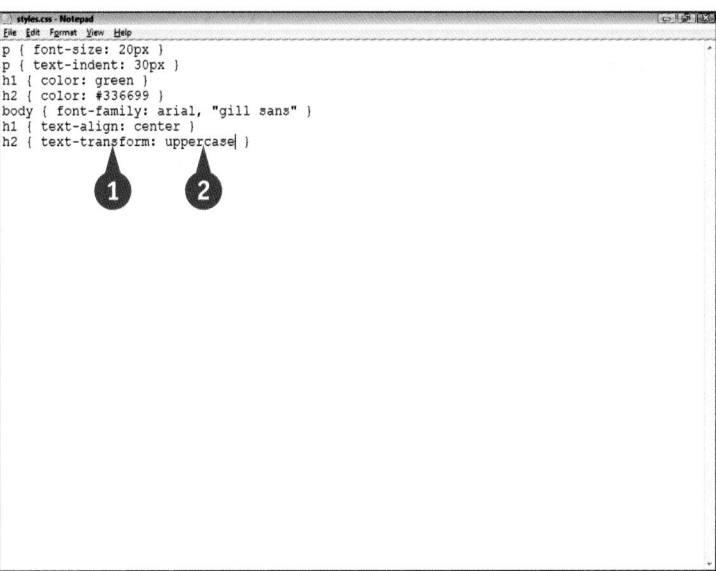

The web browser assigns the text case to the content.

● In this example, the `<h2>` content appears in uppercase letters.

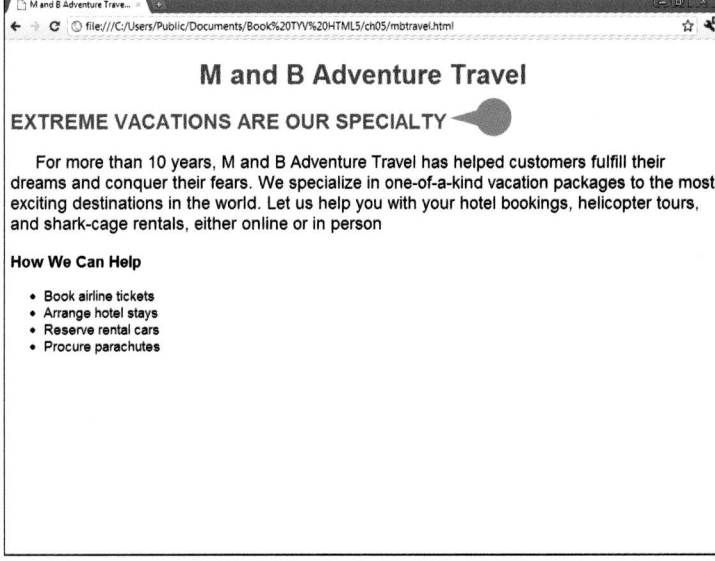

Control Line Spacing

You can use the `line-height` property to adjust the spacing, or *leading*, between lines of text. Adjusting line spacing can make your web page text easier to read. The line spacing value can be specified as a multiple of the height of the element's font. It can also be specified as an absolute value or a percentage. Be careful when applying small values because this can result in overlapping lines. Line spacing cannot have a negative value.

Control Line Spacing

1 Click inside the tag declaration and type `line-height:` and a space.

2 Type a value for the spacing.

This example uses a value of 2.0 to make the spacing two times the current font height.

You can also set a percentage or an absolute value, such as 10px, for the spacing.

Note: To learn more about writing style sheets and rules, see Chapter 4.

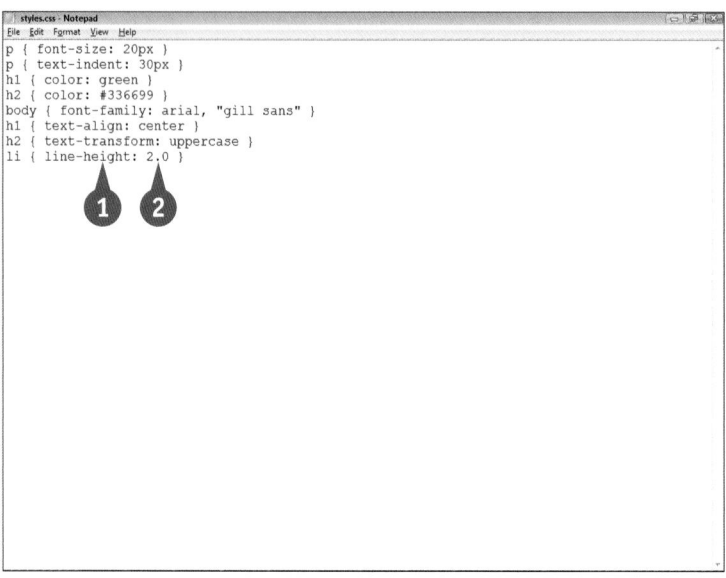

The web browser assigns the line spacing to the content.

● In this example, because of the `<li>` tags, the unordered list displays extra line spacing.

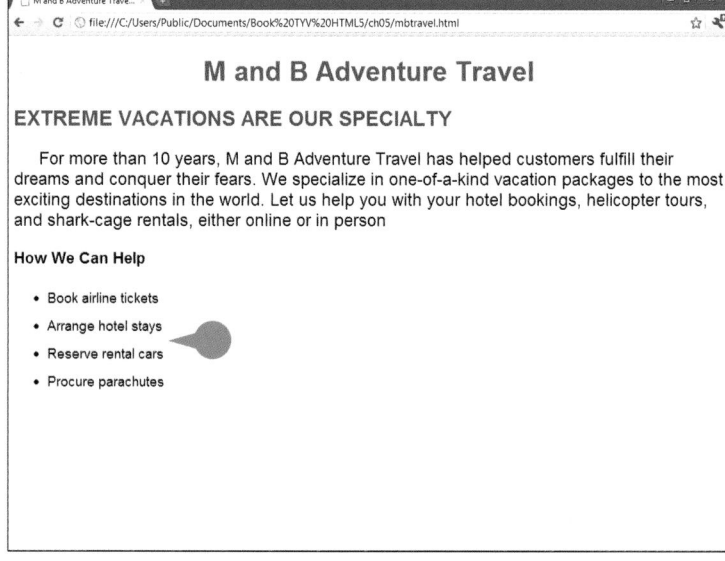

Control Letter Spacing

Y ou can control the spacing between characters, or *kerning*, using the `letter-spacing` property. Letter spacing changes the appearance of your text by increasing or condensing the space between letters.

You can specify letter spacing in points (`pt`), pixels (`px`), millimeters (`mm`), centimeters (`cm`), inches (`in`), picas (`pc`), x-height (`ex`), or em space (`em`). The specified value is added to the default spacing normally inserted between letters. Negative values condense the space between letters, with high negative values causing letters to overlap.

Control Letter Spacing

① Click inside the tag declaration and type `letter-spacing:` and a space.

② Type a value for the spacing.

Note: To learn more about writing style sheets and rules, see Chapter 4.

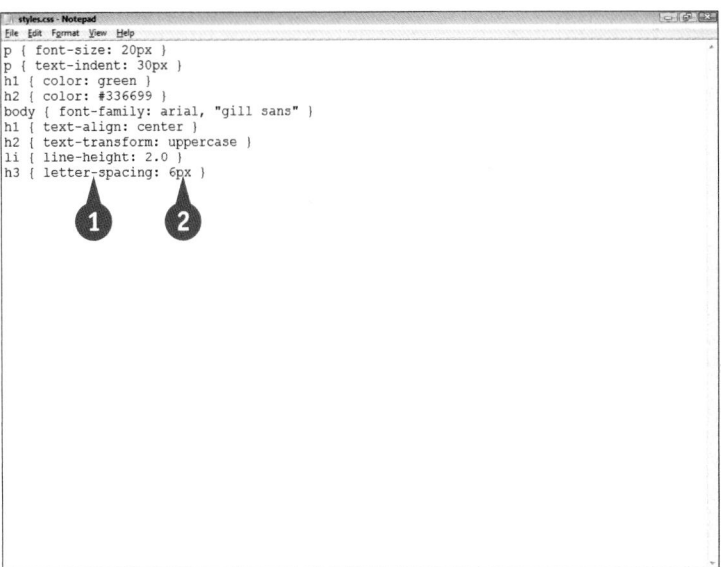

The web browser assigns the letter spacing to the content.

● In this example, letter spacing is applied to the `<h3>` content before the unordered list.

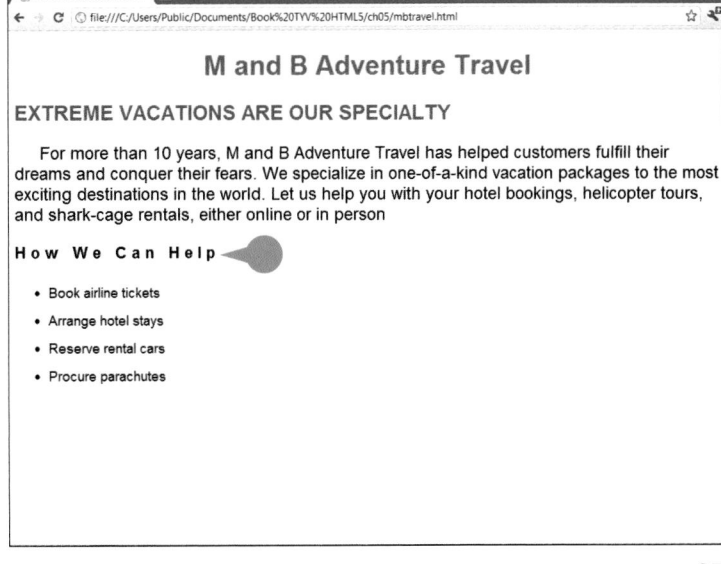

Add Background Colors

You can use the `background-color` property to change the color that appears behind the content on a page. For example, you can change the background behind text to a fluorescent color to make it appear as if the text has been highlighted with a marker. You can specify the color by name, hexadecimal color value, or RGB value. To add a background color to just a few words of a paragraph, you can apply the property using the `<span>` tag and a CSS class. To add a background color to an entire page, you can apply the property to the `<body>` tag.

Use caution when assigning a background color to an element, taking into account the color of the content in the foreground.

Add Background Colors

Add to Text

1. In the style sheet for the page, create a CSS class for the `<span>` tag.

Note: To learn more about creating classes, see Chapter 4.

2. Click inside the tag declaration and type `background-color:` and then a space.

3. Type the color name or color code you want to assign.

Note: See "Change the Color of Text" for a list of common color names. For more color options, see: www.wooldridge.net/html5

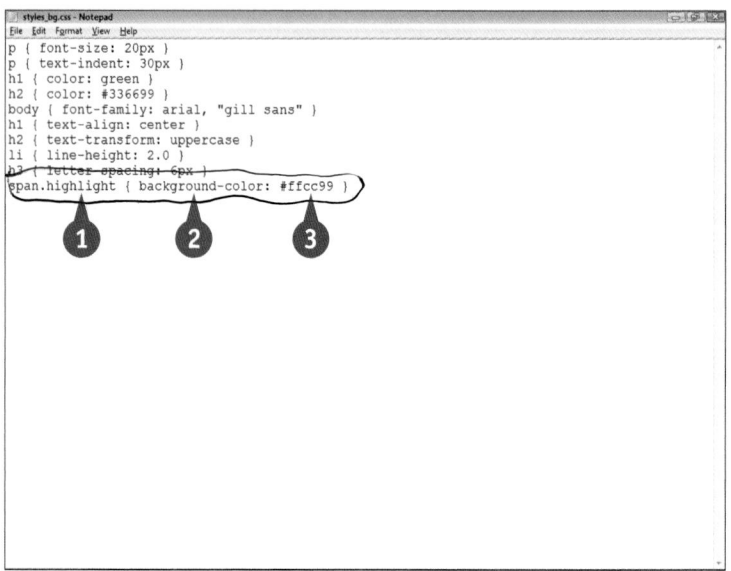

4. Type `<span>` before the text to which you want to add a background color.

5. Type `</span>` after the text.

6. Click inside the `<span>` tag, type `class="?"`, replacing *?* with the name of the class you defined in step 1.

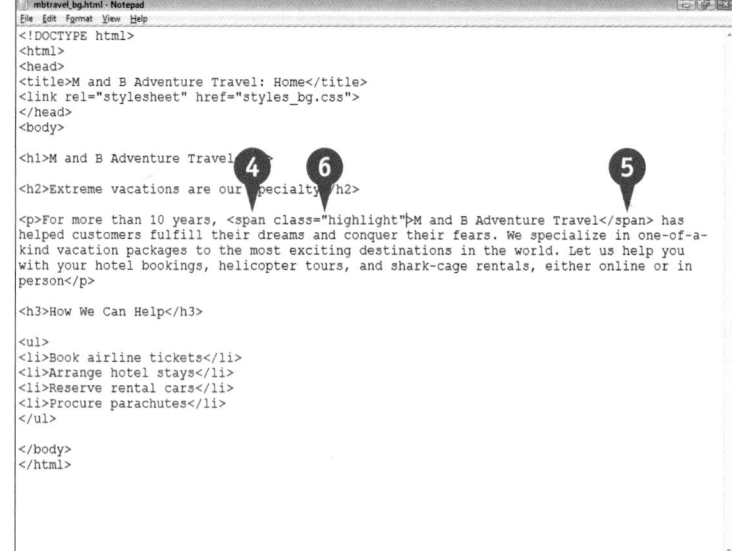

88

Add to a Page

7 In the style sheet for the page, create a CSS rule for the `<body>` tag.

8 Click inside the tag declaration and type `background-color:` and then a space.

9 Type the color name or color code you want to assign.

● Separate multiple rules with semicolons.

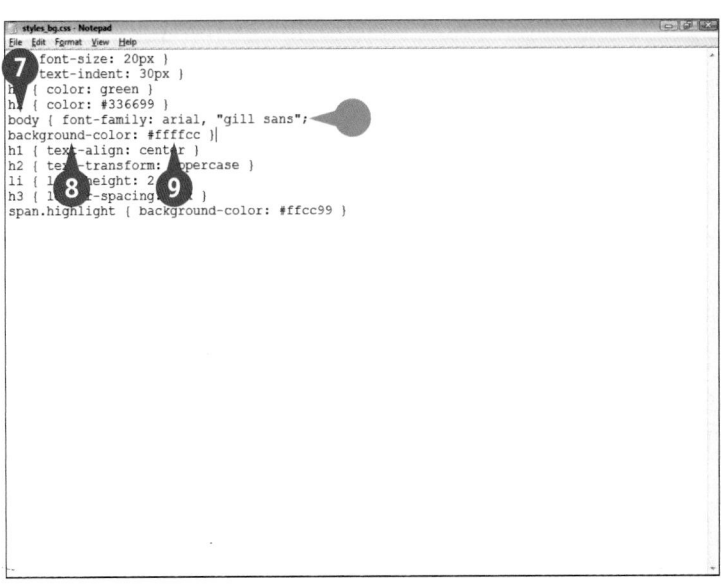

View the Page

The web browser assigns the background color to the content.

● In this example, light-orange highlighting has been added to some text.

● A light-yellow background has been applied to the entire page.

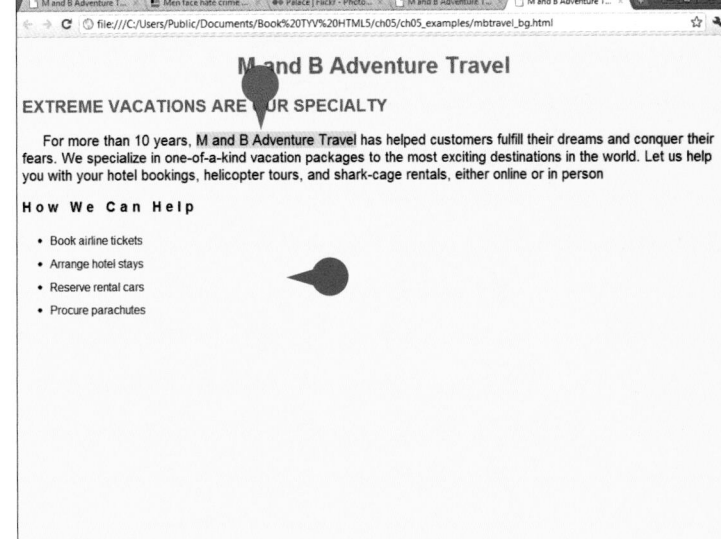

Can I use the background property to apply a background color?

Yes. In most browsers, the following CSS rule also adds a background color to text:

`span.highlight {background: pink}`

The difference between the `background` and `background-color` properties is that you can use `background` to specify additional style information such as an image to display in the background. For more information about background images, see Chapter 6.

How do you prevent certain sections of text in a paragraph from wrapping?

You can put `<span>` and `</span>` tags around the text and apply the following class:

`.nonewline {white-space:nowrap}`

You apply the class similar to how you apply the class to add a background color in the steps above. Except in this example you use `nonewline` as the `class` attribute.

Style a Bulleted List

You can add style rules to bulleted lists on your pages to change the shapes of the bullets or remove the bullets altogether. You can also change how the list items are formatted so that they appear in a horizontal line across the page instead of as a vertical list. These CSS techniques are often used when creating navigation links on a page. Navigation links are commonly defined as a list of unordered links using the `<ul>` tag.

Style a Bulleted List

Create a List

1 Create a bulleted list using the `<ul>` and `<li>` tags.

Note: To learn more about creating bulleted lists, see Chapter 3.

2 Inside the `<ul>` tag, type `class="?"`, replacing *?* with a CSS class name.

3 You can type a `<br>` tag with a `clear` style to keep the text that follows the list from wrapping. See Chapter 6 for more details.

Note: To learn more about CSS classes, see Chapter 4.

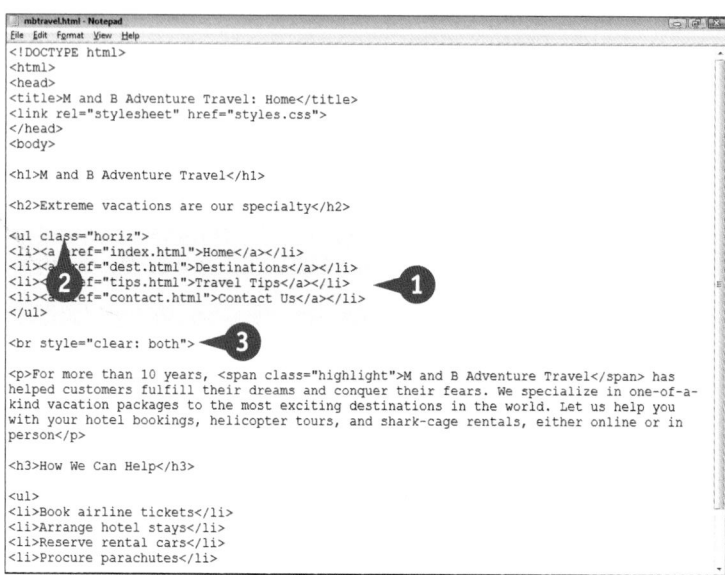

Style the List

4 Define a CSS class for the `<ul>` tag using the class name from step **2**.

5 In the declaration, type `list-style-type: ?`, replacing *?* with a bullet type.

Available bullet types are `disc`, `circle`, `square`, and `none`.

6 Type a semicolon (`;`).

7 Type `padding: 0` to remove the indenting normally added to a list.

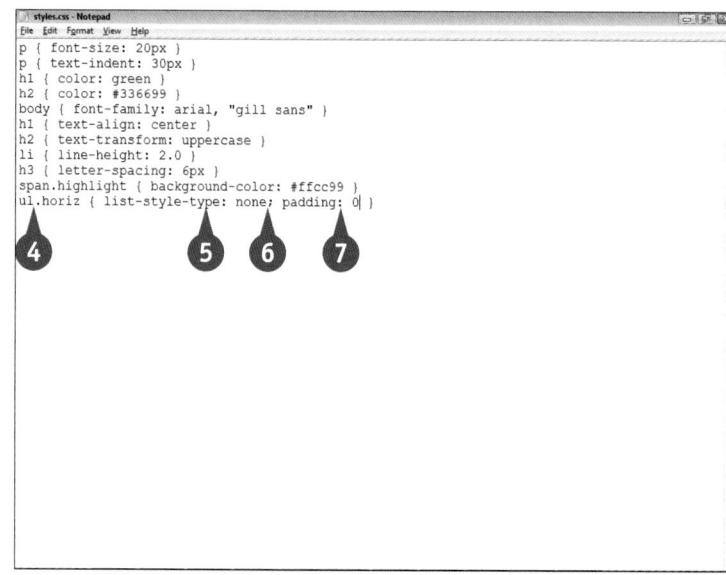

8 Define a CSS class for the <li> tag nested inside the <ul> tag.

Note: For more about defining classes based on nesting, see Chapter 4.

9 In the declaration, type float: left to align the list items to the left beside one another.

10 Type a semicolon (;).

11 To add space around the list items, type padding: ?, replacing ? with a measurement.

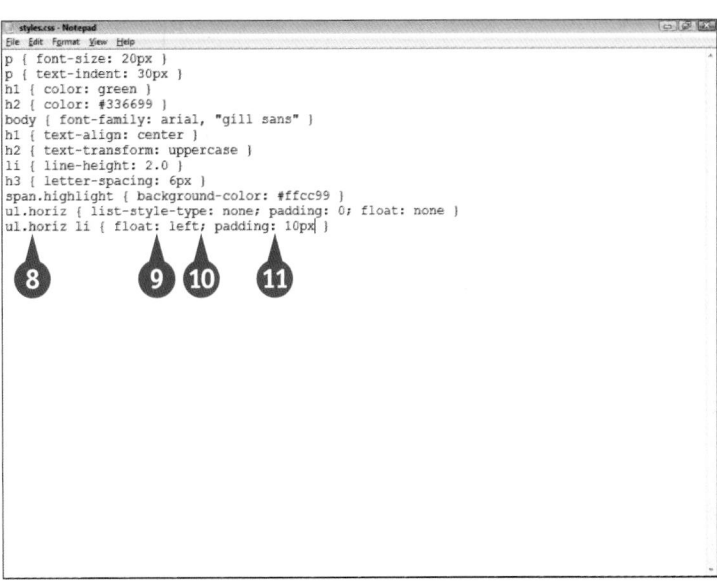

View the Result

The web browser assigns the styles to the list.

● In this example, bullets have been removed and the list items have been arranged horizontally.

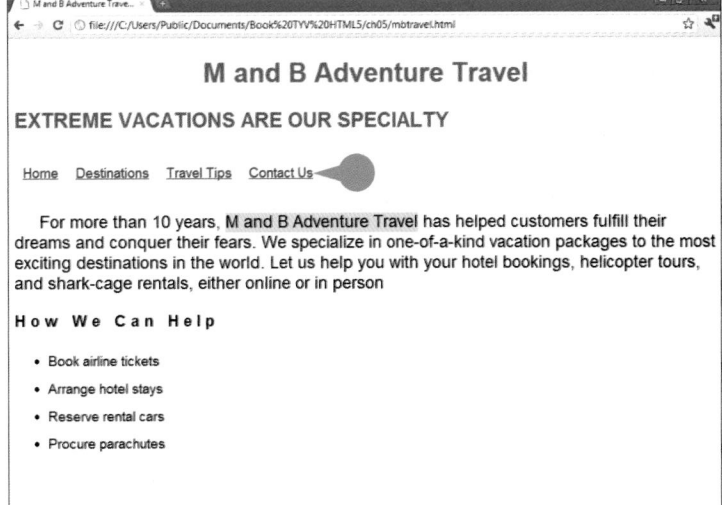

TIPS

How do I replace bullets with images?
You can create your own custom bullets in an image editor, save them as images, and apply them to your bulleted lists:

```
ul.menu {list-style-image: url(mybullet.
png)}
```

This style replaces the default list bullets with the image mybullet.png. The web browser looks for the image in the same directory as the style sheet. You can add images/ to the beginning of the image filename to have the browser look in an images subfolder.

How do I add color backgrounds to my list items?
You can add a background-color declaration to the list item style to make the items look more like buttons. The following creates items with orange backgrounds:

```
background-color: orange
```

The background-color property takes a color name or hexadecimal color code. See "Change the Color of Text" for details about setting CSS colors. To add space between the colored items, you can add margin space to the items:

```
margin: 5px
```

Adding Images

Are you ready to add images to your web page? Images include photographs, logos, clip art, backgrounds, clickable buttons, and more. You can insert images into your web page using the `<img>` tag and adjust the alignment and padding of the images using CSS style sheets. You can also use HTML5 code to add captions to your images. Understanding how to place images on a web page is important because photos and illustrations can be key to adding visual appeal.

Windsurfing

Windsurfing is an extreme watersport that combines elements of surfing and sailing. The key equipment for windsurfing includes a board, mast, boom, and sail. The size of the board and sail vary depending on the skill of the rider and weather conditions.

Types of windsurfing boards include freeride boards, which are built for mostly straight-line sailing and occasional turning, and wave boards, which are smaller and built for riding on and jumping breaking waves. In 1984 windsurfing became an Olympic event.

Understanding Web Page Images

You can use images in a variety of ways on your web pages. Images include everything from graphics and clip art to photographs and other visual objects. Images can illustrate text, show a product, provide background decoration, or act as navigational buttons for a website. Most of the images used on the web today are of one of three file formats: JPEG, GIF, and PNG. Knowing when to use each file format, and how to minimize the file size when you save an image, can help you create pages that look great and download fast.

Image File Formats

Although numerous file types are used for computer images, JPEG, GIF, and PNG are the three most popular types used on the web. The current versions of all of today's popular web browsers can display these three image types. All three formats offer file-size compression, which makes images download quickly from a web server to your computer. Another option for displaying graphical content on your pages in HTML5 is by using the new <canvas> tag, which is covered in Chapter 13.

JPEG

JPEG, which stands for *Joint Photographic Experts Group*, supports 24-bit color, allowing for millions of colors. The JPEG format is commonly used with complex images, such as photos or graphics that use millions of colors and feature lots of detail. JPEG is not a good choice for solid-color artwork because it results in a larger overall file size, which translates to longer download times. JPEG images usually use a .jpg filename extension.

GIF

GIF, which stands for *Graphics Interchange Format*, supports up to 256 colors. The GIF format is more commonly used for simple images, such as logos and graphics containing basic shapes and lines. If your image or graphic contains few colors and not a lot of detail, GIF is a good file format choice. A single GIF file can also store multiple images and display them as an animation. GIF images use a .gif filename extension.

PNG

The PNG (*Portable Network Graphics*) format offers rich color support and advanced compression schemes, so it is a good choice for a variety of image types. Like JPEG, PNG supports 24-bit color but can also be saved with fewer colors, similar to GIF. PNG is a newer format than GIF and JPEG but is fully supported by all popular browsers. PNG images use a .png filename extension.

Downloading Considerations

Browsers must download an image before users can view it on the web page. Large images can take a long time to display, especially if Internet connection speeds are slow. For this reason, consider the overall file size of an image when deciding whether or not to add it to a web page. If you fill your page with several large pictures, the download time for the page to fully display will be excessive.

Optimize Images

Most image-editing programs allow you to adjust the quality of an image to control its file size. You can also control file size by shrinking or cropping an image. If you use larger image files, for example images that weigh in at more than 100K, users with slow connections may not be willing to wait for the pictures to download. With GIFs and PNGs, you can decrease the number of colors in an image to reduce the file size. Affordable image editors include Adobe Photoshop Elements and Corel PaintShop Photo Pro. Paint, which comes free with Windows, and Preview, which comes free with Macs, also offer image-optimization features.

Alternative Text

Web users may turn off the browser's image-display setting to help speed up the downloading of web pages. Also, some visually impaired users view the web using screen readers that do not display images at all. To accommodate such users, be sure to include alternative text describing the images on your page. Alternative text can appear in place of the image and allows users to understand how the image relates to the rest of the page. Learn how to add alternative text in the section "Add Alternative Text."

Insert an Image

You can add images to your web page to increase visual interest or illustrate a topic. For example, you can add a photograph of a product or a company logo to a business's web page. HTML enables you to display images as *inline* elements, which means they appear within the body of the page along with text.

You can use image files from a digital camera or scanner, or you can create illustrations with a graphics program. You can also obtain images online from inexpensive stock-photo websites such as iStockphoto. On photo-sharing sites such as Flickr, users often allow noncommercial use of their photos.

Insert an Image

Insert a Photograph

1. Type `<img src="?">` where you want to insert a photographic image, replacing *?* with the relative path to the file you want to insert.

   In this example, because the image was saved in the same folder as the HTML file, you reference it with just the filename.

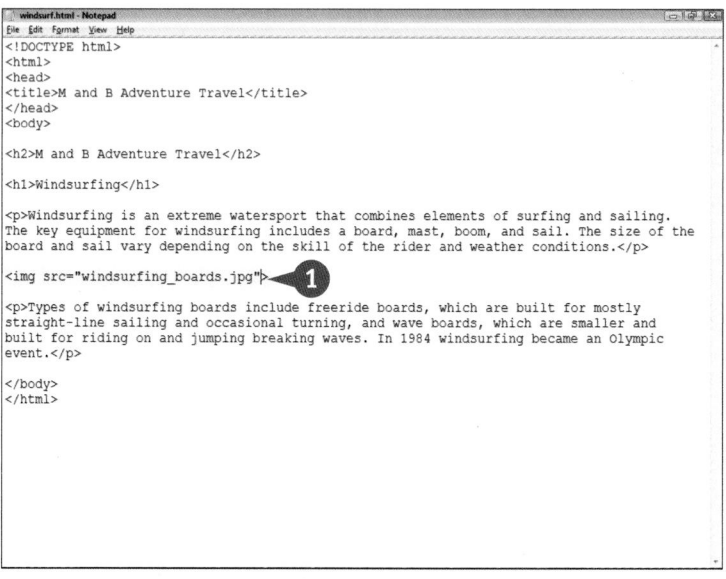

● The web browser displays the image on the page.

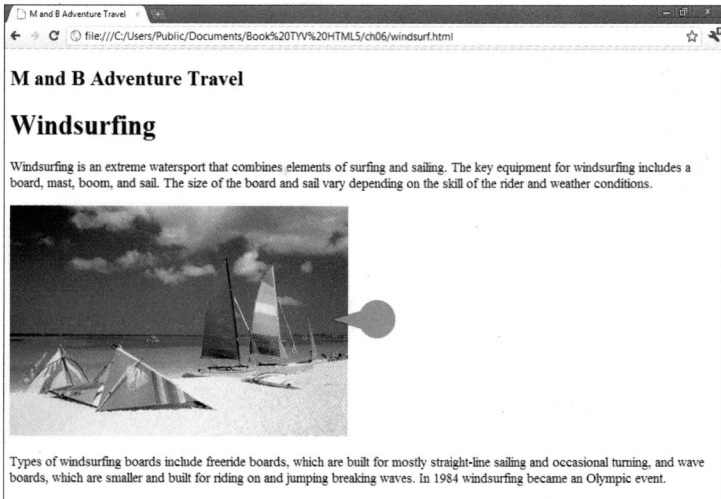

Insert a Graphic File

1 Type `<img src="?">` where you want to insert a graphic, replacing *?* with the relative path to the file you want to insert.

In this example, because the graphic was saved in an images subdirectory relative to the HTML file, you reference it with the subdirectory name followed by a forward slash (/) and then the filename.

● The web browser displays the graphic on the page.

TIPS

How can I download an image from a web page?
Chrome, Internet Explorer, Firefox, and most other web browsers enable you to copy an image from a website by right-clicking the image and selecting a Save command. If you save an image in the same folder as your HTML files, you can then use the image on your pages using the previous steps. Make sure you have permission from the image owner before using the image on your website.

How can I insert an image in my eBay auction?
Many auction sites, such as eBay, allow you to include certain HTML code in your listing descriptions. If you have your auction item's image file hosted on a web server, you can use an HTML `<img>` tag to insert the image into your auction description. Using HTML to insert an image yourself is an alternative to using eBay's photo-hosting feature. See Chapter 15 for more about moving content to a web server.

Specify an Image Size

If your image appears too big or too small on a web page, you can use HTML coding to change the size with image attributes. You can set the width and height of an image in pixels or as a percentage of the overall window size. This can enable you to combine your images nicely with the text and other content around them. Make sure to carefully test your page when resizing images using HTML because too much stretching or shrinking can cause a loss of image quality.

Specify an Image Size

① Click inside the `<img>` tag and type `width="?"`, replacing *?* with the width measurement you want to set.

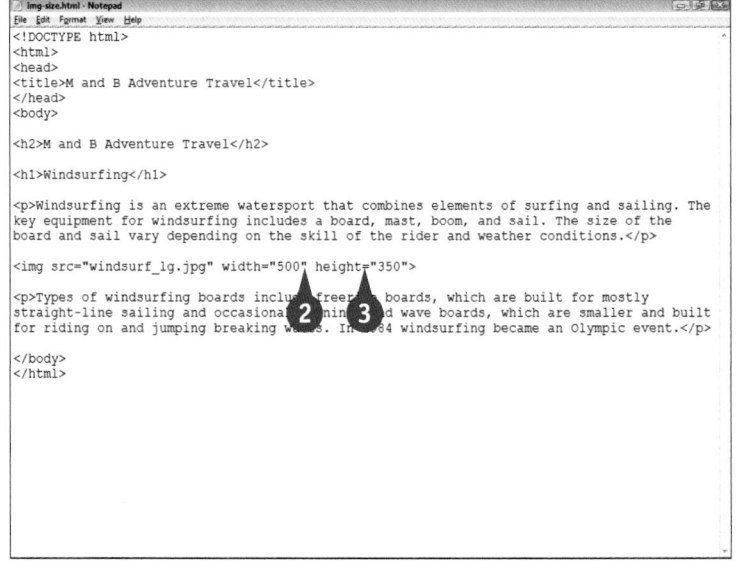

② Type a space.

③ Type `height="?"`, replacing *?* with the height measurement you want to set.

● You can also set the attribute value as a percentage. This tells the browser to display the image at a percentage of the browser window size.

When giving a percentage value, be sure to follow it with a percent sign (%).

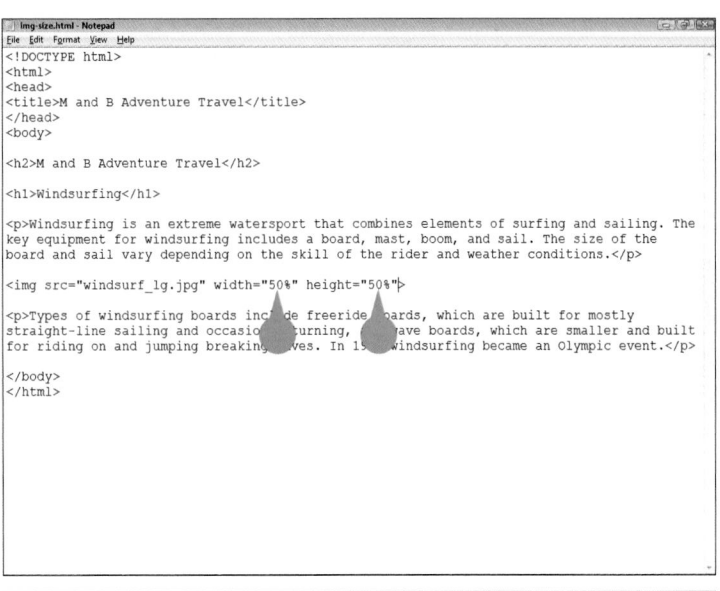

● The web browser displays the image at the specified size on the page.

Note: If you specify only one dimension, whether the width or the height, for your image, a browser sizes the other dimension proportionally based on the original size.

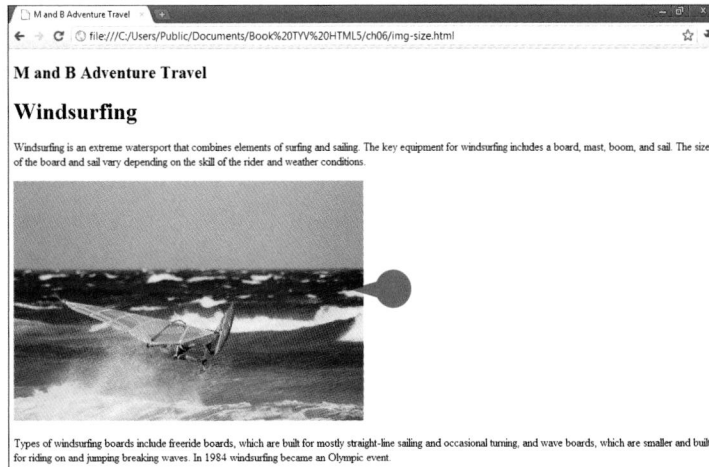

TIPS

What size should I set for a web page image?
The best size for an image depends on how you want to use it on the web page. The vast majority of web users access pages with their monitors set at least 1024 pixels in width and 768 pixels in height. At these settings, browsers can usually display images 950 pixels in width and 600 pixels in height without requiring the user to scroll. Making your images smaller can allow users to see more than one image at a time, depending on the layout.

Is it better to resize an image in an editing program or using HTML coding?
Resizing images using HTML can reduce the quality of your images, especially if you use HTML to enlarge them. Also, shrinking an image using HTML does not actually reduce its file size, which means the image does not download any faster. For these reasons, resizing images using an image editor if you have one is better. This enables you to maintain an image's quality and optimize its file size.

Add Alternative Text

For users who have images turned off in their browsers, you can add alternative text that identifies the images on your page. Alternative text, sometimes called *placeholder text*, can describe what appears in an image and is an important addition to your web page markup. Most search engines, because they process text but not images, use alternative text to better understand the content of your page. This can help improve the placement of your website in search results.

Add Alternative Text

1 Click inside the `<img>` tag and type `alt="?"`, replacing *?* with alternative text describing the image.

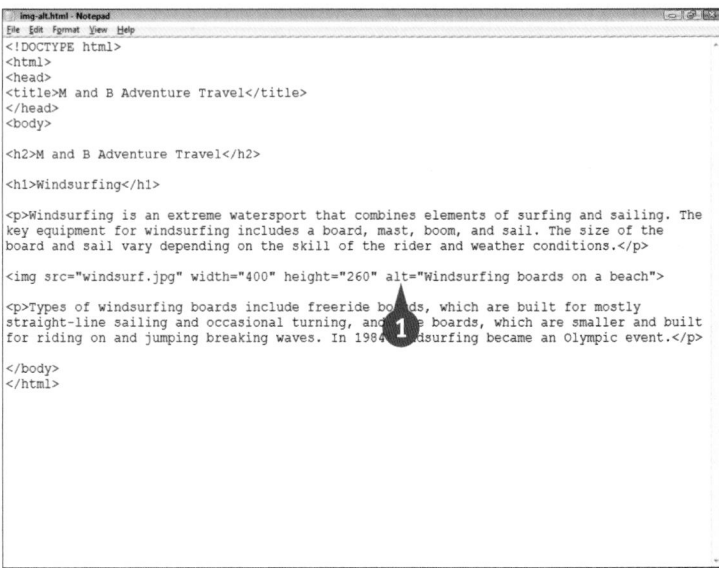

● If the user's browser has images turned off, or if the image cannot be found on the web server, the browser displays the alternative text in lieu of the image.

Note: You can combine alt information with title information in the same image. See "Create an Image Label" for more details.

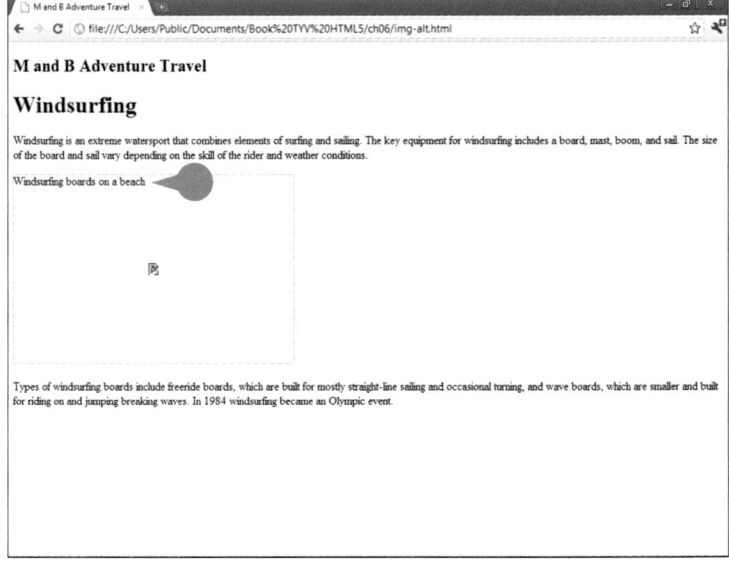

Create an Image Label

You can add a label that appears whenever the user positions the mouse pointer over a particular image on a web page. You can use labels to offer detailed information about the image.

Labels work differently from alternative text. Alternative text appears on the page itself when images are turned off. A label appears in a pop-up box when the user positions the mouse over the image. You add a label by including a `title` attribute in the `<img>` tag.

Create an Image Label

1 Within the `<img>` tag, type `title="?"`, replacing ? with the image label you want to appear.

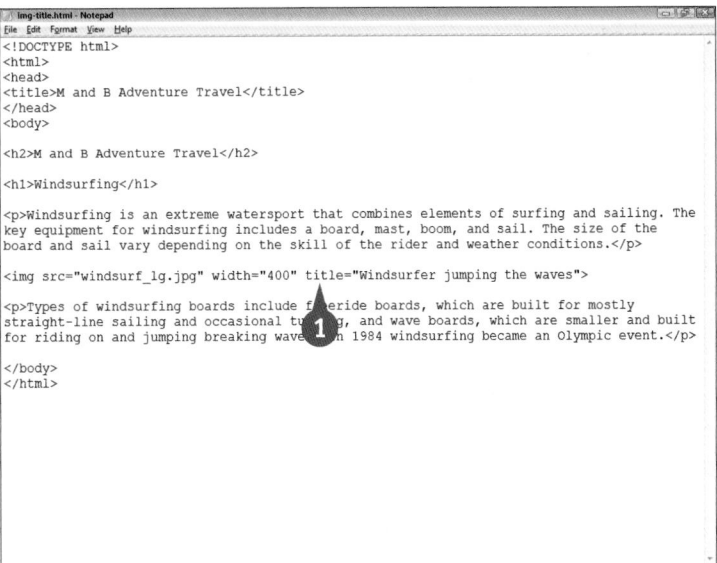

● The label appears when you position the mouse pointer over the image in the browser window.

Note: Label text can also help search engines determine the type of image content on your page.

Note: You can combine title information with alt information in the same image. See "Add Alternative Text" for more details.

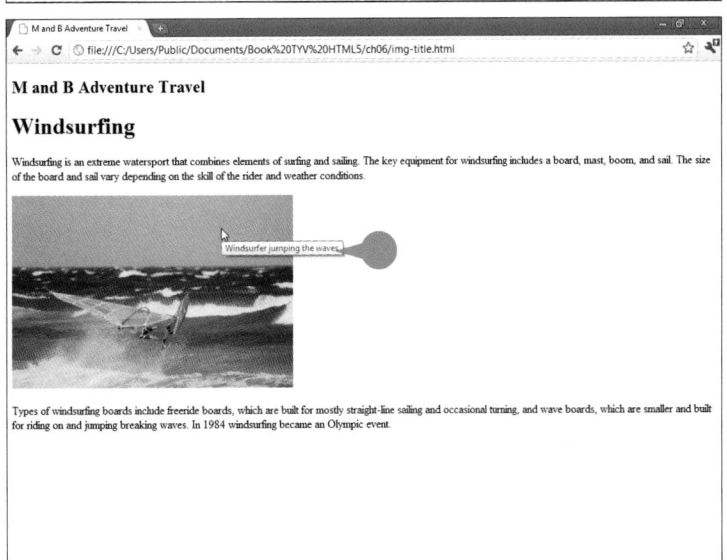

Add an Image as a Figure

You can use the `<figure>` tag to mark images that are related to the main content of your page but that could be moved out of the main flow, if needed. For example, in an academic article, you could use the tag for the images, diagrams, and charts that could possibly appear in an appendix at the end. You can add a `<figcaption>` tag inside the `<figure>` tag to specify a caption that describes the image.

The `<figure>` and `<figcaption>` tags are currently not well supported by browsers. You can add CSS styling to help them look presentable on the page.

Add an Image as a Figure

① Add an image to your document using the `<img>` tag and `src` attribute. See "Insert an Image" for details.

② Type `<figure>` before the `<img>` tag.

③ Type `</figure>` after the `<img>` tag.

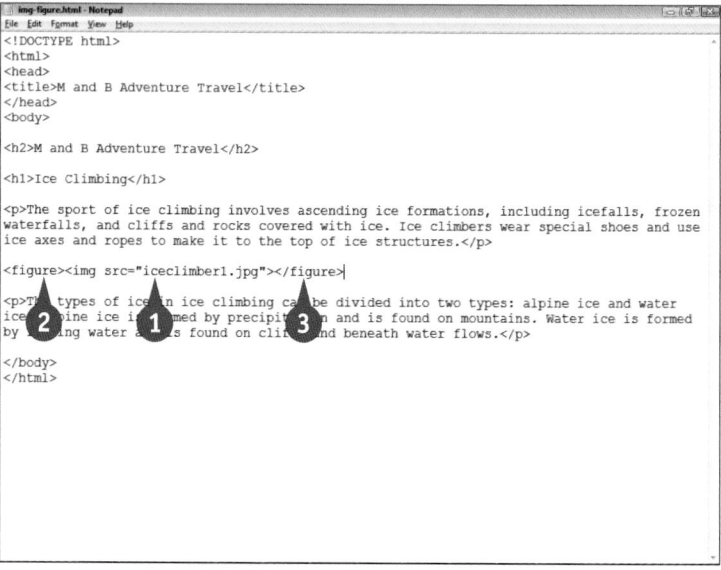

④ Inside the `<figure>` and `</figure>` tags, type `<figcaption>`.

⑤ Type the caption text.

⑥ Type `</figcaption>`.

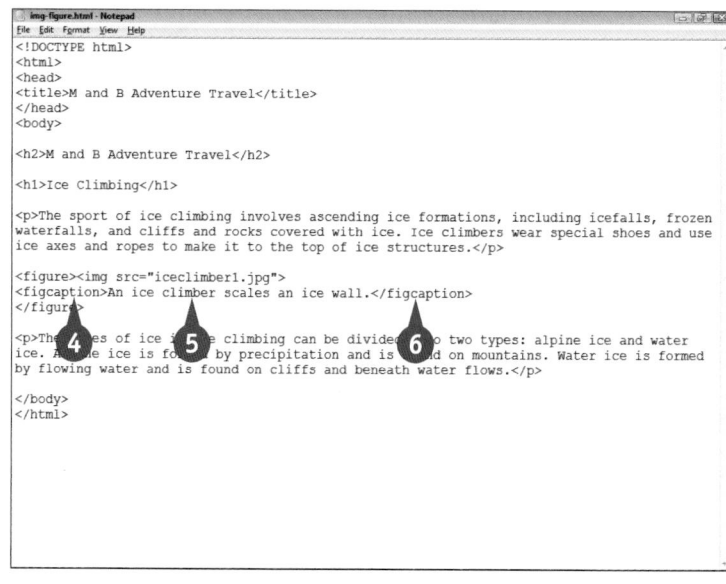

7 You can optionally create a style rule for the figure container using a `figure` selector.

8 You can create a style for the caption using a `figcaption` selector.

Note: For more about CSS rules and selectors, see Chapter 4.

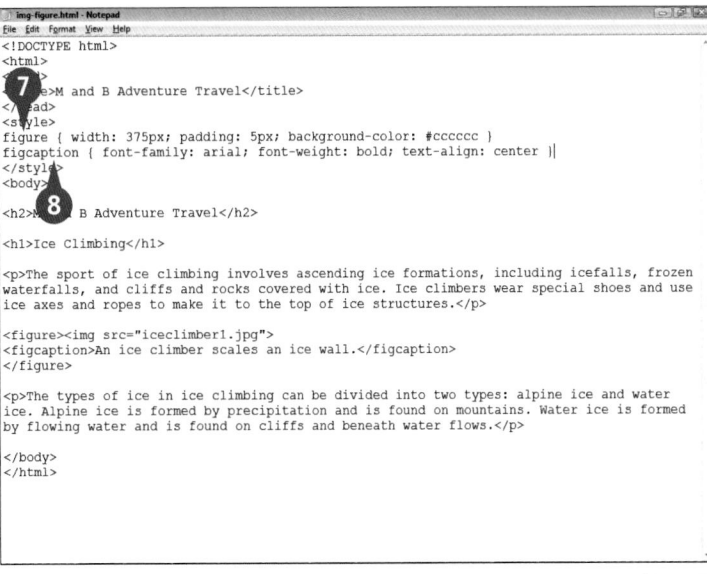

● The web browser displays the image and the caption.

An ice climber scales an ice wall.

TIPS

How can I put the figure caption on the left or right side of the image?
You can apply the `float` property to the figure image, for example:

`figure img {float: right}`

This moves the image to one side and puts a caption following it on the other side. You can set the `width` property to the figure to keep the caption and image next to one another. For example:

`figure {width: 500px}`

Can I put multiple images and captions inside my <figure> tag?
According to the HTML5 specification, a maximum of one `<figcaption>` element is allowed within the `<figure>` tag. But the tag can hold multiple images and even text, tables, and other content.

Align an Image Horizontally

You can use the CSS `float` property to control the horizontal positioning of an image on a page. The `float` property also determines how text wraps around the image. When you float an image to the left, text after it wraps to the right, and vice versa for right alignment.

You can center-align an image using the `<div>` tag. See "Center an Image" for details. You can also add space around the image to make text or other content wrapping around the image more readable. See "Add Space around an Image" for details.

Align an Image Horizontally

1 Create a CSS class for the `<img>` tag.

Note: See Chapter 4 for more about CSS classes.

2 Type {.

3 For the class declaration, type `float: ?`, replacing *?* with `right` or `left`.

4 Type }.

5 Inside the `<img>` tag, type `class="?"`, replacing *?* with the class name from step **1**.

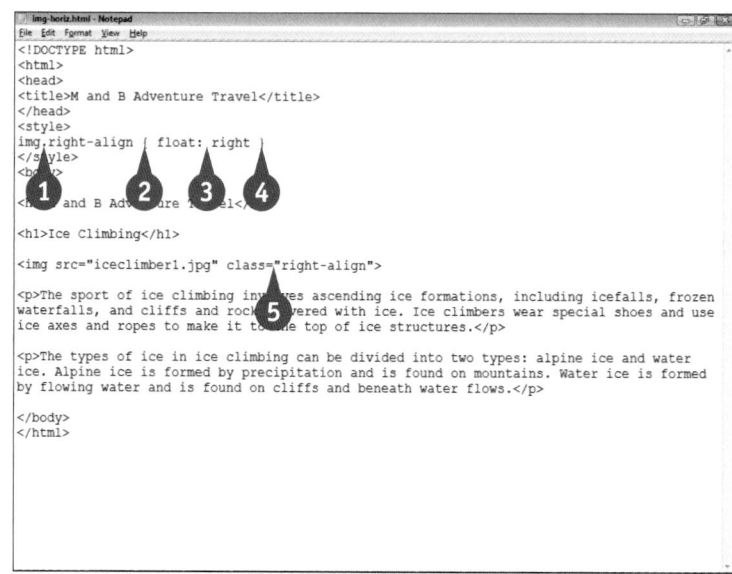

The web browser aligns the image as specified.

● In this example, the image is aligned to the right.

Note: To center-align an image, see the section "Center an Image."

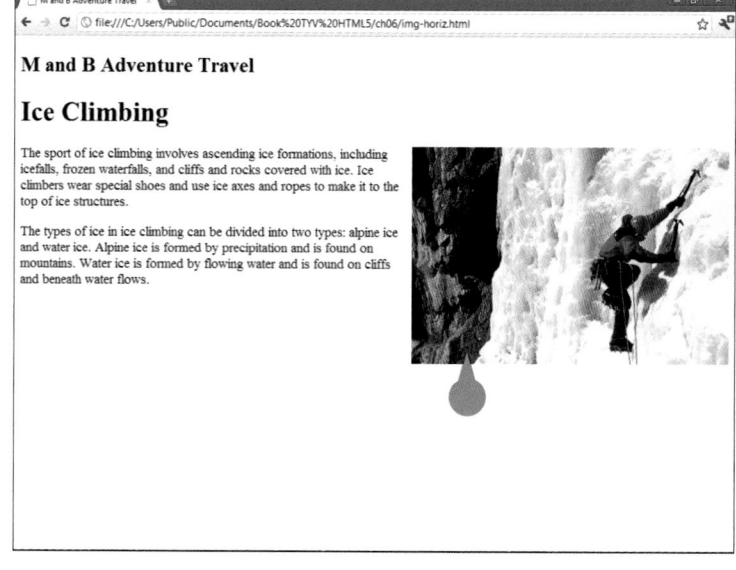

Align an Image Vertically

You can use the `vertical-align` CSS property to control the vertical positioning of an image on a page relative to text next to it. Common alignment values are `top`, `middle`, and `bottom`. This can be useful when adding short caption text to an image.

You can also align an image horizontally on a page. See the section "Align an Image Horizontally" to learn more.

Align an Image Vertically

1 Create a CSS class for the `<img>` tag.

Note: See Chapter 4 for more about CSS classes.

2 Type {.

3 For the class declaration, type `vertical-align: ?`, replacing *?* with `top`, `middle`, or `left`.

4 Type }.

5 Inside the `<img>` tag, type `class="?"`, replacing *?* with the class name from step **1**.

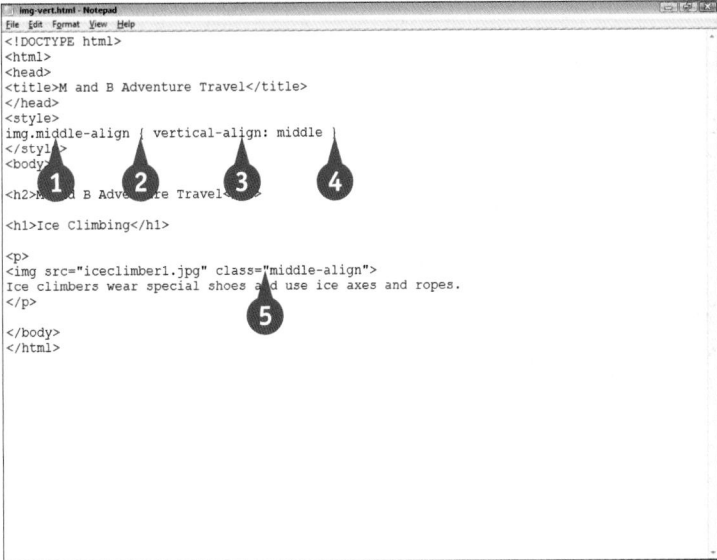

The web browser aligns the image as specified.

● In this example, the image is middle-aligned with the adjacent text.

Note: Another useful way to associate a caption with an image is with the `<figure>` and `<fig caption>` tags. See "Add an Image as a Figure" for details.

Center an Image

You can center your image on the page using a `<div>` tag and the `align` attribute. Centering an image can give it more emphasis and help it stand out from the text or other page elements. You can center an image at the top of a web page to give the page a fancy or colorful title. You can also align an image horizontally or vertically on the page. See the other sections in this chapter for details.

Center an Image

1 Create a CSS class for the `<div>` tag.

Note: See Chapter 4 for more about CSS classes.

2 For the class declaration, type `text-align: center`.

3 Before the `<img>` tag, type `<div class="?">`, replacing *?* with the class name from step **1**.

4 After the `<img>` tag, type `</div>`.

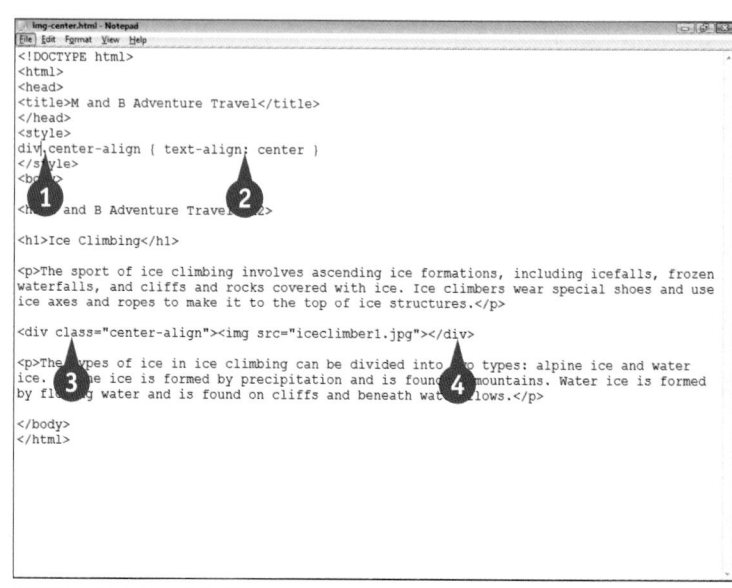

● The image appears centered on the web page.

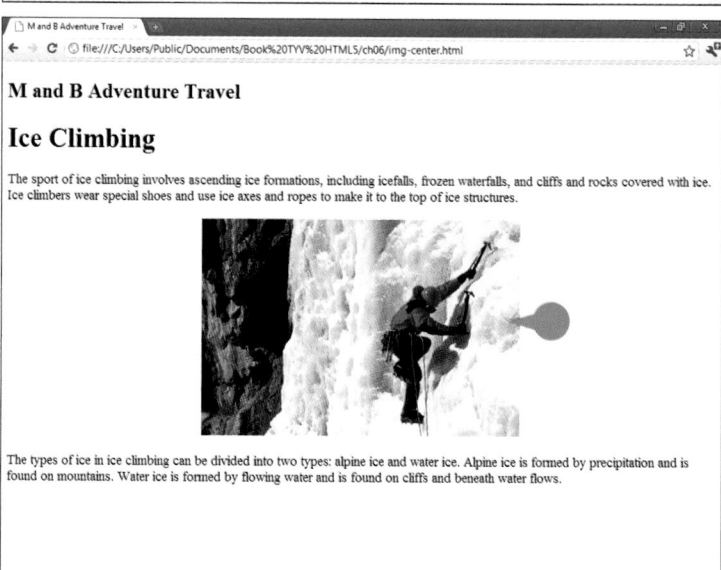

Stop Text Wrap

You can stop text wrapping around your images by applying a `<br>` tag that has the `clear` property set to `both`. This CSS causes the text or other content following the `<br>` tag to begin at the bottom of the image. You can cause text to wrap around your image in the first place by aligning the image using the `float` property. See "Align an Image Horizontally" for details.

Stop Text Wrap

1 Click where you want to end the text wrap and type `<br style="clear: both">`.

The `clear` property also accepts the values `left` and `right`, to stop wrapping to just one side.

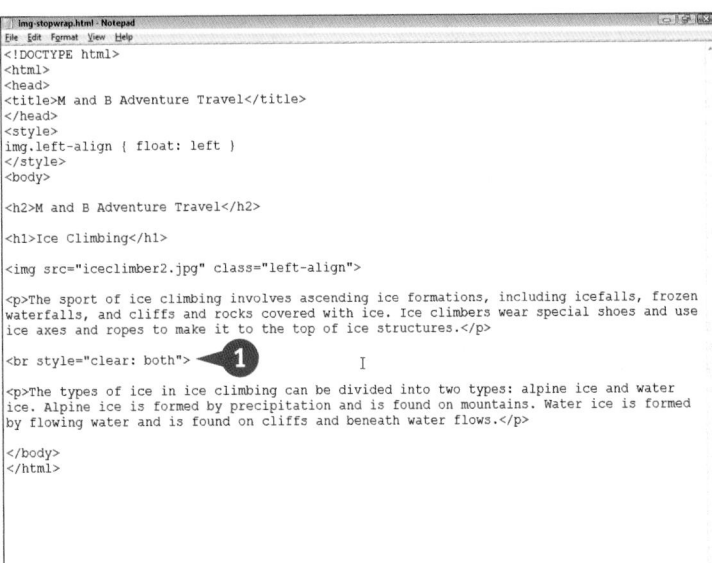

The text wrapping ends at the selected point on the page.

● In this example, the next paragraph starts on a different line from the image.

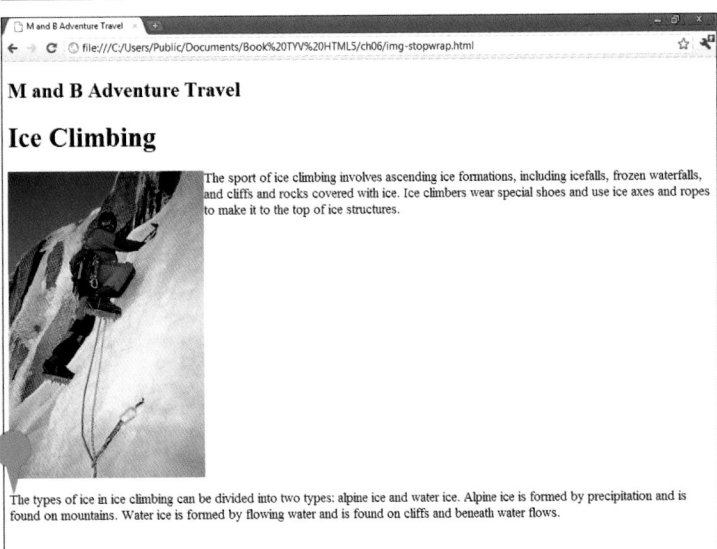

Add Space around an Image

Most web browsers display only a small amount of space between images and text. You can increase the amount of space, also called *padding*, to make the page more visually appealing and easier to read. You can control padding on all sides of an image at once with the `padding` property. You can also apply padding on just one side with the `padding-top`, `padding-bottom`, `padding-left`, and `padding-right` properties. Padding can add whitespace between the image and its caption.

Add Space around an Image

1 Create a CSS class for the `<img>` tag.

Note: See Chapter 4 for more about CSS classes.

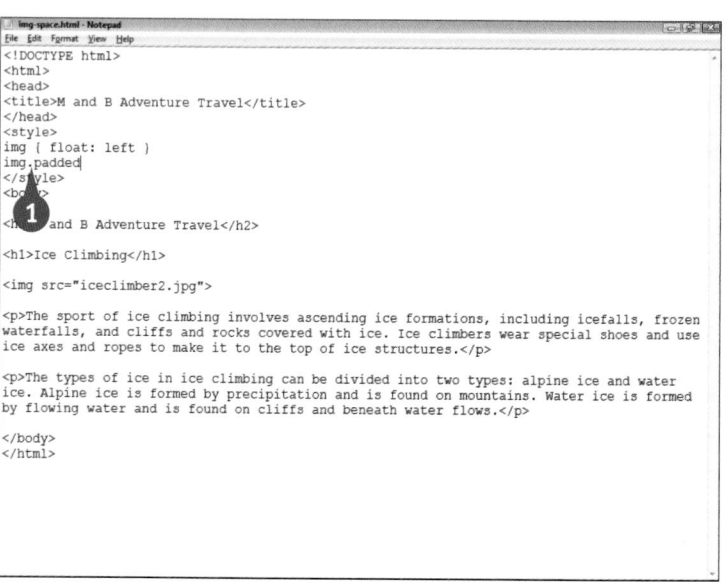

2 For the class declaration, type `padding: ?`, replacing *?* with the amount of padding.

To put padding on just one side of the image, you can use the `padding-left`, `padding-right`, `padding-top`, or `padding-bottom` property.

You can define the padding in pixels (`px`), points (`pt`), millimeters (`mm`), centimeters (`cm`), inches (`in`), picas (`pc`), x-height (`ex`), or em space (`em`).

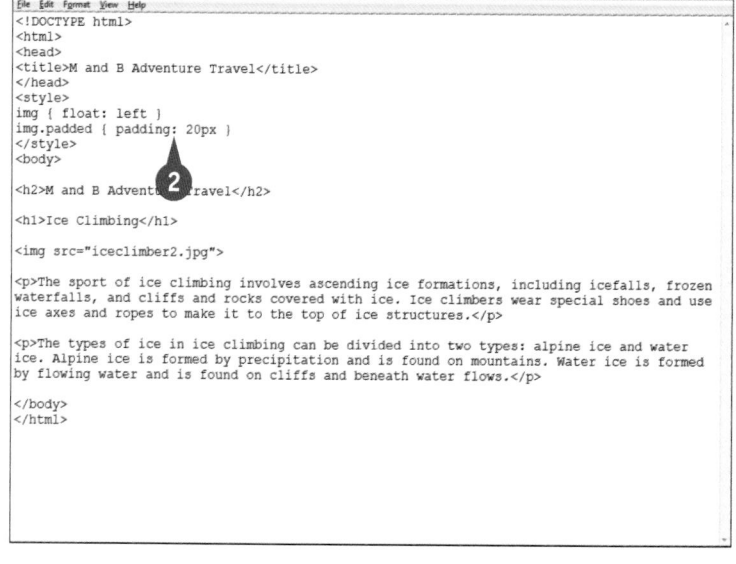

③ Inside the <img> tag, type class="?", replacing *?* with the class name from step **1**.

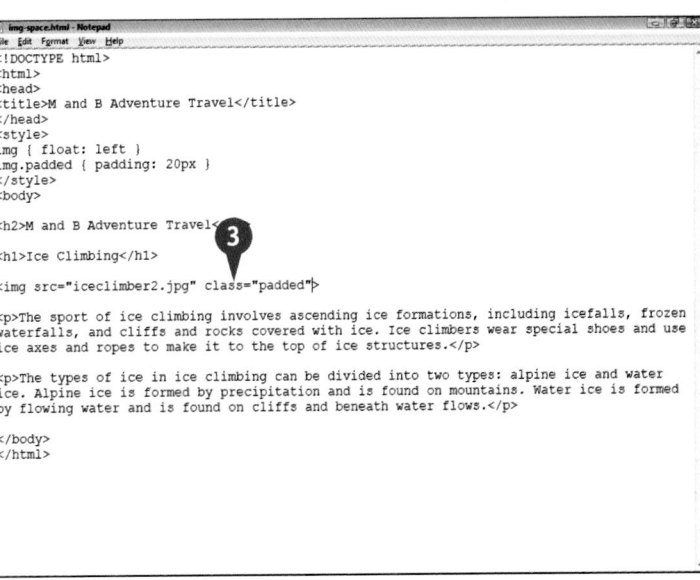

● The web browser displays the image with the specified amount of space around it.

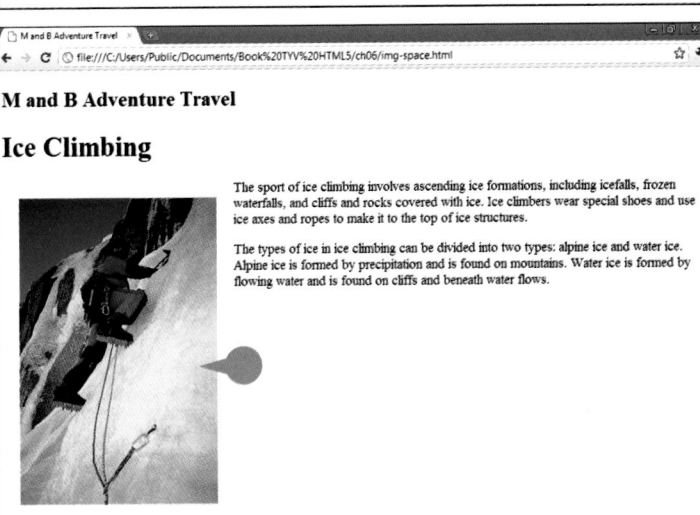

How do I apply different padding to all sides of my image at once?

You can set four measurements for the padding property to set the top, right, bottom, and left padding. The measurements are separated with spaces:

img {10px 10px 5px 0}

The rule above sets the top and right padding to 10 pixels, the bottom to 5 pixels, and the left to no padding.

Can I set the padding for an image to a percentage?

Yes. But the padding will be a percentage of the height or width of enclosing the page element, not the height or width of the image itself. If the enclosing element is the page body, the actual padding added can be hard to predict.

Add a Background Image

You can turn an image into a background for your web page by setting a value for the `background-image` property. When selecting an image for a background, try to factor in how your text will appear against the image. You may need to change the color of the text to make it legible. See Chapter 5 for details about changing the text color.

If you use a large image file, it can fill the entire background. If you use a smaller image, the browser by default tiles the image across and down the page to fill the background with a repeating pattern. You can change the tiling behavior with the `background-repeat` property.

Add a Background Image

1 Place the image you want to use as your background in the same directory as your HTML file.

2 Type `body { }` to create a style rule for the `<body>` tag.

```
img-bg.html - Notepad
File  Edit  Format  View  Help
<!DOCTYPE html>
<html>
<head>
<title>M and B Adventure Travel</title>
</head>
<style>
img { float: left }
img.padded { padding: 20px }
body { }
</style>
<body>

<h2>M and B Adventure Travel</h2>

<h1>Ice Climbing</h1>

<img src="iceclimber1.jpg" class="padded">

<p>The sport of ice climbing involves ascending ice formations, including icefalls, frozen
waterfalls, and cliffs and rocks covered with ice. Ice climbers wear special shoes and use
ice axes and ropes to make it to the top of ice structures.</p>

<p>The types of ice in ice climbing can be divided into two types: alpine ice and water
ice. Alpine ice is formed by precipitation and is found on mountains. Water ice is formed
by flowing water and is found on cliffs and beneath water flows.</p>

</body>
</html>
```

3 To insert the image as a background, type `background-image: url('?');`, replacing `?` with the path to the image.

```
img-bg.html - Notepad
File  Edit  Format  View  Help
<!DOCTYPE html>
<html>
<head>
<title>M and B Adventure Travel</title>
</head>
<style>
img { float: left }
img.padded { padding: 20px }
body { background-image: url('iceberg_bg2.jpg') }
</style>
<body>

<h2>M and B Adventure Travel</h2>

<h1>Ice Climbing</h1>

<img src="iceclimber1.jpg" class="padded">

<p>The sport of ice climbing involves ascending ice formations, including icefalls, frozen
waterfalls, and cliffs and rocks covered with ice. Ice climbers wear special shoes and use
ice axes and ropes to make it to the top of ice structures.</p>

<p>The types of ice in ice climbing can be divided into two types: alpine ice and water
ice. Alpine ice is formed by precipitation and is found on mountains. Water ice is formed
by flowing water and is found on cliffs and beneath water flows.</p>

</body>
</html>
```

④ To control how the image repeats, type background-repeat: ?, replacing *?* with repeat, repeat-x, repeat-y, or no-repeat.

The repeat-x value tiles the image horizontally, whereas repeat-y tiles the image vertically. The default is repeat.

The repeat value, which is the default, tiles the image in both directions.

The no-repeat value displays the image once.

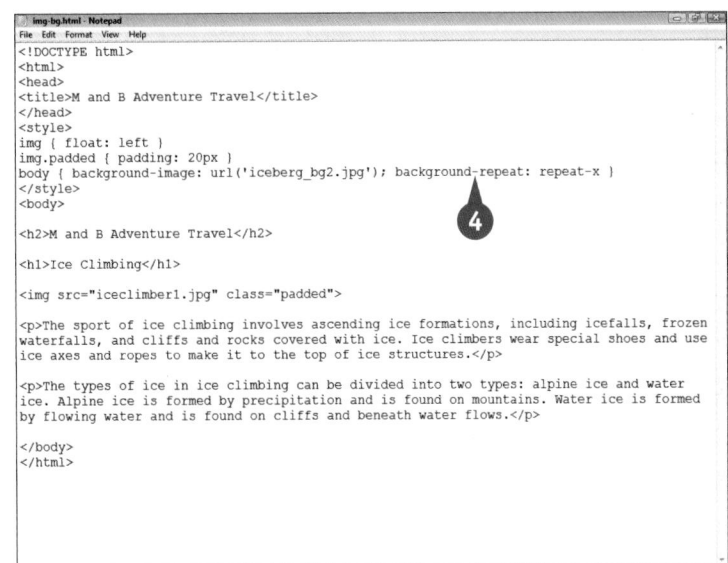

● The web browser displays the image as the background with the specified repeat style which is horizontal.

In this example, the text formatted with the heading tags in the body of the page overlays the tiling background images.

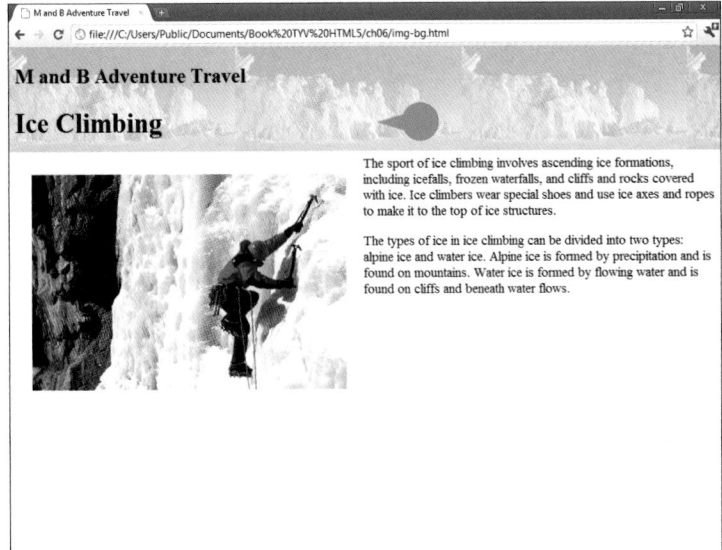

TIPS

How do I create a background image that appears once on my page?
You can assign a no-repeat value to the background-repeat property to place the image once in the background. Then you can specify the location of the image using the background-position property. A center value places the image in the center of the web page. You can use percentage values to place the image relative to the entire height and width of the window or numeric values to place it at pixel coordinates. The first value is always the horizontal position, whereas the second value is the vertical.

How do I keep a background image from scrolling with the page?
To control whether or not your background image scrolls with the page content, you can assign a background-attachment property. Assigning a scroll value, which is the default, allows the background image to scroll, whereas fixed keeps the background image fixed as the page content moves. This feature works with the different repeat and positioning settings described in this section.

Add a Meter Image

You can add the `<meter>` tag to your page to display a value within a range of values. For example, the tag can show a person's test score within a range of test scores or how much memory has been used on a hard disk. On most browsers, the `<meter>` tag displays a horizontal bar with the bar colored a certain amount based on the value. The `<meter>` tag is new in HTML5. You set the range using the `min` and `max` attributes.

To adjust the overall size of a meter bar, you can set `width` and `height` properties for the `<meter>` tag with CSS rules. See Chapter 10 for more about setting dimensions.

Add a Meter Image

1 Type `<meter>`.

2 Type the meter value. This value will be displayed by browsers that do not recognize the `<meter>` tag.

3 Type `</meter>`.

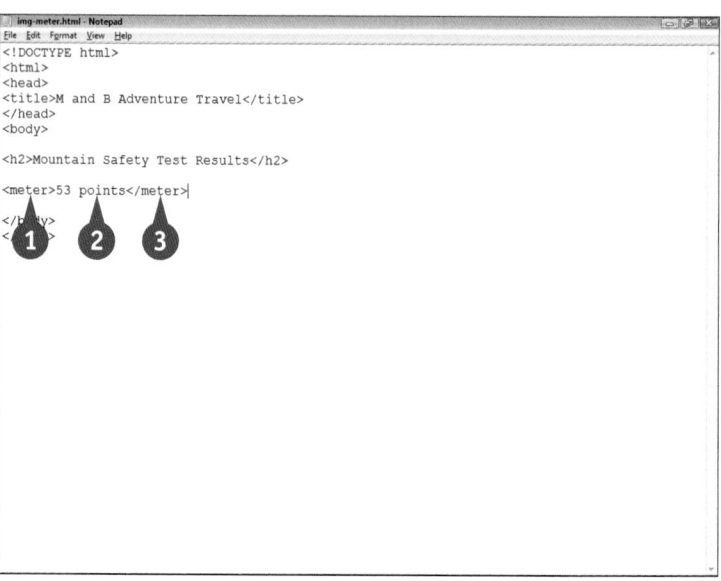

4 In the `<meter>` tag, type `value="?"`, replacing ? with the numeric value in step **2**.

5 Type `min="?"`, replacing ? with the minimum possible value of the range.

6 Type `max="?"`, replacing ? with the maximum possible value of the range.

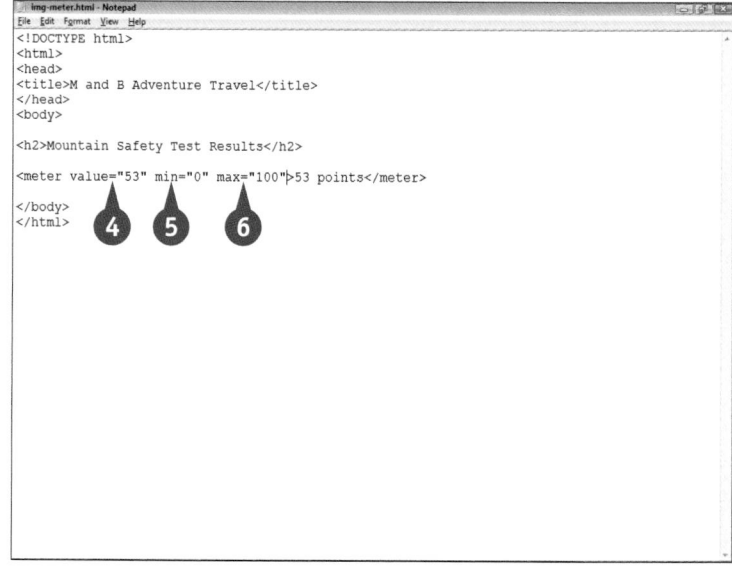

⑦ Type `low="?"`, replacing ? with the lowest realized value in the range.

⑧ Type `high="?"`, replacing ? with the highest realized value in the range.

⑨ Type `optimum="?"`, replacing ? with the range optimum.

Some browsers change the meter color based on how close the value is to the optimum.

⑩ You can optionally type more meter content to display on the page.

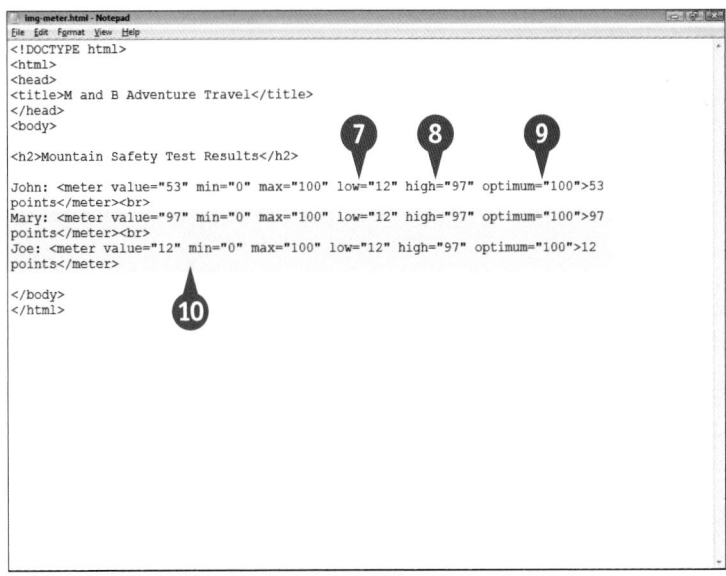

● The web browser displays a graphic showing the position of the value within the range.

In this example, the browser also shows two other meter graphics.

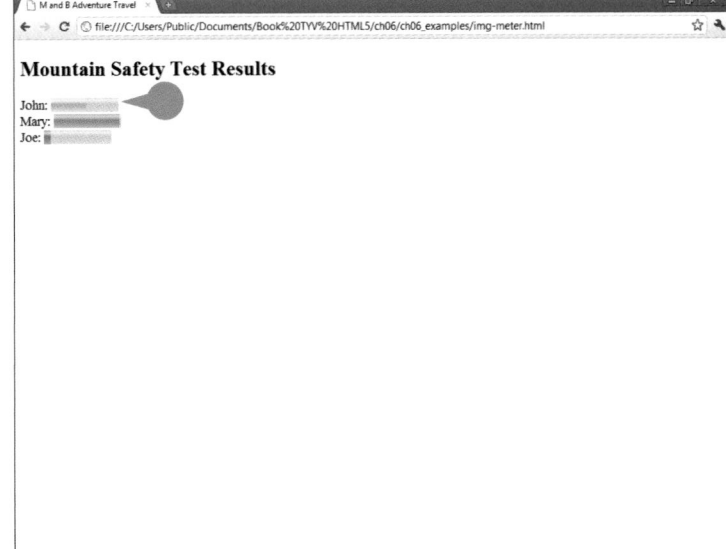

TIP

How can I visually display progress toward a goal?

If you can measure that progress in numbers, you can use the `<progress>` tag. Similar to the `<meter>` tag, it displays a colored, horizontal bar. The color (●) represents how far a current value is from a goal. The tag takes a `max` attribute, representing the goal, and a `value` attribute. For example, a fundraiser page might display this:

```
$0 <progress value="850"
max="1000">$850</progress> $1000
```

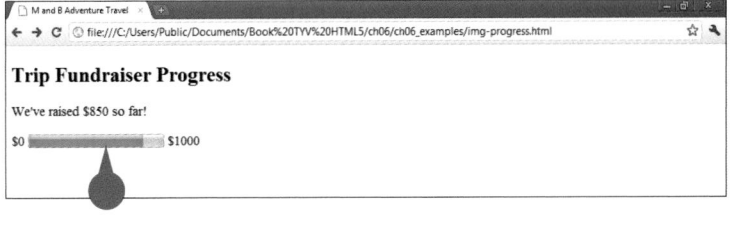

Adding Links

Are you ready to start adding links to your web pages? This chapter shows you how to create links in your HTML5 documents to allow users to jump to other websites or to other pages within your own site. You learn how to add e-mail links and control the appearance of links. You also get an introduction to URLs, which are the web addresses that define the destinations of your links. Links are created using `<a>` "tags in combination with the `href` attribute.

Understanding Links

Hyperlinks, or *links* for short, are what make web pages different from other computer documents. Any publicly accessible web page can be connected to another by creating a link. Links enable users to navigate from one topic to the next on a website, and from one website to another. The user clicks the link and the browser opens the destination page. You create links with the <a> tag and `href` attribute.

Types of Links

Links can be text, images, or multimedia. Text links typically appear as underlined, differently colored words on a page. Any image on a web page can be turned into a link. For example, graphical site maps and navigation buttons that appear at the top or side of a page can be turned into links to make it easy for users to access other pages on the same website. Similarly, you can place <a> tags around video and audio content to make them links. When a user positions the mouse pointer over a link, the pointer takes the shape of a pointing hand, indicating the presence of an active, clickable link.

Link Destinations

You can use links on your web page to direct users to other pages on the Internet. For example, you might include a link on your company web page to a local city directory detailing activities and hotels in the area. If your website consists of more than one page, you

can include links to other pages on the site. For example, your main page may provide links to pages about your business, products, and ordering information as well as to a map of your location. You can also provide links to different areas on the same page. This can be useful if a page is particularly long. It allows users to jump right to the information they want to view without having to scroll.

Absolute and Relative Links

You can use two types of links in your HTML5 documents: absolute and relative. *Absolute links* use a complete web address, or *URL*, to point to a specific page on a specific web server:

```
<a href="http://www.example.com/page.html">Click here</a>
```

Relative links use shorthand to reference a page and do not specify the server. You generally use relative links to reference documents on the same website:

```
<a href="page.html">Click here</a>
```

Understanding URLs

Every page on the web has a unique address called a URL. Short for *Uniform Resource Locator*, a URL identifies the domain name of the web server and the directory path to the file on that server. Absolute links specify a complete web page URL, whereas relative links use shorthand to specify pages relative to the page containing the link.

HTTP Prefix

All URLs for web pages include the standard HTTP (Hypertext Transfer Protocol) prefix, as in http://www.example.com. Although most browsers automatically insert the http:// prefix for you when you type an address such as www.example.com, you must include the prefix when referencing URLs in your HTML. There may be times when you use a prefix other than HTTP in your URLs. If you are linking to a document that resides on a file transfer site, you use the FTP prefix (ftp://). If you want to create a link that opens an e-mail program, allowing a user to send an e-mail message, you use the MAILTO prefix (mailto:). There is also an encrypted version of the HTTP prefix, https://, which you use when linking to secure areas of websites, such as those involving payment transactions.

Domain Name

Following the prefix in a URL is the domain name of the web server where the page is stored. Typically, domain names correspond to the company or organization hosting your web page files. Hosts can include commercial companies, educational institutions, and government agencies. In the URL http://www.example.com, "example.com" is the name of the domain, with "www." specifying a web server at that domain. Occasionally you may use a numeric IP (Internet Protocol) address such as 208.215.179.146 in your URL instead of a domain name.

Directory Path

Following the domain name in a URL is information about the directories in which the page is stored on the server. You use slashes (/) to separate the domain name, directories, and filename. Directory information does not exist in a URL if the HTML document for the page is stored in a web directory's main, or *root*, directory.

Filename

For basic web pages, the URL ends with the name of the HTML file. This information tells the web server what document to retrieve and return to the

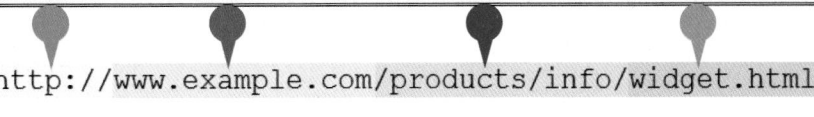

http://www.example.com/products/info/widget.html

web browser. You may see additional information at the end of URLs for pages generated dynamically, such as those on sites that use technologies such as PHP or Java. When you reference a website's home page, you often omit the path and filename from a URL, such as in http://www.example.com. In such cases, the server returns a default page for the site, usually titled index.html, located in the web server's root directory.

Link to Another Page

You can create a link in your HTML document that, when clicked, takes the visitor to another page on the web. You can link to a page on your own website or to a page elsewhere on the web. You create a link using the `<a>` tag with an `href` attribute. You surround the content that you are turning into a link with an opening and closing `<a>` tag.

To create a link, you must first know the URL of the page to which you want to link, such as http://www.wiley.com/index.html. For details about URLs, see "Understanding URLs."

Link to Another Page

Insert a Text Link

1 Type the text you want to use as a link.

2 Type `<a href="?">` in front of the text, replacing *?* with the URL of the page to which you want to link.

3 Type `</a>` at the end of the link text.

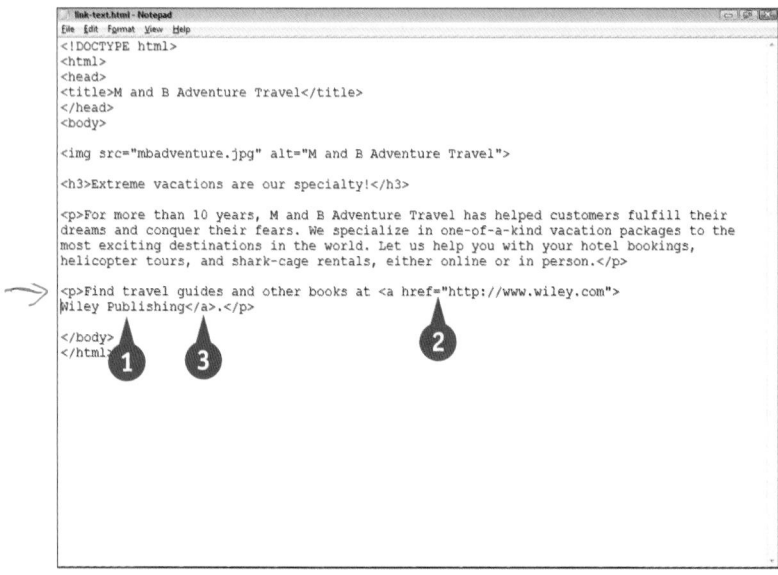

● The web browser displays the text as an underlined link.

● The mouse pointer (⇱), when positioned over the link, takes the shape of a hand pointer (☝), indicating a link.

● The URL for the link appears at the bottom of the browser.

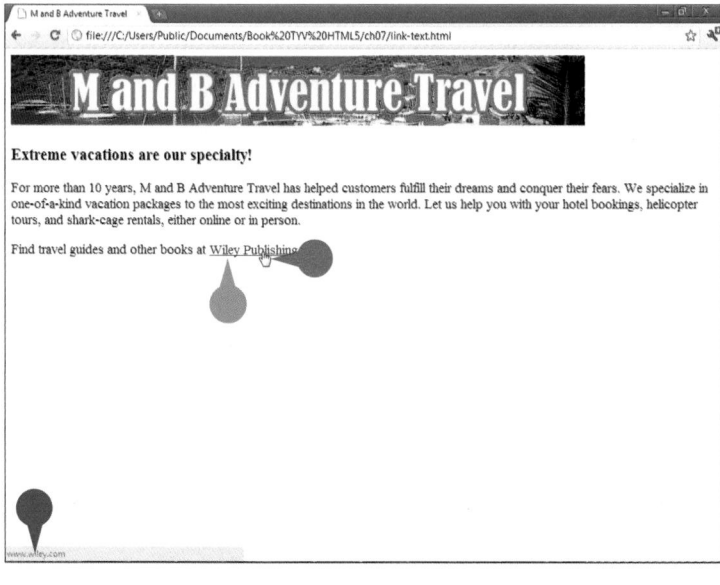

Insert an Image Link

1 Add the image you want to use as a link using the `<img>` tag.

Note: To learn how to add images to a page, see Chapter 6.

2 Type `<a href="?">` in front of the image code, replacing *?* with the URL of the page to which you want to link.

3 Type `</a>` after the image code.

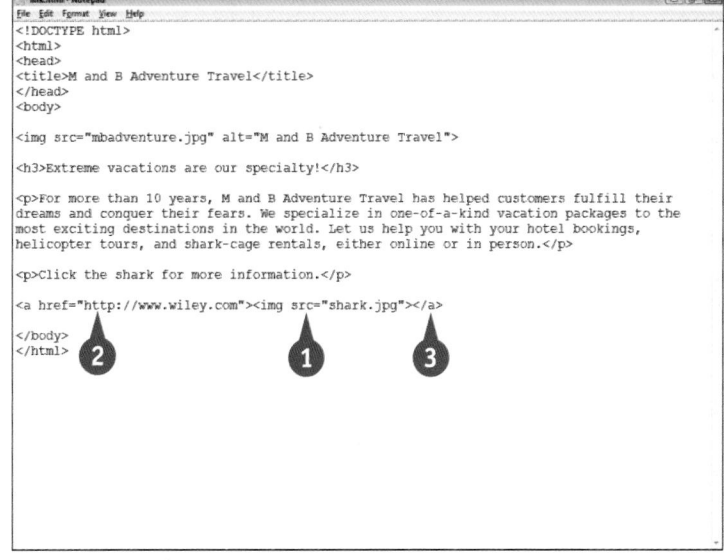

● The web browser displays the image as a link.

● The mouse pointer (⌖), when positioned over the link, takes the shape of a hand pointer (⍓), indicating a link.

● The URL for the link appears at the bottom of the browser.

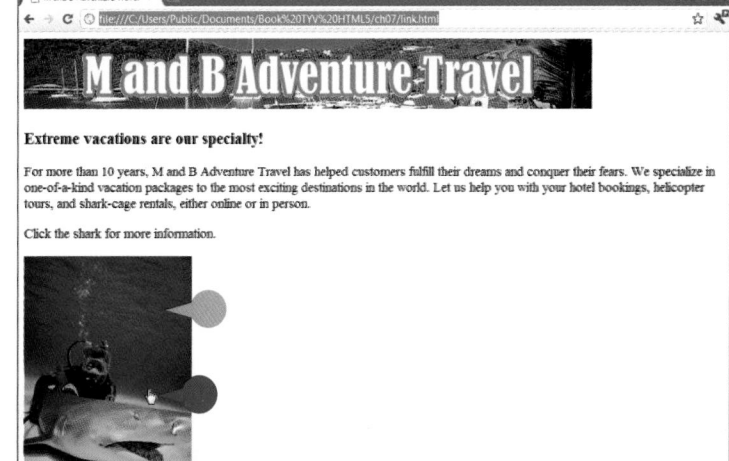

TIPS

How do I link to another page on my website?
You can link to another page on your site using a relative link. In a relative link, you specify the location of the destination page relative to the page that contains the link without specifying the domain name of the server. If the destination page is located in the same directory as the containing page, you can simply specify the filename, as in `<a href="photos.html">`. If the destination page is in a subdirectory relative to the containing page, you need to specify that subdirectory as well, as in `<a href="media/photos.html">`.

What HTML document appears when I do not specify one in the URL, such as for http://www.example.com?
When you request a URL that does not include a specific HTML document, the web server attempts to retrieve a default HTML document for that server. The default document is often index. html or default.htm. Some URLs specify a directory on a web server, such as the URL http://www.example.com/pages/, but not an HTML document. In such cases, the server retrieves the default document from the specified directory, if one exists. If the default document does not exist, the server returns an error page.

Open a New Window with a Link

You can add instructions to an HTML link that tell the browser to open the linked page in a new browser window. You may add this instruction if you want to keep a window to your own site open so the user can easily return to your page.

You use a `target` attribute within the `<a>` link tag to open links in new windows. To make all the links on your page open in new windows, you can use the `<base>` tag. To learn more about how links and URLs work, see the sections at the beginning of this chapter.

Open a New Window with a Link

Link to a New Window

1 Click within the `<a>` tag for the link you want to edit and type `target="?"`, replacing *?* with a name for the new window.

Other links on your web page can reference the same `target` name to open pages in the same new window.

If you want the link to open in a new, unnamed window, type `_blank` for the target name.

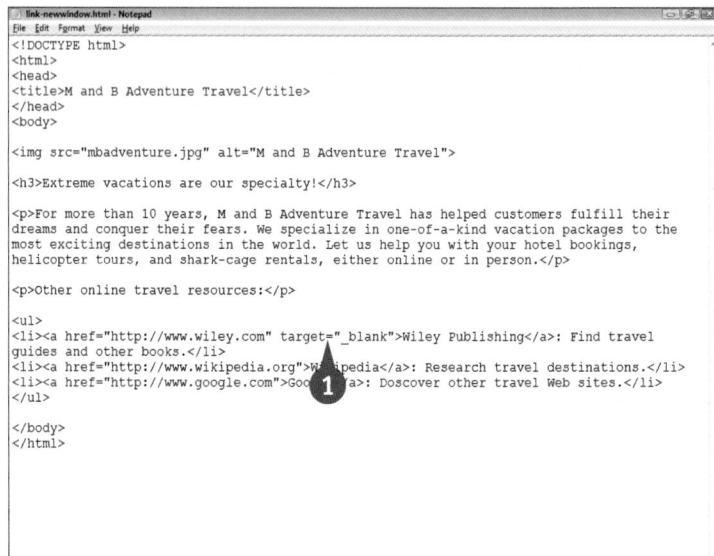

When the link is clicked, a new browser window opens.

● In the Chrome browser, the window appears in a new browser tab.

● The original tabbed window remains open.

Make All Links Open New Windows

1 Click between the `<head>` and `</head>` tags and type `<base target="?">`, replacing *?* with a name for the new window, such as `main`.

If you want the links to open in new, unnamed windows, type `_blank` for the target name.

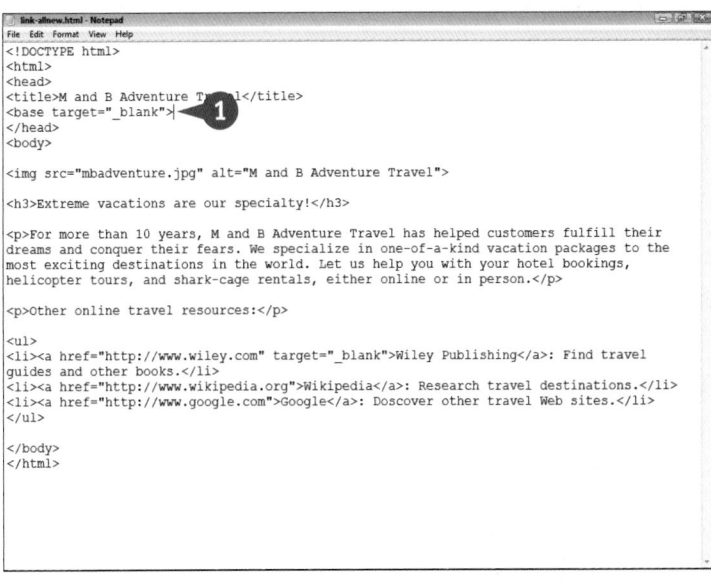

● When a user clicks any of the links on the page, a new browser window opens.

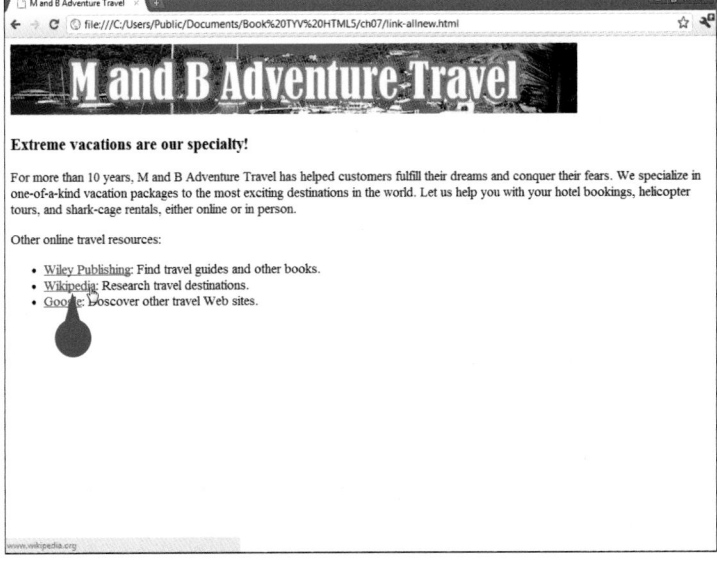

Can I make multiple links on a page open in the same window?

Yes. Just use the same `target` value for the links, for example `target= "new1"`. The first time a user clicks one of the links, a "new1" window opens. Subsequent link clicks open pages in the same window.

Should I open new windows for every link?

Probably not. If a new window opens every time a link is clicked on your pages, users may quickly become overwhelmed by the number of open windows. You may want to open new windows only when links lead to a page outside the current website. That way, the current website remains open on the user's computer.

Link to an Area on the Same Page

You can add links to your page that take the user to another place on the same page. This is particularly useful for longer documents. For example, you can add links that take the user to different headings in your document. This saves the user from having to scroll.

To link to places on the same page, you must assign names to the areas to which you want to link. In HTML5, you can do this with the *id* attribute. To learn about using the id attribute with style sheets, see Chapter 4.

Link to an Area on the Same Page

Identify an Area

1 Click inside the tag to which you want to create a link and type `id="?"`, replacing *?* with a unique name for the area.

Keeping your names short and simple is best, using only letters and numbers in the names.

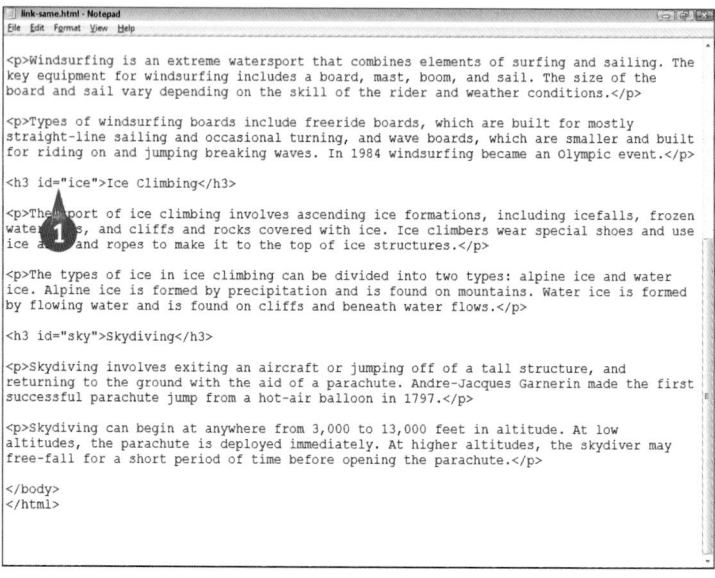

Create a Link to the Area

1 In front of the text or image you want to turn into a link, type `<a href="#?">`, replacing *?* with a name of the section to which you want to link.

Note: Be sure to include the pound sign (#) when linking to other areas of a page.

2 Type `</a>` after the link text.

Note: To use an image as a link, see the section "Link to Another Page" to learn more.

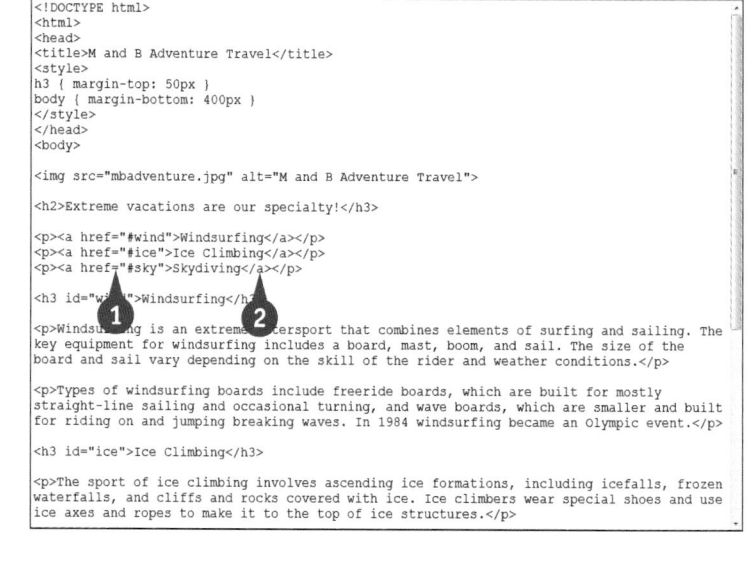

3 Click the link.

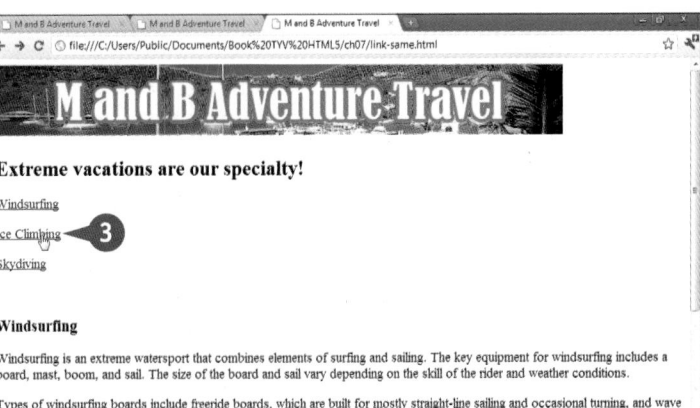

● The browser scrolls to the designated section of the page.

Can I place a link at the bottom of my page that returns the user to the top of the page?

Yes. Adding a link to the bottom of a long page to help the user navigate to the top again without having to scroll is a good idea. To create such a link, add an `id` attribute to an HTML tag at the top of the page following the steps shown in this section, and then insert a link that references that `id` value. Good text to use for such a link is "Return to Top" or "Back to Top."

How do I link to a specific location on another page on my website?

You can use the same technique shown in this section to link to a section on another page. First, name the area on the other page using the `id` attribute, and then create a link to the page, adding a `#` and then the id value to the relative link, such as `<a href="page.html#section1">`.

Link to Another File Type

You can add links to non-HTML resources, such as PDF files, spreadsheet files, image files, compressed files, and more. To make such files web accessible, you must store them in the same locations on the web server as your HTML files. Then you can reference them with a URL just as you do an HTML page.

Thanks to special plug-ins, some web browsers can open certain non-HTML files. For a file that it cannot open, a browser may prompt users to save the file on their computers.

Link to Another File Type

① Type the text for the link.

It is good form to include a description on the page that identifies what type of file the link opens.

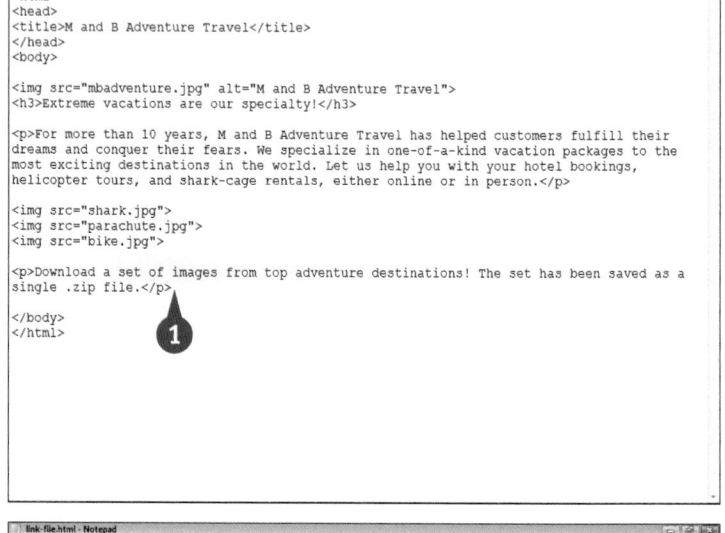

② Type `<a href="?">`, replacing *?* with the relative path and name of the file.

③ Type `</a>` at the end of the link text.

● The link appears on the web page.

When the link is clicked, the browser may display the file in the browser window.

Note: To open the file in a new window, see the section "Open a New Window with a Link."

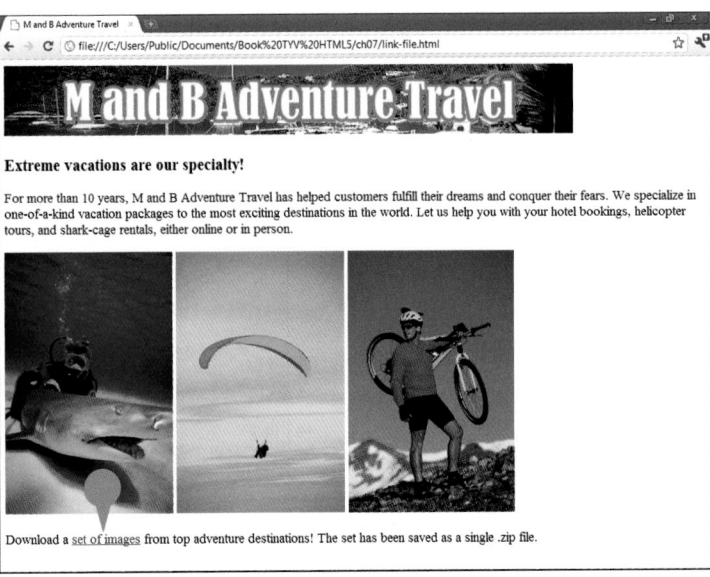

If it cannot open the file, the browser may automatically download it to a directory on your computer.

● In Chrome, you can click here to view the downloaded file.

Some browsers may prompt you to specify the download directory. See your browser documentation for details.

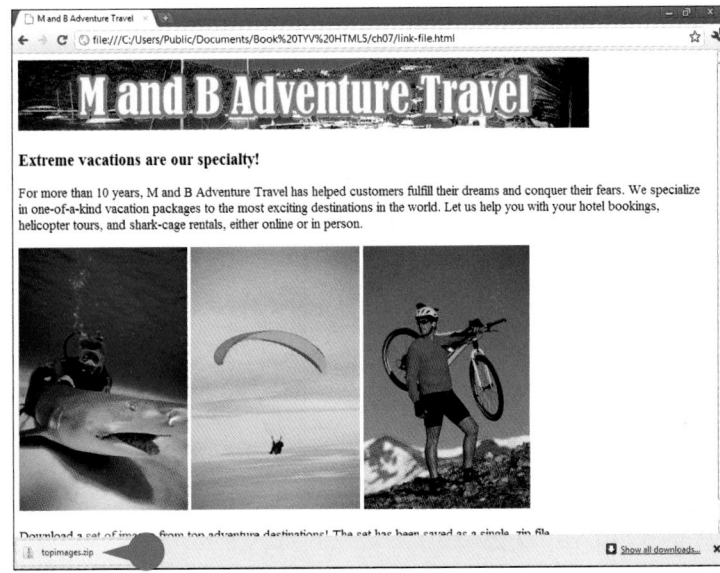

Can I include links to plain text files?
Yes, and most browsers can open and display such files. Because browsers do not read plain text files as HTML files, browsers display the text without formatter and without inline images or other features. This can be useful if you want to deliver raw text data that viewers can easily save in their browser.

What happens if the user cannot download or open the file?
If the user encounters problems accessing a non-HTML file, his or her browser or computer may display an error message. To help with possible problems that might occur, be sure to include information about the file format and size on the web page; also include links to any useful tools that can help the user work with the file. For example, if the link is to a PDF file, include a link to the Adobe website where the user can download the Adobe Reader program, which can read PDFs.

Link to an E-Mail Address

Y ou can create a link in your web page that allows users to send an e-mail message. In most browsers, clicking an e-mail link opens a new message in the default e-mail client program. The user can fill out a subject and message and then send the information to the address specified in the link. Adding e-mail links is a good way to solicit feedback and questions from your website visitors. An alternative way to allow users to send you information is with a form. See Chapter 9 for details about forms.

Link to an E-Mail Address

1 Type the text you want to use as an e-mail link.

It is standard practice to use the e-mail address as the text link.

2 In front of the link text, type `<a href="mailto:?">`, replacing *?* with the e-mail address you want to use.

3 Type `</a>` at the end of the link text.

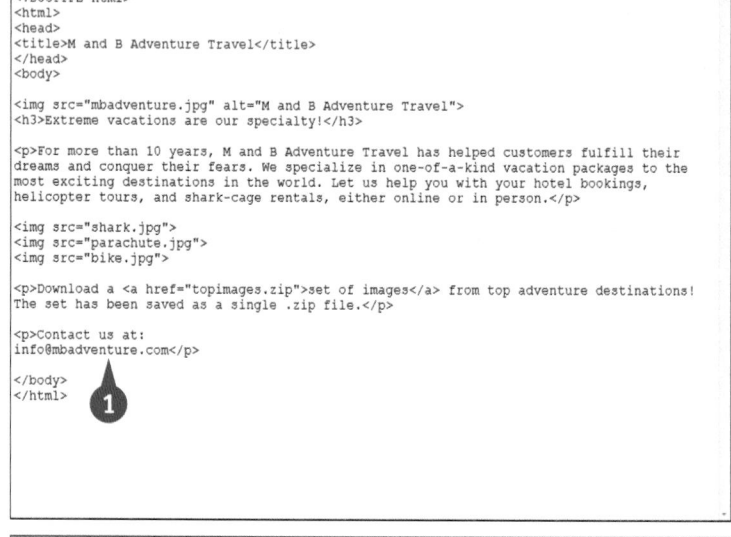

● The link appears in the web browser.

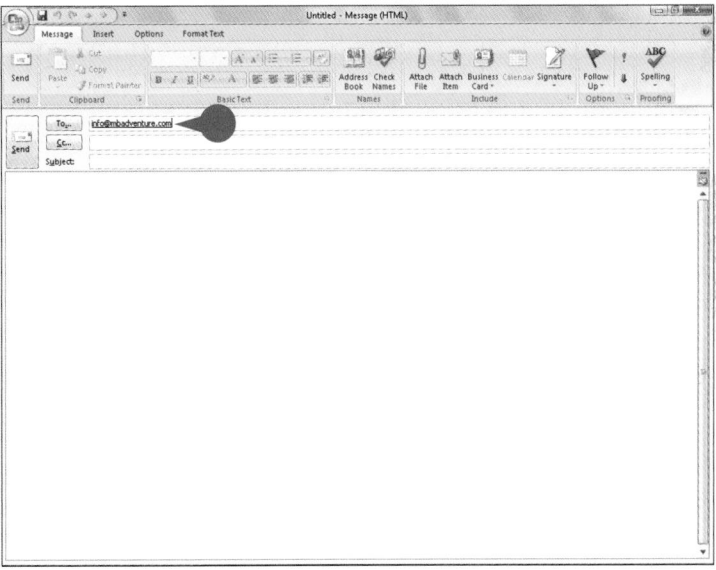

● When the link is clicked, the user's e-mail editor opens with the To field prefilled with the e-mail address.

TIPS

Can I specify a subject for an e-mail message?

Yes. You can use the ?subject parameter within the link tag to include a subject line with the e-mail message. When the user clicks the link and the e-mail client opens, the subject area is prefilled. You can use this technique to help recognize e-mail generated from your website. For example:

```
<a href="mailto:webmaster@example.com
?subject=Comments">E-mail a comment</>
```

Is it safe to use my e-mail address in a link?

You should use caution when placing a personal e-mail address on a web page. E-mail addresses on web pages are notorious magnets for unsolicited e-mail because such addresses can be harvested automatically by spamming tools that crawl the web. For this reason, you may want to create a separate e-mail account just for your web-generated e-mail messages. Gmail, Yahoo! Mail, and Hotmail are popular e-mail services that offer free accounts.

Change Link Colors

You can control the appearance of links throughout your web pages using a style rule. You can change the color of unvisited, visited, and active links to make them match the theme of your website. You can specify one of 16 predefined HTML colors, a hexadecimal color value, or an RGB value. You can also remove the default underlining that normally appears beneath a link using the *text-decoration* property. To change the color of a link or turn on underlining when the cursor is positioned over it, see "Change Link Hover Effects."

Change Link Colors

① Type a:? { } to identify the link tag, replacing *?* with the type of link you want to change (link, visited, or active).

Note: To learn more about writing style sheets and rules, see Chapter 4.

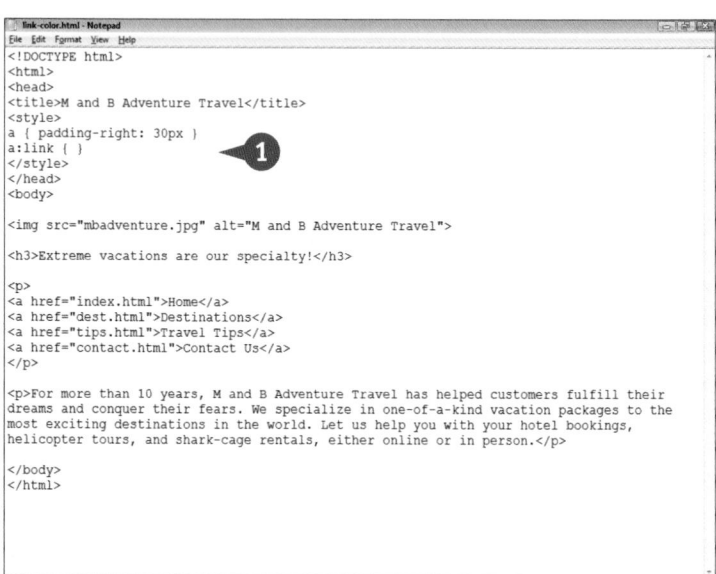

② Click between the { } and type color: and a space.

③ Type the color name, hexadecimal code, or RGB value you want to assign.

Note: To view a table of color values, see "Change the Color of Text" in Chapter 5.

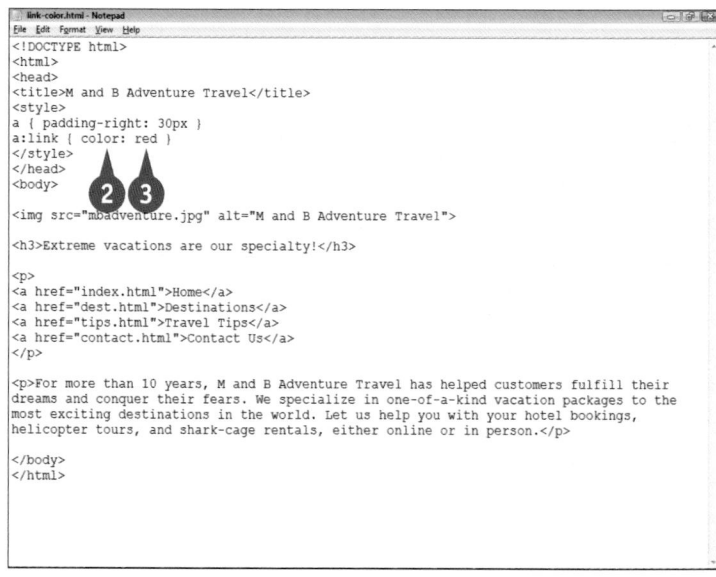

④ Repeat steps **1** to **3** for the other link types.

⑤ You can add a `text-decoration: none` property-value pair to the `a:link` declaration to remove the underlining from a link type.

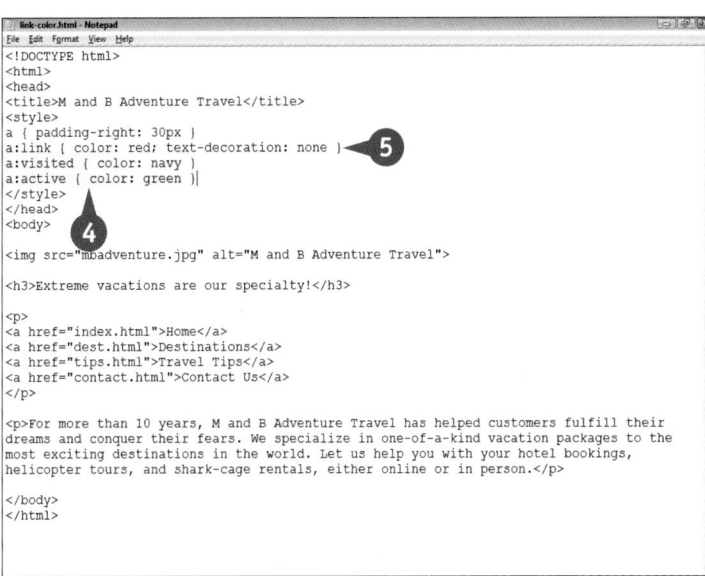

● The web browser displays the links on the page in the styles you specified.

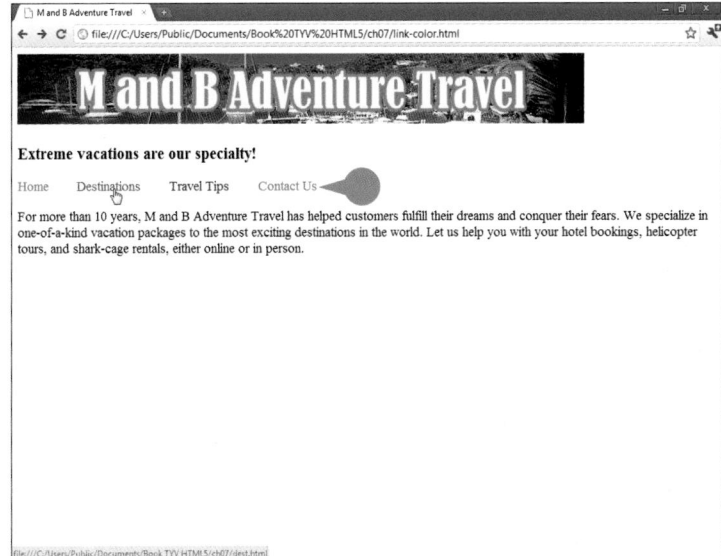

What other style sheet properties can I apply to links?
You can use the `background` and `font-family` properties to control the appearance of your links. Here is an example of a style rule with other properties assigned:

`a:link {background: yellow; font-family: Arial}`

Any time you type more than one property-value pair in a style rule, be sure to separate them with semicolons.

What is an RGB value?
An RGB value is a way of specifying a precise color in CSS. The color is defined by its mix of red, green, and blue components. You specify each color using a number between 0 and 255 or a percentage. For example, `rgb(255, 255, 0)` or `rgb(100%, 100%, 0%)` creates yellow. For more about creating colors for web pages, see Chapter 4.

Change Link Hover Effects

You can use a style rule to control how link text appears when the mouse pointer is positioned over it. For example, you can change the font style of the text, add a border, or change the background color. If you have created another rule that removes the underlining from your links, you can use a hover style to make the underlining reappear. For more about changing the color of links, see "Change Link Colors" earlier in this chapter.

Change Link Hover Effects

1 Type a:hover { } to define the hover style selector.

Note: To learn more about writing style sheets and rules, see Chapter 4.

```
link-color.html - Notepad
File  Edit  Format  View  Help
<!DOCTYPE html>
<html>
<head>
<title>M and B Adventure Travel</title>
<style>
a { padding-right: 30px }
a:link { color: red; text-decoration: none }
a:visited { color: navy }
a:active { color: green }
a:hover { }
</style>
</head>
<b
<img src="mbadventure.jpg" alt="M and B Adventure Travel">

<h3>Extreme vacations are our specialty!</h3>

<p>
<a href="index.html">Home</a>
<a href="dest.html">Destinations</a>
<a href="http://www.wiley.com">Travel Tips</a>
<a href="contact.html">Contact Us</a>
</p>

<p>For more than 10 years, M and B Adventure Travel has helped customers fulfill their
dreams and conquer their fears. We specialize in one-of-a-kind vacation packages to the
most exciting destinations in the world. Let us help you with your hotel bookings,
helicopter tours, and shark-cage rentals, either online or in person.</p>

</body>
</html>
```

2 Click between the { } and type one or more property-value pairs that will be applied when the mouse pointer is positioned over a link.

In this example, bold and border styles are defined.

```
link-color.html - Notepad
File  Edit  Format  View  Help
<!DOCTYPE html>
<html>
<head>
<title>M and B Adventure Travel</title>
<style>
a { padding-right: 30px }
a:link { color: red; text-decoration: none }
a:visited { color: navy }
a:active { color: green }
a:hover { font-weight: bold; border: solid red 1px }
</style>
</head>
<body>

<img src="mbadventure.jpg" alt="M and B Adventure Travel">

<h3>Extreme vacations are our specialty!</h3>

<p>
<a href="index.html">Home</a>
<a href="dest.html">Destinations</a>
<a href="http://www.wiley.com">Travel Tips</a>
<a href="contact.html">Contact Us</a>
</p>

<p>For more than 10 years, M and B Adventure Travel has helped customers fulfill their
dreams and conquer their fears. We specialize in one-of-a-kind vacation packages to the
most exciting destinations in the world. Let us help you with your hotel bookings,
helicopter tours, and shark-cage rentals, either online or in person.</p>

</body>
</html>
```

③ To add underlining, type text-decoration: underline.

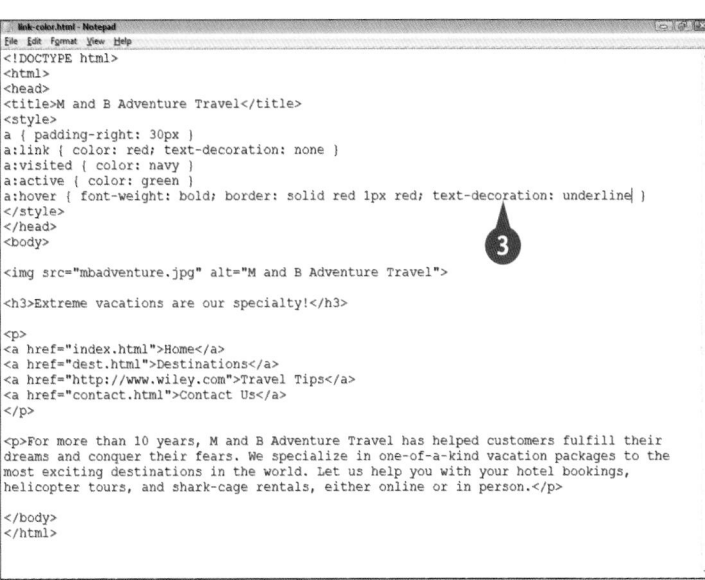

● The web browser changes the link's style when the mouse pointer hovers over it.

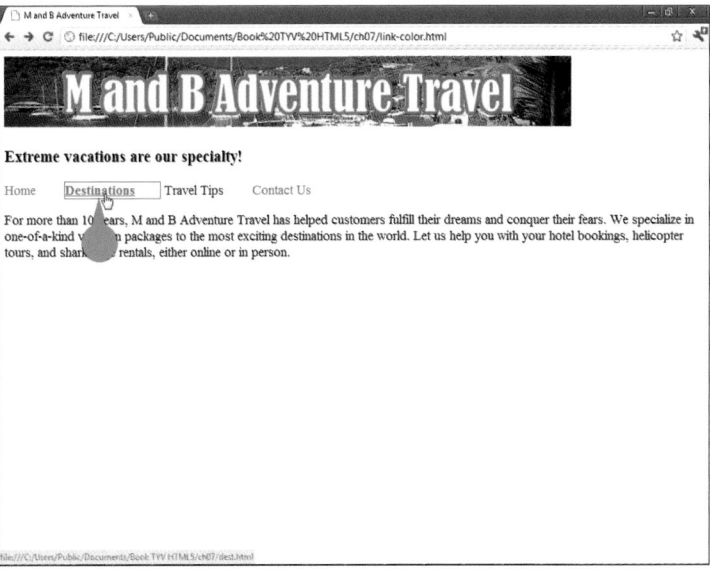

TIPS

Can I add other line decorations besides underline for my hover styles?
In addition to assigning the underline value to the text-decoration property, you can assign overline to place a line over the link text or line-through to place a line through the link text. You can also use these decorations to style regular, non-link text.

Why might I want to add a hover style using CSS?
With style sheets, you can customize your links so that they look more like regular text by changing their color and removing the underlining usually associated with text links. This may be stylistically appealing, but it can also hide the fact that elements on a page are hyperlinks. A hover style can give a user visual feedback that certain words on a page are clickable links.

Define Link Relationships

You can specify one or more relationships between a hyperlink and the current document by including a `rel` attribute inside the `<a>` tag. For example, the `rel` attribute can mark the link as belonging to the previous or next document in a series, to the website of the author of the current document, or to a copyright license for the current document. You can also use the `rel` attributes to tell search engines to ignore a link when determining the ranking of the current page. Search engines often analyze the outgoing links on pages to help categorize the pages the links are on.

The `rel` attribute is also used when defining links to external CSS style sheet files. See Chapter 4 for more details.

Define Link Relationships

Add Links to a Page

1 Add links to the content on your page using the `<a>` tag and `href` attributes.

Note: To learn more about creating links, see "Link to Another Page."

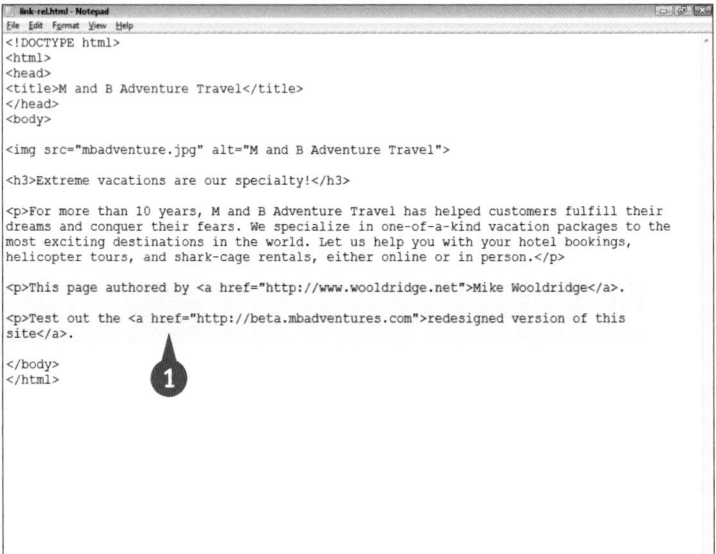

Define a Single Relationship

2 Inside the `<a>` tag for a link, type `rel="?"`, replacing *?* with a relationship type.

In this example, an `author` relationship is defined. The link leads to a web page about the author of the current page.

Note: For a list of relationship types, see the tip on the next page.

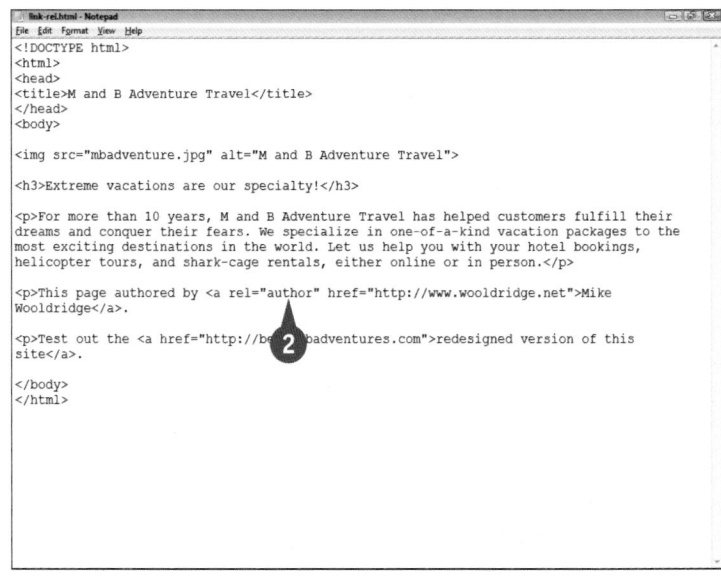

Define Multiple Relationships

③ Inside another <a> tag for a link, type rel="?", replacing *?* with multiple relationship types. Separate the types with spaces.

In this example, the external value specifies that the link leads to an external site. The nofollow value specifies that search engines should not consider the link when ranking the current page.

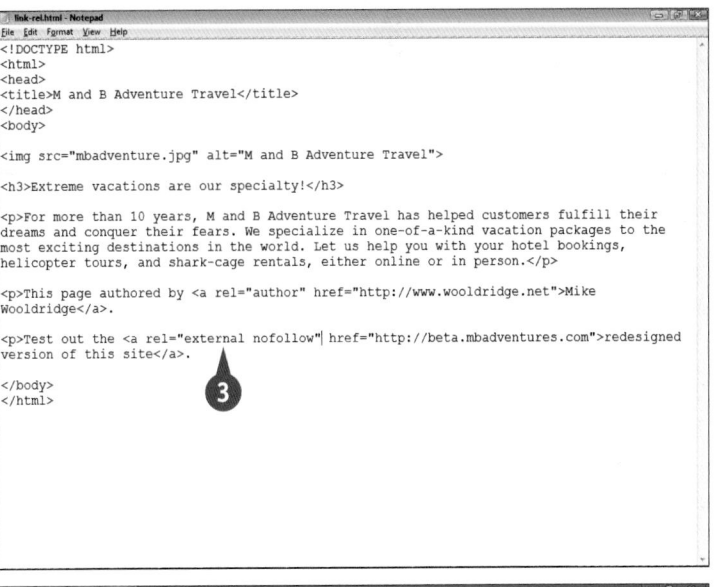

View the Links

● The web browser displays the page content with the links.

Note: Typically web browsers do not style links with rel values any differently than links without rel values.

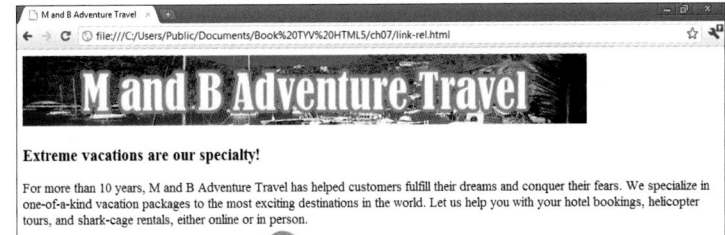

TIP

What are some link relationship types?

The following are values that can be used with the rel attributes in <a> tags:

alternate	Link to an alternate representation of the current document
author	Link to the author of the current document
external	Link to a document at a site that is external to the site of the current document
first, prev, next, last	Links to other documents in a series of documents
help	Link to context-sensitive help
license	Link to a copyright license for the current document
nofollow	Specifies that search engines should not consider the linked document for page-ranking purposes
noreferrer	Specifies that the browser should not send referrer information when the link is clicked
search	Link to a search page for the current document
tag	Link to a tag or keyword describing the current document

Working with Tables

Are you looking for a way to organize data on your web page into rows and columns? This chapter shows you how to use HTML tables to do this. You create tables using an outer `<table>` tag and various other tags within it. A `<tr>` tag defines a row in a table, and `<td>` tags define data cells within the row. In addition to organizing data with tables, you can add color or background images behind the data in tables. You can also use tables as layout tools to organize sections of content on your page.

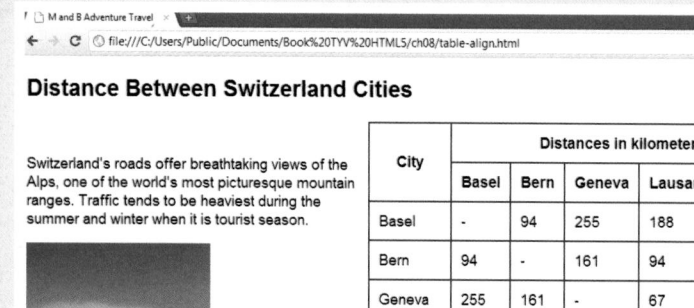

Distance Between Switzerland Cities

Switzerland's roads offer breathtaking views of the Alps, one of the world's most picturesque mountain ranges. Traffic tends to be heaviest during the summer and winter when it is tourist season.

City	Distances in kilometers				
	Basel	Bern	Geneva	Lausanne	Zurich
Basel	-	94	255	188	85
Bern	94	-	161	94	122
Geneva	255	161	-	67	283
Lausanne	188	94	67	-	216
Zurich	85	122	283	216	-
1 km = 0.6215 miles					

Understanding Table Structure

HTML tables enable you to effectively present large amounts of data in rows and columns. Tables can include numeric data and textual content; they can also include images and multimedia. For example, you can use tables to display a company's sales results or a grid of photos in an online photo gallery. By applying CSS rules to tables on your web page, you can turn on borders as well as change the color, alignment, and size.

Table Structure

Every table is basically a rectangle containing rows and columns. The places where the columns and rows intersect are called *cells*. Each cell can hold web page content. Using CSS rules, you can set the size of an entire table as well as the size of particular cells. You can also turn borders of a table and its cells on or off, depending on whether you want to draw attention to the table's structure.

Cell Spanning

Cells can span two or more columns or rows to form bigger containers for data. For example, a table may include a title cell at the top that spans multiple columns across the table (●), or one that extends downward across several rows. When you span cells in a table, interior cell walls disappear to create larger cells.

Traditional Tables

You can use a traditional table, like the table shown here, on a web page to present data in a tabular format. For example, you might insert a table to hold a list of products and prices or to display a class roster. You can set a fixed width and height for the table to make it fit in with the rest of the page content.

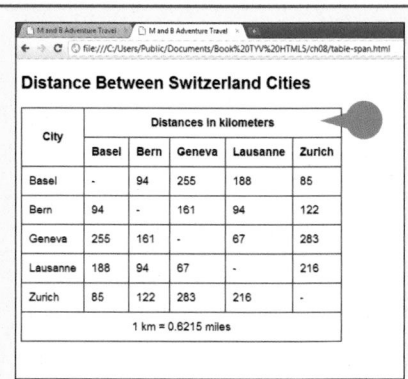

Distance Between Switzerland Cities

City	Distances in kilometers				
	Basel	Bern	Geneva	Lausanne	Zurich
Basel	-	94	255	188	85
Bern	94	-	161	94	122
Geneva	255	161	-	67	283
Lausanne	188	94	67	-	216
Zurich	85	122	283	216	-
1 km = 0.6215 miles					

Tables for Layout

You can use a presentation-style table to showcase the overall content on the page in interesting ways. Instead of defining an exact size, you can specify a table size using percentages. Whenever the user resizes his or her browser window, the table resizes as well. This allows for a more "liquid" layout. This type of table is good for page layouts as well as data tables. See "Use a Table for Page Layout" for an example of such a table.

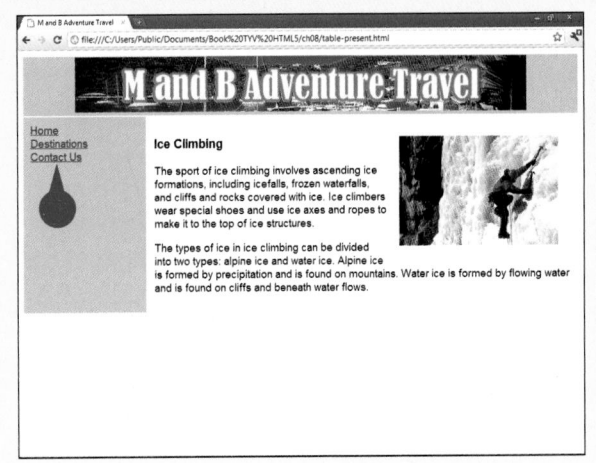

Table Elements

The building blocks of HTML tables are the `<table>`, `<tr>`, and `<td>` tags. The `<table>` tag defines the table itself. The `<tr>` tag defines a table row. The `<td>` tag defines the table data, or cell content, within each row. In addition to these codes, you can assign table headers, adjust the alignment of data, and add background colors and images.

Table Borders

You can control the width of the borders in your table using a `border` attribute. To turn off borders, you can set the `border` value to 0, or leave the attribute unset because no borders is the default in most browsers. Visible borders can be useful for traditional data tables to show where cells begin and end (●). For presentation tables, you can turn borders off so as not to call attention to the underlying page structure.

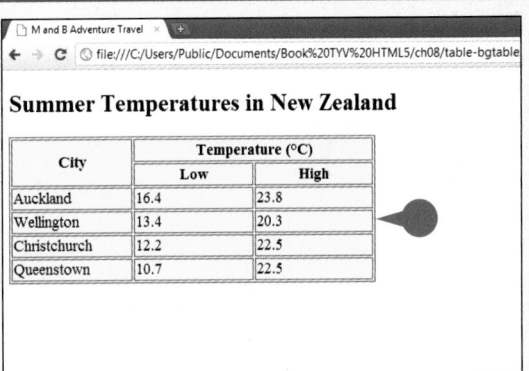

Table Backgrounds

Table backgrounds can help delineate table cell structure just like borders. You can use a different color in table heading cells to set off those cells from the data cells. In presentation tables, background colors can set off headers, navigation (●), and footer sections of a page from the main content. You can also add background images to a table just as you can to an entire web page.

Add a Table

You can insert a table onto your page to organize data or control the page layout. HTML tables are made up of cells arranged into rows and columns. You can assign different page elements to different cells to control the positioning of those elements on the page. Cells can hold text, images, and other web page content. You define the placement of a table on a page with the `<table>` tag. Inside the `<table>` tag, you can define rows with the `<tr>` tag and data cells within those rows with `<td>` tags.

Add a Table

① Type `<table>` where you want to insert a table.

② Type `<tr>` to start the first row in the table.

To make it easier to distinguish between rows, type each row tag on a new line.

③ Type `<td>` for the first cell you want to create.

④ Type the cell data.

Note: If you want your first row to include bold column labels, you can use the `<th>` tag instead of `<td>`. See the section "Add Column Labels" to learn more.

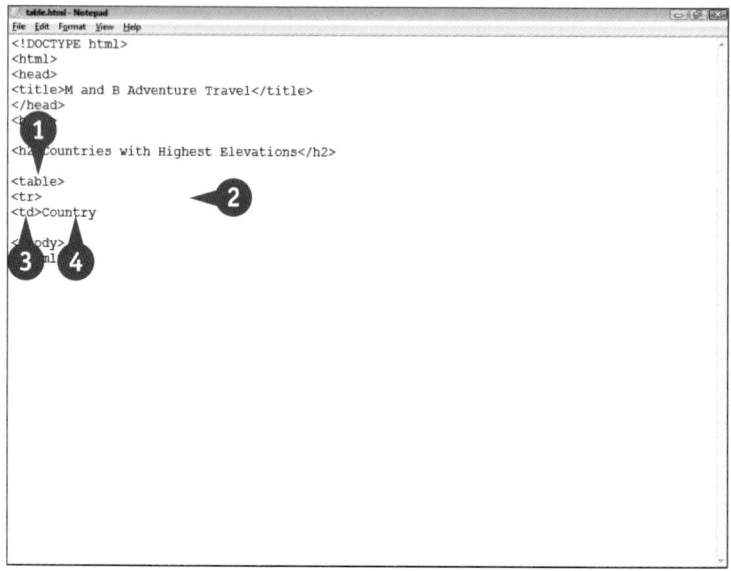

⑤ Type `</td>` to complete the cell.

⑥ Repeat steps **3** to **5** to add cells.

To make it easier to distinguish between cells, you can place each cell on a new line in your HTML document.

⑦ Type `</tr>` at the end of the first row.

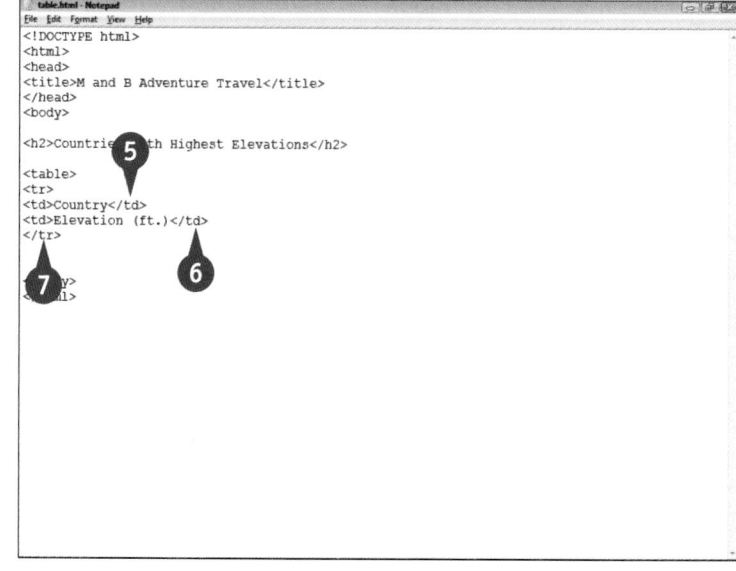

8 Continue adding rows and cell data as needed.

9 Type </table> at the end of the table data.

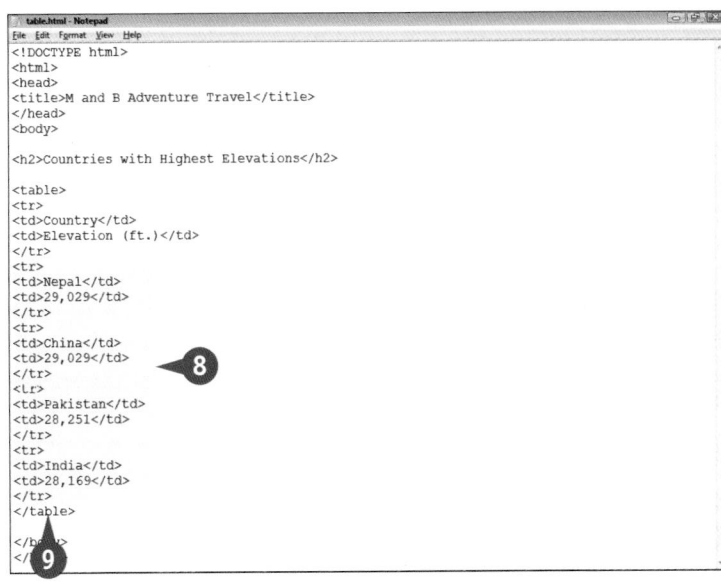

The web browser displays the data in a tabular format.

● In this example, the table cells need some padding and spacing or borders.

Note: See the sections "Add Table Borders" and "Adjust Cell Padding and Border Spacing" to learn more.

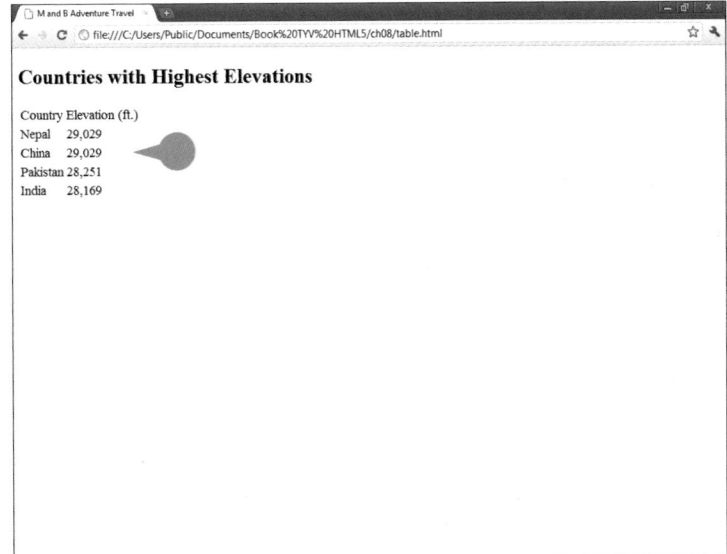

TIPS

How do I set a size for a table?
You can set the dimensions of a table as exact pixel values or as percentages of the browser window using CSS width and height properties. If you want to set a fixed size and have the entire table width visible in browsers, set the width at 960 pixels or less because most users surf the web with their monitors set to at least 1024 pixels in width. For more information, see the section "Adjust the Table Size."

How do I add extra space inside my table?
The space separating your table content from the sides of the table cells is called *padding*. You can add padding using CSS rules to increase the amount of space separating your table content. You can also set padding to 0 to make the content flush with the sides of the cells. For more details, see "Adjust Cell Padding and Border Spacing."

Add Table Borders

Table borders make your cells easier to distinguish and give the table a visible structure on a page. A border is simply a line that appears around the table or around each cell within the table. By default, a table does not have a border unless you specify one. You can use the `border` and `border-width` attributes to turn table borders on and adjust their thickness, respectively.

Applying border rules to the `<table>` tag affects the border surrounding the entire table. Applying the rules to the `<td>` tag affects the borders around each cell. The example below sets both types of borders, but you can also set just one for your table.

Add Table Borders

① In your style sheet, type `table { }` to define a table selector.

② Click between the `{ }` and type the style, size, and color for the table border, separating the values with spaces.

Common styles include `solid`, `dotted`, `dashed`, and `double`.

You can define the size in pixels (px), points (pt), millimeters (mm), centimeters (cm), inches (in), picas (pc), x-height (ex), or em space (em).

Note: See the section "Add a Table" to learn how to create a basic table.

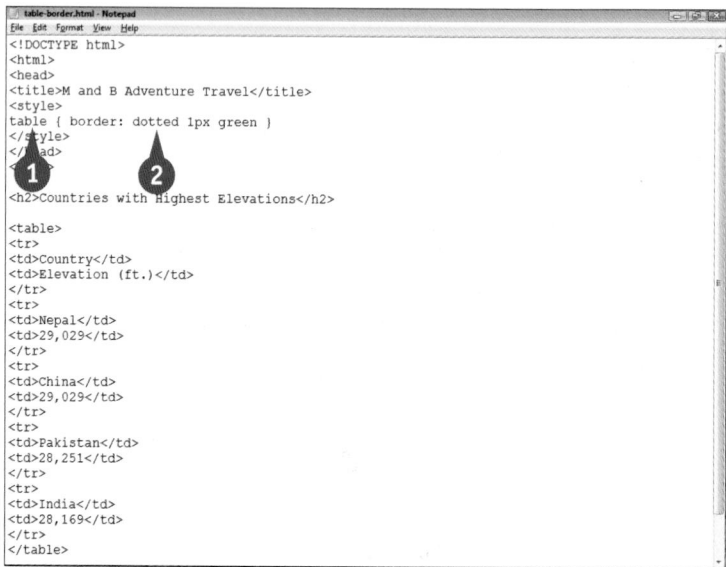

③ Type `td { }` to define a td selector.

④ Click between the `{ }` and type the style, size, and color for the table cell borders, separating the values with spaces.

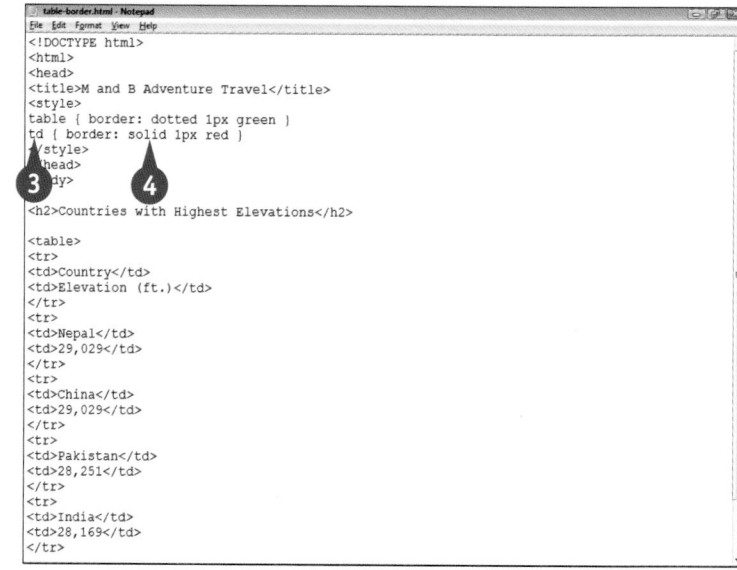

⑤ For the table declaration, type a ; and then `border-width: ?`, replacing *?* with a `width` value.

You can define the width in pixels (`px`), points (`pt`), millimeters (`mm`), centimeters (`cm`), inches (`in`), picas (`pc`), x-height (`ex`), or em space (`em`).

⑥ For the `td` declaration, type ; and then `border-width: ?`, replacing *?* with a `width` value.

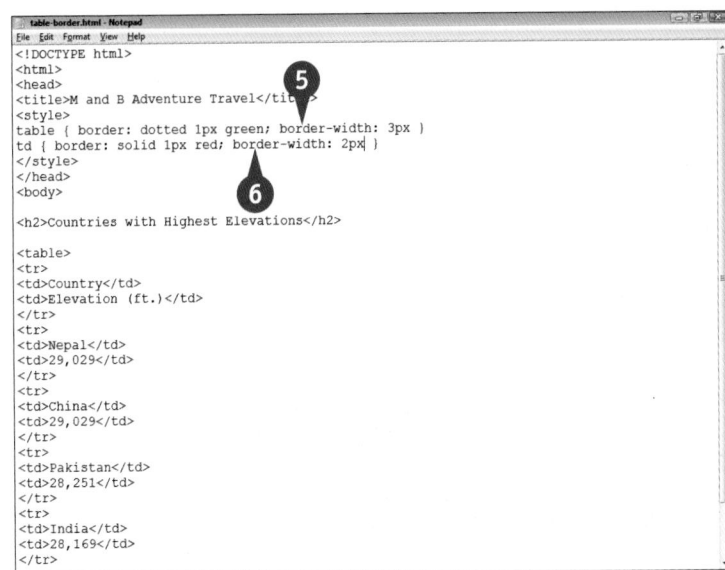

● The browser displays borders for the table and the table data cells. The outer table borders are dotted and green while the inner cell borders are solid and red. All borders are one pixel in width.

Note: For more about setting CSS color values, see Chapter 5.

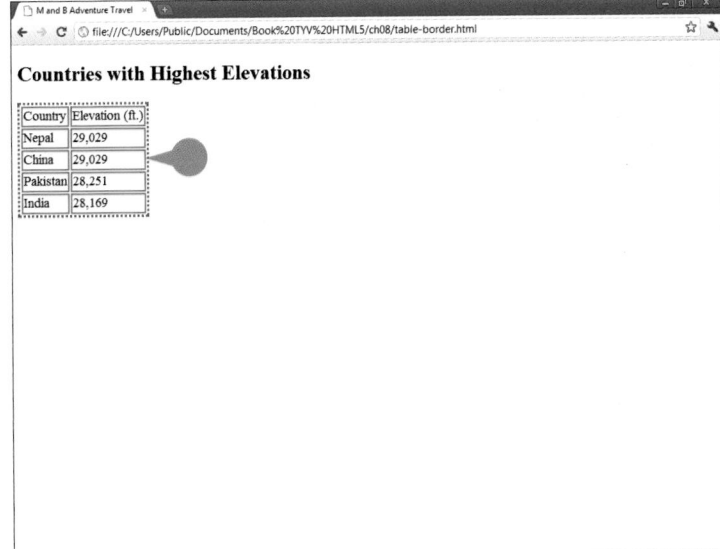

TIPS

How do I get rid of the space between table cell borders?
By default, most browsers add space between the borders of neighboring table cells and the outside border. You can remove the space by adding `border-collapse: collapse` to your rule for the `<td>` tag. This enables you to divide your table content with single lines.

How do I create 3-D borders in my tables?
You can set the border style property in steps **2** and **4** above to `groove`, `ridge`, `inset`, or `outset` to create borders with 3-D styling. The browser creates the borders using different shades of the border color to create borders that appear to pop into or out of the page.

Adjust Cell Padding and Border Spacing

You can use padding to add space between the border and the contents of a cell. Padding can make table content more legible. You can use spacing to increase the distance between cell borders. Increasing the spacing can add emphasis to the borders when you have borders turned on. If you do not define padding and spacing properties, most browsers add 1 pixel of padding and 2 pixels of spacing by default. You can also set padding or spacing settings to 0 to remove them from your tables.

Adjust Cell Padding and Border Spacing

Set Cell Padding

① In your style sheet, type `td { }` to define a td selector.

Note: To set the padding between the outer border of the table and the cells, you can define a `table` selector.

② Click between the `{ }` and type `padding: ?`, replacing *?* with the padding size.

You can define the size in pixels (px), points (pt), millimeters (mm), centimeters (cm), inches (in), picas (pc), x-height (ex), or em space (em).

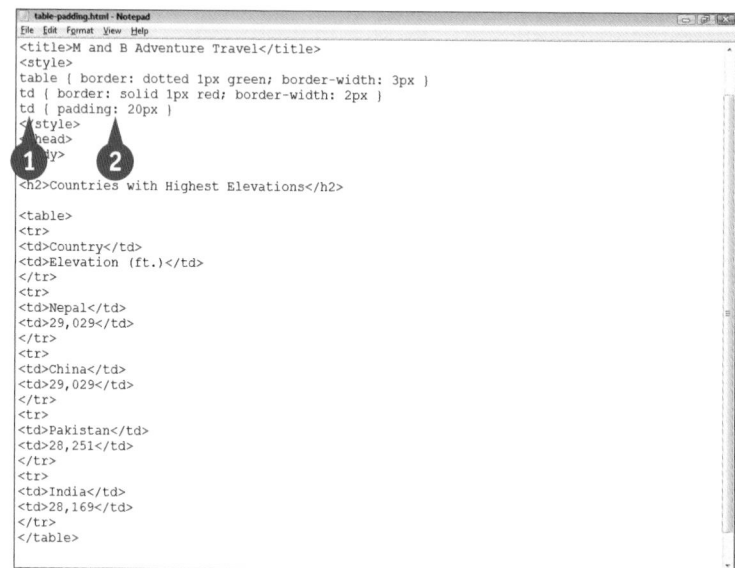

● In this example, table borders are turned on to show the padding more clearly.

● The web browser displays the designated amount of space between the cell contents and the cell borders.

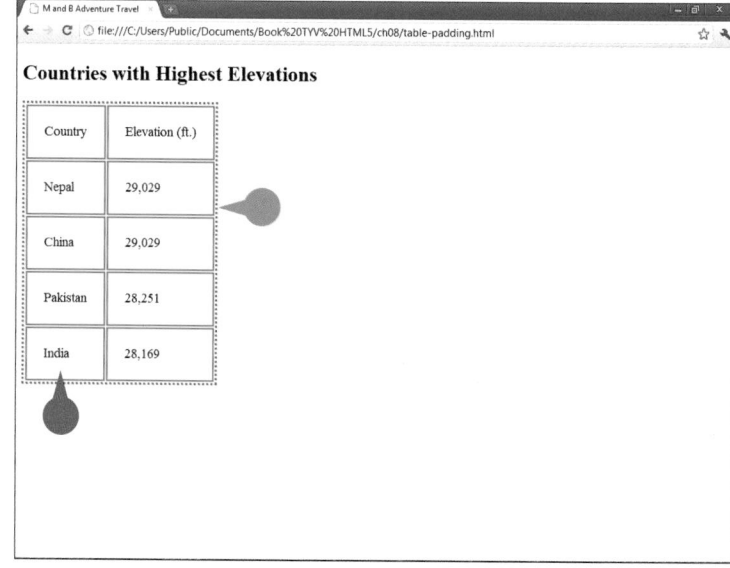

Set Cell Spacing

1 In your style sheet, type `table { }` to define a td selector.

2 Click between the `{ }` and type `border-spacing: ?`, replacing `?` with the spacing size.

You can define the size in pixels (px), points (pt), millimeters (mm), centimeters (cm), inches (in), picas (pc), x-height (ex), or em space (em).

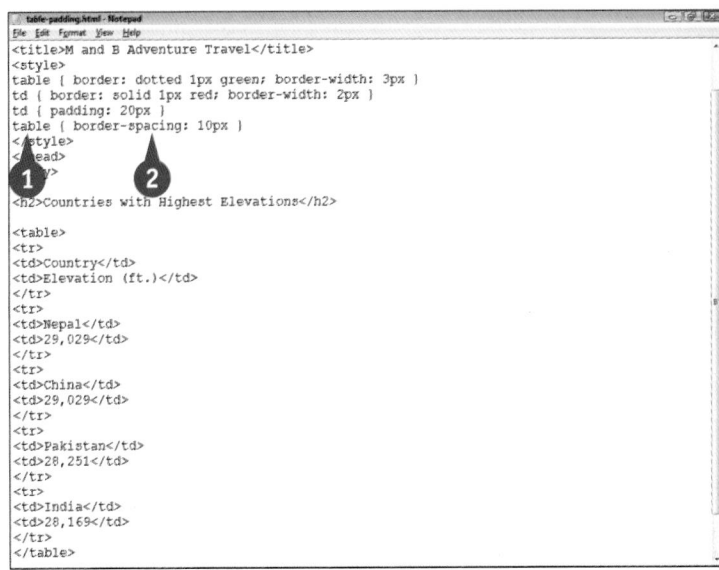

● In this example, a table border is turned on to clearly show the spacing.

● The web browser displays the designated amount of spacing for the cell borders.

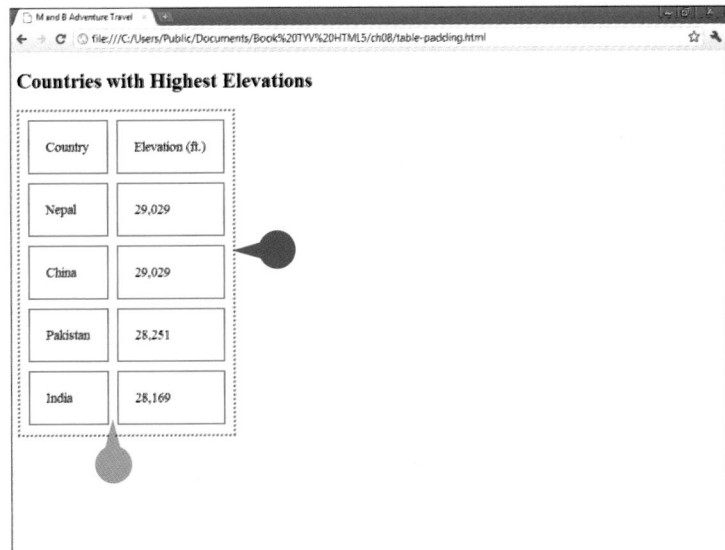

TIPS

How do I add different spacing to different sides of my table cells?

You can set your `padding` property to four different size values separated by spaces:

`td { padding: 20px 10px 0 10px }`

The values are applied to the top, right, bottom, and left sides of the table cells, respectively. If you set the property to two values, the first value is applied to the top and bottom and the second value to the left and right.

How do I control the padding on just one side of a cell?

The `padding` property applies padding to all sides of cells. To control padding on just one side of a cell, you can set the `padding-top`, `padding-bottom`, `padding-left`, or `padding-right` property. For example, the following applies 10 pixels of padding to the top of the cells of a table:

`td { padding-top: 10px }`

Adjust Cell Width and Height

You can control the width of table cells using the `width` property and the height of cells using the `height` property. This enables you to allocate more space to columns or rows that have more content. If you do not set a specific width or height, the content of the cell determines the cell's size.

You can specify dimensions using a pixel value or using a percentage relative to the width or height of the overall table. You can also specify the height and width of the overall table. See the section "Adjust the Table Size" for details.

Adjust Cell Width and Height

Set Cell Width

① In your style sheet, type `td { }` to define a td selector.

② Click between the `{ }` and type `width: ?`, replacing `?` with the size.

You can define the size in pixels (px), points (pt), millimeters (mm), centimeters (cm), inches (in), picas (pc), x-height (ex), or em space (em).

Note: See the section "Adjust the Table Size" to set the width of the entire table.

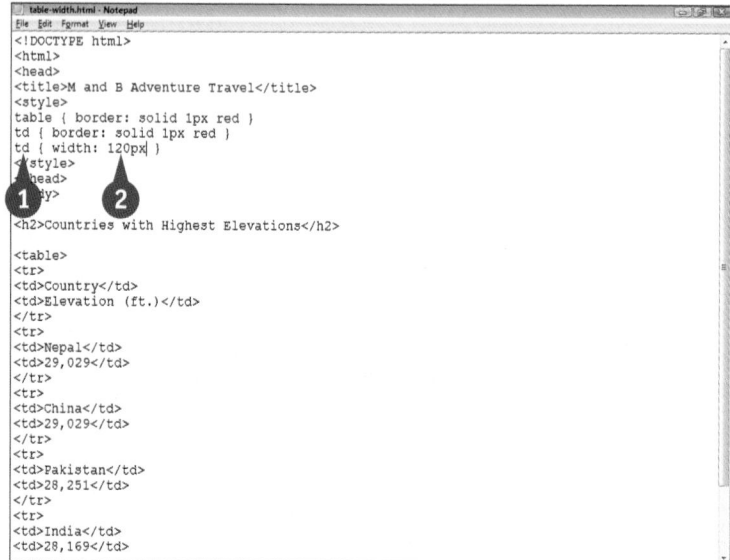

● The web browser displays a set width for the cells in the table. In this example the width is 120 pixels.

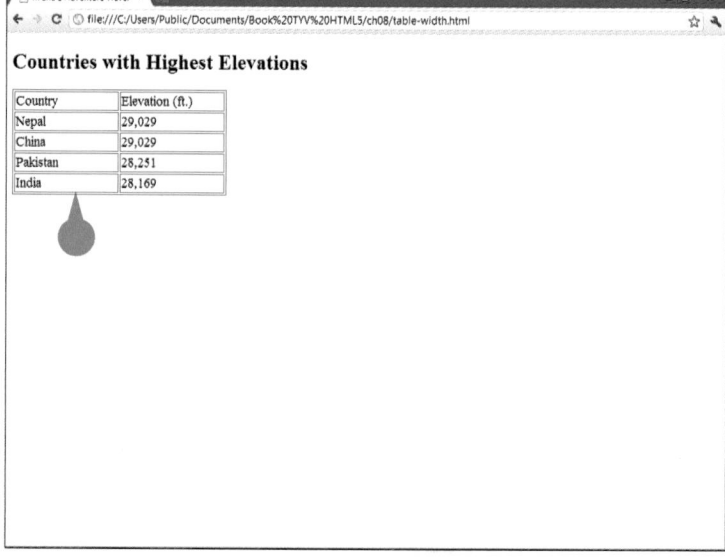

Set Cell Height

1 In your style sheet, type `td { }` to define a td selector.

2 Click between the `{ }` and type `height: ?`, replacing `?` with the size.

You can define the size in pixels (`px`), points (`pt`), millimeters (`mm`), centimeters (`cm`), inches (`in`), picas (`pc`), x-height (`ex`), or em space (`em`).

Note: See the section "Adjust the Table Size" to set the height of the entire table.

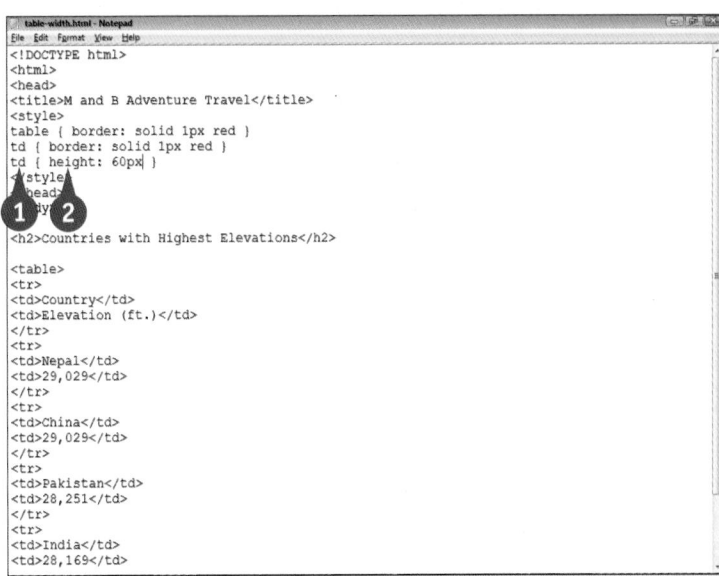

● The web browser displays a set height for the cells in the table. In this example, the height is 60 pixels.

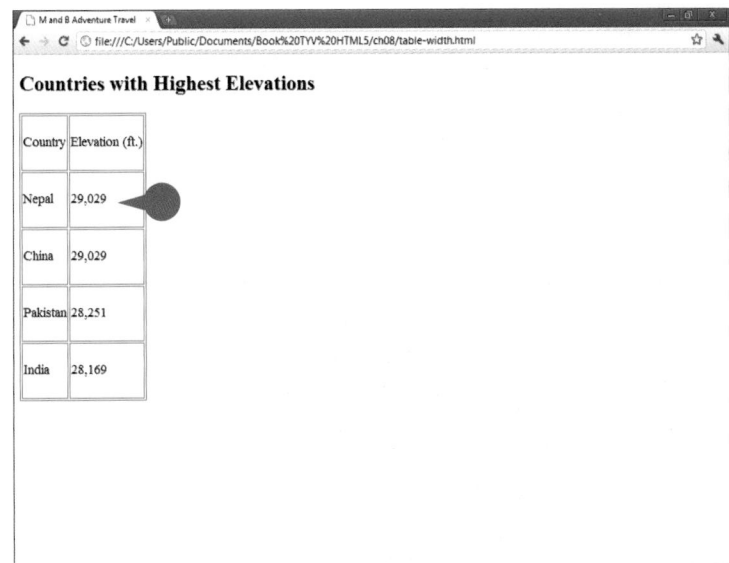

How do I set the height and width for a single table cell?
You can define the width and height as a CSS class, for example:

`td.custom { width: 100px; height: 75px }`

Then you can apply that class to the table cell:

`<td class="custom">My data</td>`

For more about CSS classes, see Chapter 4. Note that when you define the dimensions of a table cell, the dimensions are also applied to other cells in that row and column.

What if I set the height or width to a size smaller than the size of the enclosed content?
The browser shrinks the cell down to the size of the enclosed content but no further. It also preserves any padding settings you have defined. It does not shrink to smaller than the content and padding, even if you define it that way with `width` and `height` properties.

Add Column Labels

If you are building a table to populate with data, you can add descriptive labels, also called *headers*, to the top of each column using the <th> tag. For example, if your table lists products and prices, your column headers might include labels such as Product Number, Product Name, and Price. You can also add headers to the cells on the sides to label the rows of a table. In most browsers, column headers appear in bold type and are centered within each cell.

Add Column Labels

1 Type <th> after the <tr> tag for the row you want to use as your column labels.

Note: See the section "Add a Table" to learn how to create a basic table.

2 Type label text for the first column.

3 Type </th> at the end of the label.

4 Repeat steps **1** to **3** to add as many column labels as you need, ending the row with the </tr> tag.

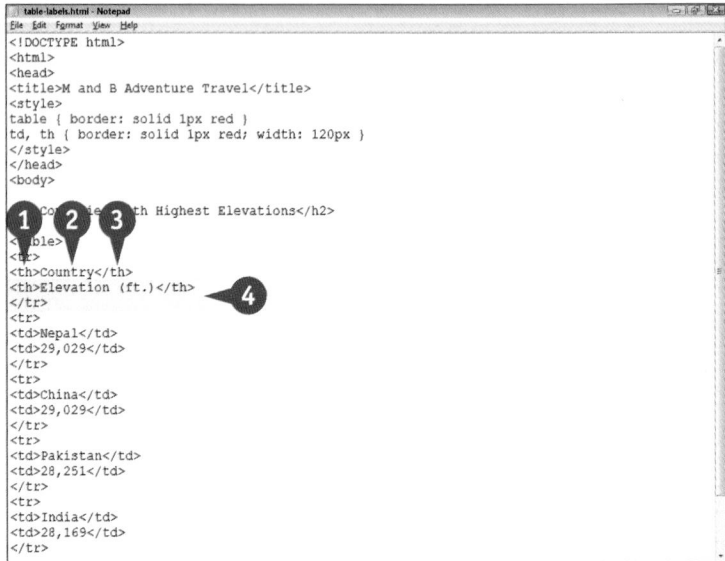

● The web browser displays the labels as column headers in the table.

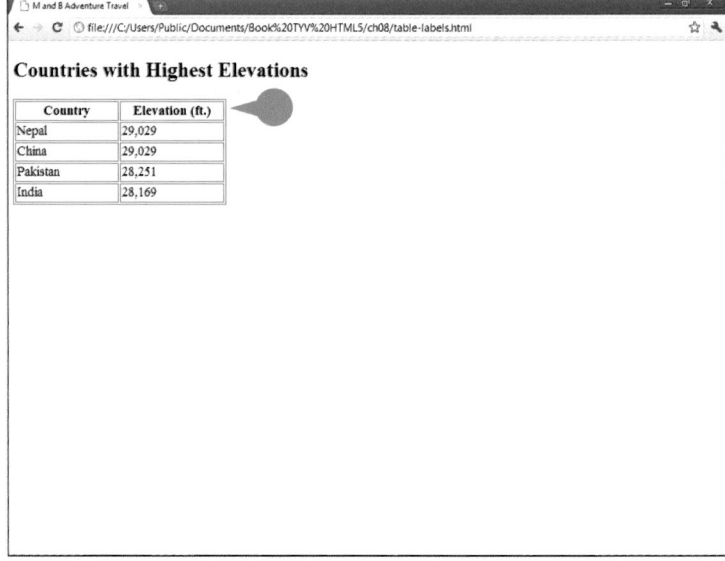

Add a Caption to a Table

You can define a caption that describes the contents of your table with the `<caption>` tag. The `<caption>` goes immediately inside your `<table>` tag and can appear only once in your table.

A browser typically displays the caption cantered, outside and above the table. You can apply style rules to the `<caption>` tag to change its size, color, alignment, and other characteristics. For more about defining style rules, see Chapter 4.

Add a Caption to a Table

① Create an HTML table.

Note: See "Add a Table" for details.

② Inside the `<table>` tag, type `<caption>`.

③ Type your caption text.

④ Type `</caption>`.

● In this example, styles have been applied to the `<caption>` tag.

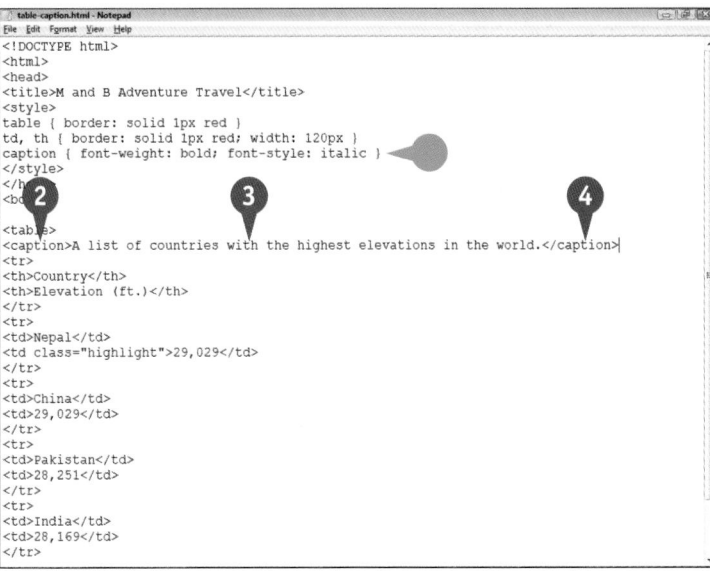

● The web browser displays a caption for your table with any associated styles.

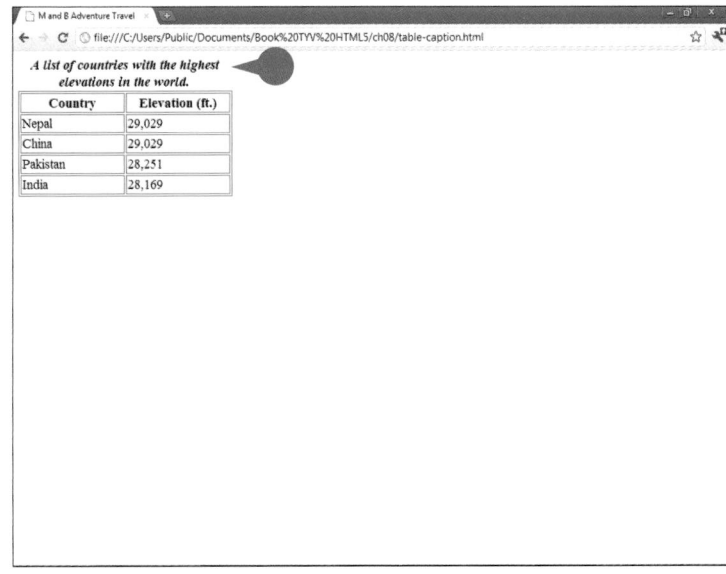

Add a Background Color to Cells

You can add color to individual cells in your table with the `background-color` CSS property. You can use background color to draw attention to the cell contents or to distinguish header cells from data cells.

When applying a background color, be careful not to choose a color that makes the table data difficult to read. See Chapter 5 to learn more about setting color values with CSS. To apply a background color to an entire table, see "Add a Background Color to a Table."

Add a Background Color to Cells

1 Create a CSS class for the `<td>` tag.

Note: See Chapter 4 for more about CSS classes.

2 Type `{`.

3 For the class declaration, type `background-color: "?"`, replacing *?* with a color name, hexadecimal value, or RGB code.

Note: See Chapter 5 to learn more about assigning color values.

4 Type `}`.

5 Inside the `<td>` tag you want to color, type `class="?"`, replacing *?* with the class name from step **1**.

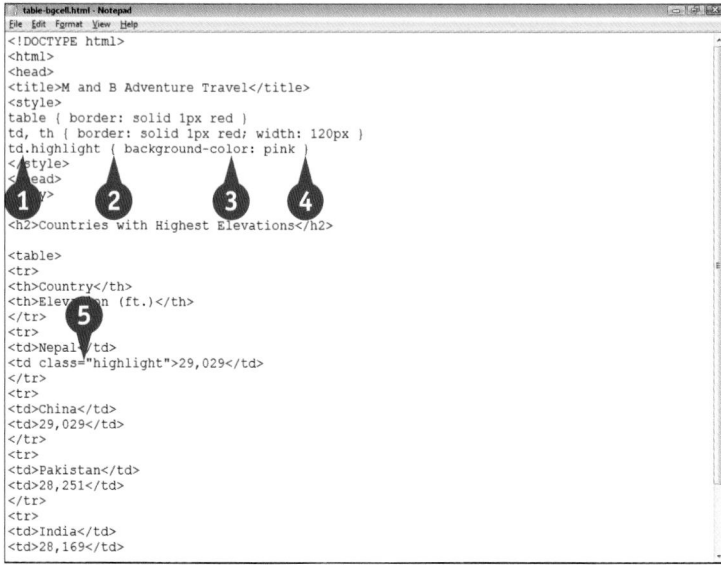

● The web browser displays the background color in the cell. In this example, the color is pink.

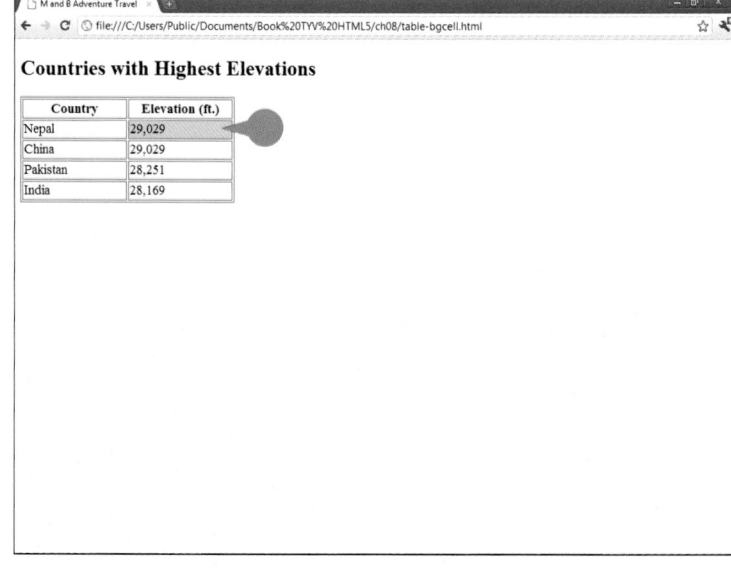

Add a Background Color to a Table

You can add a background color to an entire table with the `background-color` CSS property. You can use background color to make the table consistent with other colors on your page or to distinguish it from other tables.

When applying a background color, be careful to choose a color that works well with the color of the table data as well as with the color of any borders you have set. See Chapter 5 to learn more about setting color values in HTML. To apply a background color to a table cell, see "Add a Background Color to Cells."

Add a Background Color to a Table

1 Create a CSS class for the `<table>` tag.

Note: See Chapter 4 for more about CSS classes.

2 Type {.

3 For the class declaration, type `background-color: "?",` replacing *?* with a color name, hexadecimal value, or RGB code.

Note: See Chapter 5 to learn more about assigning color values.

4 Type }.

5 Inside the `<table>` tag for the table you want to color, type `class="?",` replacing *?* with the class name from step **1**.

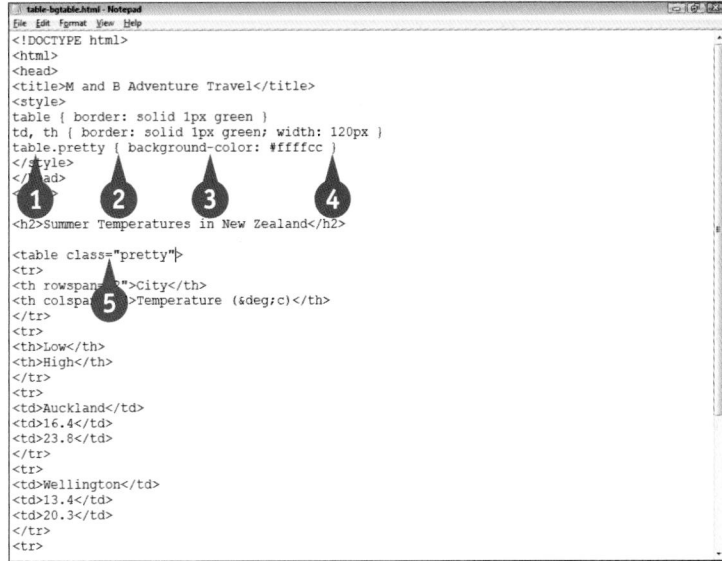

● The web browser displays the background color across the entire table.

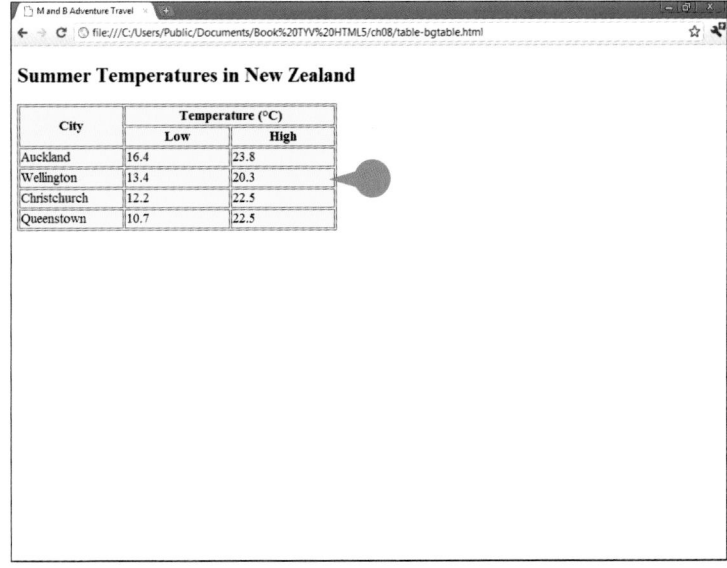

Adjust the Table Size

You can control the exact size of a table using the `width` and `height` CSS properties assigned to the `<table>` tag. You can specify a table size in pixels or set the size as a percentage of the enclosing container, which is often the browser window.

When setting a width in pixels, consider limiting the value to 960 pixels or less to ensure the table fits within a typical desktop monitor. If you prefer a more flexible table, set the size as a percentage. This allows the table to be resized if the browser window is resized.

Adjust the Table Size

Set a Table Width

1 Create a CSS class for the `<table>` tag.

Note: See Chapter 4 for more about CSS classes.

2 Type `{`.

3 For the class declaration, type `width: "?"`, replacing *?* with a size value.

You can define the size in pixels (`px`), points (`pt`), millimeters (`mm`), centimeters (`cm`), inches (`in`), picas (`pc`), x-height (`ex`), or em space (`em`). You can also define it as a percentage (`%`).

4 Type `}`.

5 Inside the `<table>` tag for the table you want to size, type `class="?"`, replacing *?* with the class name from step **1**.

● The web browser displays the table at the specified width. In this example, the width is 60% of the browser window.

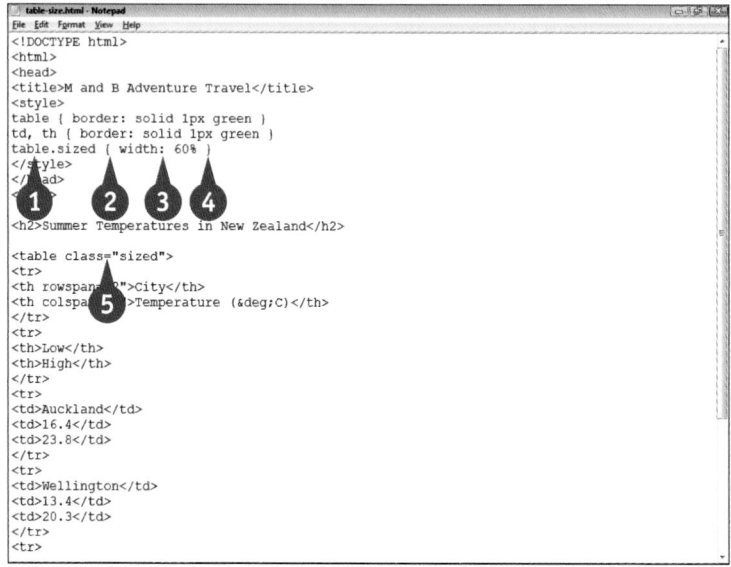

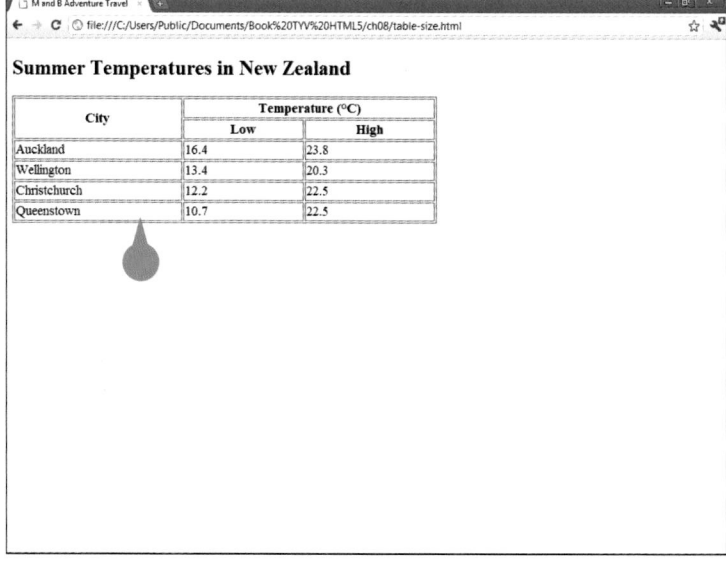

Set a Table Height

1️⃣ Create a CSS class for the `<table>` tag.

Note: See Chapter 4 for more about CSS classes.

2️⃣ Type {.

3️⃣ For the class declaration, type `height: "?"`, replacing *?* with a size value.

4️⃣ Type }.

5️⃣ Inside the `<table>` tag for the table you want to size, type `class="?"`, replacing *?* with the class name from step 1.

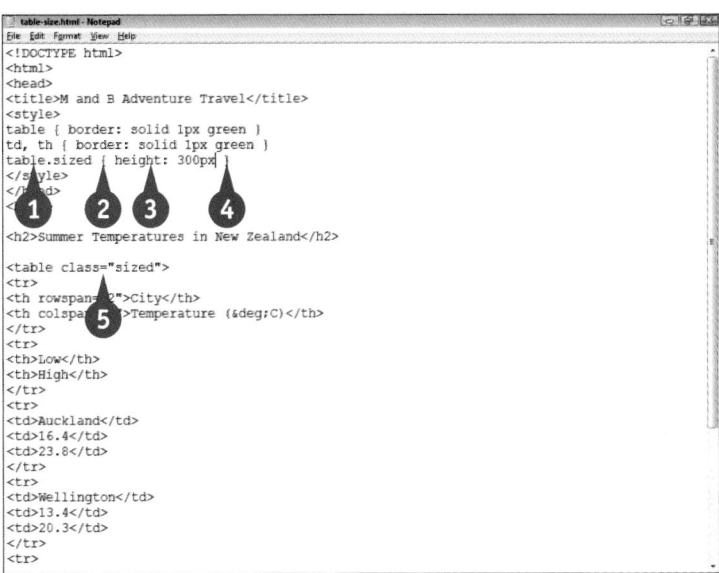

● The web browser displays the table at the specified size. In this example, the height is 300 pixels.

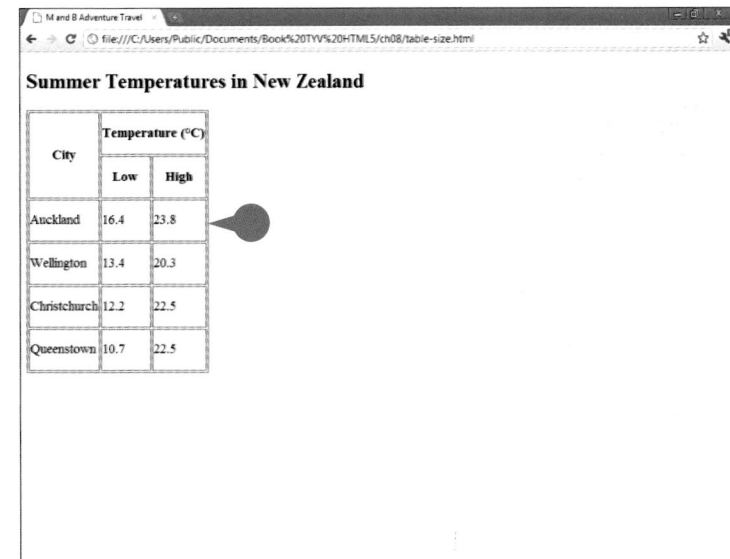

TIPS

Is it possible to set a table too small for its contents?
No. If you accidentally set a size too small for the contents, the browser ignores the measurements and tries to make the table fit as best it can. On the other hand, if you set a table too wide, users can be forced to scroll to see parts of the table. To keep a table fully visible in most desktop browsers, do not make your table wider than 960 pixels.

To what size does a browser set my table if I do not specify width?
If you do not set a width CSS rule, the browser sizes the table based on the cell contents. When a table contains text, the browser expands the table far enough to fit its largest contents, but not past the right edge of the browser window. If a table contains large images, it may have to extend beyond the browser's viewing area to accommodate the images.

Change Cell Alignment

You can control the alignment of data within your table cells with CSS rules using the `text-align` and `vertical-align` properties. The `text-align` property controls horizontal alignment: `left`, `center`, and `right`. By default, all table data you enter into cells is left-aligned. The `vertical-align` attribute controls vertical alignment: `top`, `middle`, and `bottom`. By default, the table data is vertically aligned to appear in the middle of each cell.

You can align content in a single cell by applying style rules to the `<td>` or `<th>` tag. You can align content in a row or in an entire table by applying style rules to the `<tr>` or `<table>` tags, respectively.

Change Cell Alignment

Set Horizontal Alignment

1 Create a CSS class for the table tag whose content you want to horizontally align.

Note: See Chapter 4 for more about CSS classes.

2 Type `{`.

3 For the class declaration, type `text-align: "?",` replacing *?* with `left`, `center`, or `right`.

4 Type `}`.

5 Inside the tag specified in step **1**, type `class="?",` replacing *?* with the class name.

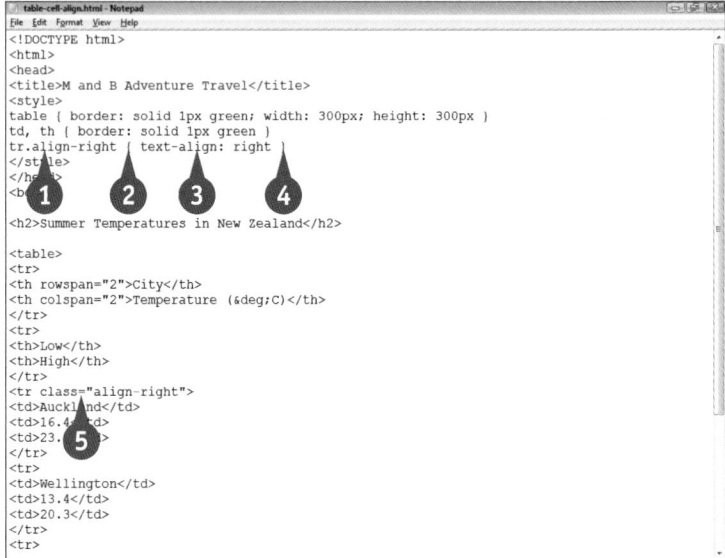

● In this example, applying a style to a `<tr>` tag aligns content in a row to the right.

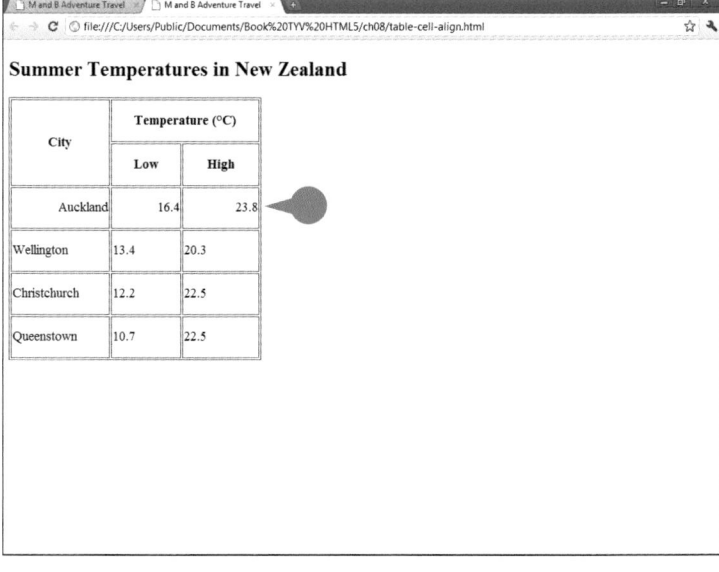

Set Vertical Alignment

1 Create a CSS class for the `<table>` tag whose content you want to vertically align.

2 Type `{`.

3 For the class declaration, type `vertical-align: "?"`, replacing *?* with `top`, `middle`, or `bottom`.

4 Type `}`.

5 Inside the tag specified in step **1**, type `class="?"`, replacing *?* with the class name.

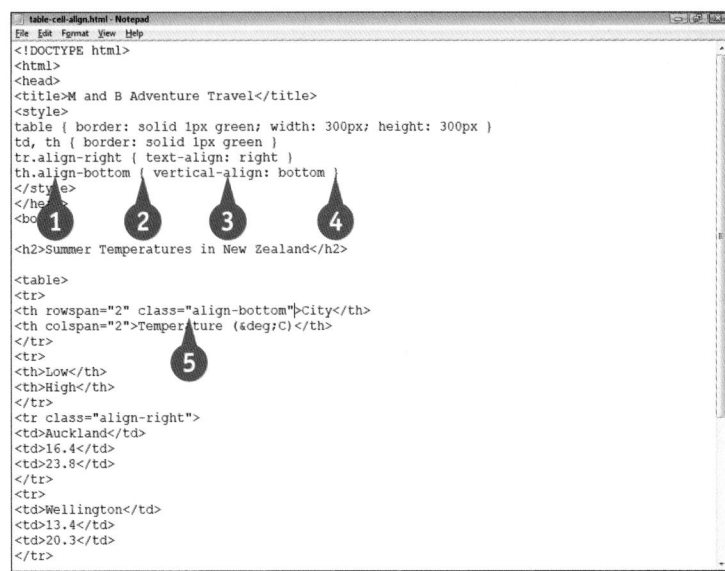

● In this example, applying a style to a `<th>` tag aligns content in a header cell to the bottom.

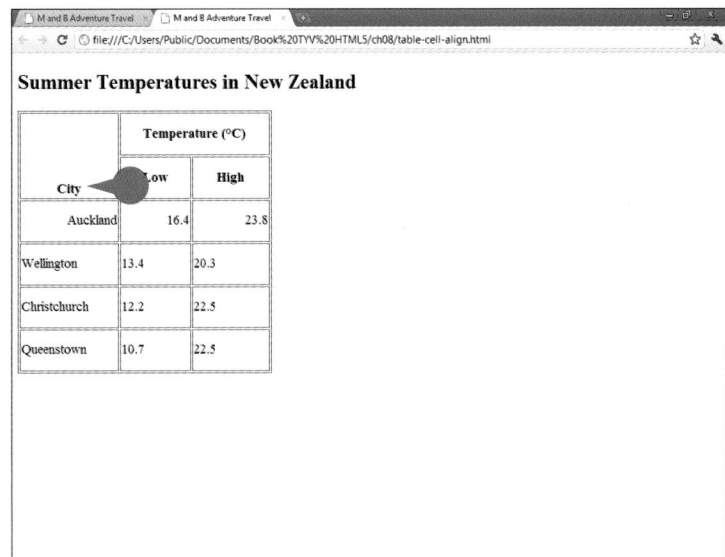

TIPS

How do I justify data in a table cell?
Justification sets both left and right alignment and stretches the text to span the area between the cell borders. You can justify text in a cell by setting the `text-align` property to `justify`.

How can I align all the content in my table to the right except for one cell?
You can set the `text-align` property to `right` for the `<table>` tag and then apply a different `text-align` property to the cell's `<td>` tag using a class. See Chapter 4 for more about CSS classes. Because the `<td>` tag is within the `<table>` tag, style rules applied to the `<td>` tag override those of the outer `<table>` tag.

Change Table Alignment

You can control the positioning of a table on your web page with CSS rules. To align a table to the left or right on your page, you can set the `float` property. To align a page to the center, you can set the `margin-left` and `margin-right` properties. Aligning a table can help you use the space on your page more efficiently or present table data more prominently on your page.

You can use these CSS techniques to align other content on your page as well. For more about aligning images on your page, see Chapter 6.

Change Table Alignment

Align to the Side

1 Create a CSS class for the `<table>` tag.

Note: See Chapter 4 for more about CSS classes.

2 Type `{`.

3 For the class declaration, type `float: ?`, replacing ? with `right` or `left`.

4 Type `}`.

5 Inside the `<table>` tag for the table you want to align, type `class="?"`, replacing ? with the class name from step **1**.

The web browser aligns the table.

● In this example, the table is right-aligned, with text and an image wrapping around the left side.

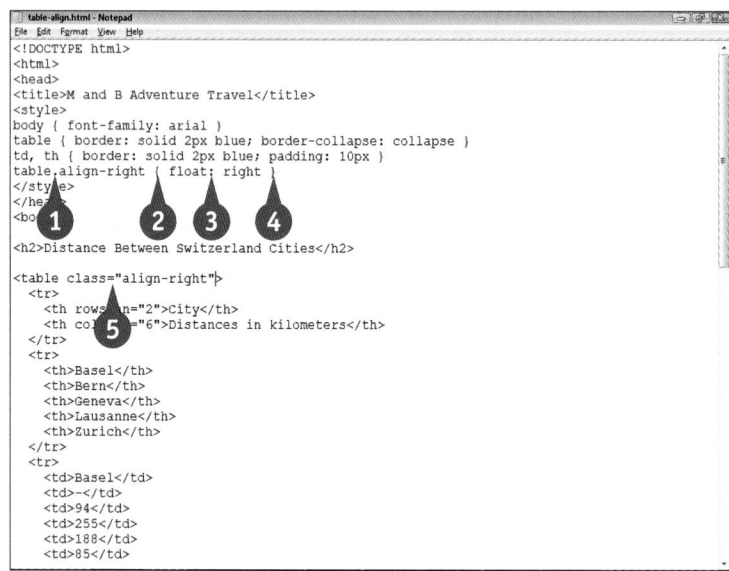

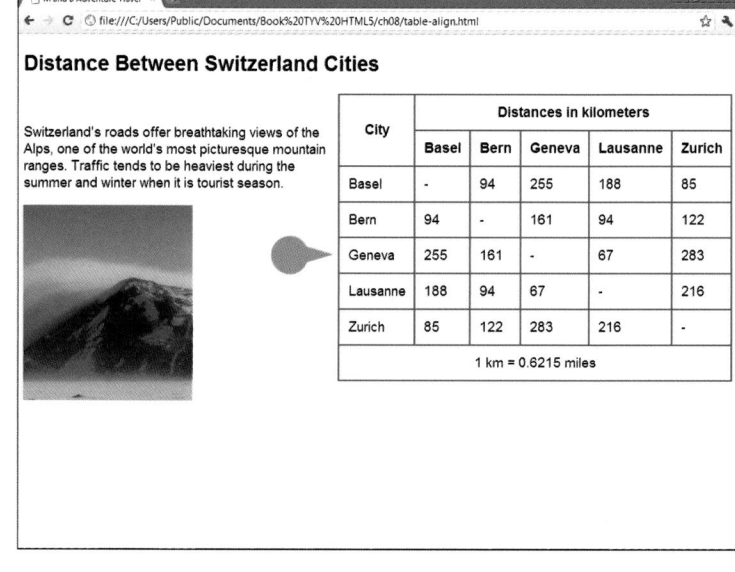

Distance Between Switzerland Cities

Switzerland's roads offer breathtaking views of the Alps, one of the world's most picturesque mountain ranges. Traffic tends to be heaviest during the summer and winter when it is tourist season.

City	Distances in kilometers				
---	Basel	Bern	Geneva	Lausanne	Zurich
Basel	-	94	255	188	85
Bern	94	-	161	94	122
Geneva	255	161	-	67	283
Lausanne	188	94	67	-	216
Zurich	85	122	283	216	-
1 km = 0.6215 miles					

Align in the Center

1 Create a CSS class for the `<table>` tag.

Note: See Chapter 4 for more about CSS classes.

2 Type {.

3 For the class declaration, type `margin-left: auto`.

4 Type ; and then type `margin-right: auto`.

5 Type }.

6 Inside the `<table>` tag for the table you want to align, type `class="?"`, replacing *?* with the class name from step **1**.

● The web browser aligns the table to the center.

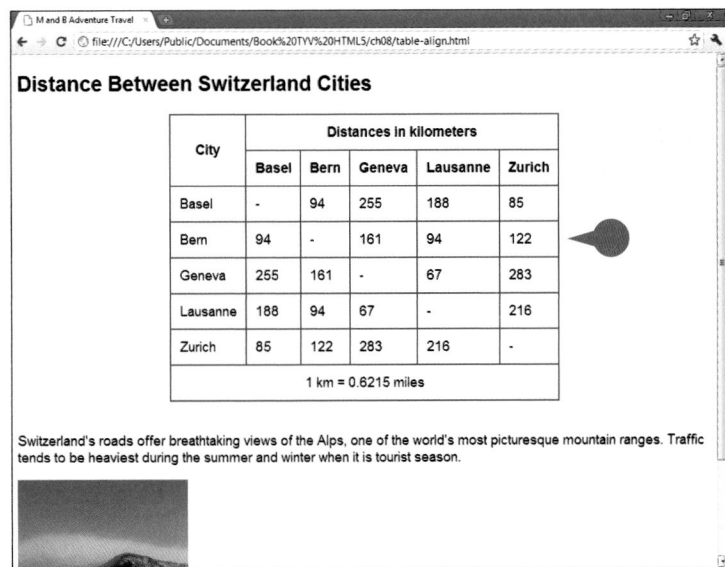

TIPS

How do I format a table so that it stretches the entire width of the browser window?

You can set the `width` property of your table to `100%` to stretch the table the entire width of the browser window. For example:

```
table { width: 100% }
```

The table shrinks or expands as you change the dimensions of the browser.

How can I indent a table aligned to the side?

You can indent such a table using the `margin-left` or `margin-right` properties along with the `float` property in your CSS rule. For example, you can set the following:

```
table { float: left; margin-left: 10px }
```

This rule indents a left-aligned table 10 pixels from the left side. For more about setting margins, see Chapter 10.

Extend Cells Across Columns and Rows

You can create a larger cell in your table by extending the cell across two or more columns or rows. The ability to span cells, also called *merging cells,* enables you to create unique cell structures within your table. For example, you might include a large cell across the top of a table to hold a heading or an image. You can merge multiple cells in a column to apply a single label to several rows. You merge cells by applying the `colspan` or `rowspan` attributes to `<td>` tags in your table.

Extend Cells Across Columns and Rows

Extend Cells Across Columns

① Click inside the tag for the cell you want to extend across columns.

② Type `colspan="?"`, replacing *?* with the number of columns you want to span.

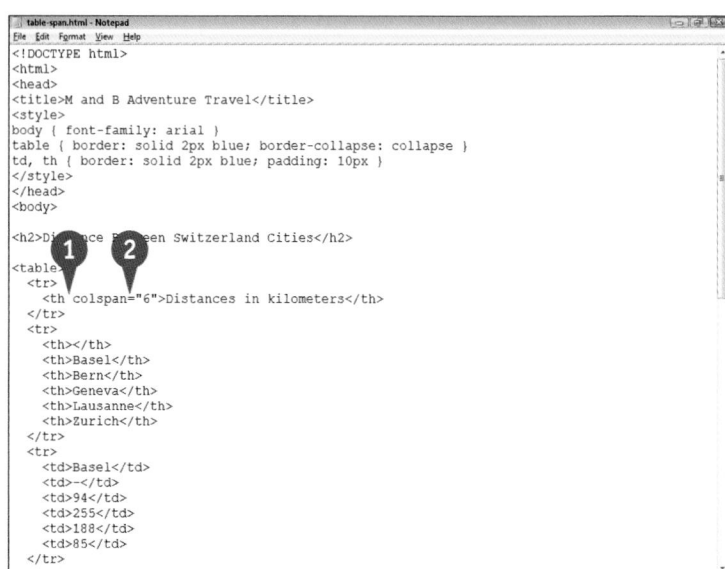

The web browser displays the cell spanning the designated number of columns.

● In this example, a heading column spans the top of the table.

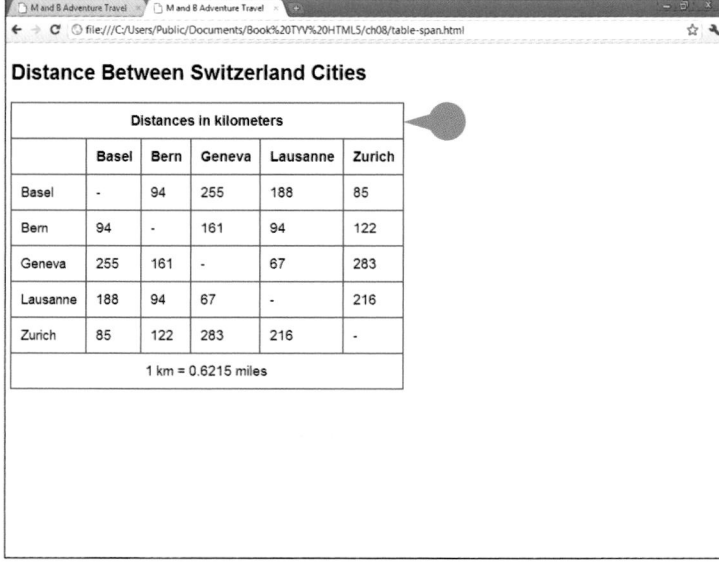

Extend Cells Across Rows

① Click inside the tag for the cell you want to extend across rows.

② Type `rowspan="?"`, replacing *?* with the number of rows you want to span.

If you are using the HTML from the previous example, also remove the blank data cell in the City row.

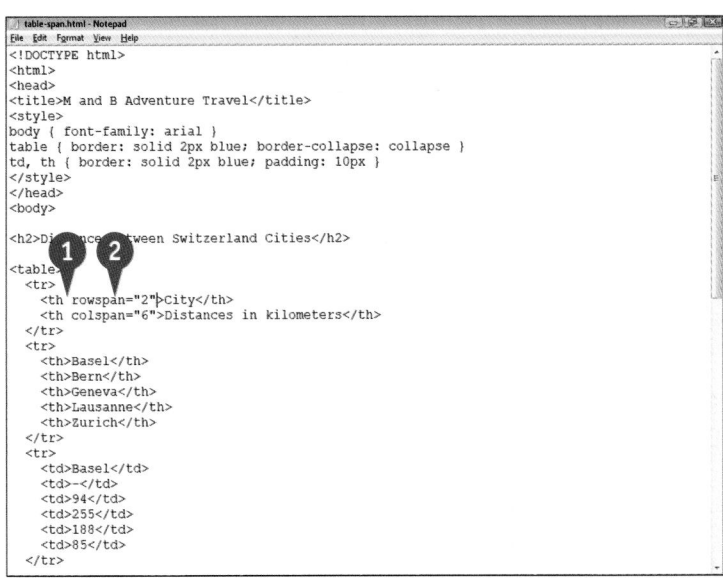

The web browser displays the cell spanning the designated number of rows.

● In this example, a heading spans two rows at the top of the table.

● In this example, a heading also spans five columns. You can combine column and row spanning to create complex table designs.

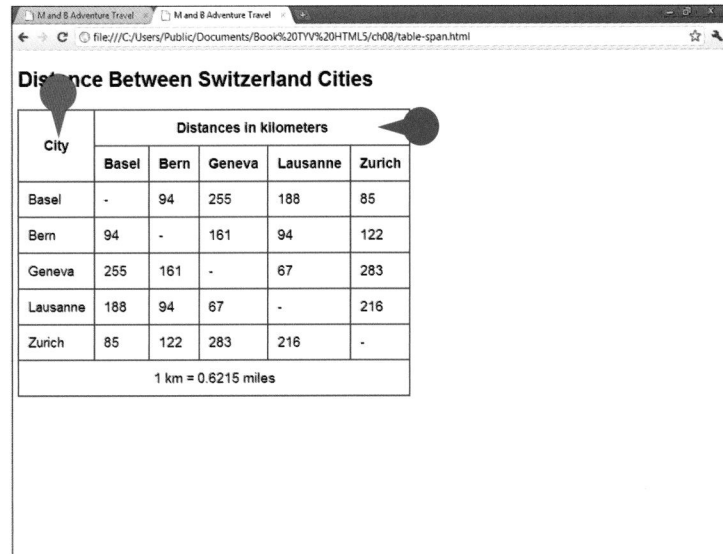

TIPS

Can I extend a cell across columns and rows at the same time?

Yes. If you add the `colspan` and `rowspan` attributes to the same row or header tag, you can make a cell span across and down in the table. Just remember to remove cells in the columns and rows that you want the current cell to span.

How can I set off a row that spans the top of my table?

You can create a title cell for a table by creating a top cell that spans all the cells beneath it. To set that cell off from the others, you can add a background color. See the section "Add a Background Color to Cells" for more information. You can also make that cell a header cell by using the `<th>` tag. See the section "Add Column Labels" for details.

Use a Table for Page Layout

In addition to using tables to display sets of numeric or textual data, you can use tables to organize the overall content on your web page. The cells of a table can be used to hold sections of content such as page titles, navigation links, paragraphs of text, and images. You can keep borders turned off to make the underlying table structure invisible to the user.

Note that the preferred way of organizing the overall content on a page, according to HTML5 specification, is with semantic HTML5 tags and CSS rules instead of with tables. For more about creating a page with semantic tags and CSS, see Chapter 11.

Use a Table for Page Layout

① Type `<table>`.

② For each row in your table, type `<tr>` and then `</tr>`.

This presentation table has two rows of content.

③ Type `</table>`.

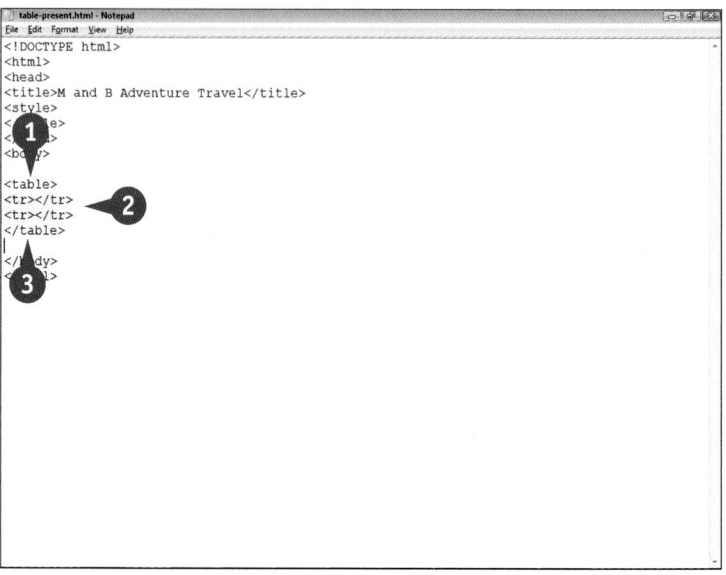

④ Type `<td>` and then `</td>` to create a table cell for a section of content.

⑤ Inside the `<td>` and `</td>` tags, type the content.

⑥ You can type `rowspan` or `colspan` attributes in a `<td>` tag to extend table cells across other cells.

Note: For details about spanning rows and columns, see "Extend Cells Across Columns and Rows."

⑦ Repeat steps 4 to 6 for each section of content on your page.

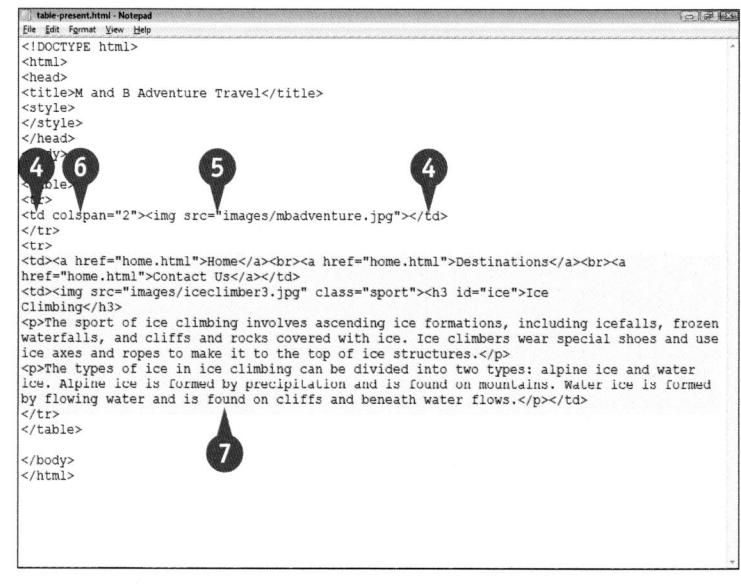

8 Create a CSS class for a `<td>` tag that defines a section.

Note: See Chapter 4 for more about CSS classes.

9 Define the CSS properties for the section. For example, you can set a `width` or `height` to constrain how large each section appears on the page. You can set `padding` to add blank space around your sections.

Note: See Chapters 5 and 11 for more about CSS properties.

10 Apply the CSS classes using the `class` attribute.

11 Repeat steps **8** to **10** for each section in your page.

The web browser displays the presentation table.

The table in this example includes a header, navigation column, and a main content section.

Because the table width is set to a percentage rather than a fixed value, the width adjusts if you resize the browser window.

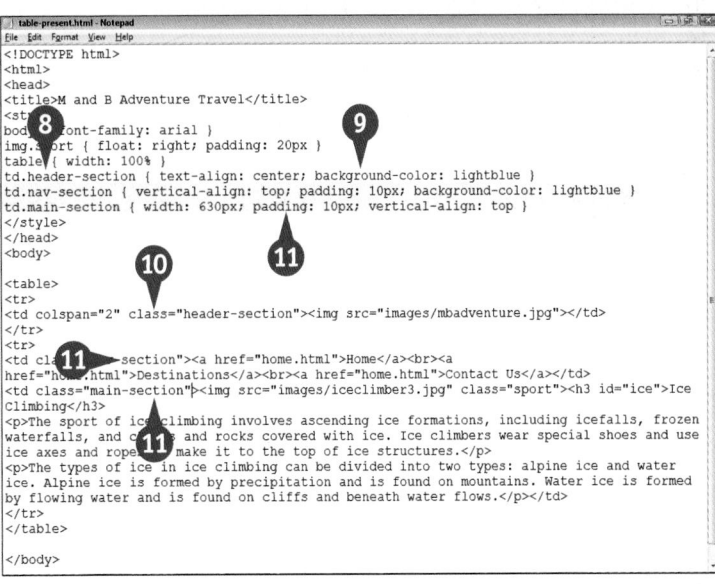

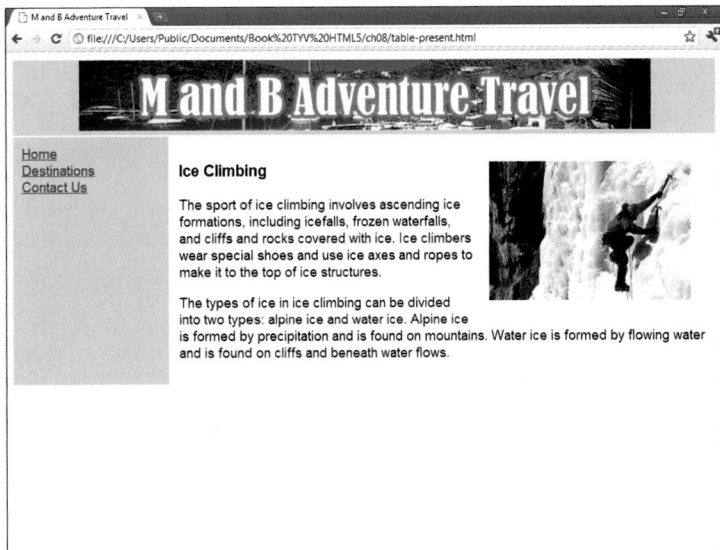

TIPS

In a layout table, how do I make the section content start at the top of my table cells?

By default, content in a table cell is middle-aligned. In your CSS rule for a cell, you can apply the `vertical-align` attribute with a value of `top` to make content start at the top of a table cell. For more information, see "Change Cell Alignment."

How can I use borders with my layout table?

You can turn on borders while you are building a layout table so you can see its design more clearly in the browser. For example, you can set the following to turn on a red border for your cells:

```
td { border: solid 1px red }
```

Once your table appears how you like it, you can remove the `border` declaration to turn off the borders.

CHAPTER 9

Creating Forms

Looking for a way to allow your website visitors to communicate with you? This chapter shows you how to build forms that gather information from users and send it to web servers for processing. You can build forms that allow users to send feedback about a site or buy products by submitting credit card information. To create a form, you can use a variety of input fields, including text fields, check boxes, drop-down menus, and radio buttons. The sections in this chapter describe how to add these fields and when to use them.

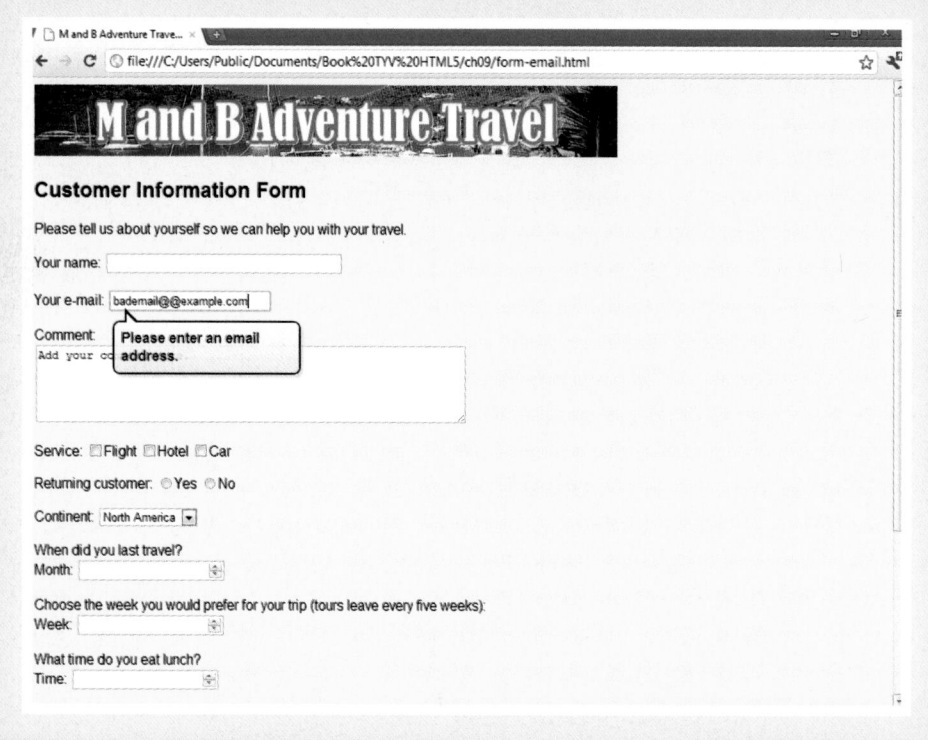

Understanding Forms

You can use forms to collect information from the people who visit your website. For example, you might enable visitors to send you feedback, post comments on articles, or purchase goods or services from your business. You collect information by creating an HTML5 form on your page. When the user submits the form information, the information is sent back to the web server for processing. Forms are an important way to make a site interactive instead of just a collection of static pages with text and images.

Forms and Scripts

In an HTML5 form, input elements such as text fields, menus, and check boxes collect data from a website user. After a user fills in the data, he or she clicks a button to submit the form, and the browser sends the data back to the web server. The web server typically handles the data by processing it with a program known as a *common gateway interface*, or CGI, script. For example, you can write CGI scripts to parse the data and send back a custom web page in response or store the data in a database. You can examine the database to see what information users have submitted.

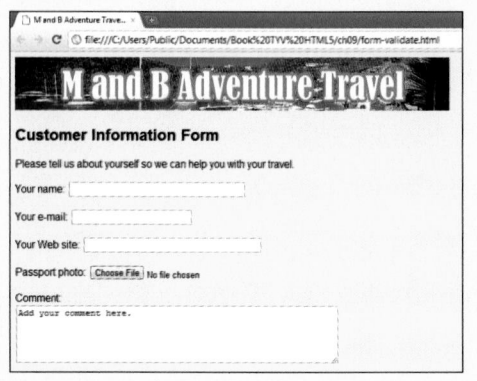

Implementing CGI Scripts

You can write your own CGI scripts if you know a programming language such as Perl, PHP, or Java, or you can adapt one of the many free CGI scripts available on the web. Sites like the CGI Resource Index (http://cgi.resourceindex.com), Matt's Script Archive (www.scriptarchive.com), and HotScripts.com (www.hotscripts.com) are good places to start. Many web hosts also make CGI scripts accessible to their customers. The place where CGI scripts are stored on a web server is usually called a CGI-bin directory (the directory may be called something else, depending on the server).

```
logs.pl - WordPad
File  Edit  View  Insert  Format  Help
#!/usr/bin/env perl

print "Content-type: text/html\n\n";

print "<HTML><BODY style=\"font-
family:Arial,Helvetica,sans-serif\">\n";

print "<table border=\"1\" cellpadding=\"2\"
cellspacing=\"0\">\n";

my @logs = <logs/*>;
@logs = reverse(sort(@logs));
my $lastline;
my @data;

foreach my $log (@logs) {
    open(INFILE, "$log") or die "Can't open @ARGV[
0 ] $!";
    my $id = substr $log, 5, 14;
    if ($id=="last.txt") {
        next;
    }
    while (<INFILE>) {
        $lastline = $_;
    }
    @data = split(/\|/, $lastline);
```

HTML for Forms

Web page forms have three important parts: a `<form>` tag, form input elements, and a Submit button. When designing and building a form, you write HTML to define the different objects that allow users to type or select information. These objects can include text fields, radio buttons, check boxes, and more. All forms should include a Submit button for sending the data to a web server for processing. The `<form>` tag usually specifies the script that processes the form information on the web server.

```
form-url2html - Notepad
File  Edit  Format  View  Help
<form method="post" action="cgi-bin/customer.cgi">

<p>Your name:

<input type="text" name="customername" size="40" maxlength="50"></p>

<p>Your e-mail:

<input type="email" name="emailaddress" size="25" maxlength="254"></p>

Your Web site:

<input type="url" name="webaddress" size="40" maxlength="200">

<p>Comment:<br>

<textarea name="customercomment" rows="5" cols="60" wrap="hard">
Add your comment here.
</textarea></p>

<p>Service:

<input type="checkbox" name="flight" value="yes">Flight
<input type="checkbox" name="hotel" value="yes">Hotel
<input type="checkbox" name="car" value="yes">Car</p>
```

Types of Forms

You can create different types of forms to enable different types of interaction. For example, you can create a search form that allows users to search your website for information by submitting keywords. You can add data-collection forms to gather information from users, such as names, postal addresses, and e-mail addresses. Your form can allow users to comment on and rate the articles posted on your website. You can also use forms to help customers add items to an online shopping cart and make a purchase on your site.

Confirmation

After the form data is processed, a script typically sends a confirmation page back to the browser window noting whether or not the form data was sent successfully. You might also code your script so that it sends a confirmation message by e-mail. It is always good practice when collecting form data to provide visitors with a confirmation or assurance that some sort of action will be taken based on their submission.

Sending Data to Databases

Another use for CGI scripts is to send form data to a database. Database systems are designed to store and manage large amounts of information. CGI scripts can translate form data from the web server into a format that a database can read. If you plan to use your form data in conjunction with a database, you need to learn more about how databases work with the web. Popular database systems include MySQL, Microsoft SQL Server, and Oracle.

Sending Data to an E-Mail Address

If you do not want to use a CGI script, you can use a command directly in your <form> tag that tells a browser to send form data to an e-mail address. When a user submits the form, the browser inserts a list of field names and values in an e-mail message, which the user can then send. This option is useful only if the form is simple; more complex forms require scripts or databases to process and make sense of the information. To learn more about sending form data via e-mail, see the section "Send Form Data to an E-Mail Address."

Types of Form Elements

Forms are made up of a variety of input elements. Some elements, such as text boxes, give users a way to add information in a free-form manner. Others, such as radio buttons, constrain what the user can submit. You can mix different types of input elements in a single form. At the end of a form is usually a submit button that allows the user to send the entered information back to the web server. A script then processes the information on the web server.

Text Boxes

Text boxes are input fields designed specifically for users to type data into, such as typing a name or comment. A text box can be a single line to collect a limited amount of characters, such as a phone number or postal code. Text boxes can also be large, multiline fields that allow for submitting paragraphs of input. In single-line text boxes, you can control the maximum number of characters a user can type. New in HTML5, some text boxes can hold a specific type of text content such as an e-mail address or a URL.

Radio Buttons

Radio buttons are the small, circular buttons found on forms. Like check boxes, radio buttons are used to present several choices to the user. Unlike with check boxes, however, users may select only one radio button in a set, similar to how the buttons on old automobile radios work. For example, if you include a feedback form on your page that rates your website, you might include radio buttons for the values Excellent, Good, Average, and Poor. The user can select only one of the four options.

Check Boxes

Check boxes enable a user to select one or more options from a list. For example, if you want to collect information about a user's familiarity with computers, you can place a set of check boxes next to a list of computer applications. When designing a form, you have the option of presenting check boxes as already checked.

Menu

A menu enables you to present a large set of choices in a form. In a drop-down menu, a user clicks a box to open a list of options from which he or she can select only one. For example, users often choose from a drop-down menu when selecting their state or country in an address form. New in HTML5, you can define menus that hold time and date information such as months, weeks, and days.

File Upload

With a file upload, you can enable users to send you photos, word-processing documents, or spreadsheets in addition to plain text information. When you add the upload element, a Choose File button appears with the field, allowing users to locate the file they want to send.

Range Slider

To offer an interactive way to select from a set of numbers, you can display a range slider, which is new in HTML5. Users can choose a number within the range by clicking and dragging a horizontal slider. By adding some JavaScript to your form, you can display the current number set by the slider.

Date and Time Fields

HTML5 introduces several new field types for presenting chronological information such as month, week, and time fields. Users can select the values in these fields by clicking Up and Down scroll arrows. To constrain what dates and times can be selected, you can set a minimum value, a maximum value, and a step value that determines the values in between.

Submit Button

Users need a way to send their data to the web server. They can do this using a submit button, which usually appears at the end of the form input elements. Data is collected only after the user clicks this button.

Reset Button

You can add a reset button to your HTML form that allows the user to reset all the input fields and start over. This button usually appears at the end of the form, next to the Submit button.

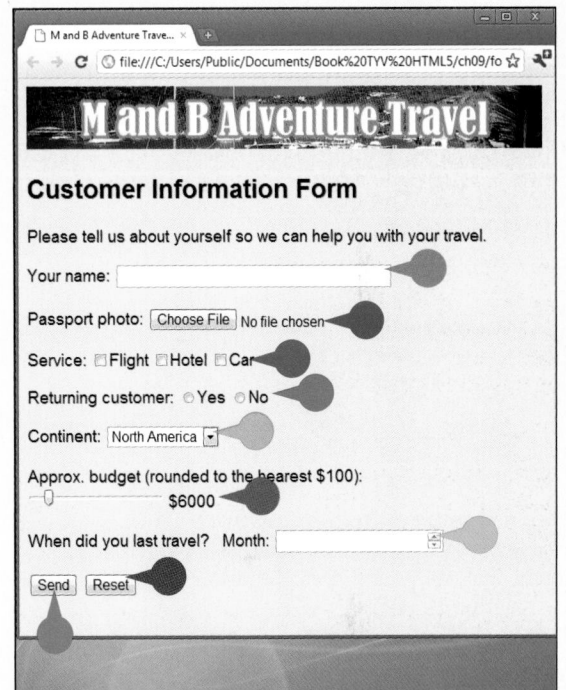

Create a Form

You can use a form to gather information from the people who visit your website. To create a form, you use the `<form>` tag to point to the CGI script that will process the form, define the form elements, and display a Submit button to send the data to the script.

Most forms use a CGI script to instruct the web server to process the collected information. Consult your web host to find out the location of a directory where you can store your script on the server. You can also forego a CGI script and send the form data to an e-mail address. See the section "Send Form Data to an E-Mail Address" to learn more.

Create a Form

① Click where you want to insert a form and type `<form method="?"`, replacing ? with `post` or `get`.

The type of method to use can depend on the information you are collecting or the script that processes the form data.

If you are including a file upload element in your form, use the `post` method.

② Type a space and `action="?">`, replacing ? with the name and location of the CGI script you want to use to process the form data.

Note: You may need to contact your web host to determine the name and path of the CGI script.

③ Type `</form>`.

You can now add input elements to your form between the `<form>` and `</form>` tags.

Note: See the remaining sections in this chapter to learn more about adding input elements.

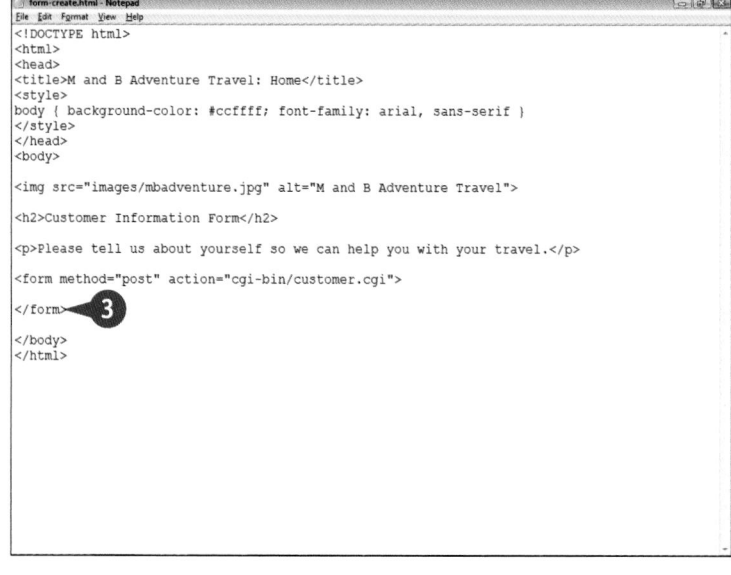

Send Form Data to an E-Mail Address

You can instruct the browser to send form data to an e-mail address. When the user clicks the Submit button for the form, a new e-mail message opens in the default e-mail client. Data from the form is inserted into the e-mail message as name/value pairs; for example, `month=May`. You might use this type of form if your web server does not support CGI scripts. Note that e-mail-based forms may not work for all users because the forms require that the browser be correctly configured to use an e-mail client and that the e-mail client supports this feature.

Send Form Data to an E-Mail Address

① Click where you want to insert a form and type `<form method="post"`.

② Type a space and `enctype="text/plain"`.

③ Type a space and `action="mailto:?">`, replacing `?` with the e-mail address to which you want to send the form data.

④ Type `</form>`.

You can now add input elements to your form between the `<form>` and `</form>` tags.

Note: See the remaining sections in this chapter to learn more about adding input elements.

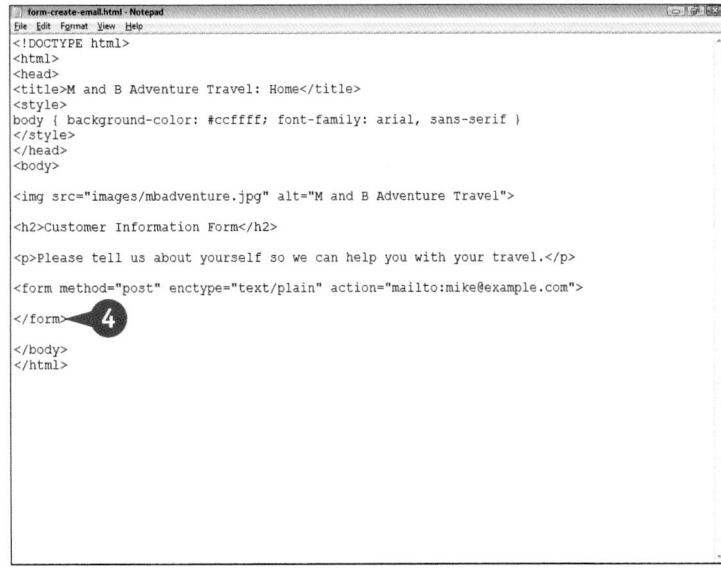

Add a Text Box

You can add a text box to your form to allow users to type a single-line reply or response. When creating a text box, you must identify the input field with a unique name. You can also control the text box size and the maximum number of characters a user can type in the field.

By default, browsers display the text box field at a width of 20 characters. You can make the text box wider using the `size` attribute. You can control the number of characters allowed in a text box by specifying a value with the `maxlength` attribute. To create custom text fields for e-mail or URLs, see the other sections in this chapter.

Add a Text Box

1 Between the `<form>` and `</form>` tags, add a new line for the text box.

2 Type `<input type="text"`.

3 Type a space and `name="?"`, replacing ? with a unique identifier for the text box.

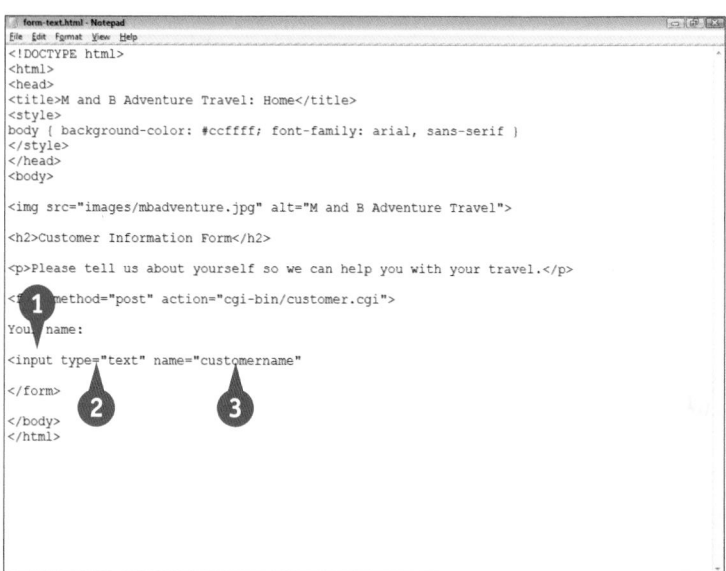

4 Type a space and `size="?"`, replacing ? with a width in characters.

5 To define a maximum number of characters for the field, type `maxlength="?">`, replacing *?* with the maximum number of characters allowed.

Note: Do not forget to type a closing bracket (>) at the end of your input element tag.

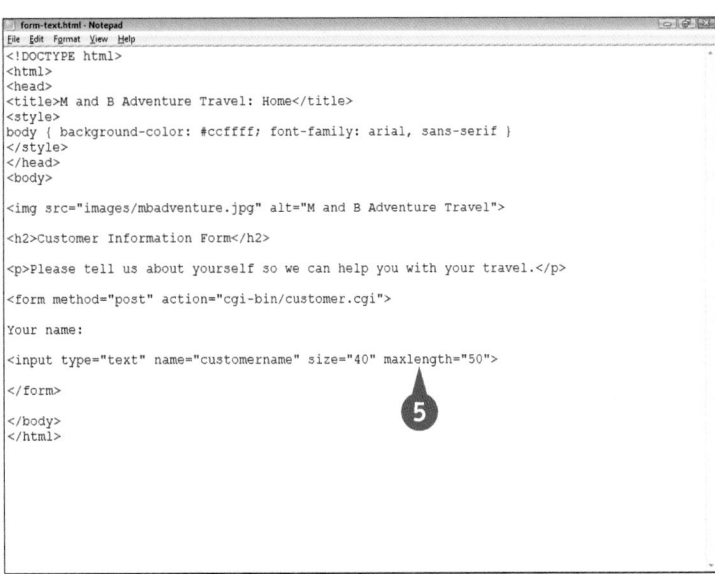

● The web browser displays the text box in the form.

● The user can click inside the text box and type the required information.

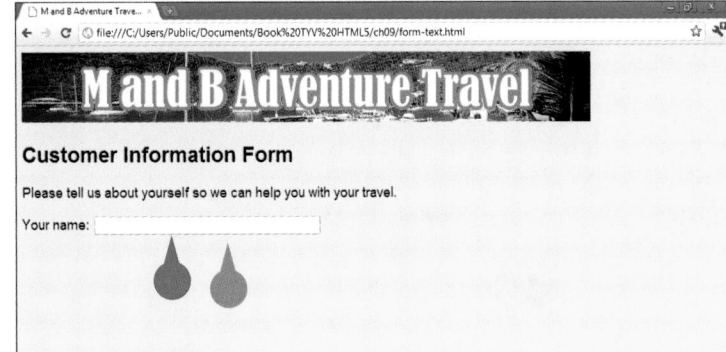

TIPS

Can I add a default value to a text box?
Yes. A default value is text that appears in the text box when the user views the form. You can use default values to initially define a popular choice or response. To specify a default, you can add the `value` attribute to the `<input>` tag. For example:

```
<form method="post" action="/cgi-bin/feedback.pl">

<input type="text" name="fullname" value="Enter your
first and last names">

</form>
```

You can also define a placeholder for a text field. A placeholder appears in the field but does not count as a value for that field. See "Add a Placeholder" for details.

How do I create a password text box?
Password text boxes are similar to regular text boxes with one difference. Rather than displaying the characters that are typed, the input field displays the data as asterisks (*) or bullets (•). This prevents others from seeing the password text. To create a text box for password entry, you specify the password type in the `<input>` tag. For example:

```
<input type="password"
name="secret" size="45">
```

Add a Large Text Area

If your form requires a large text-entry box, you can create a large text area that holds multiple lines of text. For example, if you create a feedback form, you can use a large text area to allow users to type paragraphs of text, rather than limiting them to a smaller space.

When defining a text area, you can control the size of the text box and how text wraps within the field. Text area size is measured in rows and columns, with the measurement based on the number of characters that can be displayed.

Add a Large Text Area

① Between the `<form>` and `</form>` tags, add a new line for the large text box.

② Type `<textarea`.

③ Type a space and `name="?"`, replacing ? with a unique name for the text area.

Note: You can use the `<br>` or `<p>` tag to separate input elements onto different lines in your form.

④ Type a space and `rows="?"`, replacing ? with the number of rows you want to specify to determine the height of the text area.

⑤ Type a space and `cols="?"`, replacing ? with a number of character columns to determine the width of the text area.

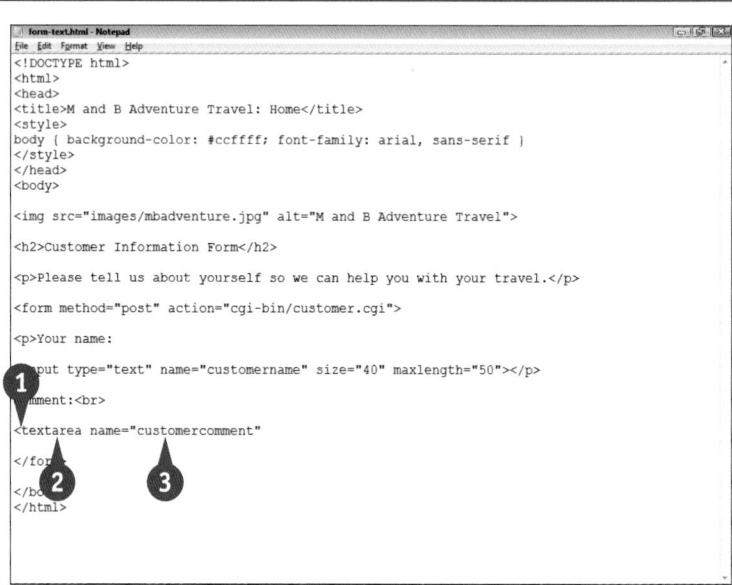

6 Type a space and `wrap="?">`, replacing *?* with a text wrap control.

`soft` wraps text within the text area but does not wrap text in the form results.

`hard` wraps text within both the text area and the form results.

`off` turns off text wrapping, forcing users to create new lines of text as they type.

7 Type `</textarea>`.

● You can add a default message between the `<textarea>` and `</textarea>` tags.

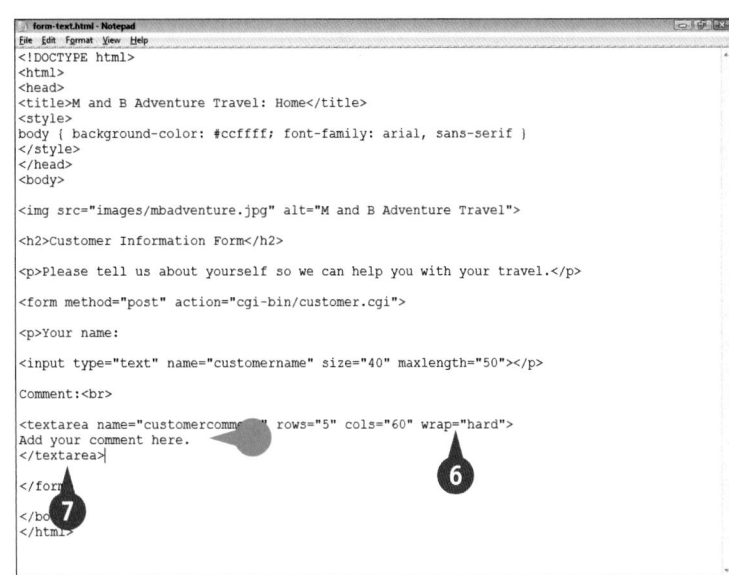

● The web browser displays the text area in the form. In this example, the text area has 5 rows and 60 columns.

● The user can click inside the text box and type information.

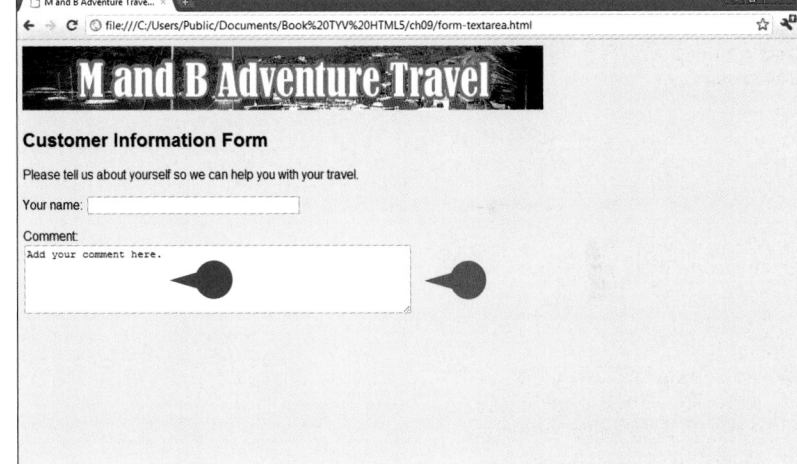

TIPS

What happens if the user types more than can be viewed in the text area?
If the user types more text than is visible in the text area, scroll bars appear at the side of the text box. Scroll bars allow the user to scroll and view the text. The text area automatically holds as much text as the user needs to type, up to 32,700 characters.

Is there a way to keep users from typing text into a large text area?
Yes. You can use the `readonly` attribute if you want to display default text in a text area and do not want users to move or edit the text. For example, you might use a large text area to explain something about your form or display terms of service about your site. You can place the `readonly` attribute within the `<textarea>` tag. The attribute does not require a value.

Add Check Boxes

You can add check boxes to your form to allow users to select from one or more options. You might use check boxes to find out what types of services a user is interested in. When a user selects a check box and submits the form, the browser sends information associated with the check box to the web server as a name/value pair; for example, `flight=yes`. Check box values are often set to `yes` or `true` to denote that boxes were selected, but they can have other values as well. To force your users to select a single option, see "Add Radio Buttons."

Add Check Boxes

① Between the `<form>` and `</form>` tags, type `<input type="checkbox"`.

② Type a space and `name="?"`, replacing *?* with a unique name for the check box.

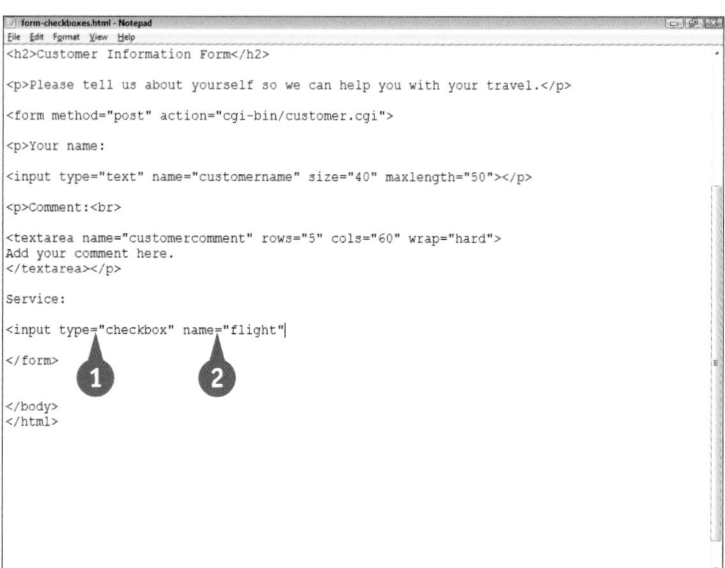

③ Type a space and `value="?">`, replacing *?* with a value to be assigned if the check box is checked.

Note: The check box value does not appear on the form.

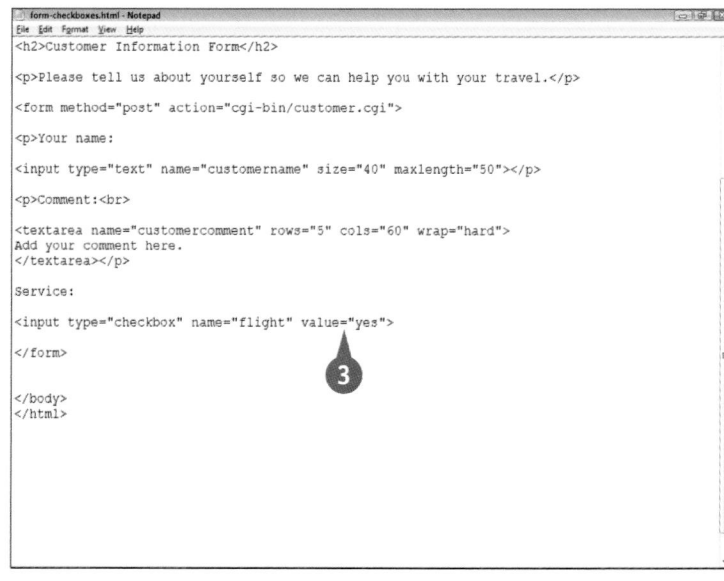

4 Type the text you want to appear beside the check box.

5 Repeat steps **1** to **4** to create more check boxes for a group of check box options.

Note: You can optionally use `<br>` or `<p>` tags to separate input elements onto different lines in your form.

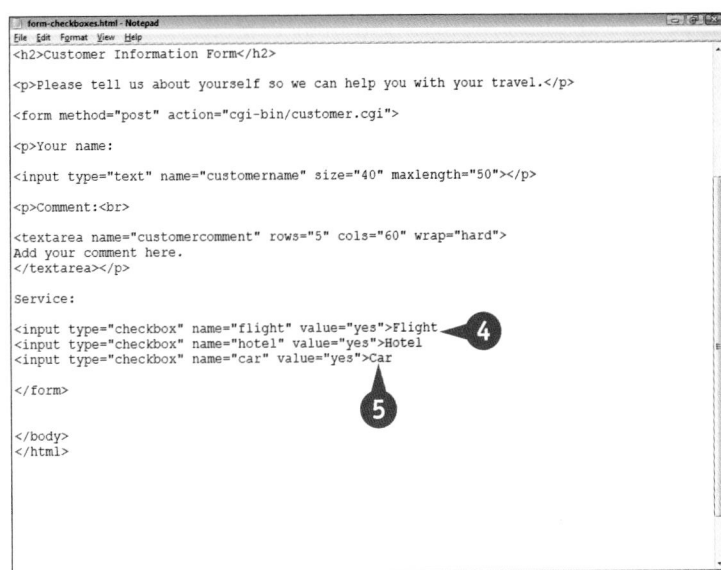

- The web browser displays the check boxes in the form.

- The user can click the box to insert a check mark.

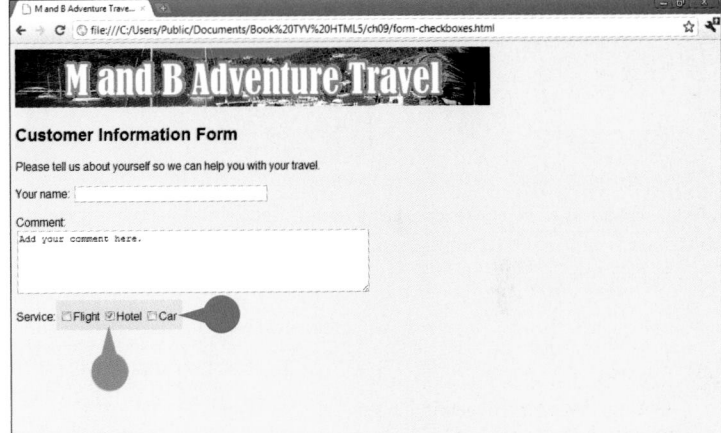

TIPS

How do I automatically show the check box as selected?

You can use the `checked` attribute to show a check box as selected by default when the user views that page. You add the `checked` attribute to the `<input>` tag:

```
<form method="post" action="/
cgi-bin/questionnaire.pl">
<input type="checkbox"
name="newsletter" value="yes" checked>
</form>
```

How do I get the check boxes onto separate lines?

You can use the `<p>` or `<br>` tag. Your code might look like this:

```
<form method="post" action="/cgi-bin/questionnaire.
pl">
<p>What type of movie do you like the best?</p>
<br><input type="checkbox" name="drama" value="true">
<br><input type="checkbox" name="comedy" value="true">
<br><input type="checkbox" name="action" value="true">
</form>
```

Add Radio Buttons

You can use radio buttons if you want to allow users to choose only one item from a group. The user clicks a button to activate the selection. You might use radio buttons to enable users to answer yes-or-no questions in a form. When a user selects a radio button and submits the form, the browser sends information associated with the selected radio button to the web server as a name/value pair; for example, `returning=yes`. If you want your users to be able to select multiple options, you should use check boxes. See "Add Check Boxes" for details.

Add Radio Buttons

1 Between the `<form>` and `</form>` tags, type `<input type="radio"`.

2 Type a space and `name="?"`, replacing *?* with a unique name for the radio button group.

3 Type a space and `value="?">`, replacing *?* with a value describing the radio button.

Note: The radio button value does not appear on the form.

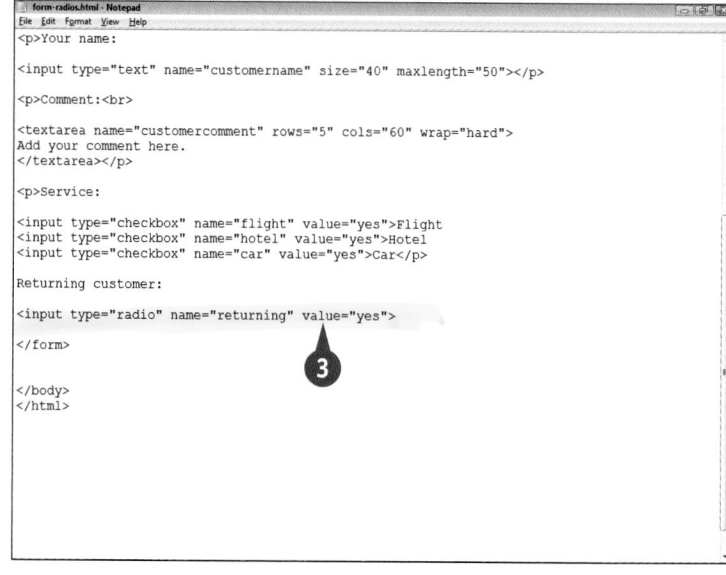

4 Type the text you want to appear beside the radio button.

5 Repeat steps 1 to 4 to add more radio buttons to the group, using the same name for all the buttons in a set.

Note: You can optionally use <br> or <p> tags to separate input elements onto different lines in your form.

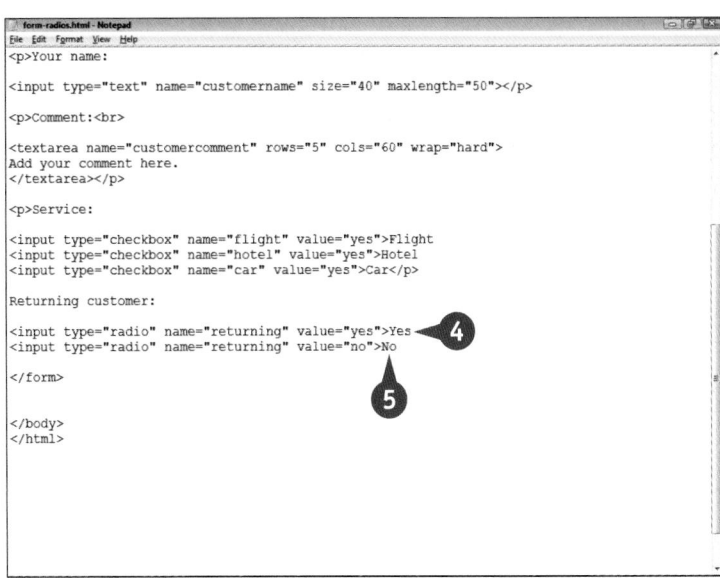

● The web browser displays the radio buttons on the form.

● The user can click the radio button to select that option.

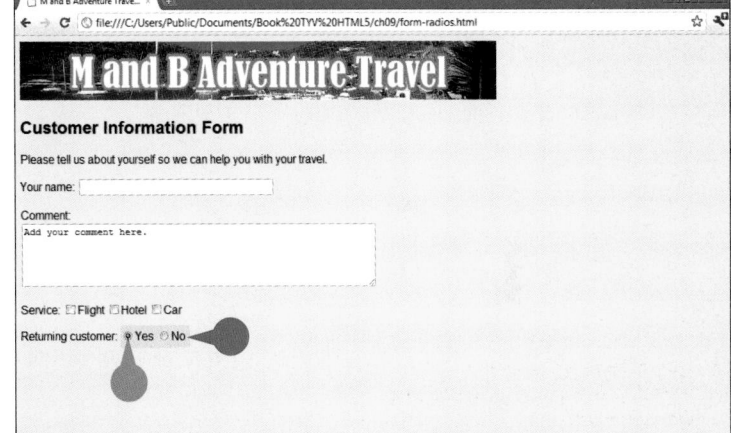

What happens if I give radio buttons in a set different names?

When radio buttons have different name attributes, the browser treats them as parts of different radio button sets. This means the user is able to turn more than one of them on at a time by clicking. Make sure all the radio buttons in a set have the same name attribute to avoid this.

Can I show a particular radio button as selected by default?

Yes. You can use the checked attribute to show one radio button in the group as selected by default. The checked attribute is inserted after the value attribute in your HTML code. Your code might look like this:

```
<form method="post" action="/cgi-bin/
questionnaire.pl">

<input type="radio" name="agerange"
value="40-50" checked>

</form>
```

Add a Menu List

You can add a menu list to a form to give users a list of choices. Menus enable you to display choices as a drop-down list that appears when the user clicks the list. By storing a long list of choices as a drop-down list, you can free up space for other input items in the form. When a user selects a menu item and submits the form, the browser sends information associated with the menu and the selected item to the web server as a name/value pair; for example, `continent=africa`.

Add a Menu List

① Between the `<form>` and `</form>` tags, type `<select name="?",` replacing *?* with a unique name for the menu.

② Type a space and `size="?">,` replacing *?* with the height, measured in character lines, for the menu input.

If you want to display a drop-down menu, set the height to `1`.

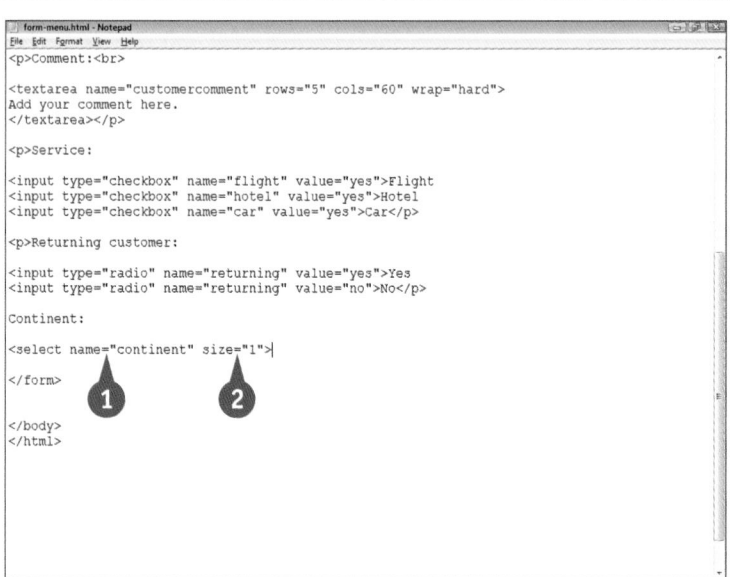

③ Start a new line and type `<option value="?">,` replacing *?* with a descriptive word for the menu item.

④ Type the text you want to appear in the menu list.

⑤ Repeat steps **3** and **4** to add more menu items to the list.

⑥ To make one menu item appear as selected in the list, type `selected` after the `value` attribute.

⑦ Type `</select>`.

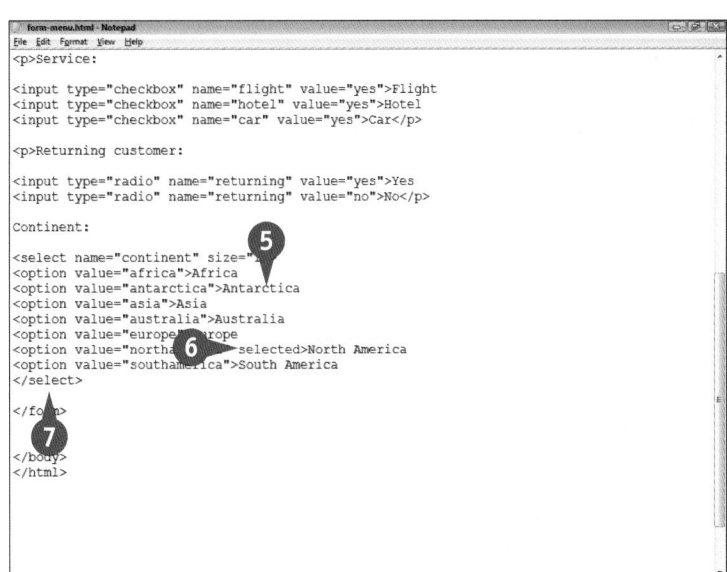

The web browser displays the menu on the form.

● The user can click here to display the drop-down list.

● The user can click a list item to make a selection.

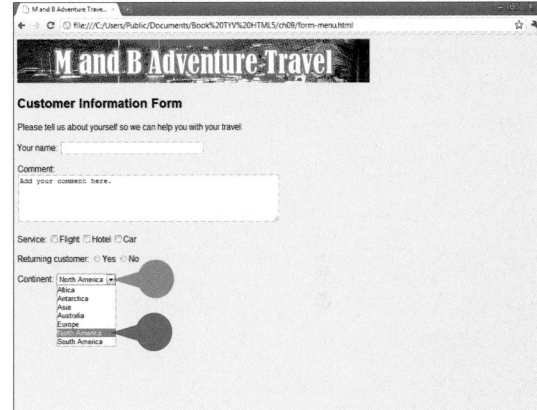

How do I display a menu of items on my form as a scrollable list?

Type the number of menu entries to display at a time as the `size` attribute value. This makes the menu appear as a rectangular box that displays the items as a list. If the number of menu items is more than the display size, users can scroll to view the entire list. If the menu size is 1, a drop-down menu appears.

How can I create a submenu?

Use the `<optgroup>` tag and the `label` attribute (note that not all browsers support the `<optgroup>` tag):

```
<p>What is your favorite sport?</p>
<select name="favoritesport">
<optgroup label="Summer">
<option value="Diving">Diving
<option value="Biking">Biking
</optgroup>
<optgroup label="Winter">
<option value="Skiing">Skiing
<option value="Ice Climbing">Ice Climbing
</optgroup>
</select>
```

Add a Date and Time Input

You can add various date and time menus to help your users choose from preset times. Depending on what questions you are asking, you can allow a user to choose a week, a specific date, or a start time. By using the `step` attribute, you can increment a user's choices by regular intervals. This gives your users limited choices based on a set of parameters. For example, you can have users select from meeting times which begin every two hours, and only on days beginning at one date and ending at another.

Add a Date and Time Input

① Between the `<form>` and `</form>` tags, type `<input type=?`, replacing ? with a date or time input type.

Common date and time input types are `month`, `week`, and `time`.

② Type a space and `name="?"`, replacing ? with a unique name for the input field.

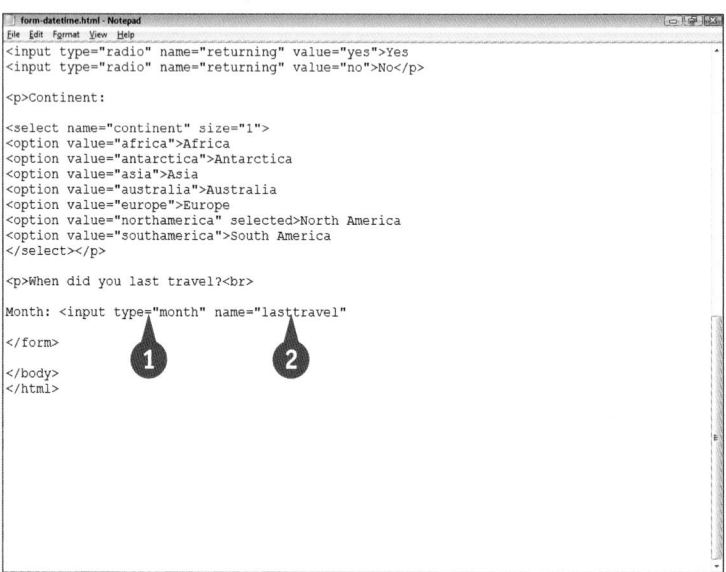

③ Type a space and then `min="?"`, replacing ? with the earliest option you want to accept.

For a `month` type, use the format YYYY-MM (June of 2011 would be 2011-06).

For a `week` type, use YYYY-WNN (the third week of 2012 would be 2012-W03).

For a `time` type, use HH:MM in a 24-hour format (2:00 p.m. would be 14:00).

④ Type a space and `max="?"`, replacing ? with the latest option you want to accept.

5 Type a space and then `step="?">`, replacing *?* with the number of units you want to increment by in the menu.

For a `month` type, step values are in months.

For a `week` type, step values are in weeks.

For a `time` type, step values are in seconds. The value `3600` would create increments one hour apart.

Note: Do not forget to type a closing bracket (>) at the end of your input element tag.

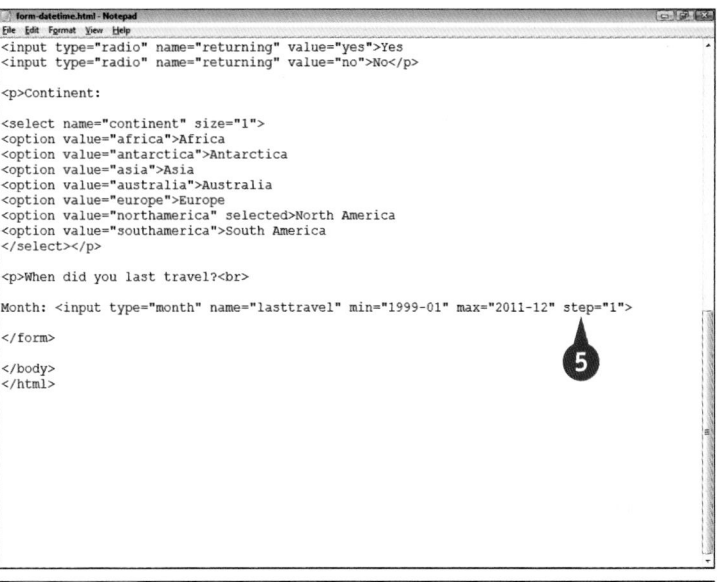

● The web browser displays the date or time elements.

● In this example, additional inputs were created for weeks and time.

● The user can click the up or down arrows to choose an option.

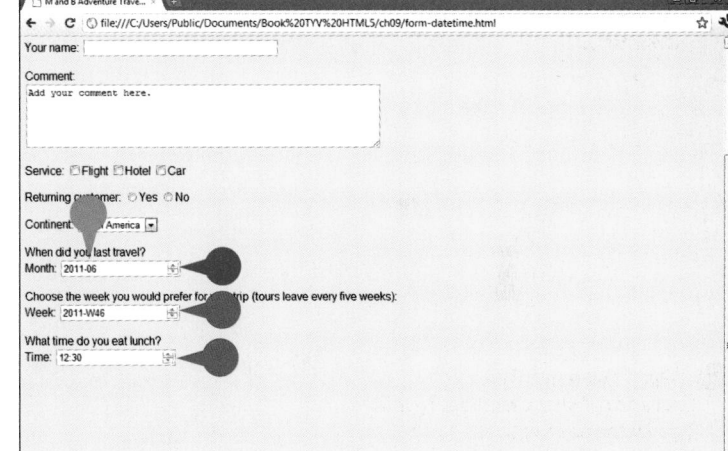

TIPS

How can I create a text field that accepts only numbers?

You can add a form input field of the type `number`. The field will accept only numeric data. You can set a `min` attribute for a minimum, a `max` attribute for a maximum, and a `step` attribute to define the acceptable numbers in between. For example:

```
<input type="number" name="age" value="21"
min="1" max="120" step="0.5">
```

The `number` input appears as a text field with clickable scroll arrows for selecting a number. The default `step` value is 1 and the default starting value for the field is 0. If you submit something other than a number in the field, the browser cancels the submission and displays an alert.

How do I submit data with my form that I do not want displayed to the user?

You can define a form input field of type `hidden`. For example:

```
<input type="hidden"
name="specialcode" value="abc123">
```

The hidden data is submitted with the other data in the form but does not appear on the page. In the above case, specialcode=abc123 is submitted. Note that users can still view the hidden data by viewing the page source, so you should not use hidden fields for secret or private data.

Add an E-Mail Field

By adding an e-mail field, you can allow your users to submit an e-mail address in your form. You might use this feature to allow users to sign up for a mailing list or a newsletter, or simply to give you a way to contact them. Note that it is standard practice to let users know if you will be sharing their e-mail address with anyone else after you collect it.

The e-mail field looks like a regular text field when displayed in a form. After the form is submitted, the browser checks whether the field data is a valid e-mail address. For other ways to validate your form data, see "Validate Input with a Pattern."

Add an E-Mail Field

① Between the `<form>` and `</form>` tags, add a new line for the e-mail input.

② Type `<input type="email"`.

③ Type a space and `name="?"`, replacing *?* with a unique identifier for the e-mail field.

④ Type a space and `size="?"`, replacing *?* with a width in characters.

180

5 To define a maximum number of characters for the field, type `maxlength="?">`, replacing *?* with the maximum number of characters allowed.

Note: Do not forget to type a closing bracket (>) at the end of your input element tag.

The web browser displays the text box in the form.

● The user can click inside the text box and type an e-mail address.

● If the user types an invalid e-mail address and submits the form, an alert appears.

Note: Browser support for validation of e-mail fields varies.

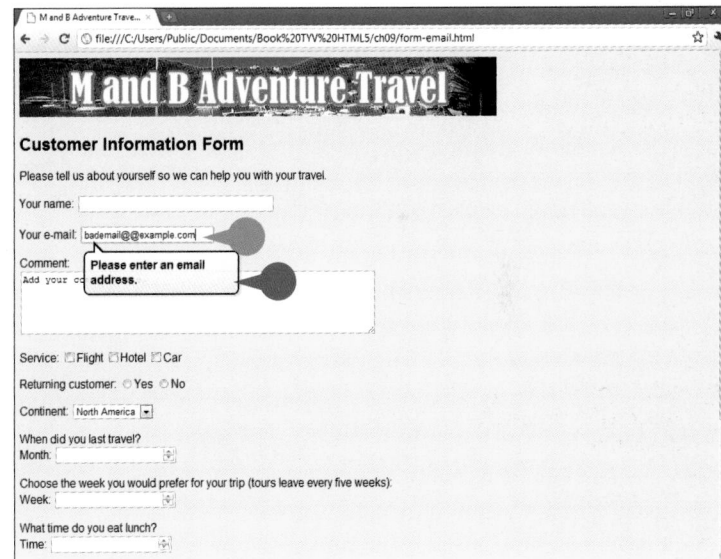

TIPS

How do I create an input field for a telephone number?
You can add a `tel` input type to a form to give users a place to enter their telephone number. For example:

`<input type="tel" name="phone">`

This feature is new in HTML5. Note that, because the accepted format of telephone numbers varies widely from country to country, browsers do not validate that data submitted in this field match a particular format. So the field behaves like a normal text input field.

Can I prevent a text box from autocompleting?
Autocompletion is when a browser displays suggestions for input data based on past data submissions. For sensitive information, you probably do not want the user's browser to display suggestions. To prevent this from happening, you can set the `autocomplete` attribute to `off`. For example:

`<input type="text" name="ssn"`
`autocomplete="off">`

Add a URL Field

By adding a URL field, you can allow your users to submit a web address in your form. You might use this feature to allow users to specify their personal or company website when submitting a form. New in HTML5, this feature is useful because validating long web addresses can be tricky.

The URL field looks like a regular text field when displayed in a form. After the form is submitted, the browser checks whether the URL data is a valid web address. For other ways to validate your form data, see "Validate Input with a Pattern."

Add a URL Field

1 Between the `<form>` and `</form>` tags, add a new line for the URL input.

2 Type `<input type="url"`.

3 Type a space and `name="?"`, replacing *?* with a unique identifier for the URL field.

4 Type a space and `size="?"`, replacing *?* with a width in characters.

5 To define a maximum number of characters for the field, type `maxlength="?">`, replacing *?* with the maximum number of characters allowed.

Note: Do not forget to type a closing bracket (>) at the end of your input element tag.

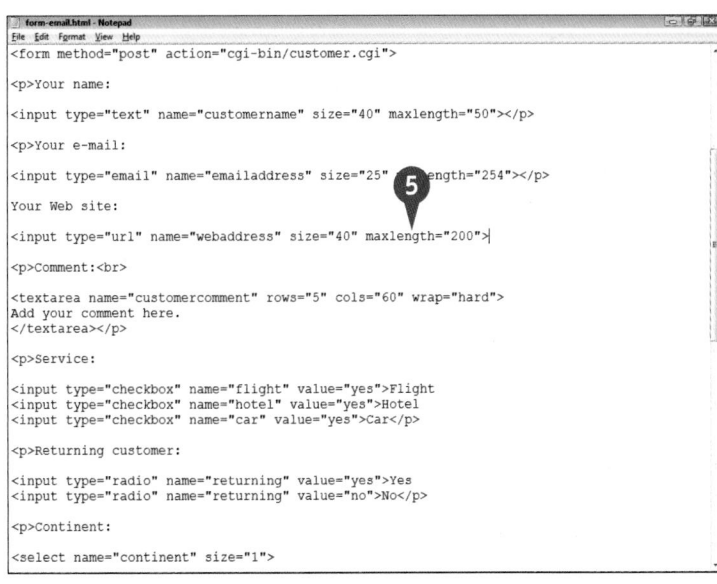

The web browser displays the URL field in the form.

● The user can click inside the text box and type a web address.

● If the user types an invalid URL and submits the form, an alert appears.

Note: Browser support for validation of URL fields varies.

Note: See Chapter 7 for more about URLs.

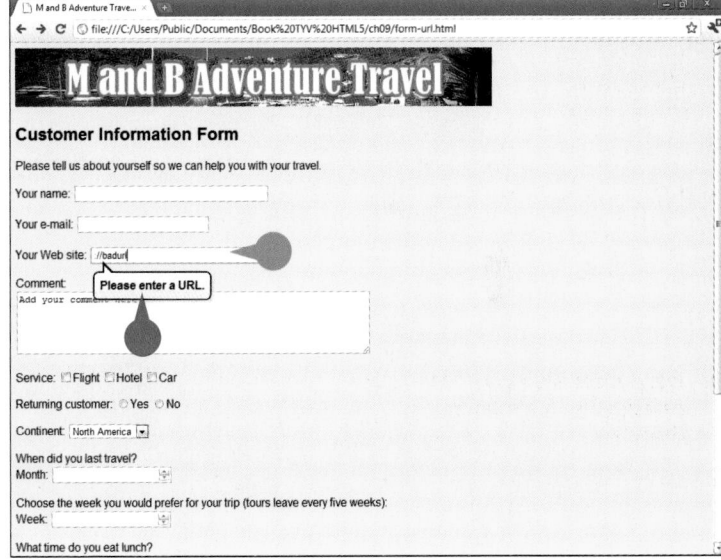

In a URL field, what URLs are considered invalid by browsers?
Current browsers perform very basic checks to determine if text in a URL field is valid. Google Chrome checks if the text includes "://" with alphabetical text before and alphanumeric text or a period after. Such validation does not guarantee that the URL actually works, but it will recognize simple typing errors.

How can I create a URL field with more stringent validation rules?
You can add a `pattern` attribute to the `<input>` tag to perform additional validation. For example, adding the following requires that the URL also begin with "http":

`pattern="http.*"`

For more about using the `pattern` attribute, see "Validate Input with a Pattern."

Add a Range Slider

If you want your users to select from a range of values, you can add a range input field to your form. In most browsers, the range input appears as a slider that a user can click and drag horizontally to select a value.

You can set a minimum and maximum to your range. You can also determine at what increments values exist within the range. For example, you can present a range slider that enables users to choose any multiple of 5 between 25 and 85. Or, if you were selling a product which came in packages of four, you could use a slider to force users to select only multiples of four. The range input is new in HTML5.

Add a Range Slider

① Between the `<form>` and `</form>` tags, add a new line for the range input.

② Type `<input type="range".`

③ Type a space and then `min="?"`, replacing *?* with the minimum value for your slider.

④ Type a space and then `max="?"`, replacing *?* with the maximum value for your slider.

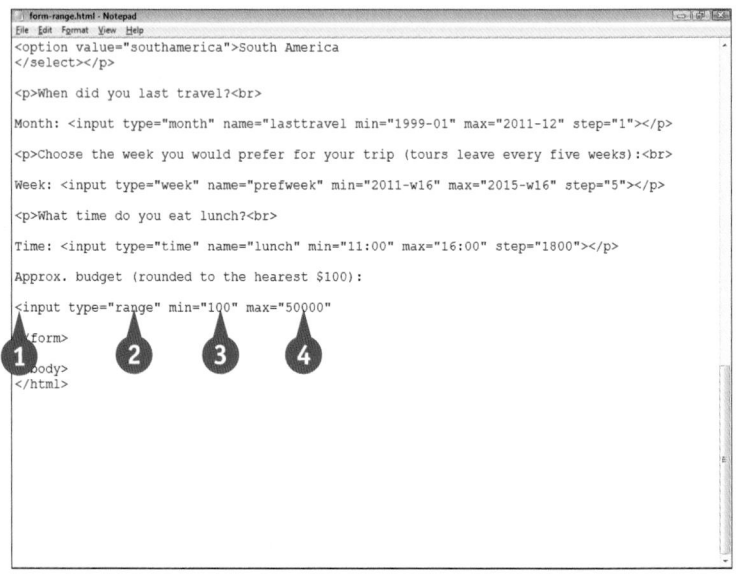

⑤ Type a space and then `step="?"`, replacing *?* with the range increment.

6 Type a space and `value="?"`, replacing *?* with the default value for the slider.

Note: Do not forget to type a closing bracket (>) at the end of your input element tag.

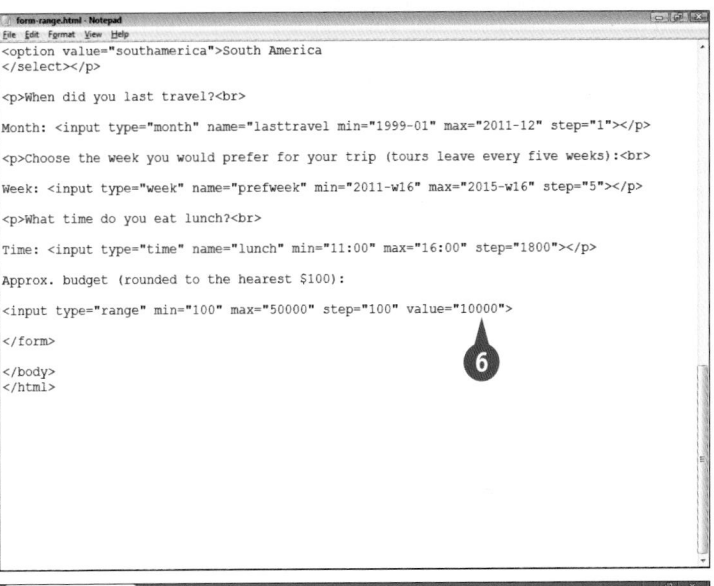

- The web browser displays the range slider.

- You can click and drag the slider to select from the range of numbers.

  To display the current value of the slider in your form, see the tip below.

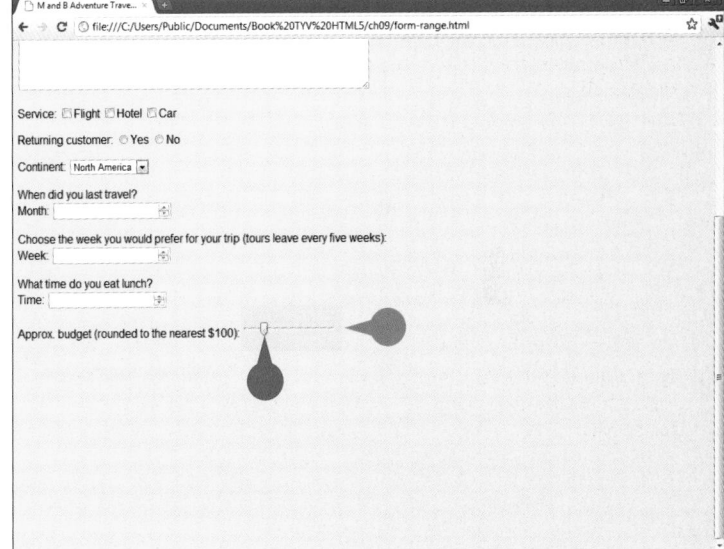

How do I display the current value of the slider?

As currently implemented by most browsers, the range input field is shown as a slider without the current value of the slider being displayed. You can display the current value using a `<span>` tag and JavaScript code:

1 Next to the range `<input>` tag, type `<span id="display">?</span>`, replacing *?* with the default value of the slider.

2 Inside the `<input>` tag, type `onchange="document.getElementById('disp').innerHTML = this.value"`.

The browser displays the initial value of the slider and then changes that value as the slider is clicked and dragged.

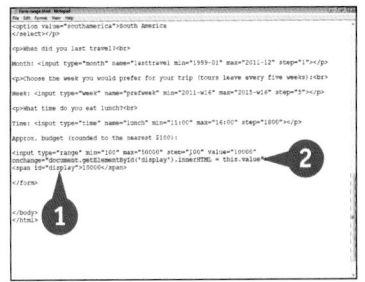

Add a File Upload

If you want users to send you files, such as resumes or photos, you can add a file upload element to your form. When you add the upload element, a Browse button appears with the field, allowing users to quickly locate the file they want to send. You can even limit what file types are allowed.

The upload element works only if your `<form>` tag's `method` attribute is set to `post`. See the section "Create a Form" to learn more about specifying a method.

Add a File Upload

① Make sure the `<form>` tag method is set to `post`.

② Within the `<form>` tag, type `enctype="multipart/form-data"`.

③ Type the text you want to appear before your file upload element.

④ Type `<input type="file"`.

5 Type a space and then
name="?">, replacing ? with a
name for the input field.

Note: Do not forget to type a closing
bracket (>) at the end of your input
element tag.

The web browser displays the upload
element on the form.

● Users can click a button to select a
file. The button label varies from
browser to browser.

● Clicking the button opens an Open
dialog box.

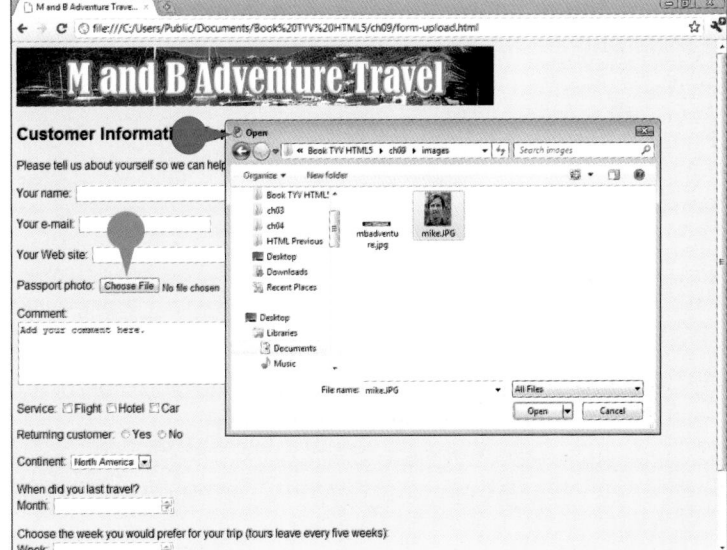

Add a Submit Button

You can add a submit button to your form so users can send you the data they enter into the form. It is common practice to add the submit button to the bottom of the form, below the text boxes, check boxes, radio buttons, and other elements. You can choose any label you want for the button. It is a good idea to choose a label that conveys to users that they need to click the button to submit their data. If you do not include a label, most browsers display "Submit" or similar text on the button.

Add a Submit Button

① Between the `<form>` and `</form>` tags, type `<input type="submit"`.

② Type a space and type `value="?">`, replacing ? with the text you want to appear on the button.

● The browser displays the submit button on the form.

When the user clicks the button, the form data is sent to the value of the `action` attribute specified in the `<form>` tag.

Note: For more about the `<form>` tag, see "Create a Form."

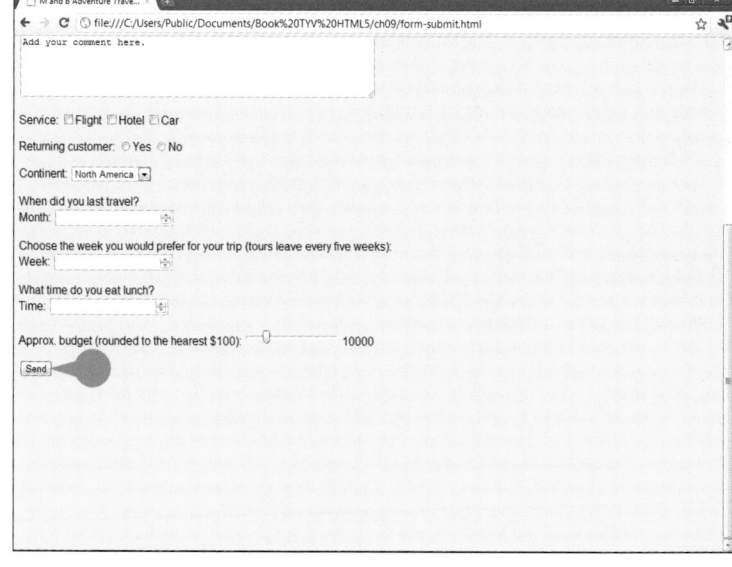

Add a Reset Button

You can add a reset button to your form to allow users to clear the data they have entered. For example, the user may want to type different information, or change his or her mind about submitting the information. A reset button lets users erase all the information they typed into the various input fields. It is standard practice to put the reset button at the bottom of the form, next to the Submit button.

Add a Reset Button

1 Between the `<form>` and `</form>` tags, type `<input type="reset"`.

2 Type a space and `value="?">`, replacing *?* with the text label you want to appear on the button.

If you do not include a label, most browsers display "Reset" on the button.

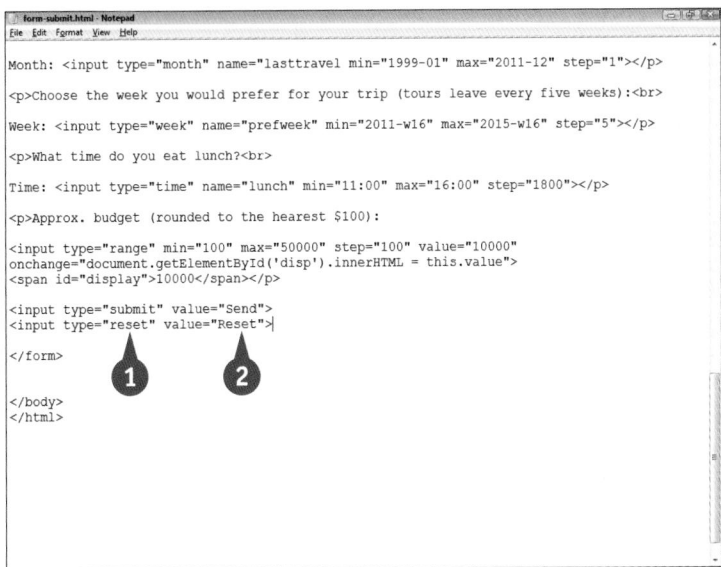

● The browser displays the reset button on the form.

When the user clicks the button, the form is reset to its original settings.

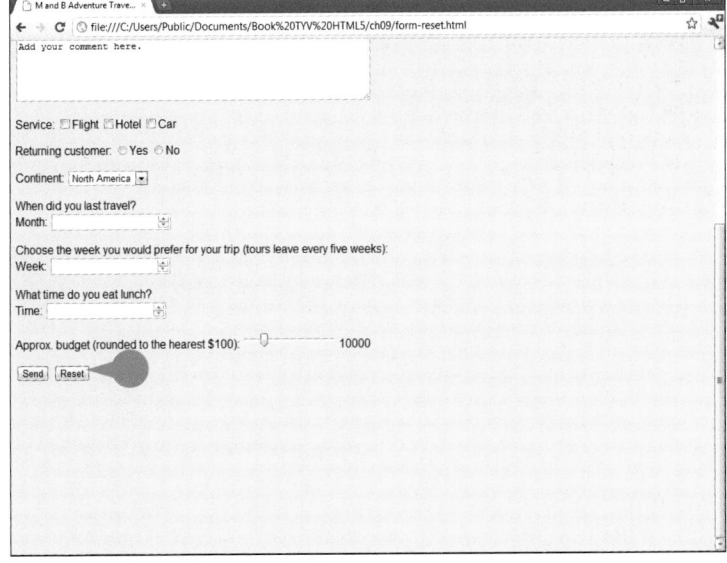

Require a Field

For some forms, you need users to fill in specific fields for form submission to be successful. For example, you may require a name and an e-mail in the submission of a contact form. You can mark these fields in your form using the `required` attribute. If you set a field to required, your users cannot submit the form until they have entered valid data in that field. In browsers that support this new HTML5 feature, attempting to submit the form without filling in a required field results in an error and the browser displaying an alert.

Require a Field

1 In the `<input>` tag for the field you want to require, type `required`.

In this example, the customer name field is required.

The `required` attribute does not require a value associated with it.

● Submitting the form without the required field filled in results in the browser canceling the submission and displaying an alert message.

Note: Browser support for required fields in forms varies.

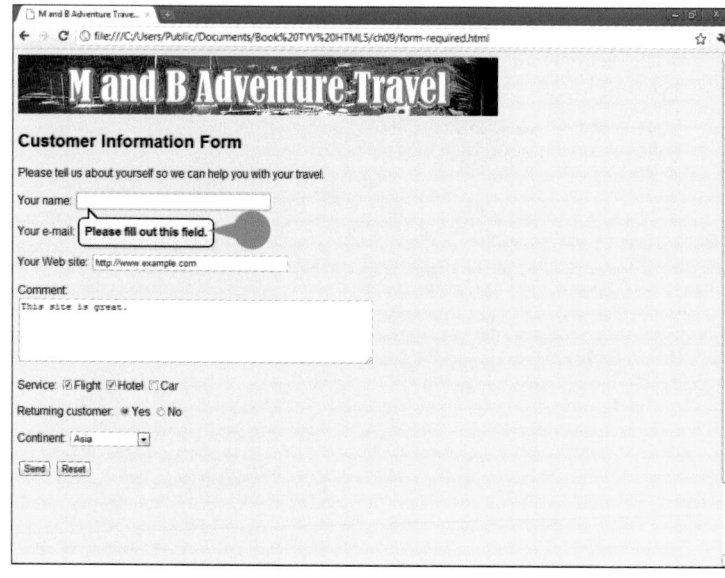

Add a Placeholder

You can add placeholder text to your form fields to add instructions to your users about how they should add data to the fields. The text appears inside the form field when the form first appears. If a user clicks inside the field, the placeholder text disappears and the user can type in the field as usual. In the past, web developers could add such a feature using JavaScript. With HTML5, you can add it by simply applying an attribute.

Add a Placeholder

1 Inside the `<input>` tag for the field to which you want to apply a placeholder, type `placeholder="?"`, replacing *?* with the placeholder text.

You can add placeholders to single-line and multiline text fields.

● The browser displays the placeholder in the text field when the form is first loaded.

Clicking in the text field causes the placeholder to disappear.

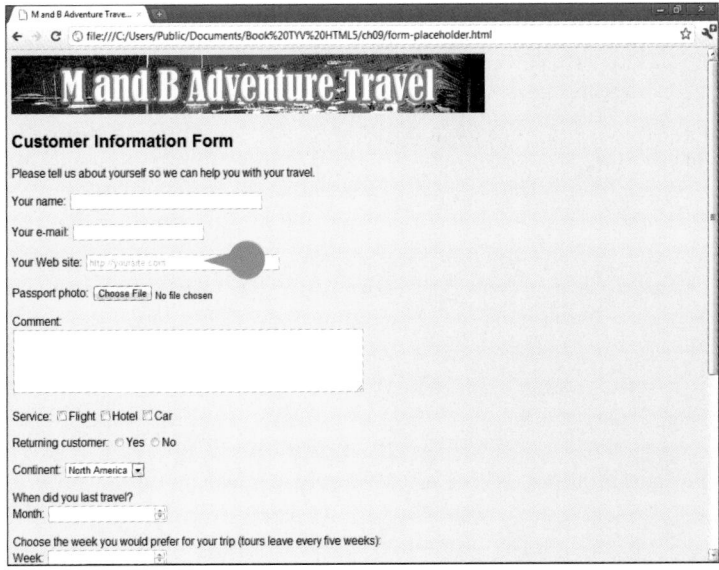

Validate Input with a Pattern

You can create custom text-field validation in your forms by including the `pattern` attribute in your `<input>` tags. The browser will check to see if the data in the field matches the defined pattern before submitting the form to the server. If there is no match, the browser aborts the form submission and displays an alert. You create a pattern using a language known as *regular expressions*.

This validation is just like what occurs with e-mail and URL text fields described earlier in this chapter. With the `pattern` attribute, you can create your own custom validations for specific types of text fields, in addition to e-mail addresses and URLs.

Validate Input with a Pattern

Accept Only Letters and Numbers

1 In the `<input>` tag for the field you want to validate, type
`pattern="[A-z0-9]*"`.

In this pattern, the brackets (`[]`) surround the characters you accept.

The `A-z` specifies you accept all uppercase and lowercase letters. You can use `A-Z` for only uppercase or `a-z` for only lowercase.

The `0-9` specifies you also accept numbers.

The asterisk (`*`) specifies that you accept any number of the characters specified inside the brackets, including none at all.

● If a user submits data that includes nonalphanumeric data, the browser cancels the submission and displays an alert.

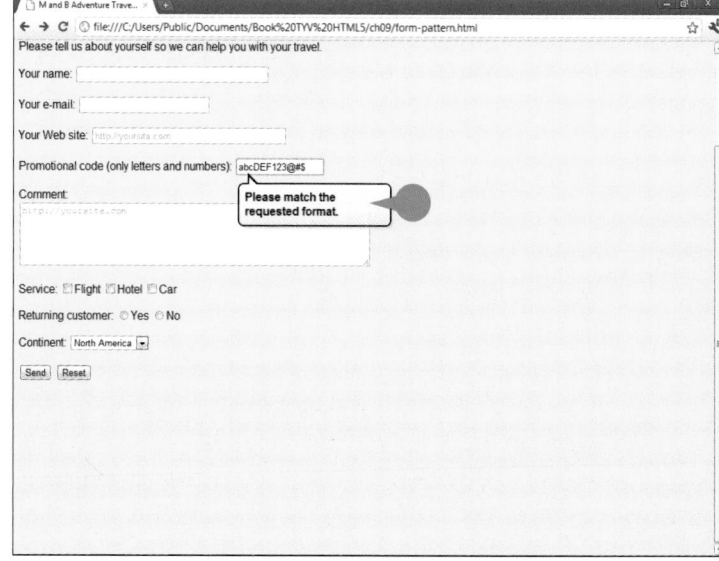

Accept a Phone Number Pattern

① In the `<input>` tag for the field you want to validate, type `pattern="?"`, replacing *?* with a pattern representing a phone number.

In this example, the form accepts a sequence of three digits, a hyphen, three digits, a hyphen, and four digits.

For each group of numbers, brackets (`[]`) surround the type of characters you accept. The `0-9` specifies that only numbers are accepted.

The braces (`{}`) describe how many times the numbers in the brackets should repeat.

The hyphens (-) not inside the brackets represent normal hyphens.

If a user submits data that matches the phone-number pattern, for example "555-555-1234", the validation succeeds.

● If the user submits anything else, the browser cancels the submission and displays an alert.

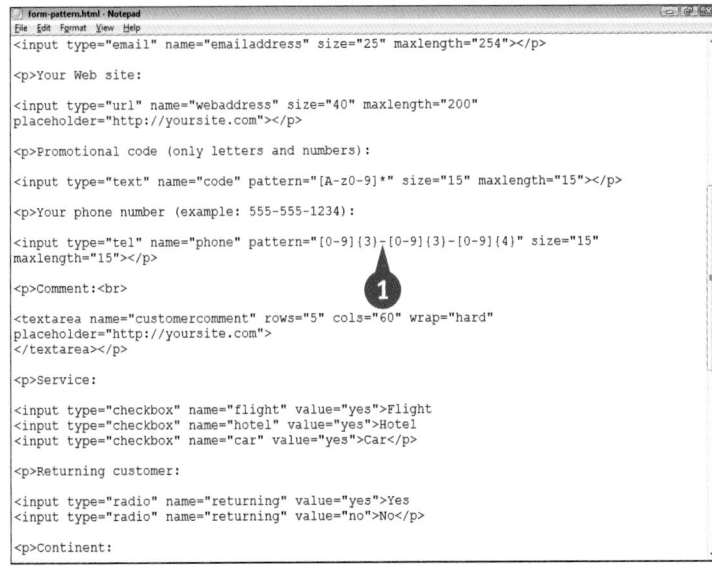

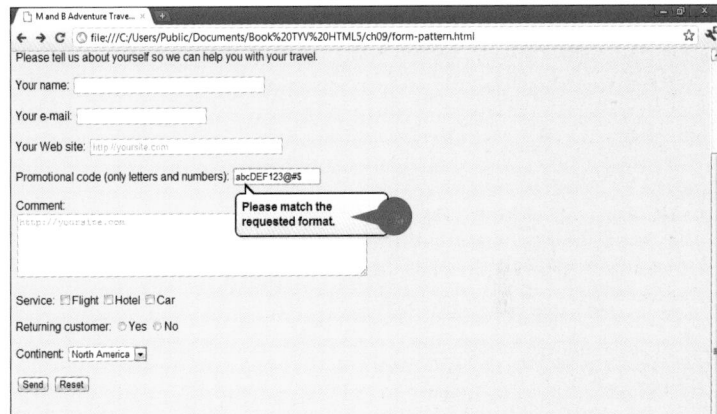

TIP

What are some regular expressions that I can use in my patterns?
The following are common regular expression patterns. For more information, see: www.wooldridge.net/html5

.	Any character, including letters, numbers, symbols, and whitespace.
[a-z]	Any lowercase letter.
[A-Z]	Any uppercase letter.
[A-z]	Any letter, lowercase or uppercase.
[0-9]	Any number.
*	Any number of instances of the character preceding it, including zero instances.
+	One or more instances of the character preceding it.
?	One or zero instances of the character preceding it.
{N}	N instances of the character preceding it, where N is a positive number.

Controlling Page Layout

Want to create complex layouts on your web pages, beyond what is possible using HTML5 alone? This chapter shows you how to precisely position text, images, and other elements on your pages using style sheets. Style sheets enable you to place content at set coordinates within your layout. You can also control the spacing around your page elements, wrap text around images and tables, and even overlap content.

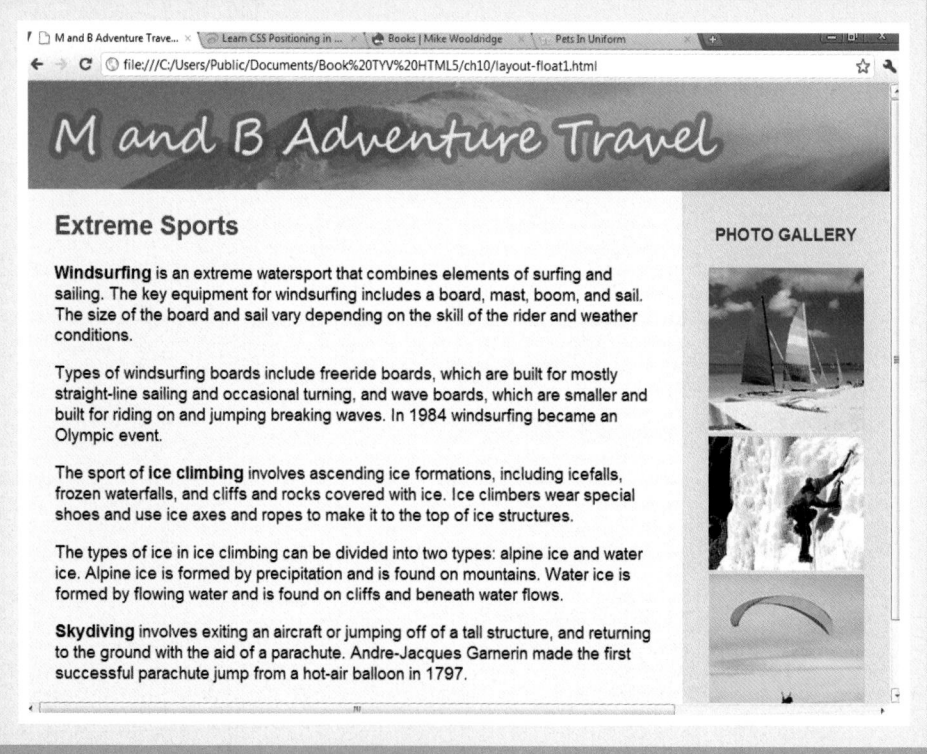

Control Layout

Y ou can use style sheets to organize text, images, and other elements on your web page in precise ways. This enables you to create more complicated layouts than those you can create with HTML tags. Style sheets allow you to specify where in a page to put different types of content by defining coordinates within the browser window. You can also precisely control the space around different elements and even overlap content on your pages.

By combining layout techniques with other CSS styles covered in Chapter 5, you can produce pages that look like they were created using a page layout program.

Box Model

The key to understanding layout using style sheets is the "box model" of web page layout, where each element on a page exists in its own rectangular box. Style sheets enable you to control the dimensions of the box using height and width attributes, where the box is placed on the web page, and how the box aligns or overlaps with other boxes on the page.

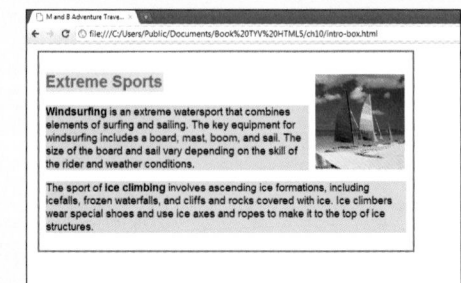

HTML5 Block Tags

You define boxes for your content using block-level HTML5 tags. Block-level tags place new lines before and after the content they enclose. The <p>, <h1>, and <table> tags are examples of block-level tags. So are the new semantic HTML5 tags such as <section>, <article>, <header>, and <footer> covered in Chapter 11, which enable you to define different sections of content on your page.

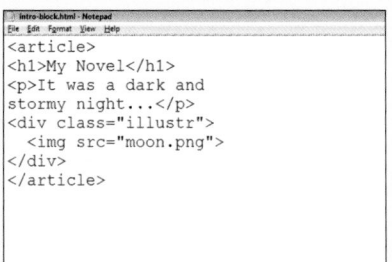

Positioning Content

You can use different types of positioning to place the boxes of content on your pages. *Relative* positioning places content on the page relative to the normal flow of the other content on the page. *Absolute* positioning places content on absolute points on the page relative to the containing block. *Fixed* positioning places content relative to the browser window and keeps it fixed as a user scrolls.

Mountain Biking   **Skydiving**

Offsetting Content

You can offset content on your web page from its normal position using top, left, right, and bottom style sheet properties. This enables you to place content in a precise position within the browser window. You can even place content completely outside of the browser window by using a large or negative offset value. You can also overlap content in the browser window by placing an element at the same window coordinates as another element.

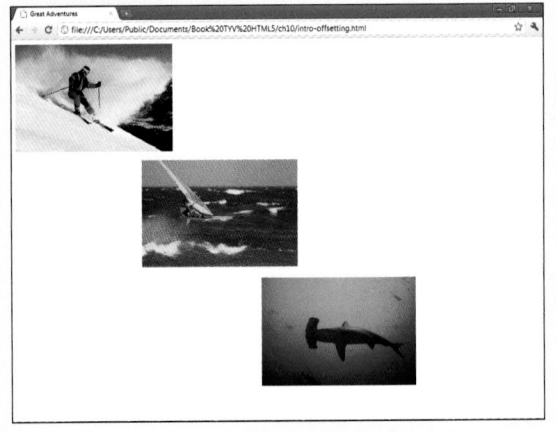

Padding and Margins

You can control the space that surrounds content inside each box on your page. Space outside the edge of the box is known as *margin* (●), whereas space inside the edge of the box is called *padding* (●). Style sheets enable you to control space on the top, left, right, and bottom of the boxes independently. You can also turn on borders, which appear where the margin and padding meet.

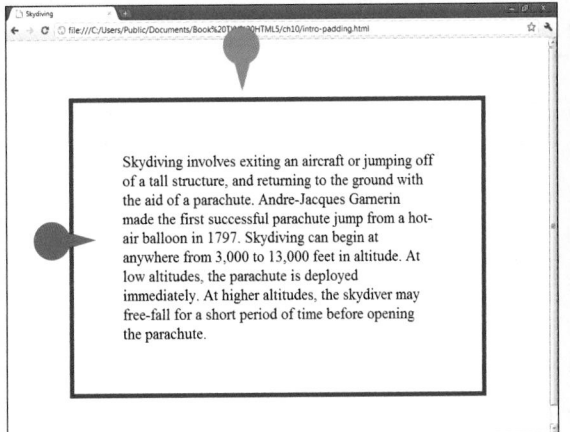

Floating Content

The float CSS property takes a box out of the normal flow of your page and moves it to the right or left side of the enclosing box. Content that follows then wraps around the floated element. Floating enables you to align images, paragraphs, page sections, and other content.

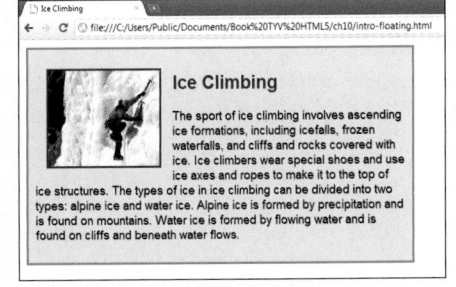

Set Width and Height for an Element

You can use the `width` and `height` properties in your style sheet to set the dimensions of your web page elements. For example, if you want certain paragraphs to take up a fixed amount of space in your page flow, you can apply a style rule as a class. See Chapter 4 to learn more about style sheet classes.

You can also specify a size based on a percentage. Percentage sizes are measured relative to the browser window or enclosing HTML tag. You can use the `float` property to make page content wrap around a resized element. See "Align Elements Horizontally" for details.

Set Width and Height for an Element

Define an Absolute Size

1 Click inside the tag declaration and type `width: ?; height: ?,` replacing *?* with absolute sizes for the width and height.

You can specify values in points (`pt`), pixels (`px`), millimeters (`mm`), centimeters (`cm`), inches (`in`), picas (`pc`), x-height (`ex`), or em space (`em`).

● In this example, the style is applied by assigning a class to a `<p>` tag. For more about using classes, see Chapter 4.

2 Type `class="?"` inside the HTML tag, replacing *?* with the class name.

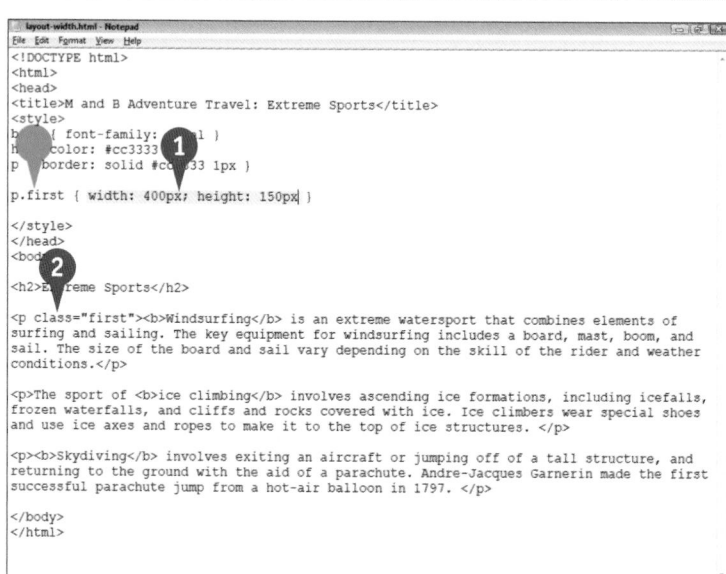

● The web browser displays the element with an absolute width and height.

In this example, borders are turned on to show the dimensions of the content boxes.

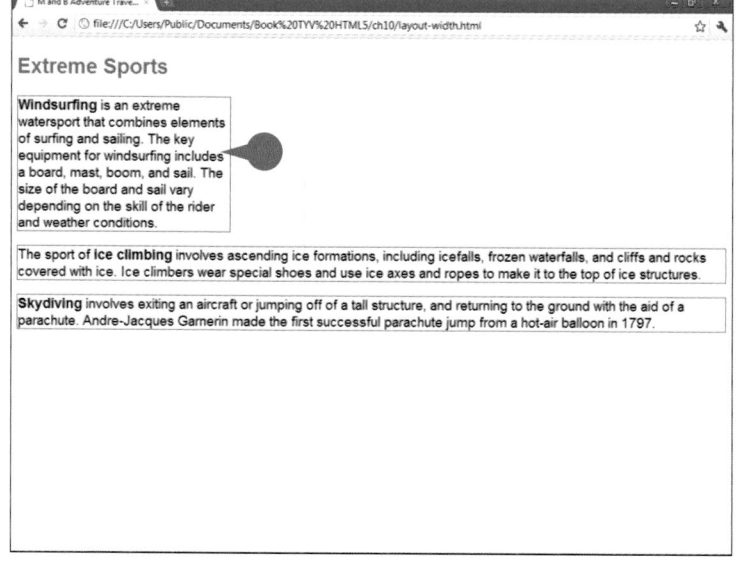

Define a Relative Size

1 Click inside the tag declaration and type `width: ?;` replacing *?* with a percentage size for the width.

Note: For percentage values, the height property is not supported consistently across browsers.

2 Type `class="?"` inside the HTML tag, replacing *?* with the class name.

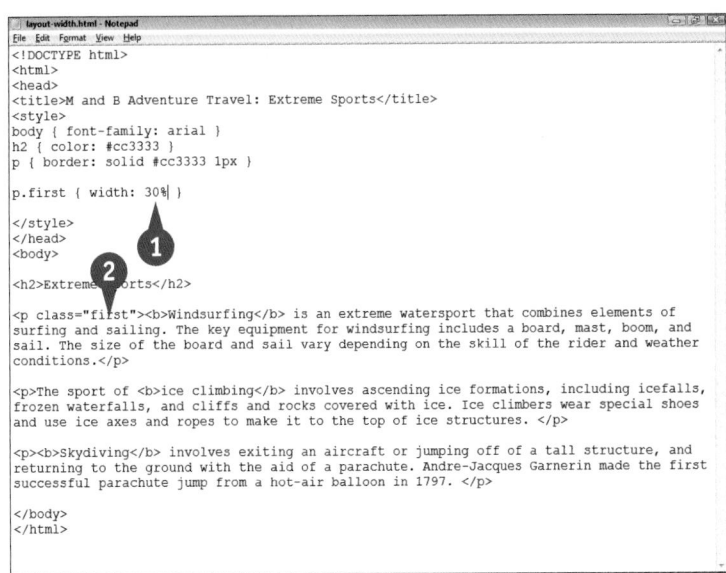

● The web browser displays the element with a width relative to the size of the enclosing box.

In this case, the enclosing box is the `<body>` tag, so the content is resized based on the browser window dimensions.

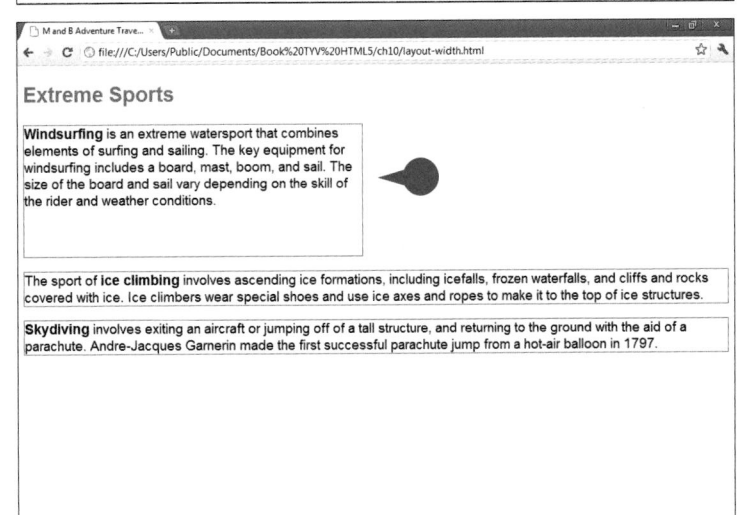

TIPS

What are the em and ex style sheet measures?
The em and ex measures enable you to define sizes on your pages based on the size of the surrounding text. The concept comes from typography, where em represents the width of the capital letter *M* and ex represents the height of the lowercase *x*. If you set a style sheet measurement to 2em, text will be twice the size of the normal font. If viewers adjust the font size of their browser, the content sized on your page using em also adjusts. The ex measure works similarly but on a smaller scale.

How do I control what happens to text that extends outside a CSS box?
You can control how text outside a box is handled using the `overflow` property. Setting the property to `visible` causes the text to be rendered outside the box. A `hidden` value hides the text outside the box. Both `scroll` and `auto` values display scroll bars for viewing the content, if needed. You can assign the `overflow` property to the `<p>`, `<div>`, and other block-level tags.

Use Relative Positioning

You can apply *relative* positioning to elements on your web page to place content relative to other content on the page. If you offset a relatively positioned element using the `top`, `left`, `right`, or `bottom` property, the element is offset relative to the point where it would normally begin.

For example, setting the `left` property to `50px` adds that much space to the left side of your page content, moving it to the right.

Use Relative Positioning

Apply Relative Positioning

1 Click inside the tag declaration and type `position: relative`.

● In this example, the positioning is applied to all the paragraphs on a page by defining a style for the `<p>` tag.

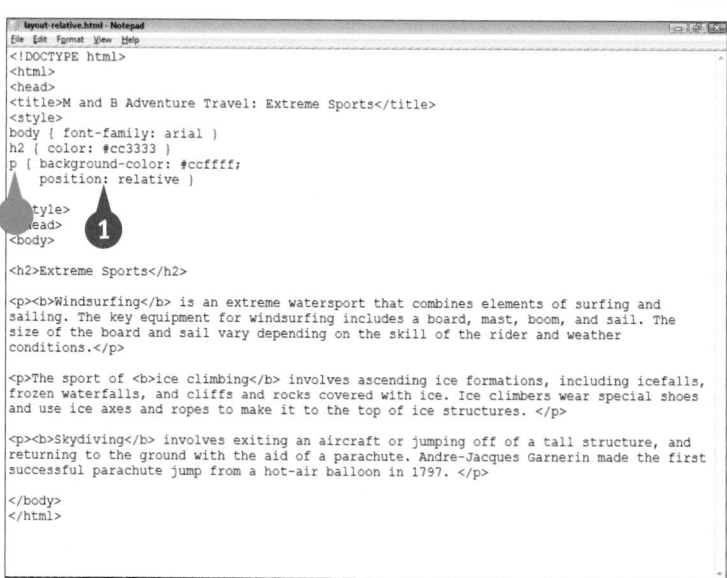

● The web browser displays the elements with relative positioning, one after the other.

In this example, a background color is applied to the paragraphs to show the dimensions of the content boxes.

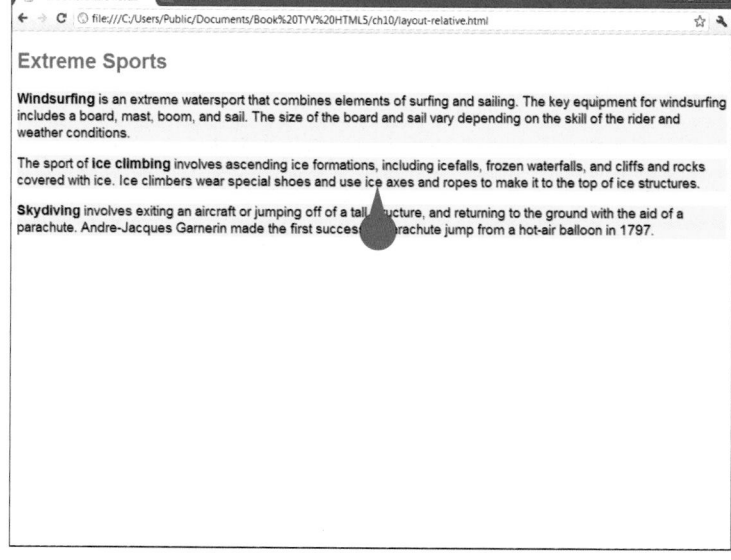

Apply an Offset

1 Click inside the tag declaration and type `top: ?;`, replacing *?* with the amount you want to offset the elements from the top of the normal page flow.

2 Click inside the tag declaration and type `left: ?`, replacing *?* with the amount you want to offset the element from the left of the normal page flow.

You can specify values in points (`pt`), pixels (`px`), millimeters (`mm`), centimeters (`cm`), inches (`in`), picas (`pc`), x-height (`ex`), or em space (`em`).

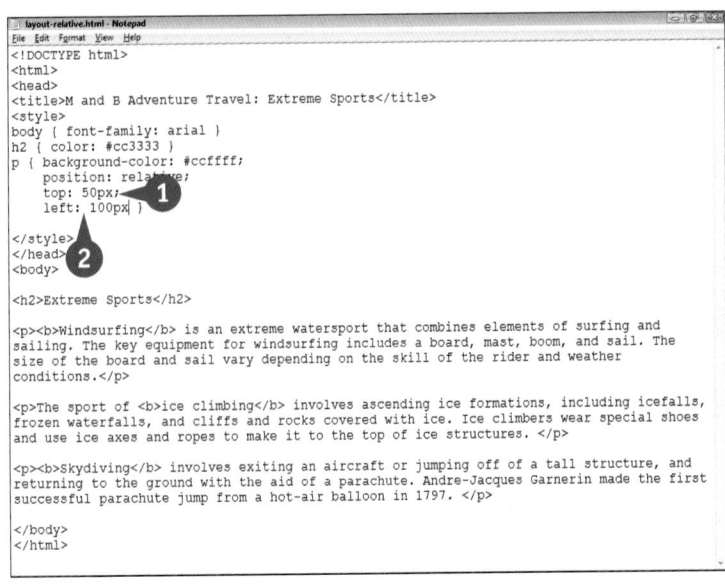

● The web browser displays elements with offsets applied. In this example, the paragraphs are offset relative to their normal position in the page flow.

Note: You can narrow elements on your page so that they appear within the browser window by setting their dimensions. See "Set Width and Height for an Element."

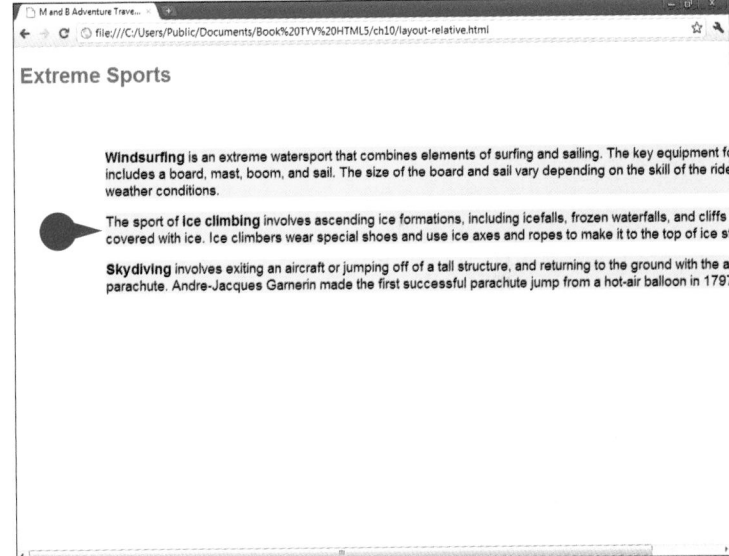

TIPS

Can I offset content from the bottom or the right?
Yes, but note that offsetting from the bottom may obscure the page content above the positioned element, and offsetting from the right can move content beyond the left edge of the browser window.

How can I position content outside the browser window?
You can apply a high positive or negative positioning value to the content. For example, you could set the `left` property to −5000px to move it far to the left, outside of view. You might want to do this for descriptive content that you want search engines to see but that you want to hide from human visitors. Another way to provide descriptive information for search engines is to add metadata. See Chapter 2 for details.

Use Absolute Positioning

You can apply *absolute* positioning to place an element at exact coordinates on a page, independent of elements that came before it. The coordinates are determined relative to the box that encloses it. This enables you to precisely fit together boxes of text, images, and other content on a page, like a jigsaw puzzle. You can set the coordinates using the `top`, `left`, `right`, and `bottom` properties.

Absolute positioning removes an object from the normal flow of page content. Its size and position have no effect on the position of content that follows it.

Use Absolute Positioning

1 Click inside the tag declaration and type `position: absolute`.

Note: In this example, absolute positioning is applied to an image using a style sheet class. For more about using classes, see Chapter 4.

```
layout-absolute.html - Notepad
File  Edit  Format  View  Help
<!DOCTYPE html>
<html>
<head>
<title>M and B Adventure Travel: Extreme Sports</title>
<style>
body { font-family: arial }
h2 { color: #cc3333 }
p { background-color: #ccffff; width: 600px }
img.right-align { position: absolute }

</style>
</head>
<body>

<h2>Extreme Sports</h2>

<img src="windsurfer.jpg" class="right-align">

<p><b>Windsurfing</b> is an extreme watersport that combines elements of surfing and
sailing. The key equipment for windsurfing includes a board, mast, boom, and sail. The
size of the board and sail vary depending on the skill of the rider and weather
conditions.</p>

<p>The sport of <b>ice climbing</b> involves ascending ice formations, including icefalls,
frozen waterfalls, and cliffs and rocks covered with ice. Ice climbers wear special shoes
and use ice axes and ropes to make it to the top of ice structures. </p>

<p><b>Skydiving</b> involves exiting an aircraft or jumping off of a tall structure, and
returning to the ground with the aid of a parachute. Andre-Jacques Garnerin made the first
successful parachute jump from a hot-air balloon in 1797. </p>

</body>
</html>
```

2 Click inside the tag declaration and type `left: ?`, replacing *?* with the amount you want to offset the element from the left.

Separate multiple style sheet rules with semicolons.

In this example, the image is offset 620 pixels from the left side of the page which will place it to the right of several paragraphs of text.

```
layout-absolute.html - Notepad
File  Edit  Format  View  Help
<!DOCTYPE html>
<html>
<head>
<title>M and B Adventure Travel: Extreme Sports</title>
<style>
body { font-family: arial }
h2 { color: #cc3333 }
p { background-color: #ccffff; width: 600px }
img.right-align { position: absolute;
              left: 620px }

</style>
</head>
<body>

<h2>Extreme Sports</h2>

<img src="windsurfer.jpg" class="right-align">

<p><b>Windsurfing</b> is an extreme watersport that combines elements of surfing and
sailing. The key equipment for windsurfing includes a board, mast, boom, and sail. The
size of the board and sail vary depending on the skill of the rider and weather
conditions.</p>

<p>The sport of <b>ice climbing</b> involves ascending ice formations, including icefalls,
frozen waterfalls, and cliffs and rocks covered with ice. Ice climbers wear special shoes
and use ice axes and ropes to make it to the top of ice structures. </p>

<p><b>Skydiving</b> involves exiting an aircraft or jumping off of a tall structure, and
returning to the ground with the aid of a parachute. Andre-Jacques Garnerin made the first
successful parachute jump from a hot-air balloon in 1797. </p>

</body>
</html>
```

③ Click inside the tag declaration and type `top:  ?`, replacing *?* with the amount you want to offset the element from the top.

④ Type `class="?"` inside the HTML tag to apply the style, replacing *?* with the class name.

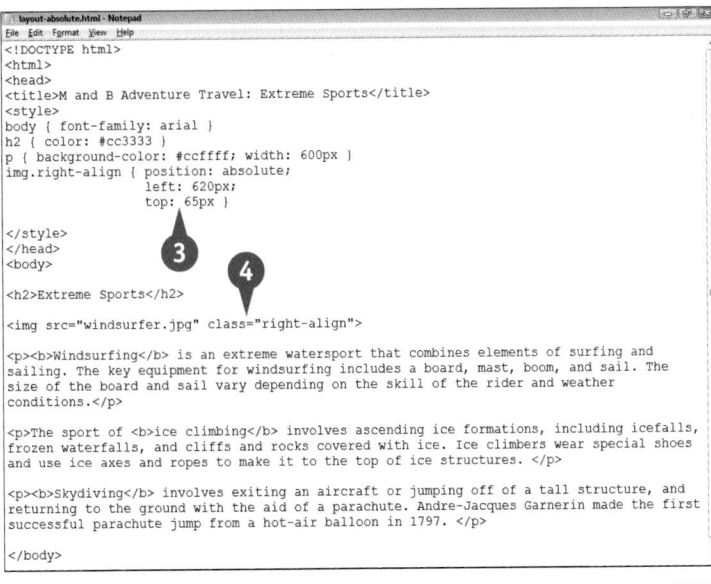

● The web browser displays the element with offsets applied.

The element is offset relative to the enclosing box, which in this example is the browser window.

In this example, the paragraphs are narrowed using a `width` property to make space for the image on the right.

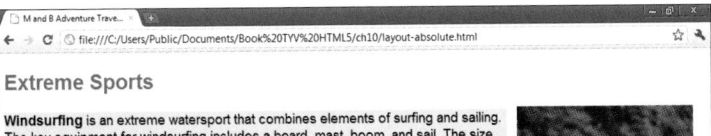

How can I apply absolute positioning to an image and a caption?

You can apply absolute positioning to an image and caption text by surrounding both with a single block-level tag such as `<figure>`, `<p>`, or `<div>`. Create a class that defines the absolute coordinates, and then apply it to the block-level tag using the `class` attribute. For more on creating classes with CSS, see Chapter 4.

How do I place an image in the bottom right corner of the browser window?

Create a class with absolute positioning similar to that in the example above, but set the bottom and right properties to 0. Apply the class to your image using a block-level tag such as `<figure>`, `<p>`, or `<div>`.

Use Fixed Positioning

Y ou can apply *fixed* positioning to place an element at exact coordinates on a page and have it remain fixed while a viewer scrolls. This is one way to keep navigation links visible as visitors view content on a long page. In contrast to relative and absolute positioning, fixed positioning is supported only in newer web browsers. Using fixed positioning on some page elements but not others can result in content overlapping when the user scrolls. How the elements overlap is determined by the z-index of the page elements. For more information about the z-index, see "Control the Overlap of Elements."

Use Fixed Positioning

1 Click inside the tag declaration and type position: fixed.

Note: In this example, fixed positioning is applied to a set of navigation links using a class. For more about using style sheet classes, see Chapter 4.

```
layout-fixed.html - Notepad
File  Edit  Format  View  Help
<!DOCTYPE html>
<html>
<head>
<title>M and B Adventure Travel: Extreme Sports</title>
<style>
body { font-family: arial }
h2 { color: #cc3333; position: relative; width: 600px; left: 200px }
p { position: relative; width: 600px; left: 200px; padding: 10px 0 }
ul { list-style-type: none; padding: 0 }
nav.left-side { position: fixed }

</style>
</head>
<body>

<nav>
<ul>
<li><a href="sports.html">Extreme Sports</a></li>
<li><a href="locations.html">Exciting Locations</a></li>
<li><a href="insurance.html">Travel Insurance</a></li>
</ul>
</nav>

<h2>Extreme Sports</h2>

<p><b>Windsurfing</b> is an extreme watersport that combines elements of surfing and
sailing. The key equipment for windsurfing includes a board, mast, boom, and sail. The
size of the board and sail vary depending on the skill of the rider and weather
conditions.</p>

<p>Types of windsurfing boards include freeride boards, which are built for mostly
straight-line sailing and occasional turning, and wave boards, which are smaller and built
for riding on and jumping breaking waves. In 1984 windsurfing became an Olympic event.</p>
```

2 Click inside the tag declaration and type left: ?, replacing *?* with the amount you want to offset the element from the left.

Separate multiple style rules with semicolons.

```
layout-fixed.html - Notepad
File  Edit  Format  View  Help
<!DOCTYPE html>
<html>
<head>
<title>M and B Adventure Travel: Extreme Sports</title>
<style>
body { font-family: arial }
h2 { color: #cc3333; position: relative; width: 600px; left: 200px }
p { position: relative; width: 600px; left: 200px; padding: 10px 0 }
ul { list-style-type: none; padding: 0 }
nav.left-side { position: fixed; left: 10px }

</style>
</head>
<body>

<nav>
<ul>
<li><a href="sports.html">Extreme Sports</a></li>
<li><a href="locations.html">Exciting Locations</a></li>
<li><a href="insurance.html">Travel Insurance</a></li>
</ul>
</nav>

<h2>Extreme Sports</h2>

<p><b>Windsurfing</b> is an extreme watersport that combines elements of surfing and
sailing. The key equipment for windsurfing includes a board, mast, boom, and sail. The
size of the board and sail vary depending on the skill of the rider and weather
conditions.</p>

<p>Types of windsurfing boards include freeride boards, which are built for mostly
straight-line sailing and occasional turning, and wave boards, which are smaller and built
for riding on and jumping breaking waves. In 1984 windsurfing became an Olympic event.</p>
```

③ Click inside the tag declaration and type top: ?, replacing ? with the amount you want to offset the element from the top.

④ Type class="?" inside the HTML tag to apply the style, replacing ? with the class name. In this example, the style is applied to a <nav> tag.

In this example, navigation links are fixed to the left of several paragraphs of text. The paragraphs of text are shifted to the right using relative positioning.

The web browser displays the element with offsets applied.

The element is offset relative to the enclosing box, which in this example is the browser window.

⑤ Scroll down the page.

Note: You may have to make your browser window smaller for the scroll bar to appear.

● The fixed content stays in the same place while the rest of the page content moves.

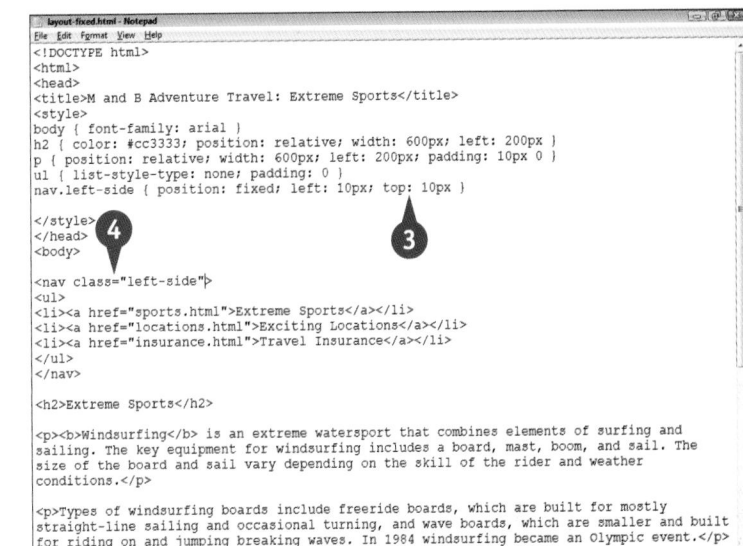

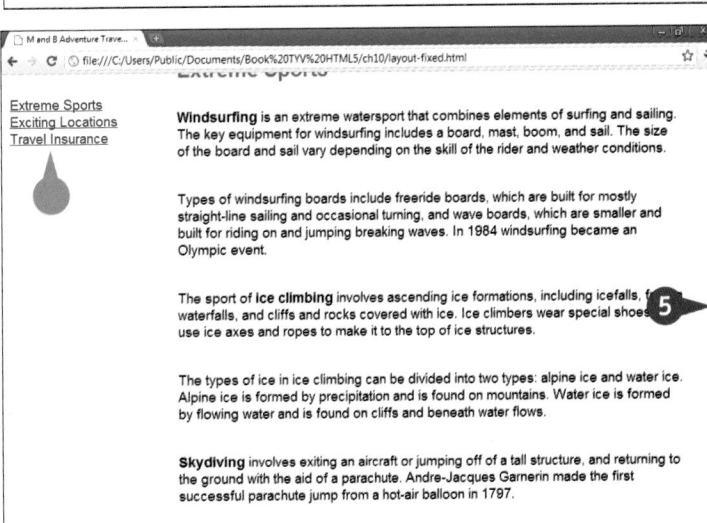

TIPS

What is static positioning?
When an element has its position property set to static, the element is placed in the normal page flow without any special relative, absolute, or fixed positioning. The static value is actually the default value for position. If you want to position content using left, top, and similar properties, be sure to explicitly set the position property to something other than static. Otherwise that positioning information is ignored.

What happens when fixed content and scrolling content overlap?
The scrolling content flows over or under the fixed content depending on the order the content is placed on the page and the z-index setting of the content. For more information setting the z-index, see "Control the Overlap of Elements."

Set Margins

You can control the margins of your web page elements using the `margin` properties. You can set margin values for the top, bottom, left, and right margins around a web page element. The margin is the spacing on the outside of a page element's border, whether or not the border is visible. To control the spacing inside the border, see "Add Padding."

You can set margin sizing using points (`pt`), pixels (`px`), millimeters (`mm`), centimeters (`cm`), inches (`in`), picas (`pc`), x-height (`ex`), or em space (`em`).

Set Margins

1 Click inside the tag declaration and type `margin-?:` and a space, replacing ? with the margin you want to adjust (`top`, `bottom`, `left`, or `right`).

2 Type a value for the margin spacing.

Typing `margin:` and then a spacing value adds that spacing around all sides of an element.

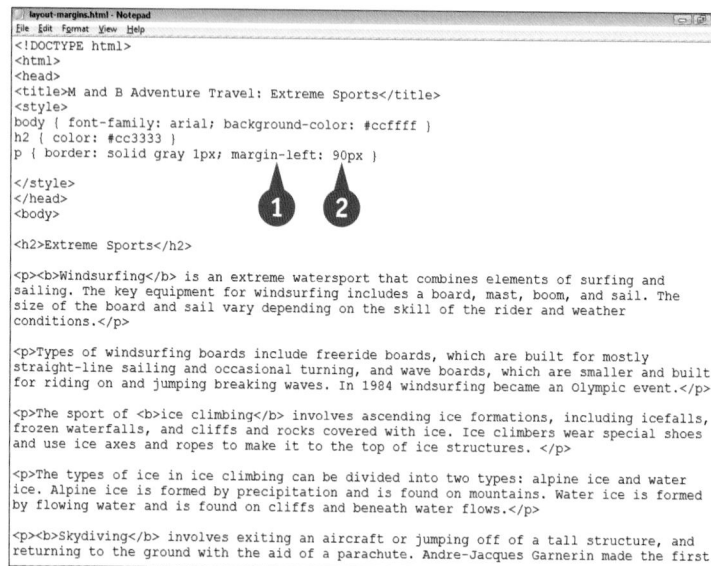

The web browser assigns margins to the web page element.

● In this example, 90-pixel margins are assigned to the left of the paragraphs on a page.

In this example, borders are turned on. Margin spacing exists outside an element's border.

Note: See "Add Padding" to learn how to add spacing inside borders.

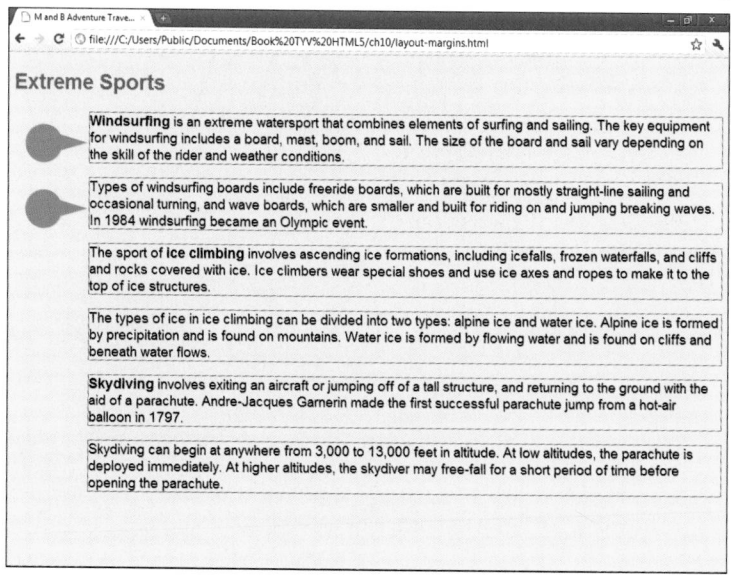

Add Padding

Y ou can use the `padding` property to add space around web page content. Adding padding can be useful for making text elements readable when they abut one another in a page layout. Padding is the spacing on the inside of a page element's border, whether or not the border is visible. To control the spacing outside the border, see "Set Margins."

You can specify padding in points (`pt`), pixels (`px`), millimeters (`mm`), centimeters (`cm`), inches (`in`), picas (`pc`), x-height (`ex`), or em space (`em`).

Add Padding

1 Click inside the tag declaration and type `padding:` and a space.

2 Type a value for the spacing.

To add padding to just one side, you can type `padding-?:`, replacing *?* with `top`, `bottom`, `left`, or `right`.

The web browser uses the assigned padding for the element to which the tag is applied.

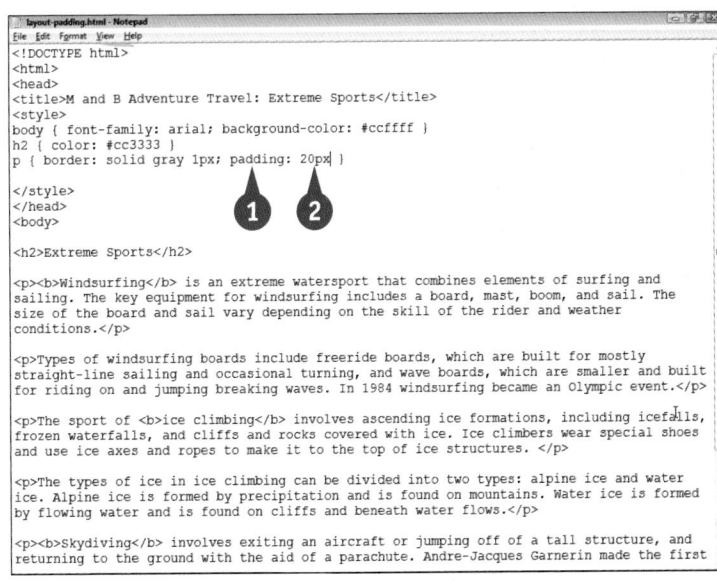

● In this example, 20 pixels of padding is assigned to the paragraphs on a page.

In this example, borders are turned on. Padding spacing exists inside an element's border.

Note: See "Set Margins" to learn how to add spacing outside borders.

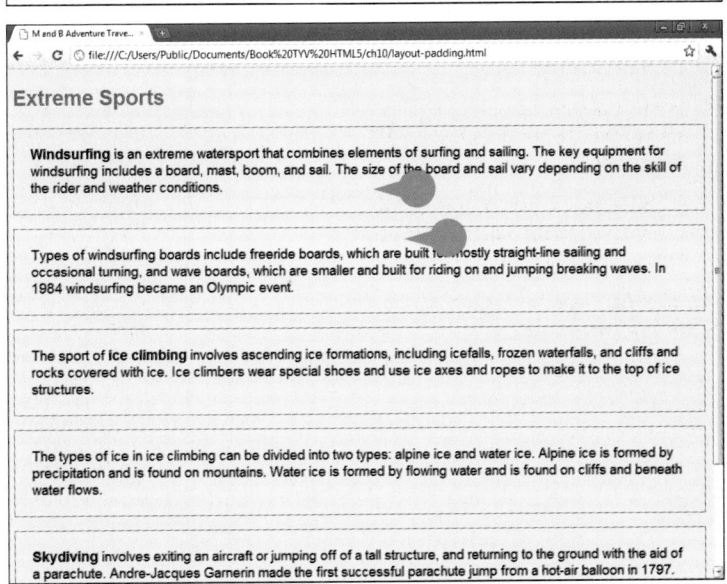

Align Elements Horizontally

You can use the `float` property to align sections of your page to the side of the browser window. The `left` value floats an element to the left side of the browser window or containing HTML tag, and the `right` value floats an element to the right side. Content that comes after the floated element in your HTML wraps around the other side. Using float techniques, you can create sidebars on your pages to display navigation, pull quotes, and other secondary content. By floating several smaller, rectangular elements to the same side, you can create a grid arrangement, which is useful for creating photo galleries. The `float` property does not work with elements for which you have assigned an absolute or fixed position.

Align Elements Horizontally

Create a Sidebar

1 Create the page content, placing the section to be floated before the wrapping content.

In this example, a narrow column defined with an `<aside>` tag and a `right-align` CSS class is floated to the right side. For more about the `<aside>` tag, see Chapter 11.

2 Click inside the tag and class declaration for the content and type `float:` and a space.

3 Type `left` to float the element to the left side, or type `right` to float the element to the right side.

● A margin has been added to the `<aside>` element to separate it from the content that wraps around it.

Note: See "Set Margins" for details about setting margins.

The web browser floats the element as directed.

● In this example, the `<aside>` element floats to the right of the text content.

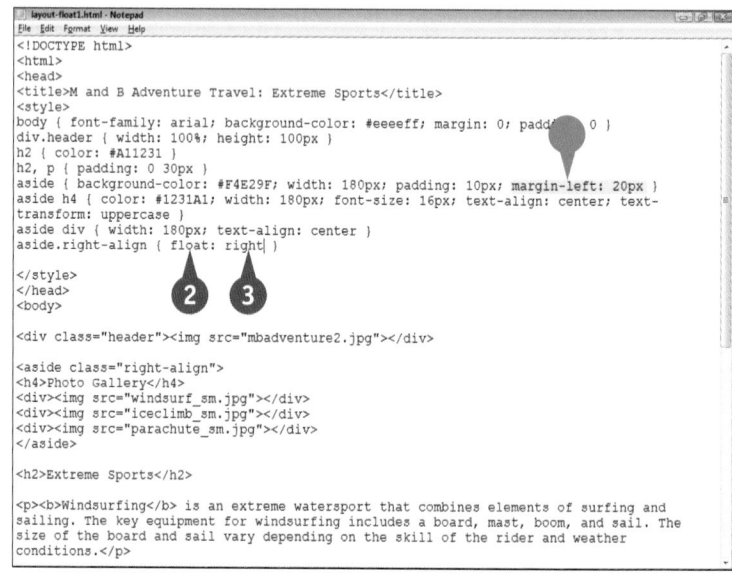

Create a Content Grid

1 Create the page content, placing the grid sections in sequence.

● In this example, images and captions are organized inside <div> tags with photo CSS class. For more about the <div> tag, see "Apply Styles with a <div> Tag."

2 Click inside the tag and class declaration you want to control and type float: and a space.

3 Type left to set the element to the left side of the text, or type right to set the element to the right side of the text.

● Padding has been added to the <div> elements to separate the images and captions from their containers.

Note: See "Add Padding" for details about setting padding.

The web browser floats the elements as directed.

● In this example, the <div> elements float to the left in a row until the space runs out in the browser window. Then another row begins.

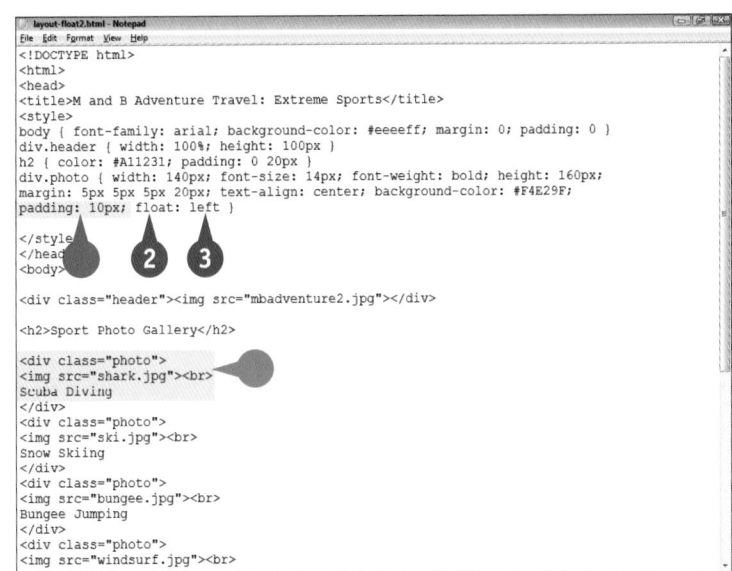

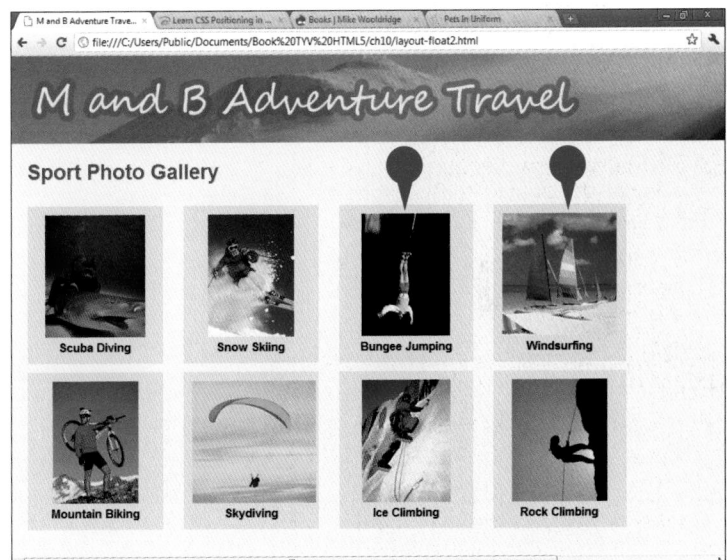

TIPS

How can I remove space between the edge of the browser window and my content?

You can set the padding and margin of the <body> tag to 0 and the margin of the content to 0. This removes any extra space between the browser window and the border of your content so that they are flush with one another. This technique is used in the examples above.

How can I center-align a grid of elements on my page?

You can surround the elements with a block-level tag and then set the text-align CSS property to center. For example, to center-align the photo grid in the example above, you can surround the grid elements with <div class="center-align"> and </div> tags, and then define the following CSS rule:

```
div.center-align { text-align: center }
```

Control the Overlap of Elements

You can use style sheets to overlap elements on your pages by positioning them at similar coordinates. You can then control the stacking order of those elements, adjusting the z-index property for each element. An element with a higher z-index value appears above an element with a lower z-index value. z-index values can be positive, negative, or zero.

See the "Use Absolute Positioning" section for more about setting the coordinates of a page element.

Control the Overlap of Elements

1 Create style sheet classes for the overlapping elements.

2 Use absolute positioning to arrange the elements on the page.

3 Apply the classes to the elements by typing class="?" inside the HTML tags, replacing *?* with the class names.

In this example, two images are overlapped.

Note: For more about creating style sheet classes, see Chapter 4. For more about absolute positioning, see "Use Absolute Positioning."

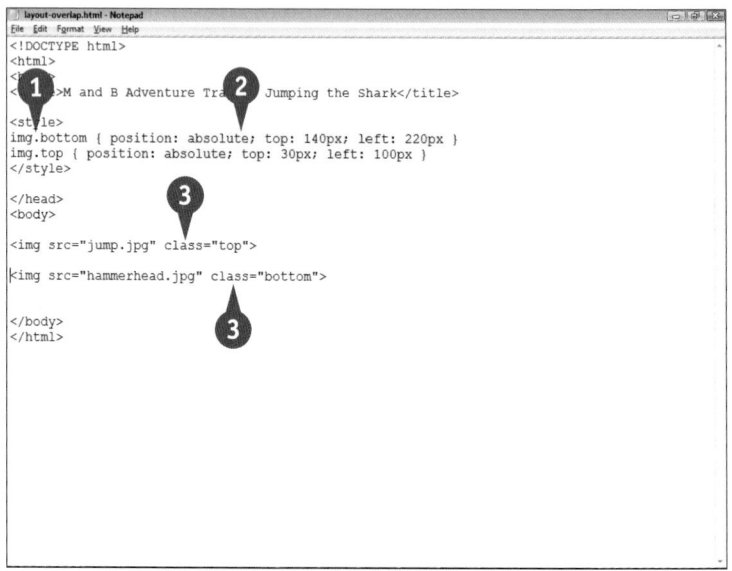

4 Inside the class declaration for the element you want on the bottom, type z-index: ?, replacing *?* with a number.

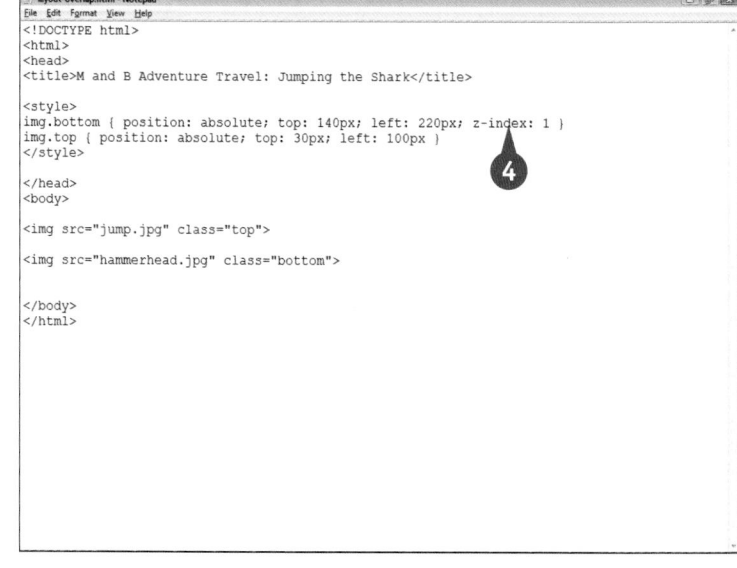

5 Inside the class declaration for the element you want on top, type z-index: ?, replacing ? with a number greater than the number in step **4**.

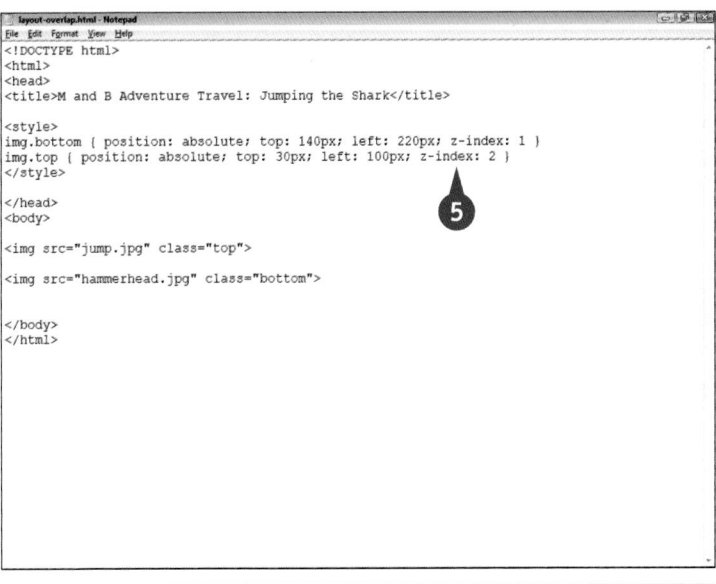

The web browser displays content with the stack order determined by the z-index values.

● In this example, the image with the z-index of 1 is on the bottom.

● The image with the z-index of 2 is on top.

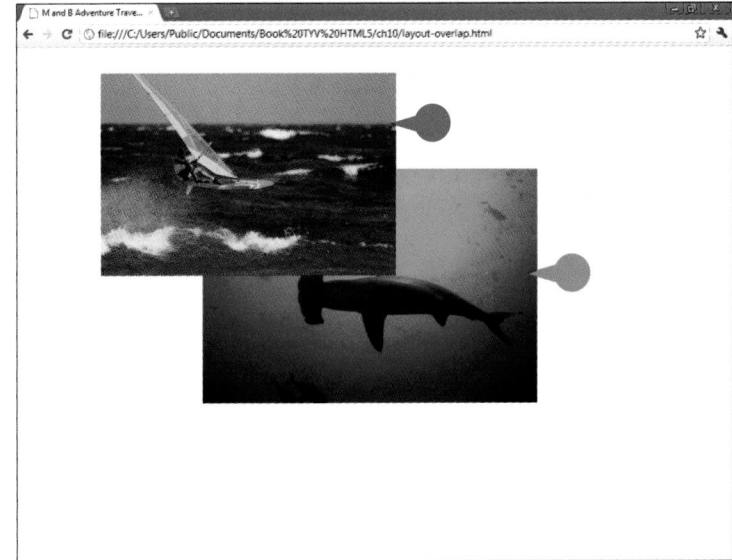

TIPS

Does it matter what actual z-index values I assign to elements on a page?
What matters are the relative values, since this determines the stacking order of elements. You may want to assign values that are spaced out to make it is easy to insert content in a stack later on. For example, if I have images with z-index values of 10 and 20, I can easily add an image between them by setting the z-index of a new image to 15.

How can I make an element transparent so that elements below it show through?
You can make content on your web page transparent by changing its opacity. However, different browsers recognize different style sheet commands for changing opacity. For Internet Explorer, you can type filter: alpha(opacity=?) in your style rule, replacing ? with a value from 0 to 100. For other popular browsers, you can type opacity: ? in your style rule, replacing ? with a fractional number from 0.0 to 1.0. You can put both properties in a declaration to make the effect compatible with as many web browsers as possible.

Apply Styles with a <div> Tag

You can use the generic <div> tag to apply styles to any block-level section of your page. Block-level sections have new lines before and after them — for example, paragraphs, headings, and tables. The <div> tag is commonly used to define areas of your page for layout purposes. For example, you can use the <div> tag to mark off the content on your page so you can fix the width or center it.

Unlike the semantic tags covered in Chapter 11, the <div> tag does not define a section of content as being of a particular type such as a header, footer, or set of navigation links. If your content is of a particular type and you want to apply styles to the content, apply the styles using a semantic tag if possible. See Chapter 11 for details.

Apply Styles with a <div> Tag

Apply the <div> Tag

1 Type <div> before the section you want to style.

2 Type </div> at the end of the section.

In this example, the tags surround all the page content.

3 To add CSS styles to the content, click inside the <div> tag and type class="?", replacing *?* with a class name.

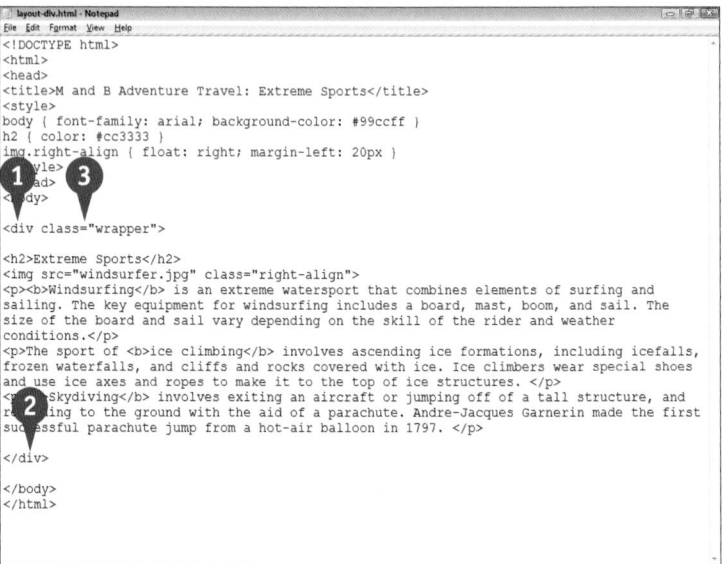

Apply Text Styles

4 In your style sheet, type div.?, replacing *?* with the name of the class.

5 Type a declaration to define styles for the text, separating multiple style rules with ; characters.

Note: For more about defining CSS style rules for text, see Chapter 5.

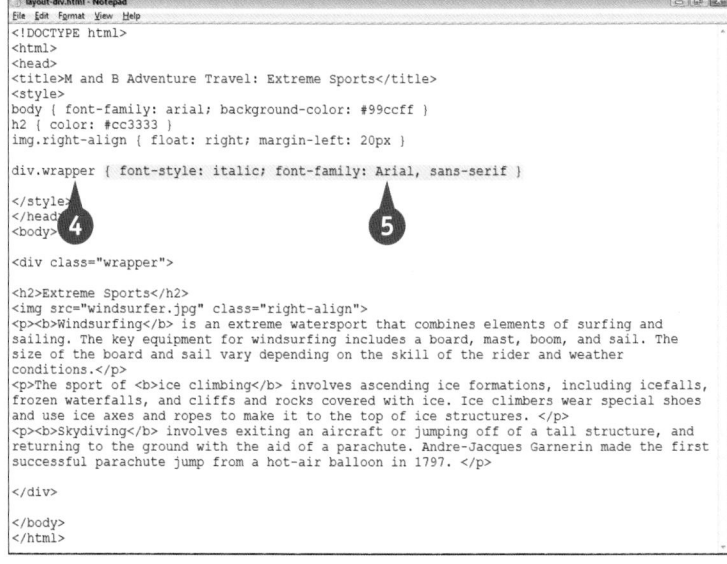

Apply Fixed-Width Centering

6 Within the style declaration, type `width: ?;`, replacing *?* with a page width.

You can specify width values in points (`pt`), pixels (`px`), millimeters (`mm`), centimeters (`cm`), inches (`in`), picas (`pc`), x-height (`ex`), or em space (`em`).

7 Type `margin-left: auto;`.

8 Type `margin-right: auto`.

Note: For more about setting widths and margins using CSS style rules, see sections "Set Width and Height for an Element," and "Set Margins."

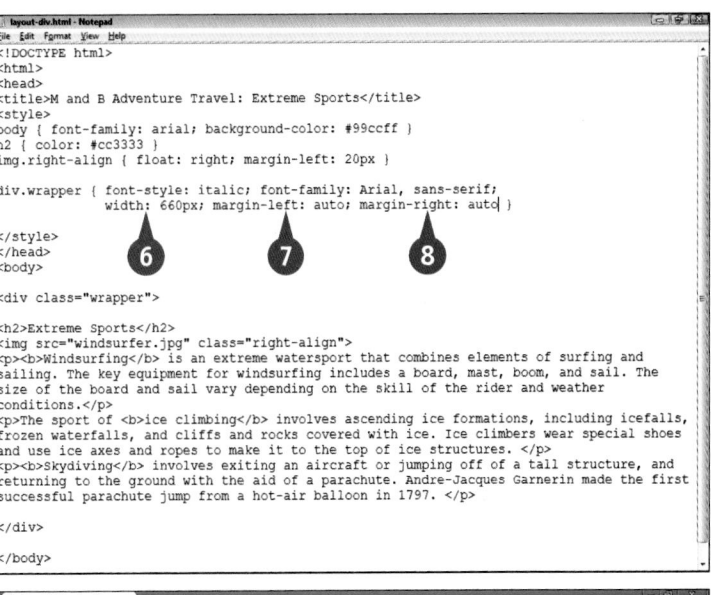

View the Page

● The web browser displays the page content as a fixed width in the center of the page.

Fixed width means that the content does not change width if you resize the browser window.

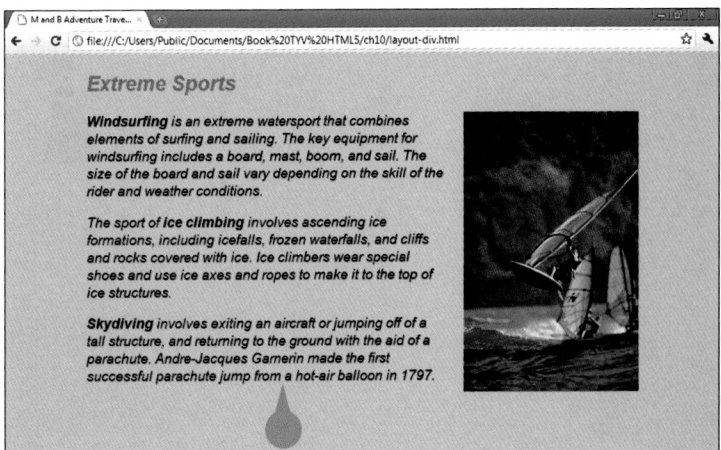

How do I apply styles to just one type of tag within a `<div>` tag?

You can be more specific in how you format the content inside your `<div>` tag by specifying a tag in your selector. For example, you can define the following style:

```
div.fancy p { text-transform: uppercase;
color: fuchsia }
```

This uppercases and colors only content inside the `<p>` tags within the `<div class="fancy">` section. See Chapter 4 for more about defining styles for nested tags.

How do I apply styles to inline content?

Inline content is text, images, or other content that appears within a line of content. The simplest example is words in a sentence. You can apply styles to inline content using the `<span>` tag. For example, the following can be used to apply CSS styles of the class "city":

```
<p>I'm going to <span class="city">Buenos
Aires</span>.</p>
```

Using the `<span>` tag keeps the text inside the sentence. If you were to use the `<div>` tag, new lines would be added before and after "Buenos Aires."

Adding Semantic Tags

Want to efficiently organize the different sections that make up your web pages? You can use the new *semantic* tags in HTML5 to define the meaning of these areas. For example, you can define part of a page as a navigation section with the `<nav>` tag and another part as a header with the `<header>` tag. Then you can create CSS rules to style those sections with colors and formatting, and then position the sections in different areas of the page.

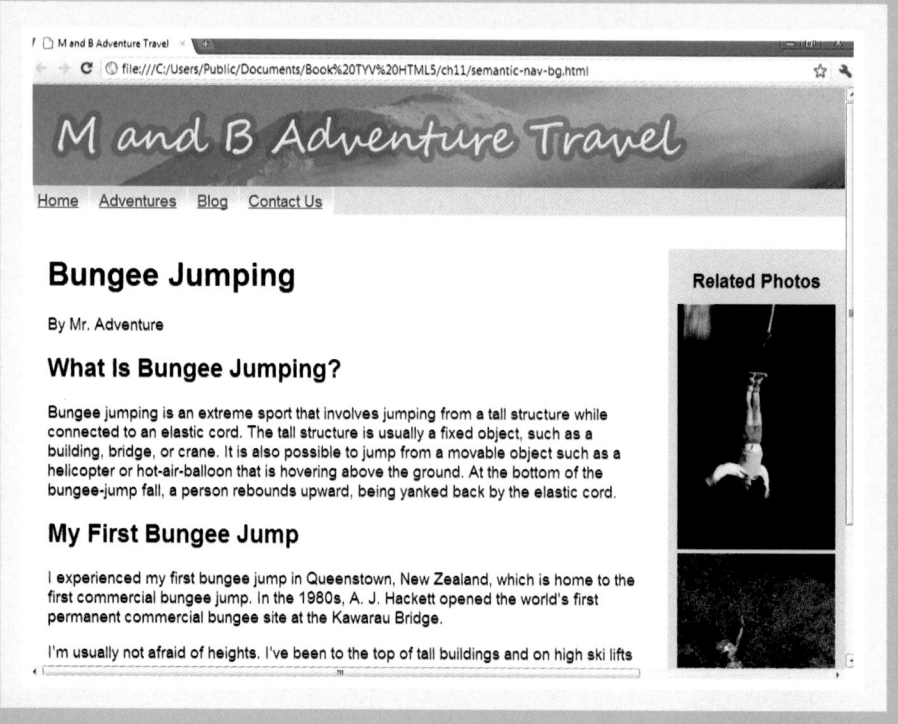

Define a Section

The `<section>` tag offers a generic way of grouping related information on a web page. The content inside the `<section>` tag typically includes a heading that tells what the section is about. You might use the `<section>` tag to define the main content on a page, or there could be several `<section>` groupings on a single page. The `<section>` tag is more specific than the `<div>` tag because the content within a `<section>` has a specific theme.

Other semantic HTML5 tags can be used instead of `<section>` when the meaning of the content is even more specific. For example, the `<article>` tag is appropriate for a newspaper story or a blog posting, whereas a group of navigation links should be enclosed in a `<nav>` tag. See the other sections in this chapter for details.

Define a Section

① Type `<section>` where you want to begin the section of content.

② Type the section content.

In this example, the `<section>` tag defines the introductory content of an article.

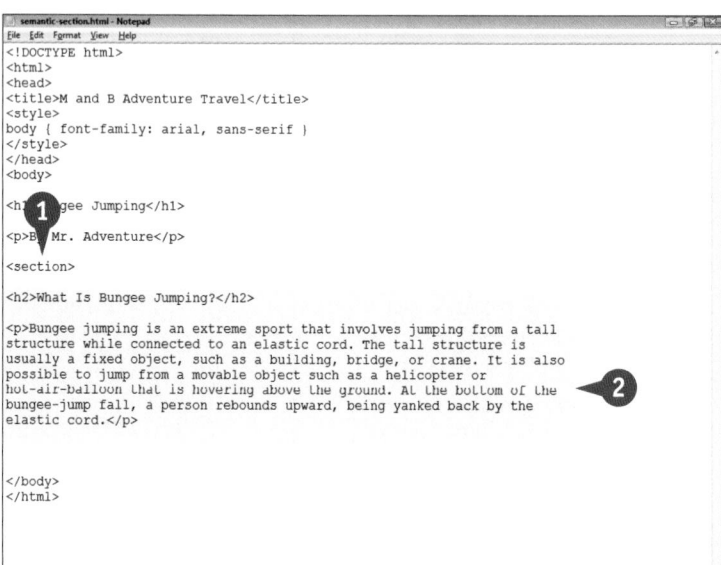

③ Type `</section>` at the end of the section content.

④ To add CSS styles to the section, click inside the `<section>` tag and type `id="?"`, replacing ? with an identifier.

The `id` attribute is used to apply style rules to a single instance of content on your page. For more details, see Chapter 4.

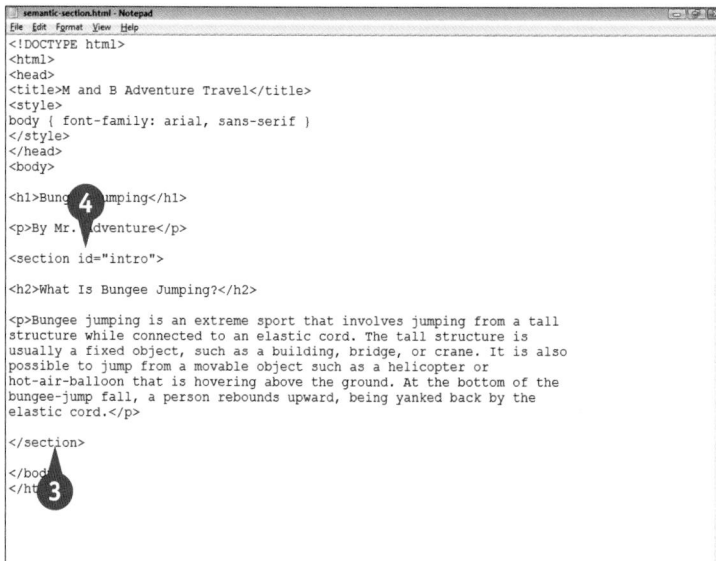

⑤ In your style sheet, type section#?, replacing *?* with the name of the identifier.

⑥ Type a declaration for the section, separating multiple style rules with ; characters.

Note: For more about defining CSS style rules, see Chapter 4.

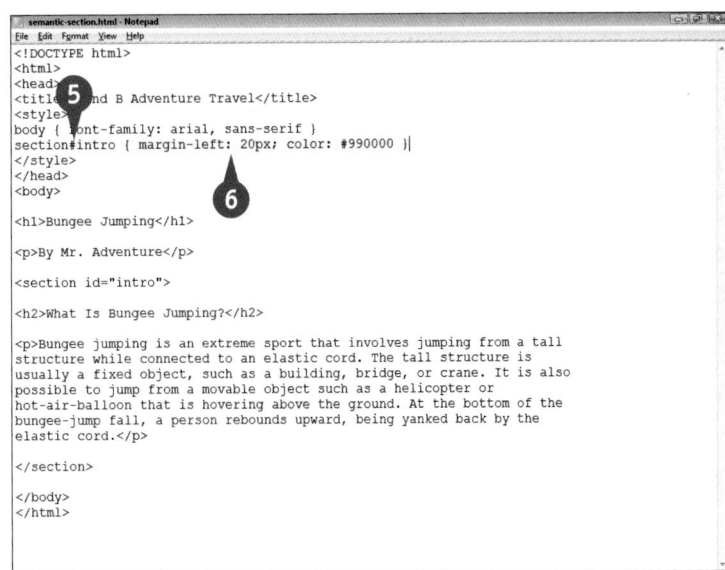

● The web browser displays the section in the page with the styles applied.

In this example, the section text is colored and indented.

You can repeat steps **1** to **6** to add more sections to the page.

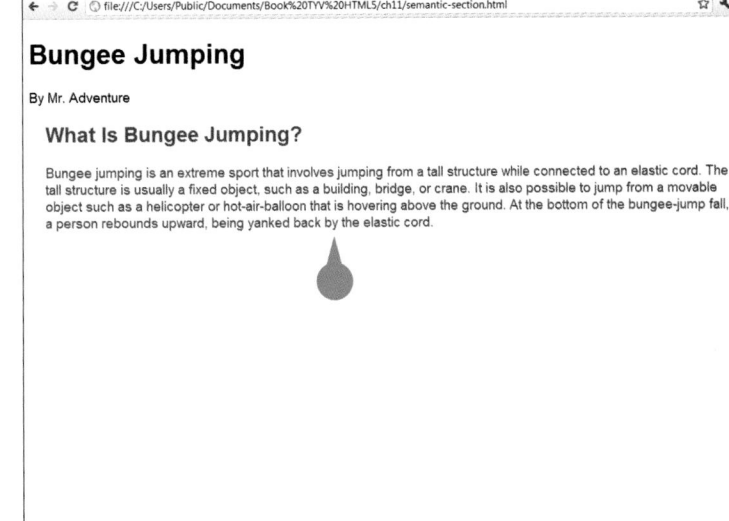

Why are semantic tags important?
Prior to HTML5, there was no standard way of defining common structures in the HTML of a web page. For example, you could define a page header with a `<div>` tag and a `header` class, but someone else might call their class `heading` or `head`. With semantic tags in HTML5, headings, navigation links, footers, and other common page elements are much easier to understand, both by computers parsing the code and web designers looking at it.

How do I apply the same styles to multiple sections on my page?
You can apply the same styles to all the sections on your page using the same CSS class. For more about defining and applying CSS classes, see Chapter 4. Or you can define styles for the `<section>` tag using `section` as the selector. Note that if you define styles for the `<section>` tag in an external style sheet and apply the sheet to multiple pages, that styling also shows up on the other pages.

Define an Article

The `<article>` tag is for defining a self-contained composition on a web page. Appropriate content for the `<article>` tag includes newspaper stories, magazine features, blog posts, or user-submitted comments. Inside the `<article>` tag are typically a title, author name, date of publication, and the main content for the article.

The `<article>` tag is more specific than the generic `<section>` tag. You can use CSS rules to style the content within an article tag. See Chapter 4 for more about applying CSS rules.

Define an Article

1 Type `<article>` where you want to begin the article.

2 Type the article content.

This example includes an article title in an `<h1>` tag, an article author, two subheadings, and several paragraphs of text.

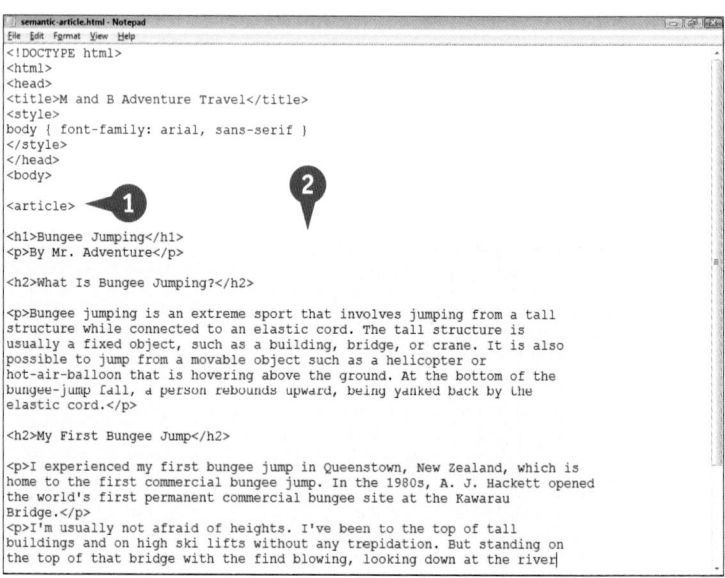

3 Type `</article>` at the end of the section content.

4 To add CSS styles to the article, click inside the `<article>` tag and type `class="?"`, replacing *?* with a class name.

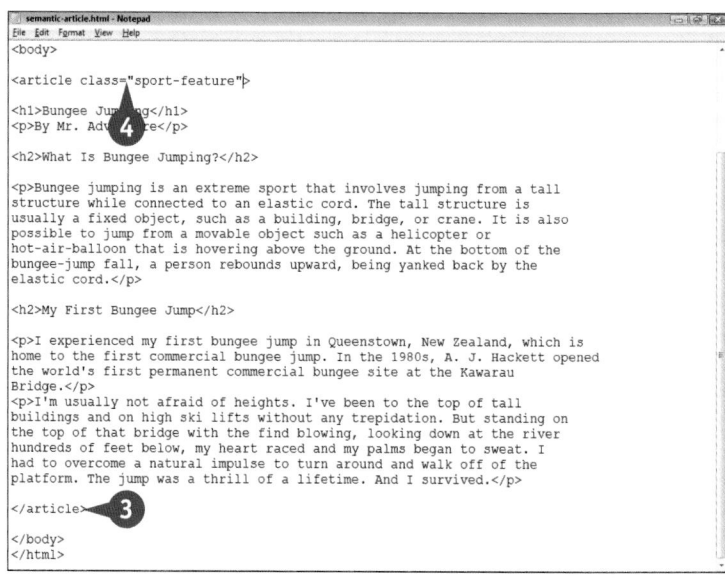

⑤ In your style sheet, type `article.?`, replacing *?* with the name of the class.

⑥ Type a declaration for the article, separating multiple style rules with ; characters.

Note: For more about defining CSS style rules, see Chapter 4.

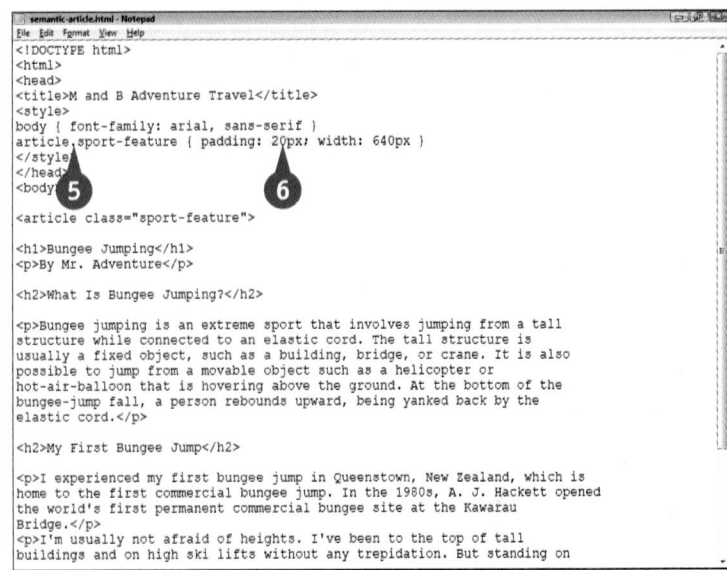

● The web browser displays the article in the page with the styles applied.

A page can have multiple articles on it. To add more, you can repeat steps **1** to **6**.

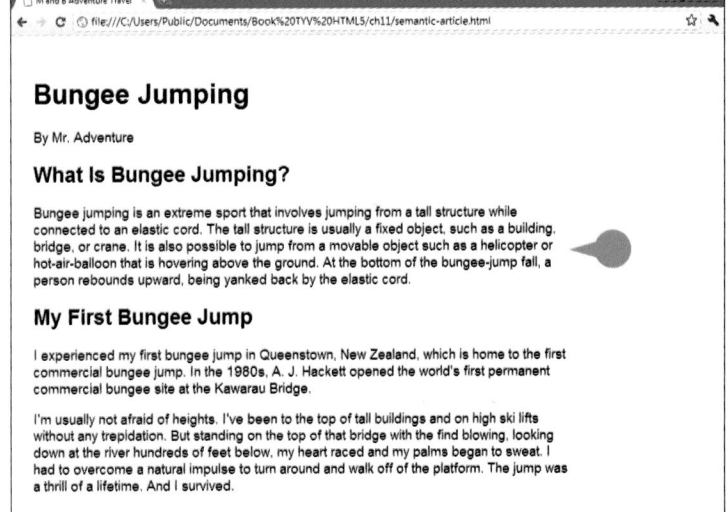

How do I define the publication date of article content?

Inside the `<article>` and `</article>` tags, you can place a `<time>` tag with a `pubdate` attribute to specify when an article was published. For example:

`<time pubdate datetime="2011-06-21"></time>`

If you want the date to appear on the page, you can add it between the `<time>` and `</time>` tags. For more information about the `<time>` tag, see Chapter 3.

Can I have articles within articles on my pages?

Yes. For example, a blog post defined with an `<article>` tag could have multiple comments associated with it. Each comment could be enclosed in its own `<article>` tag.

219

Define a Header

The <header> tag can be used to define the title of a web page or other introductory information. Typically <header> information appears at the very beginning of the body of a web page and encloses heading tags (<h1>-<h6>), an <hgroup> tag, or a header image. Common content in headers includes site names, company names and logos, and slogans. Navigation links, enclosed in a <nav> tag, can also appear in page headers. You can apply CSS rules to the <header> tag in an external style sheet and have those rules apply to instances of the header all across a site.

Define a Header

① Type <header> where you want to begin the header section.

② Type the header content.

This example shows a header displaying an image showing the website name.

③ Type </header> at the end of the header section.

④ To add CSS styles to the header, click inside the <header> tag and type class="?", replacing *?* with a class name.

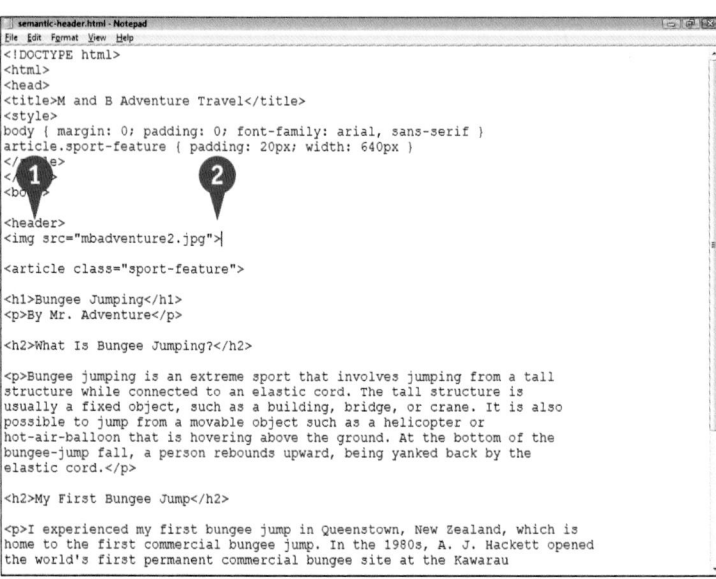

220

5 In your style sheet, type `header.?`, replacing *?* with the name of the class.

6 Type a declaration for the header, separating multiple style rules with `;` characters.

Note: For more about defining CSS style rules, see Chapter 4.

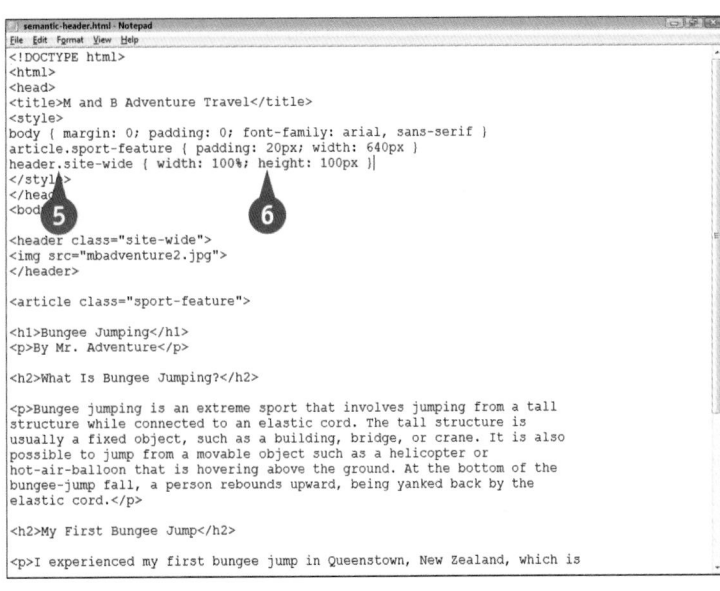

● The web browser displays the header on the page with the styles applied.

In this example, the header image stretches the entire width of the header box.

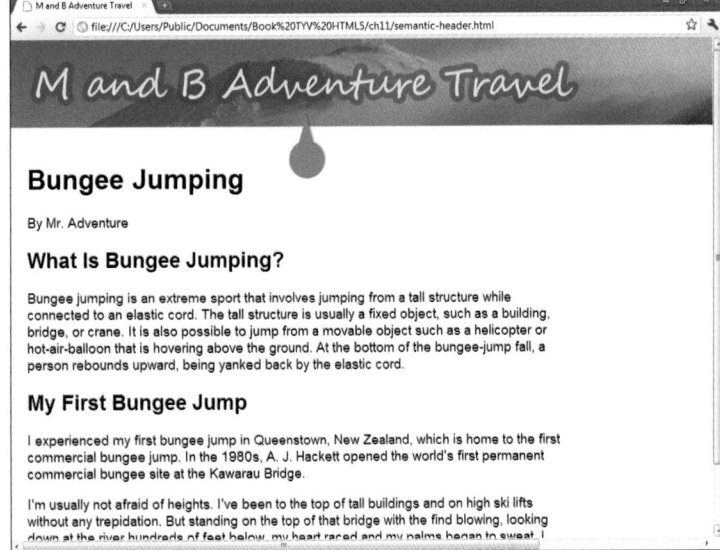

How do I use the <hgroup> tag?

The <hgroup> tag is a container for a set of two or more heading tags (<h1>-<h6>). The tag is typically used to group the title and subtitle of a page or article. For example:

```
<hgroup>
<h1>My New Blog</h1>
<h2>Enjoy my ramblings!</h2>
</hgroup>
```

The <hgroup> tag and the content it surrounds can go inside a <header> tag along with other content.

How do I make a header flush with the outside of the browser window?

By default, the <body> tag has a small amount of margin and padding associated with it that adds space between the browser window and a header. You can remove this default spacing by setting the margin and padding properties for the <body> tag to 0, as shown in the CSS rules in the example above. If you also set the margin property of the header to 0, your header content will be flush against the edges of the browser window.

Define Navigation

Y ou can use the `<nav>` tag to define a set of important navigational links to other pages on your site. By applying CSS rules to a group of `<nav>` links, you can display them in different ways — for example, as a row of buttons beneath a page header or as list in a column on the side of a page.

Defining navigational content with a special tag allows a browser to treat that content differently from the other content in your page. For example, a browser could temporarily hide the navigation if space was needed to display more essential information. For more about links in HTML5, see Chapter 7.

Define Navigation

1 Type `<nav>` where you want to begin the navigation.

2 Type the navigation links.

This example places the links in an unordered list.

3 Type `</nav>` at the end of the navigation links.

4 To add CSS styles to the navigation area, click inside the `<nav>` tag and type `class="?"`, replacing *?* with a class name.

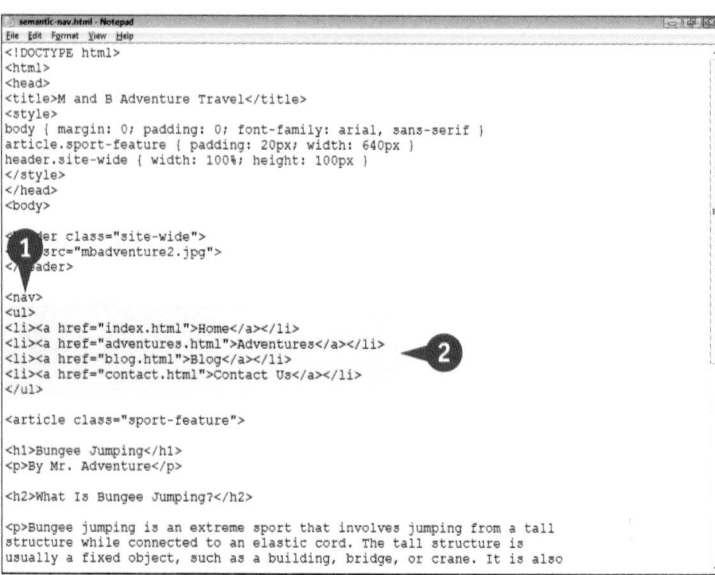

5 In your style sheet, type `nav.?`, replacing *?* with the name of the class.

6 Type a declaration for the navigation area, separating multiple style rules with `;` characters.

● This example includes styles for the `<ul>` and `<li>` tags that remove the list bullets and create a horizontal row of links.

Note: For more about styling bulleted lists, see Chapter 5.

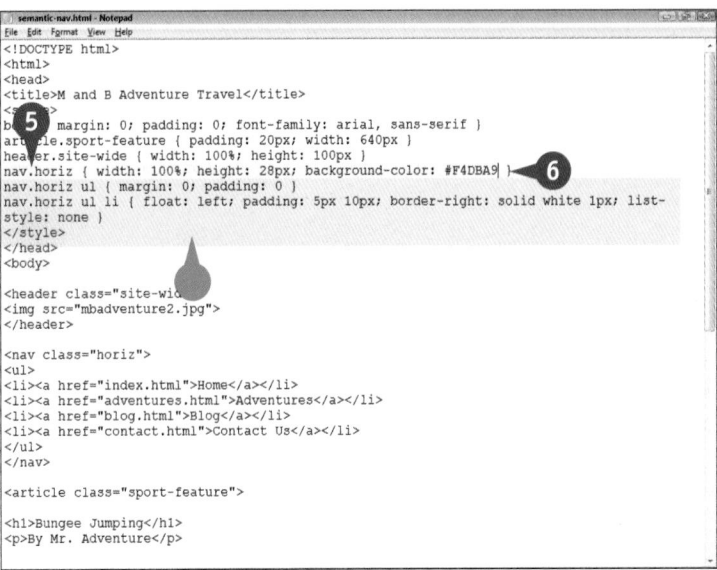

● The web browser displays the navigation area in the page with the styles applied.

Similar to the header, the navigation content spans the width of the page with the inner links aligned to the left, the default alignment.

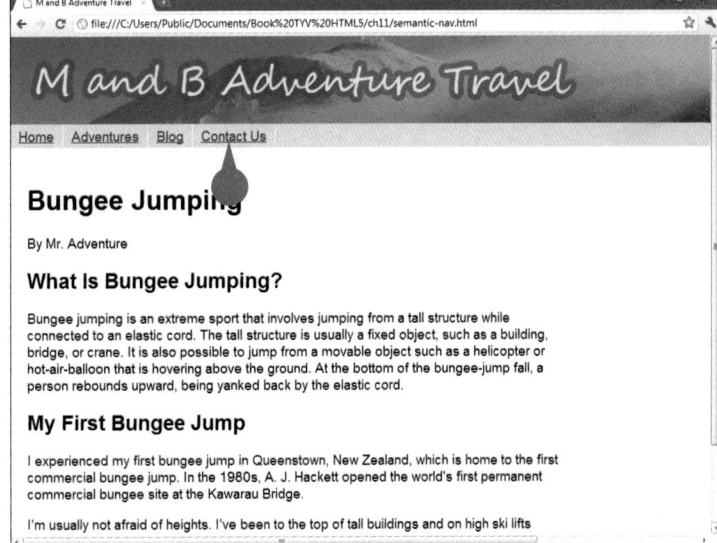

TIP

How can I give my navigation links fancy backgrounds?
You can give your navigation links fancy multicolor or gradient backgrounds by applying a background image to the links. Using the same HTML as in the example above, you can follow these steps:

1 Create and save your background image in an image editor. Save the image in a web-friendly format such as JPEG, GIF, or PNG in the same directory as your HTML file.

2 In the style declaration for the `<li>` tag, type `background-image:url('?')`, replacing *?* with the name of the image file.

Note: The web browser places the image behind the link text. For more about background images, see Chapter 6.

Define an Aside

You can mark information on your page as tangential to the main content with the `<aside>` tag. The `<aside>` tag is useful for defining pull quotes, glossary terms, or sets of links related to an article. According to the HTML5 specification, information in an `<aside>` tag should be related to the main content on the page. However, the main content should also be understandable with the `<aside>` content removed. A browser might hide `<aside>` information to save space on the screen. You can apply CSS rules to the `<aside>` tag to distinguish the information visually from the main content of the page.

Define an Aside

1 Type `<aside>` where you want to begin the aside section.

2 Type the aside content.

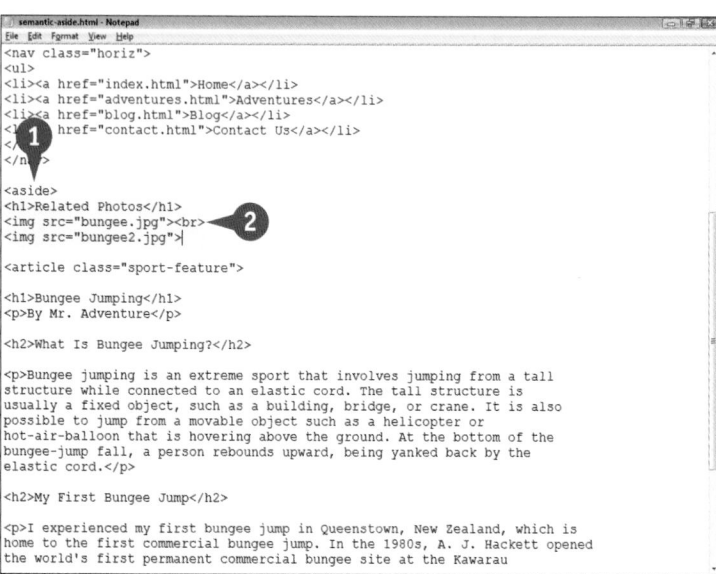

3 Type `</aside>` at the end of the aside section.

4 To add CSS styles to the aside section, click inside the `<aside>` tag and type `class="?"`, replacing *?* with a class name.

5 In your style sheet, type `aside.?`, replacing *?* with the name of the class.

6 Type a declaration for the aside section, separating multiple style rules with `;` characters.

Note: For more about defining CSS style rules, see Chapter 4.

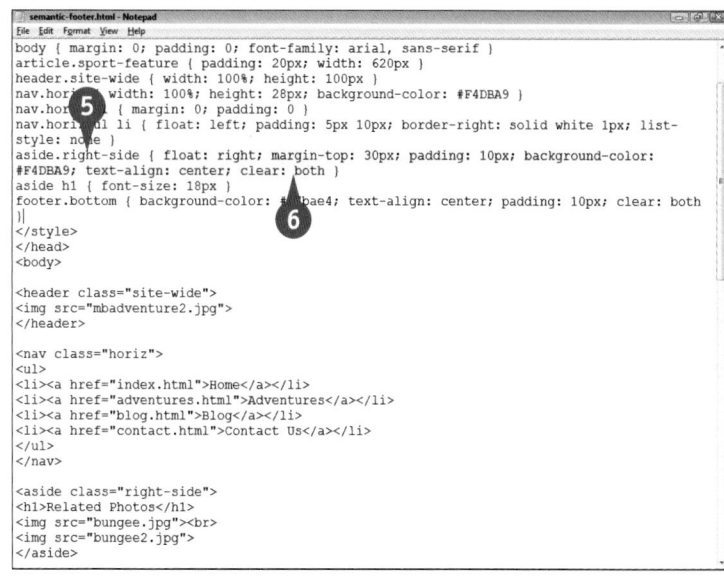

● The web browser displays the aside section on the page with the styles applied.

This example floats to the right side of the page with the article wrapped to its left.

Note: For more about using the CSS float property to align content, see Chapter 10.

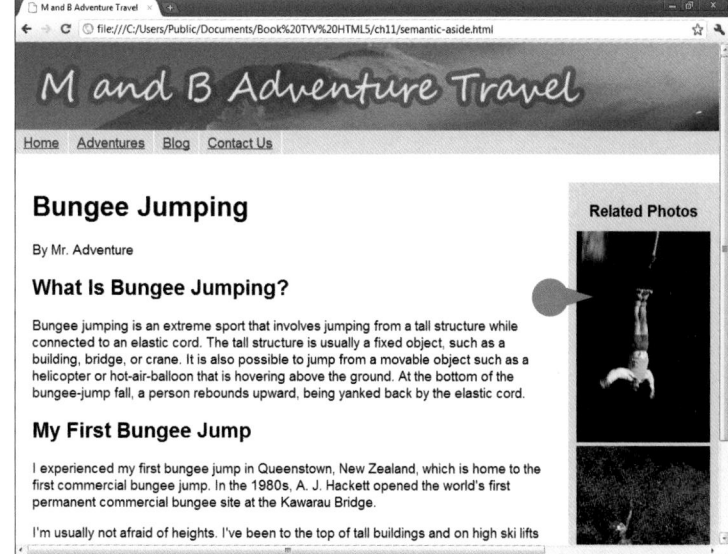

TIPS

What determines the width of my aside content?
In the example above, because no CSS `width` property is explicitly defined for the `<aside>` box, the size of the inner content determines the width along with any `padding` settings. You can widen the box by applying a `width` property to the `<aside>` CSS declaration.

How can I place columns of aside content on both sides of my page?
If you want to have columns of aside content on both the left and right side of your page, you can place two `<aside>` boxes before your main content. Then, using the CSS `float` property, align one column to the left and the other to the right. The main content coming after the aside boxes flows in between.

Define a Footer

A footer is a place to put copyright information, a contact address, links to terms of service, and other small-print items on a page. It typically goes at the end of your page, before the closing </body> tag. You can define your footer using the <footer> tag, which is new in HTML5.

The <footer> tag is a counterpart to the <header> tag, which typically goes at the top of the page. According to the HTML5 specification, a <footer> cannot contain a <header> and vice versa. Footers can go at the end of sections of your page such as articles, and you can have multiple footers on a single page.

Define a Footer

1 Type <footer> where you want to begin the footer section.

2 Type the footer content.

In this example, the footer includes a copyright notice and a link to terms and conditions.

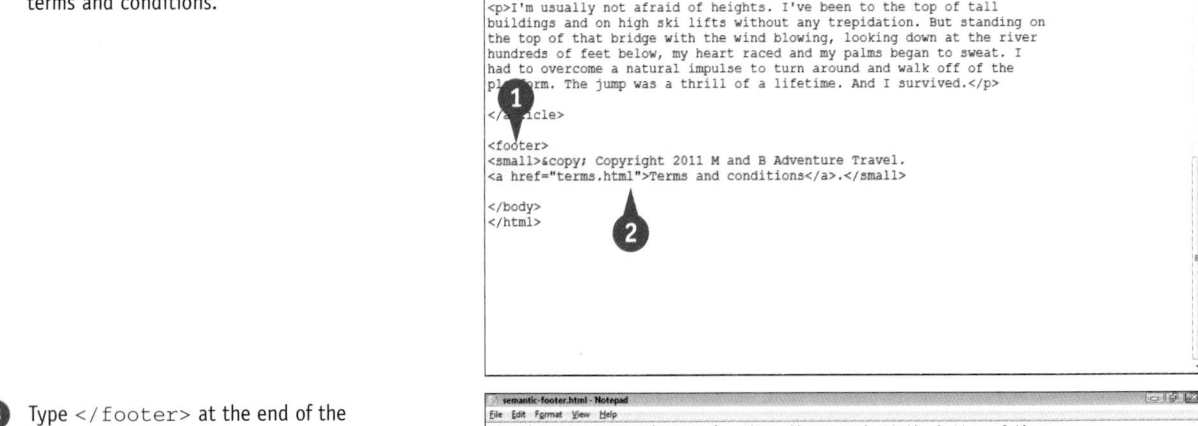

3 Type </footer> at the end of the footer.

4 To add CSS styles to the footer, click inside the <footer> tag and type class="?", replacing ? with a class name.

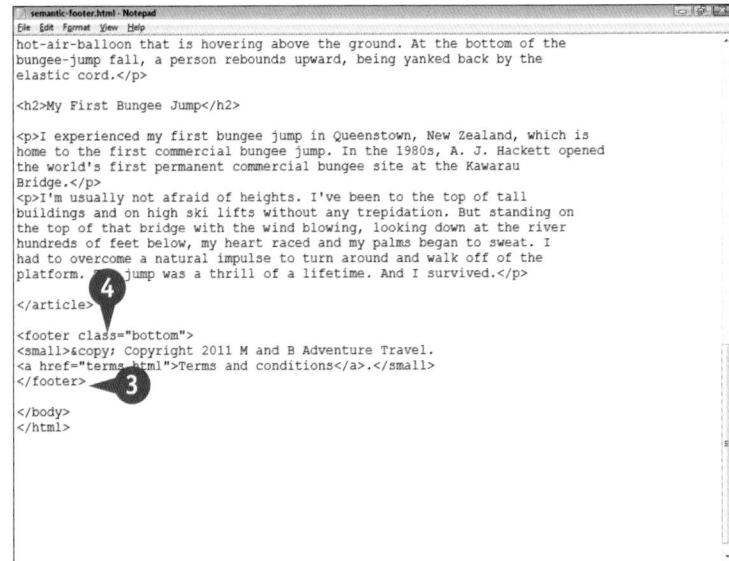

⑤ In your style sheet, type
`footer.?`, replacing *?* with the
name of the class.

⑥ Type a declaration for the footer,
separating multiple style rules with
; characters.

Note: For more about defining CSS style
rules, see Chapter 4.

● The web browser displays the footer
on the page with the styles applied.

In this example, the footer stretches
across the page below all the other
content.

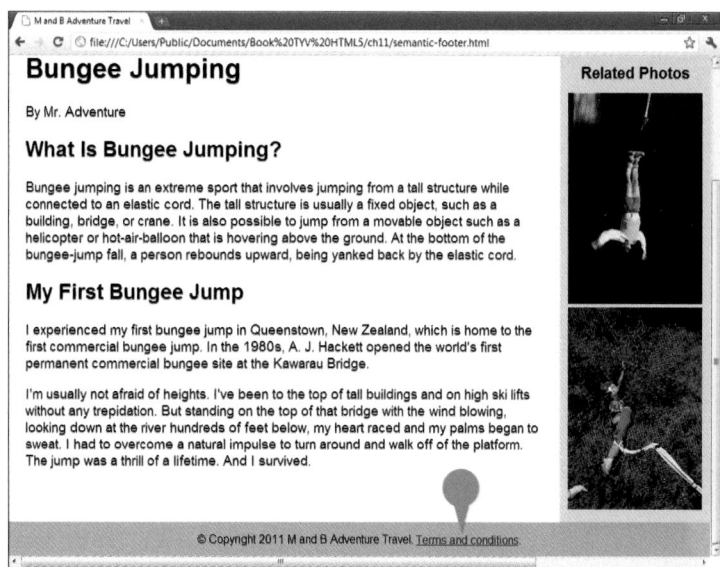

How should I style text in my footer?
Footer text is often less important information than other text
on the page. Footer text can be styled in a way that
deemphasizes it. You can use the `<small>` tag, as in the
example above, or format the text in a lighter-colored font using
CSS styles to give it a more subtle appearance.

**How do I keep a footer from appearing next to floated
content above it?**
This is a common problem. You can ensure that a footer appears
by itself on its own line on the bottom of the page by applying
the `clear: both` rule in the CSS declaration for the footer.
This tells the footer to appear below any page elements that
might be floated to the left or right above it, instead of
wrapping around those elements.

Working with JavaScript

Looking for ways to add action and interest to your website? JavaScript can help you add interactivity to your HTML5 documents. This chapter shows you how to use JavaScript code to make your pages more interesting by changing page content in response to user behavior.

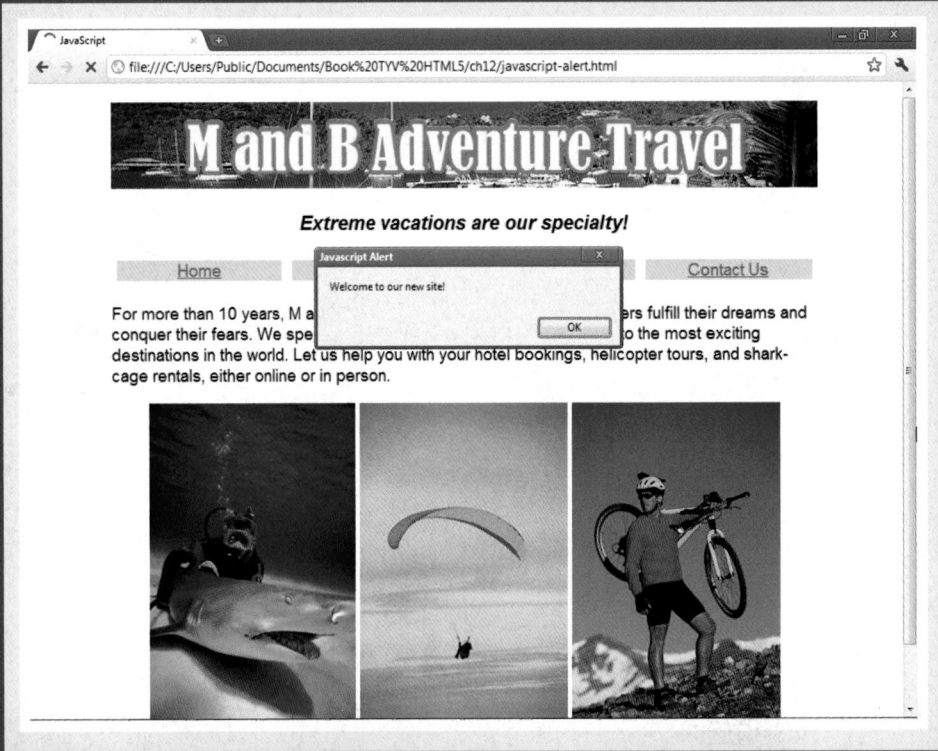

Understanding JavaScript

You can use snippets of code written in JavaScript to add dynamic effects to your web pages. Such scripts can help turn a static HTML page into a more exciting, interactive experience. You can use JavaScript to show and hide content, display message boxes, change images when a user positions the mouse over them, and more.

How Scripts Work

Scripts are short programs you can write to add interactivity to web pages. Scripting instructions can be activated when an event occurs, such as when a user clicks a link or positions the mouse pointer over an image. Scripts can also be activated automatically when the user downloads

your page. Because scripts are written in programming languages, you need to know a little bit about programming if you want to write your own scripts. To learn more about writing scripts, visit www.htmlgoodies.com/primers/jsp.

JavaScript

JavaScript is the most popular scripting language on the web, and all major browsers support it. Because JavaScript code is executed by web browsers, also known as *clients*, JavaScript is known as a *client-side* scripting language. Other scripting languages, such as PHP and Perl, run on web servers and are known as *server-side* scripting languages. Although their names are similar, JavaScript is not based on the Java programming language. Java is more complex than JavaScript and is used for different things.

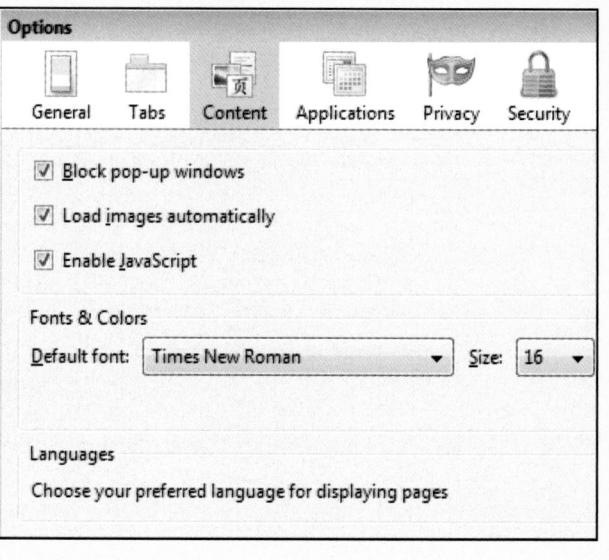

Adding Scripts to Your Pages

JavaScript code can be embedded with the HTML5 in your page or in a separate file. If you put JavaScript inside an HTML page, you need to surround it with opening and closing `<script>` tags (●). If you put your JavaScript in a separate file, you need to end the filename with a .js extension. To use code from an external file, you need to link to the file in your page using `<script>` tags and an `src` attribute (●). JavaScript is case-sensitive and requires careful placement of semicolons, single quotes, double quotes, and other punctuation, so use care when typing your scripts.

```html
<!DOCTYPE html>
<html>
<head>
<title>JavaScript</title>

<script type="text/javascript" src="browser.js"></script>

<script type="text/javascript">
function change() {
document.getElementById("tochange").innerHTML =
document.getElementById("new").value;
}
</script>

</head>
<body>

<h2 id="tochange">Extreme Sports</h2>

<input type="text" id="new">
```

Document Object Model

JavaScript can access and change your elements on a page using the *document object model*, or DOM. In the DOM, every web page is represented by a hierarchy of HTML5 tags. At the top of the document hierarchy is the document root and `<html>` tag, followed by the `<head>` and `<body>` tags, and then everything else in your page. JavaScript can access parts of your page by traversing the DOM from the `<html>` tag down, or by accessing a tag directly by its `id` attribute.

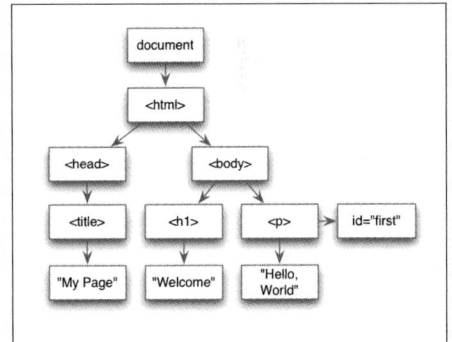

JavaScript Instructions

You work JavaScript magic by writing a set of JavaScript instructions. These instructions can read content from your document, manipulate data such as adding numbers and joining text, and make changes to elements on your page. JavaScript can also make changes to the web browser such as opening or closing windows. By stringing together instructions you can perform complicated tasks on a web page.

JavaScript Syntax

You usually write one JavaScript instruction per line, which makes the code easier to read, but you can separate multiple instructions on a line with semicolons. You often put data that you want an instruction to act on in parentheses. Usually you can use double and single quotes interchangeably in JavaScript, as long as you start and end with the same type. However, sometimes you will write JavaScript inside an HTML5

```
canvas-animate.html - Notepad
File  Edit  Format  View  Help
ctx.fillStyle = 'lightgray';
ctx.fillRect(0, 0, 600, 400);
ctx.fillStyle = 'red';
ctx.beginPath();
ctx.arc(x, y, 20, 0, Math.PI*2, true);
ctx.fill();
if (x >= w || x <= 0) {
  change = -change;
}
x = x + change;
```

attribute already surrounded by double quotes, in which case single quotes are required.

Understanding Script Events and Handlers

When you use JavaScript to add interactivity to your pages, it helps to understand when and why a script executes. Some scripts run as soon as the page downloads, whereas others require an action on the part of the web page visitor. As the website developer, you decide when a script executes. You can use event handlers to control how your scripts behave.

Script Events

Script events are actions that occur during the viewing of a web page. These events can include actions that the user takes. For example, mouse events are actions a user performs with a mouse, such as clicking, positioning the mouse pointer over an object, and releasing the mouse button after clicking it. Keyboard events include key presses on a keyboard. Form events include typing or changing information in a text field or submitting a form. The browser itself can cause an event to occur such as when it loads a new page in the browser window.

Event Handlers

You can determine what happens after an action by specifying an *event handler*. Event handlers associate an object or web page element at which the action occurs with script instructions. For example, you can use the `onclick` event handler to associate the clicking of a web page image or button with a script that pops up an alert box or changes a color on the screen. Event handlers can be defined using HTML5 tag attributes or within your JavaScript code.

```
<!DOCTYPE html>
<html>
<head>
<title>JavaScript</title>
<style>
body { background-color: #ffeecc; font-family: arial, sans-
serif }
</style>
</head>
<body>

<img src="dog.png" onclick="bark()">

<img src="cat.png" onmouseover="purr()">

<img src="bird.png" onmouseout="tweet()">

</body>
</html>
```

An Example

Imagine you want to recognize an event in which a user clicks an image and then pop up a JavaScript alert box in response. You can add an event handler to the image using the `onclick` attribute (●). The `onclick` attribute specifies what script executes when the click occurs. In this example, a JavaScript function called `showAlert` (●) is referenced. When the user clicks the image, an instruction (●) causes an alert box to pop up with the text "Clicked!" displayed.

```
javascript-example.html - Notepad
File  Edit  Format  View  Help
<!DOCTYPE html>
<html>
<head>
<title>JavaScript</title>
<script>
function showAlert() {
   alert('Clicked!');
}
</script>
</head>
<body>

<img src="sky.jpg" onclick="showAlert();">

</body>
</html>
```

Event Handler	
Event Handler	**Action**
onload	Browser loads a page when a user arrives
onunload	Browser unloads a page when a user leaves
onmouseover	User positions the mouse pointer over an element
onmousedown	User presses the mouse button
onmouseup	User releases the mouse button
onmousemove	User moves the mouse
onmouseout	User moves the mouse away from an element
onclick	User clicks an element
ondblclick	User double-clicks an element
onkeypress	User presses and releases a keyboard key
onkeydown	User presses a key
onkeyup	User releases a key
onsubmit	User clicks a Submit button

Add JavaScript to a Web Page

JavaScripts are a great way to add interactivity and dynamic content to your web pages. You can use the `<script>` and `</script>` tags to add JavaScript to your HTML5 document. The `type` attribute defines the script language. The browser reads anything between the two tags as a script. You can place your script content in the body of your HTML page.

You can also place it in the `<head>` area of your page, and reference the script using event handlers. See "Change Page Content" for an example.

Add JavaScript to a Web Page

① Type `<script type="text/javascript">` where you want to insert the script on the page.

② Type the code for the script you want to add.

In this example, the script displays the dimensions of the screen by accessing the `screen.width` and `screen.height` variables.

③ Type `</script>` at the end of the script.

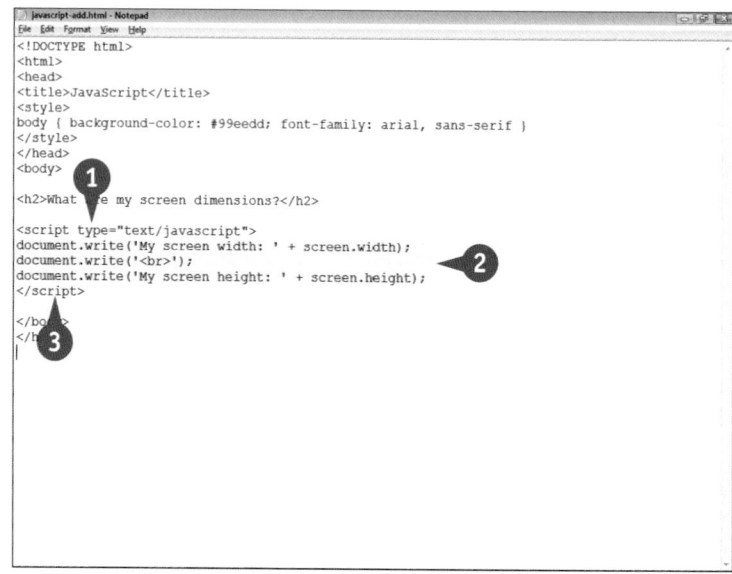

● The web browser runs the script and displays the values when the user views your page.

The screen dimensions are displayed in pixels.

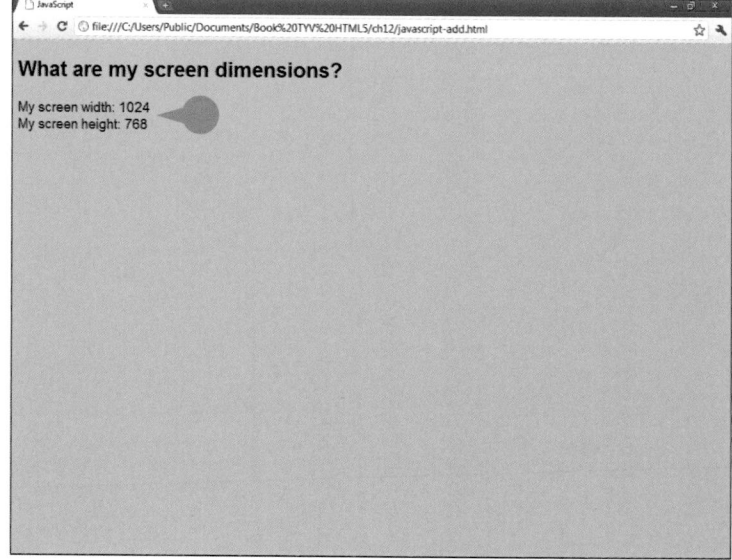

Link to a JavaScript File

Many developers prefer to save their scripts in a separate text file and link the file to the web page. Storing your scripts in a separate file can free up your HTML document to focus on web page content. When saving a JavaScript file, use the .js file extension.

When you upload your web pages to a server, be sure to include the linked JavaScript file. See Chapter 15 to learn more about publishing web pages.

Link to a JavaScript File

1 Create a new document in your text editor.

2 Type your JavaScript code.

3 Save the file using the .js file extension.

Note: See Chapter 2 to learn how to create and save documents.

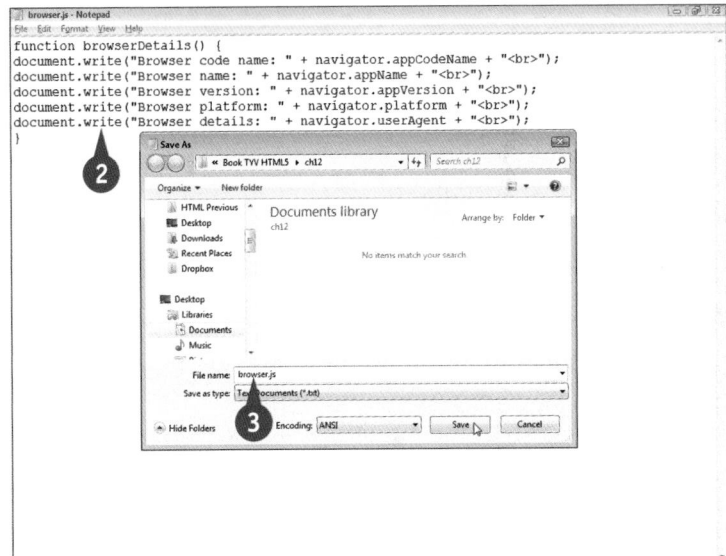

4 In your web page document, click where you want to insert the code and type `<script="text/javascript"`.

The standard place to reference external script files is in the `<head>` area of your document.

5 Type a space and `src="?">`, replacing *?* with the path to the JavaScript file.

6 Type `</script>`.

The JavaScript file is now linked to the web page.

● If the file contains JavaScript functions, you can access them from your HTML5 code.

Note: You can find many free JavaScript programs on the Internet. To use them, you must download the files and reference them in your page.

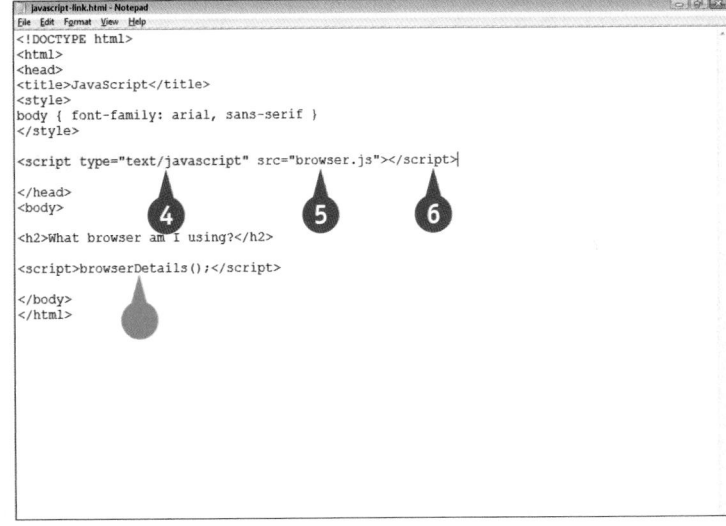

Insert the Current Date and Time

You can use JavaScript to insert the current date and time on your web page. This can help your page seem current and up to date. Unlike regular HTML5 content, the current date will change every time a user opens the page. Content that changes based on the viewing context is known as *dynamic* content.

Insert the Current Date and Time

1 Click where you want to insert the date and time on the page and add a new line.

2 Type `<script type="text/javascript">`.

3 Type `document.write(Date());`.

4 Type `</script>`.

You can keep your script on one line or break it onto multiple lines to make it easier to read.

Note: This example encloses the date and time in a `<time>` tag. For more information, see Chapter 3.

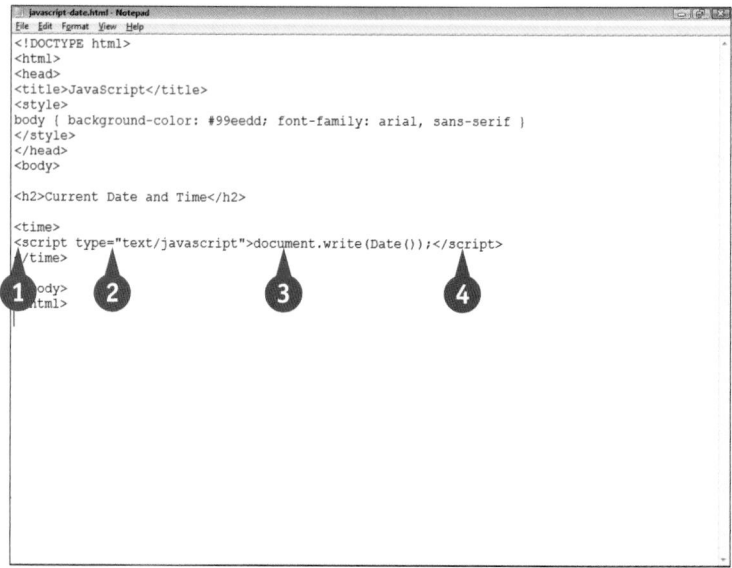

● The web browser displays the current date and time.

Display an Alert Message Box

You can use JavaScript to display an alert message box on your web page. You might use alert messages to provide special instructions about your site or to alert the user to any important information. After reading the message, the user can close the box and return to the web page by clicking a button.

In this example, the alert box is triggered by the page loading, so it always appears. To trigger a JavaScript feature based on a user action, see "Display a Pop-Up Window."

Display an Alert Message Box

① In the `<body>` tag, type
`onload="alert('?');"`.
Replace ? with the message text you want to appear in the box.

Placing the JavaScript in the `onload` event handler displays the alert box after the page has loaded.

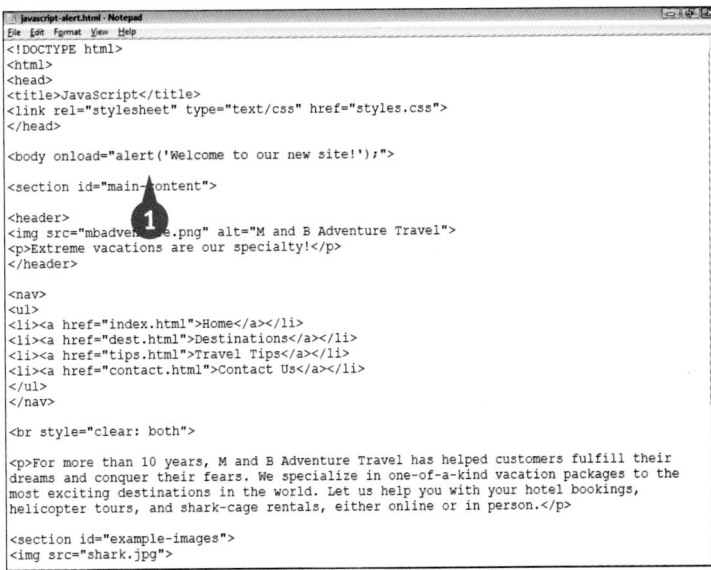

When the user displays your page in a browser, the alert message box appears.

● The user can click the OK button to close the alert box and return to the web page.

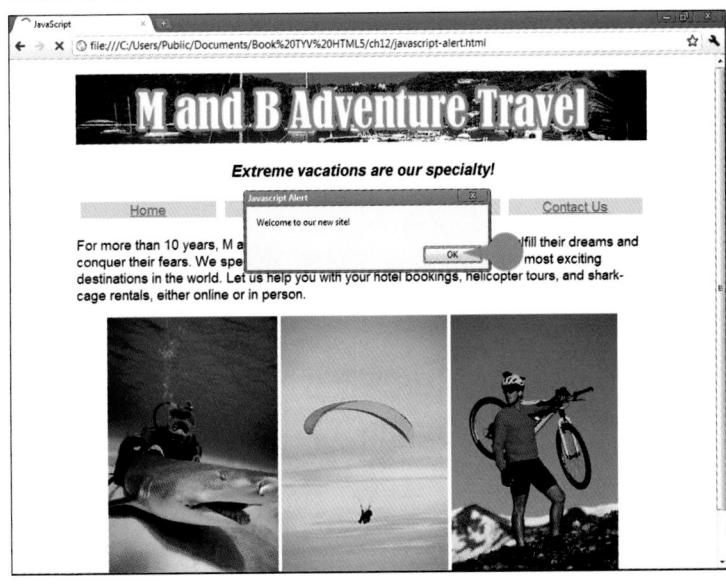

Display a Pop-Up Window

You can use JavaScript to display a pop-up window on your web page. Pop-up windows are effective ways of alerting your website visitors to special news about your site or adding help text that you want to give users the option of viewing. The window can pop up based on a user event such as in the example below. You can also display it automatically using the `onload` event handler. See "Display an Alert Message Box" for details about the `onload` event handler.

The pop-up window code references a separate HTML5 file. You need to create the file in addition to writing the JavaScript. See Chapter 2 to learn more about building HTML5 documents.

Display a Pop-Up Window

1 Create a link for opening the pop-up window.

See Chapter 7 for more about links.

2 For the link `href` attribute, type `javascript: void(0);`. This disables the normal link behavior so you can use the tag for a pop-up window.

3 Type an event-handler attribute. See "Understanding Script Events and Handlers."

This example uses an `onclick` attribute to trigger the pop-up window when the link is clicked.

4 Type `="window.open('?',,` replacing *?* with the path to the file you want to appear in the pop-up window.

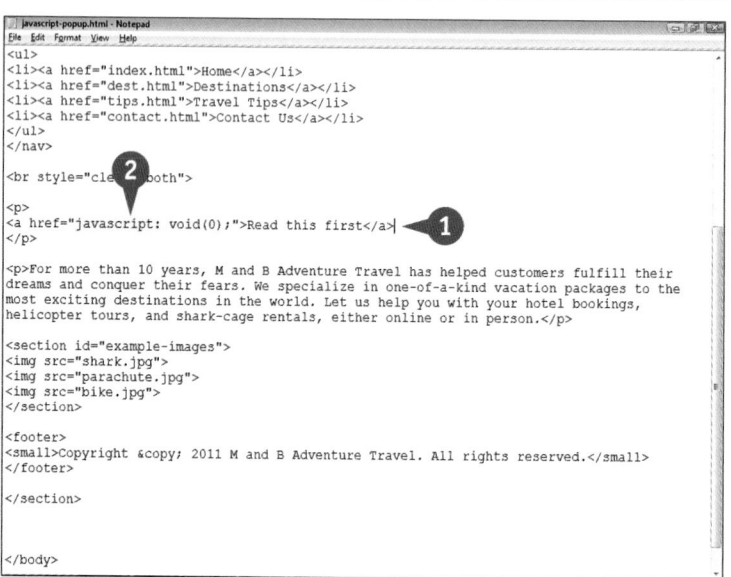

⑤ Type '?',, replacing ? with a name for the window.

⑥ Type width=?, height=?');", replacing ? with a width and height, measured in pixels, for the pop-up window.

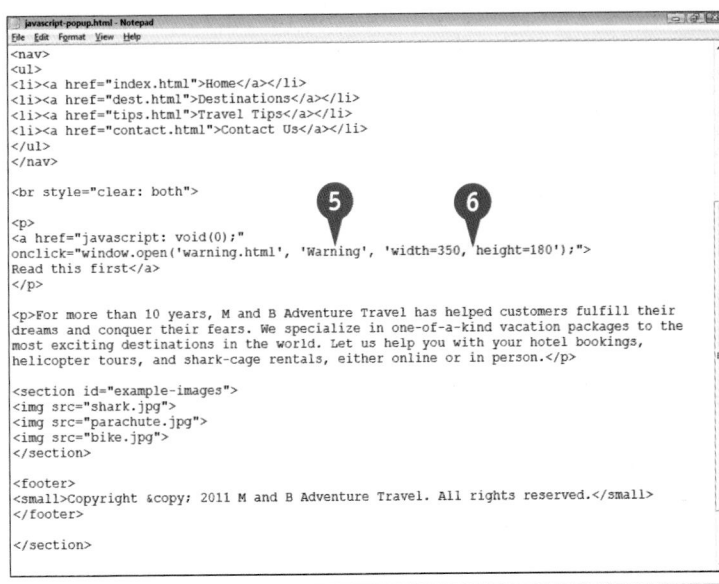

● When the user displays the page and clicks the link, the pop-up window appears.

● The user can click ✕ to close the window.

Note: Be careful about the punctuation you type in your JavaScript code. A missed comma or quote can cause an error in your script.

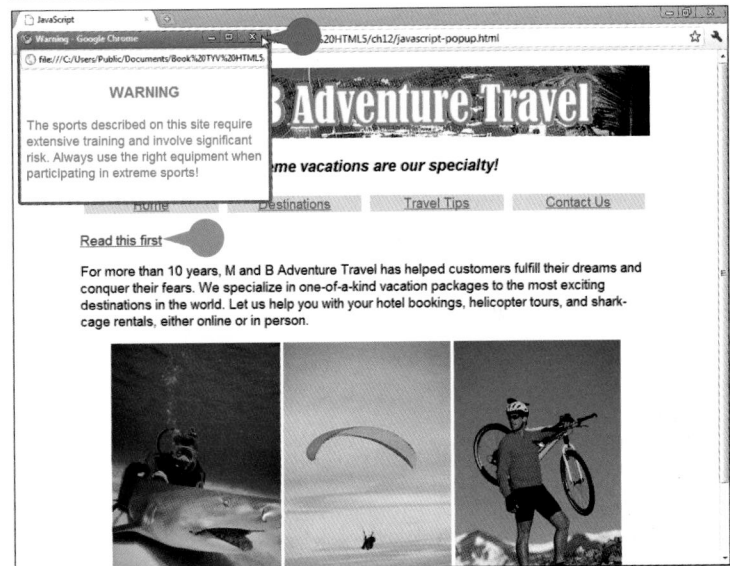

TIPS

How do I open a pop-up window in a particular location?
You can specify pixel offsets from the top and left sides of the browser window with the `top` and `left` settings. You type them next to the `width` and `height` settings. The following opens a window 200 pixels from the top and 150 pixels from the left:

```
window.open('page.html', 'pop', 'width=100,
height=100, top=200, left=150');
```

How do I make a window pop up when a user positions the mouse pointer over an image?
Create an image link instead of a text link in the example above. For details about inserting images, see Chapter 6. Also, use the `mouseover` event handler instead of the `onclick` event handler in step **3**.

Create an Image Rollover Effect

You can use JavaScript to create an image rollover effect. When the user positions the mouse pointer over the image on the web page, the image is replaced with a different one. When the user moves the mouse pointer off the image, the original image returns.

To create an image rollover, you must add two mouse event handlers to a hyperlink tag. The effect works best if the images have the same dimensions. You can resize or crop your images using an image-editing program.

Create an Image Rollover Effect

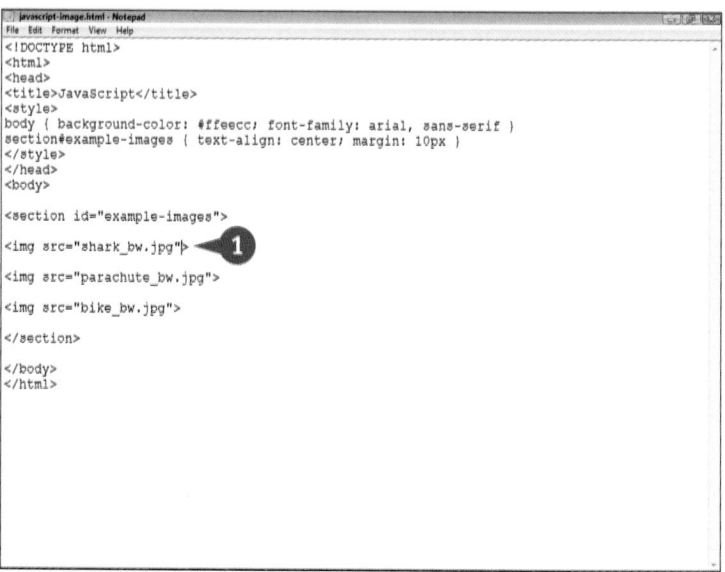

1 Add an image to your page by typing `<img src="?"`, replacing *?* with the path to the image.

Note: For more about adding images, see Chapter 6.

2 Within the `<img>` tag, type `onmouseover="this. src='?';"`, replacing *?* with the path to the image that will replace the existing image when the user rolls over the picture.

Using the `this` JavaScript keyword applies the change to the current HTML tag, in this case the `<img>` tag.

Note: Be careful to include single and double quotes where specified.

③ Type a space and then
`onmouseout="this.`
`src='?';"`, replacing *?* with the
path to the original image.

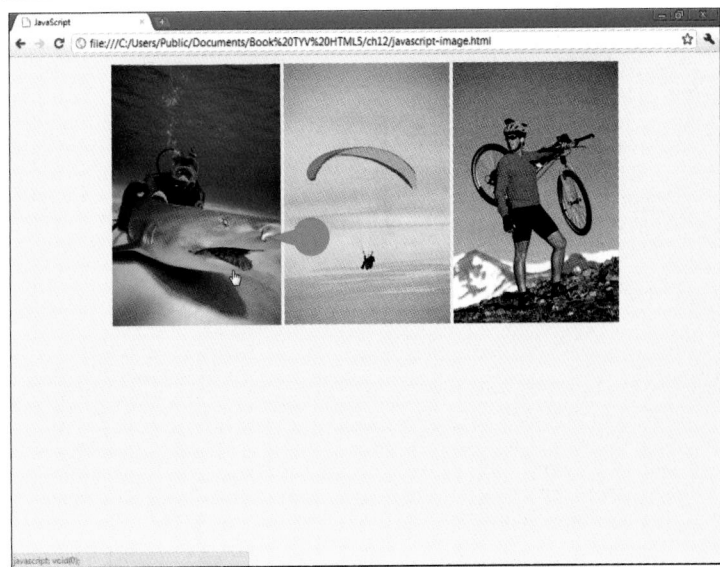

● When the user positions the mouse
pointer over the image, the web
browser replaces the original image
with the rollover image.

In this example, black-and-white
and color versions were created of
the same image in an image editor.

TIPS

How can I make my rollover effects more immediate?
You can instruct the browser to preload the rollover image using JavaScript. That way, the browser
does not have to download the rollover image when the mouse pointer rolls over the original image.
You can preload an image by adding the following script inside the `<head>` tag of your HTML:

```
<script type="text/javascript">
?=new Image(h,w)
?.src="imagepath"
</script>
```

Replace *?* with an identifier for the image, replace *h,w* with height and width values for the image,
and replace *imagepath* with the path to the image.

**How do I make my rollover
image a link?**
Surround the image with an
`<a>` tag to create a link as
you normally would. Type an
`href` attribute to define the
link destination. For more
information about creating
links, see Chapter 7.

Show a Hidden Element

You can use JavaScript to show an HTML5 element that has been hidden on a page. You can hide the element by setting its CSS display property to `none`. With JavaScript, you can change that property to `block` or `span`, which exposes the element on the page.

You can hide elements that are less important on a page to save space and make your design less cluttered. Then you can enable users who want to see that information to click links to view it.

Show a Hidden Element

① Add the HTML element that you want to hide or display to your web page. In this example, a paragraph of text is added.

Note: For more about adding text, see Chapter 3.

② Inside the element tag, type the attribute `style="display: none"` to hide the element.

Note: For more about using the `style` attribute, see Chapter 4.

③ Type `id="?"` to identify the element, replacing *?* with a descriptive name. This allows JavaScript code to reference the element and change its style.

④ Type some text to serve as a link. The user clicks the link to show the hidden element.

⑤ Before the text, type `<a href="javascript: void(0);">`.

⑥ After the text, type `</a>`.

This creates a nonfunctional link. Clicking the link does not take the user to a new page.

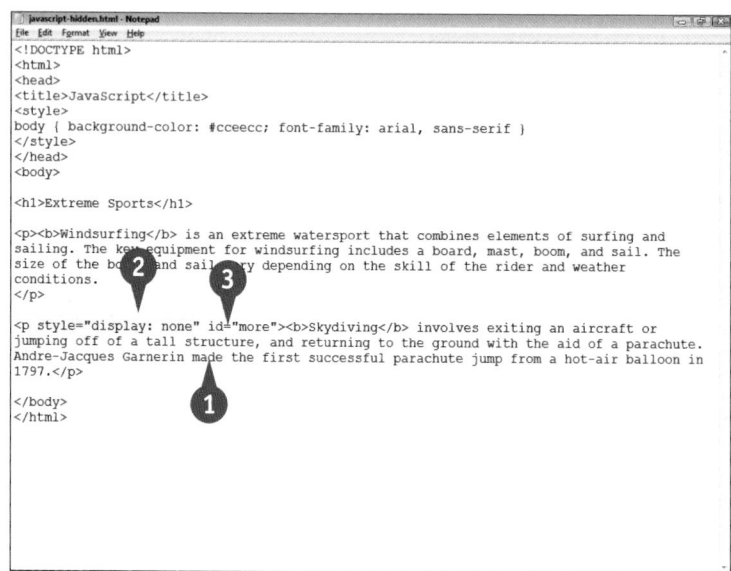

7 Inside the <a> tag, type
onclick="document.
getElementById('?'),
replacing *?* with the identifier
created in step 3.

8 Type style.display='?';",
replacing *?* with block or
inline.

The block value is for elements on
their own lines with space above
and below.

The inline value is for elements
within the flow of other text.

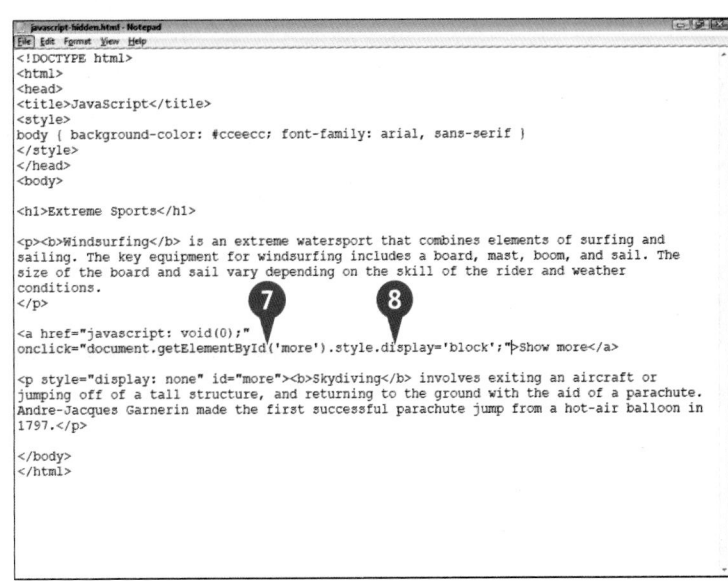

9 Click the link on the web page.

● The hidden element appears.

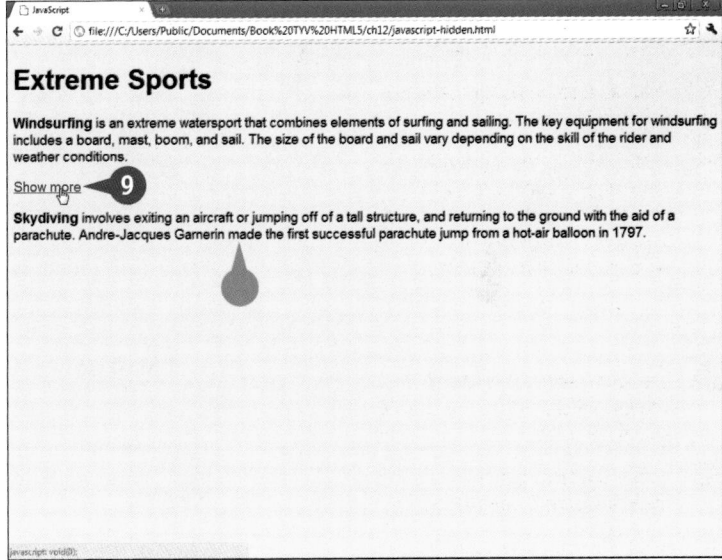

How can I hide an element on a page using JavaScript?
Use the technique just described, but set the display
property of the element to inline or block. Then use
JavaScript to change the display property to none. You can
create separate links on a page for showing and hiding to toggle
the visibility of an element.

**How can I hide an element when the mouse pointer rolls
over a hyperlink?**
Instead of using the onclick event handler, as shown
previously, use the onmouseover event handler. This causes
the element to appear when the user mouses over the link. You
can add an onmouseoff event handler to the same link to
change the display property back to none, so the element
disappears again when the user moves the mouse off the link.

Change Page Content

You can change content on your HTML5 page with JavaScript by referencing an element using the *document object model,* or DOM. The DOM organizes your page as a hierarchy of tags identified by `id` attributes. You can locate content by referencing the `id` value and change it using the `innerHTML` method.

You can use form elements to capture information from your viewers and update the content on the page based on that information.

Change Page Content

① Add the content that you want to change. In this example, text is added in an `<h2>` tag.

② Within the tag, type `id="?"`, replacing *?* with an identifier.

Note: For more about using the `id` attribute, see Chapter 4.

③ Type `<input type="text" id="?">`, replacing *?* with a different identifier. This creates a field for typing replacement content.

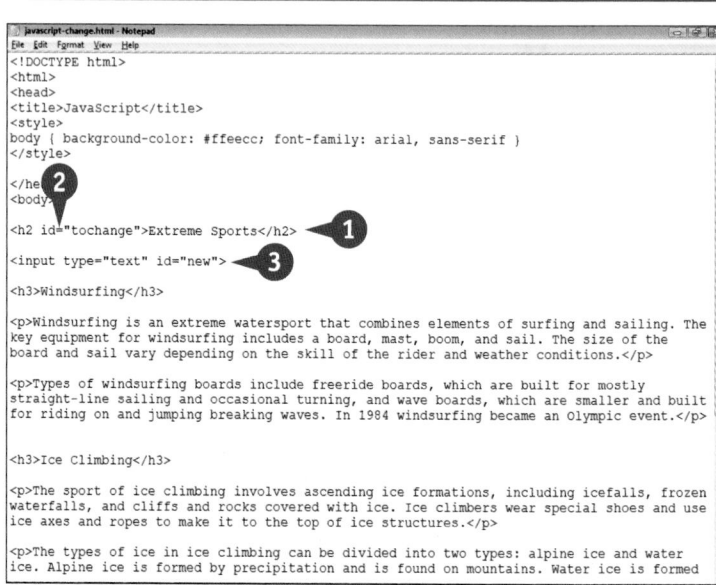

④ Type the content to serve as the event handler.

In this example, a `<button>` tag is used to create a clickable button labeled Go.

⑤ Inside the event-handler tag, type `onclick="?()"`, replacing *?* with a function name.

⑥ Type `<script>`.

⑦ Type `function ?() {`, replacing *?* with the name of the function from step 5.

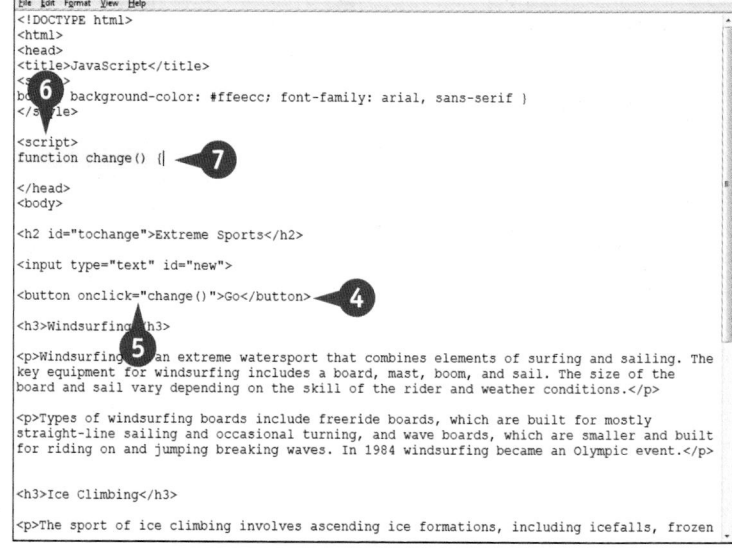

244

8   Type `document.getElementById("?").innerHTML`, replacing *?* with the identifier from step **2**.

9   Type `= document.getElementById("?").value;`, replacing *?* with the identifier from step **3**.

10 Type `}`.

11 Type `</script>`.

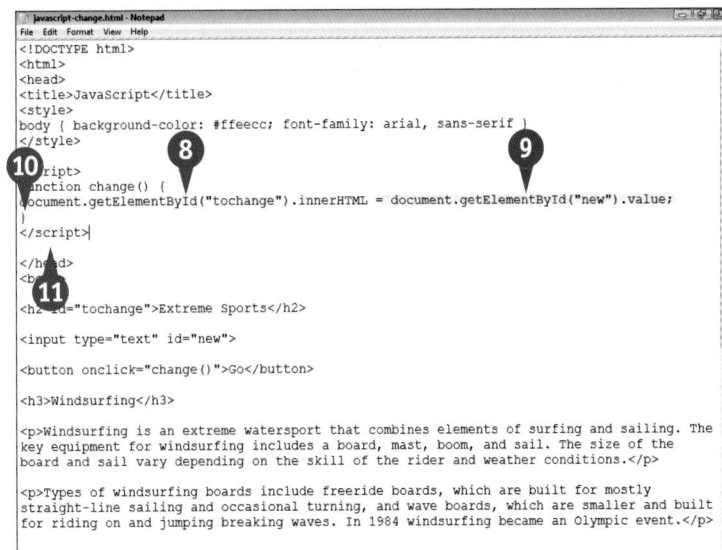

The page displays the changeable content, a text box, and a button.

12 Type the replacement text in the box.

13 Click the **Go** button.

●   The content changes.

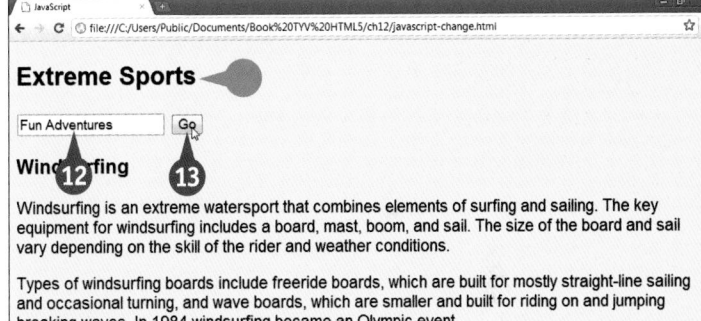

TIPS

What is the `<button>` tag?

You can use a `<button>` tag to create a generic, clickable button on your web page. You can attach JavaScript events to make the button execute JavaScript code and change content on your page, such as in the example above. Alternatively, you can set the `type` attribute of the `<button>` tag to `submit` or `reset` to create buttons for forms. See Chapter 9 for more about form buttons.

What is the visibility CSS property?

The `visibility` property is similar to the `display` property. You can set `visibility` to `hidden` to hide content on your page. However, that content, though invisible, still takes up space on the page. When the `display` property is set to `none`, the affected content does not take up space on the page.

Display a Calculation

You can use the new HTML5 `<output>` tag to display the result of a calculation on your page. The tag works with one or more form `<input>` tags that accept numeric values from the user. The `<output>` tag enables you to perform mathematical calculations for your users and easily display the results on the page.

You can optionally add CSS styles to the `<output>` tag to change its appearance. See Chapter 4 for more about applying styles to HTML5 tags.

Display a Calculation

1 Type `<form>`.

2 Type `<input type="number" step="?"` to create a number field. Replace *?* with a number by which you want the field to increment.

3 Type `name="?">`, replacing *?* with an identifier.

4 Repeat steps **2** and **3** to create a second number field.

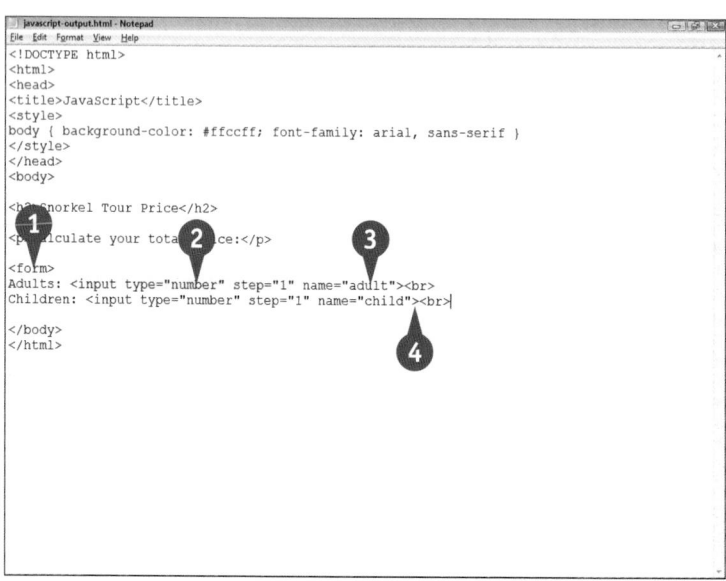

5 Type `<output name="?">`, replacing *?* with an identifier.

6 Type `</output>`.

7 Type `</form>`.

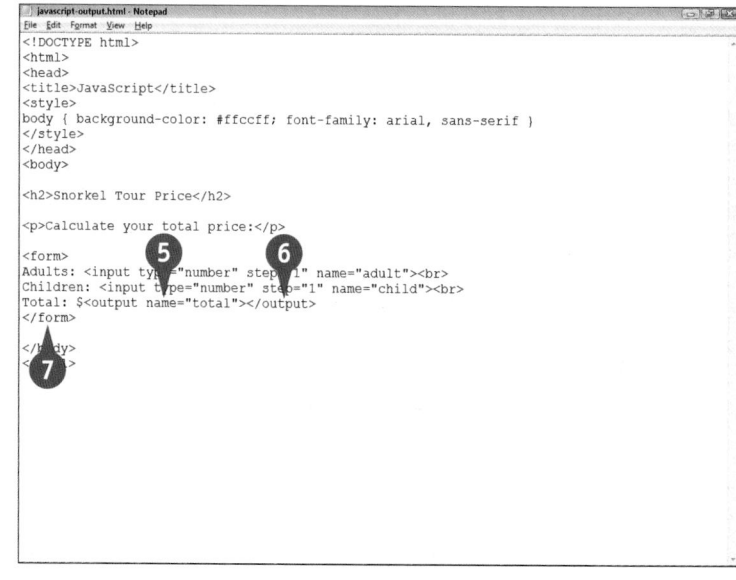

⑧ In the `<form>` tag, type `oninput="?.value =,` replacing *?* with the identifier for the `<output>` tag in step **5**.

⑨ Type `?">`, replacing *?* with any variables and operators to complete the calculation. To reference an input, type `name.valueAsNumber`, replacing *name* with a name attribute value.

In this example, the `adult` and `child` inputs are multiplied by their respective prices. The results are added together to set an output total.

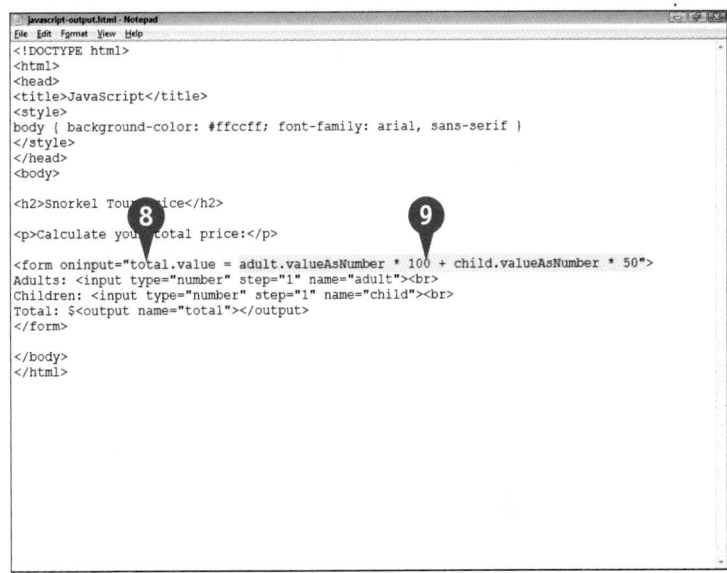

⑩ Open the web page and type values or click the up and down arrows for the input fields.

● A result is displayed by the output tag.

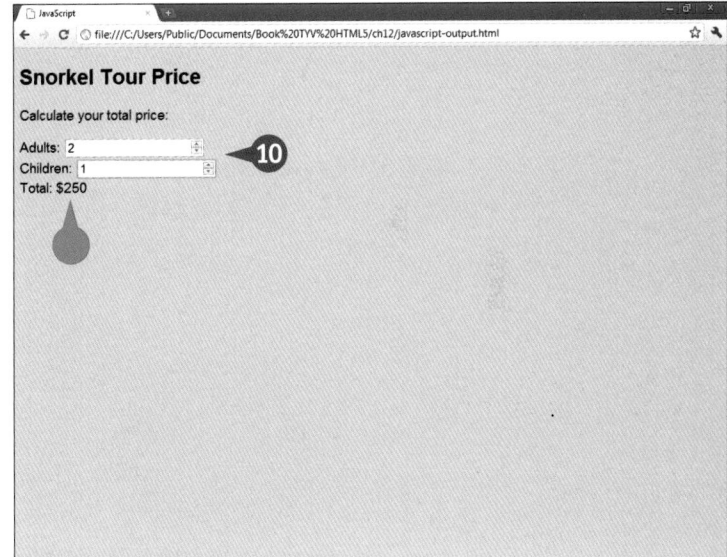

TIPS

How do I add default values to my calculation fields?
You can add a `value` attribute to the `<input>` tags to set default values to calculation fields. The default values are displayed in the fields when you initially open the page. Adding default values can help avoid having "NaN" displayed as output. "NaN" stands for "not a number" and can appear when values are missing in your equation. You can add a default output value by typing a value between the `<output>` and `</output>` tags.

What else can I use for inputting calculation values besides the number field?
You can display a range slider to allow users to click and drag an input control to select from a range of numbers. The following creates a range slider for numbers from 0 to 20:

```
<input type="range" min="0" max="20"
step="1">
```

For more about range sliders, see Chapter 9.

Adding Canvases

Want to draw shapes, lines, and words on your web pages, and add selected parts of images into the mix as well? The new HTML5 canvas enables you to combine all of these things. Canvases give you capabilities that previously you had to use your image editor for. This chapter teaches you how to set up a canvas and then draw on it using JavaScript code.

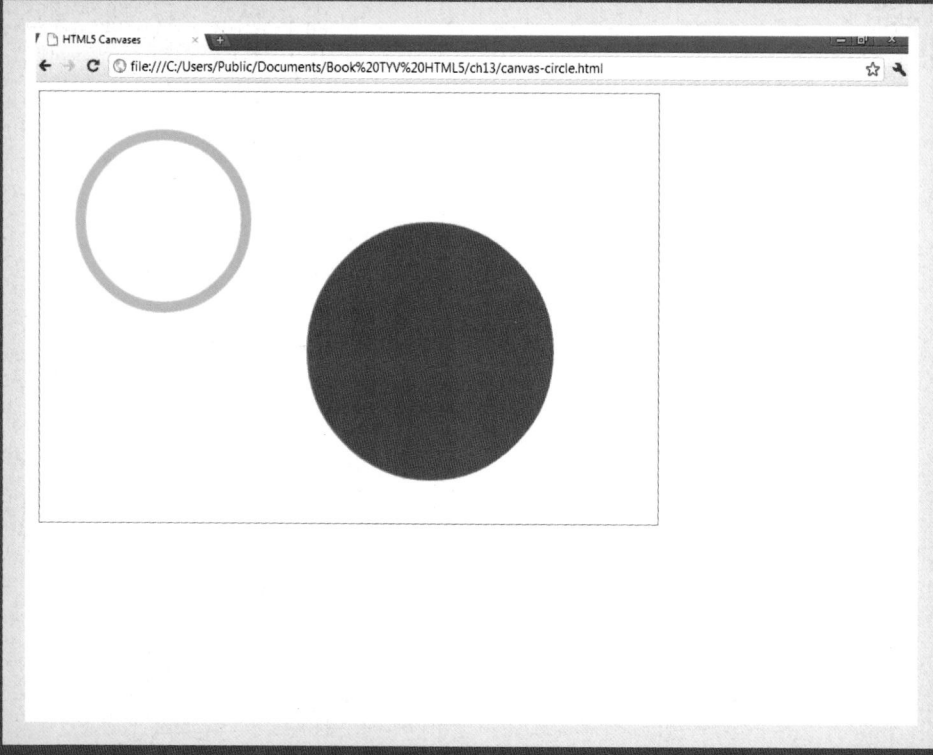

Understanding Canvases

The `<canvas>` tag enables you to define a blank drawing area on your web page. You can then draw shapes, lines, and text, insert images, create gradients, and do other interesting things on the canvas. Canvases are one of the more complicated features in HTML5 because you need to write JavaScript code to fill them with visual content. You also need to be familiar with the concept of coordinates to be able to accurately place your canvas content.

Defining the Canvas

You define a canvas on your page with the `<canvas>` tag (●). The tag accepts `width` and `height` attributes that define the size of the canvas. You also need to add an `id` attribute so your scripts can draw on the canvas. If you want, you can use CSS rules to make style and positioning changes to the canvas, just as you can with other types of tags on your page. See Chapters 4, 5, and 10 for more about CSS.

Adding Scripts

You draw on a canvas using JavaScript code. You can place JavaScript code in your HTML5 page using the `<script>` tag (●). Web browsers read the text inside `<script>` tags as scripts instead of as HTML5 tags and content. For an introduction to JavaScript, see Chapter 12.

Accessing a Canvas

Once you have a canvas on your page, you need to tell your script where the canvas is. You do this by referencing the `id` value of the canvas using the `getElementById` method and storing the result in a variable (●). For the examples in this chapter, the variable is named `cnv`, which stands for *canvas*.

Setting Up a Context

The next step in all canvas tasks is setting up the drawing context. This prepares your JavaScript code to access all the instructions it needs for adding shapes, lines, and other elements to your canvas. You set up the context using the `cnv` variable and the `getContext` method (●). In our examples, the context is stored in a variable called `ctx`, which stands for *context*.

```
<!DOCTYPE html>
<html>
<head>
<title>HTML5 Canvases</title>
<style>
canvas#mycanvas { border: solid gray 1px }
</style>
</head>
<body>

<canvas id="mycanvas" width="600" height="400"></canvas>

<script>
var cnv = document.getElementById('mycanvas');
var ctx = cnv.getContext('2d');
ctx.strokeStyle = 'orange';
ctx.lineWidth = '15';
ctx.strokeRect(160, 80, 360, 240);
</script>

</body>
</html>
```

Defining Canvas Styles

Drawing on a web page canvas is a little like painting on a real canvas. You first need to make some choices about what sort of visual content you want to apply. Similar to choosing a paint color and a brush size, a web designer can choose a color and an outline width for drawing (●). The chosen styles are applied when elements are drawn on the canvas. Note that these styles are different from the CSS styles introduced in Chapter 4.

Measuring with Coordinates

To place content on a canvas, you need to specify where that content goes. Canvases are rectangles, and you can define points within a rectangle using *coordinates*, which are pairs of numbers. When drawing on canvases, the first number in a coordinate pair is the distance from the left side of the canvas. The second number is the distance from the top of the canvas. The width and height of your canvas are defined in pixels, so coordinate values also measure distances in pixels. The coordinates 160, 80 specify a location 160 pixels from the left and 80 pixels from the top of a canvas.

Drawing Content

You specify where to draw your elements with combinations of coordinate points, widths, lengths, and rotational measurements. What values you use depends on the type of object you are drawing. Most of the instructions for creating canvas content include the words *fill*, *stroke*, or *draw*. Drawing methods are associated with the canvas context, and are accessed via the context variable — for example, ctx. strokeRect (●). The result on your HTML5 page is an object displayed on the canvas (●).

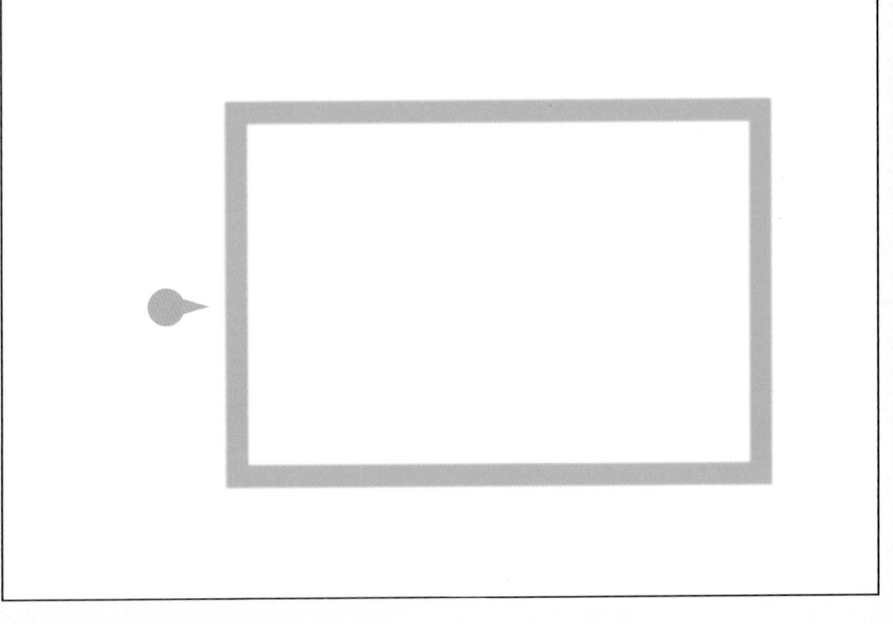

Set Up a Canvas

You can define an area on your web page as a canvas where you can draw shapes and lines, add text, and paste images. You define the area with a `<canvas>` tag. You can specify the dimensions of the drawing area with `width` and `height` attributes.

The `<canvas>` tag by itself does not create any drawn content. It reserves space on your page so you can add drawings using JavaScript code. The `<canvas>` tag is new to HTML5.

Set Up a Canvas

① Type `<canvas>` where you want to insert the drawing area on your page.

② Type `</canvas>`.

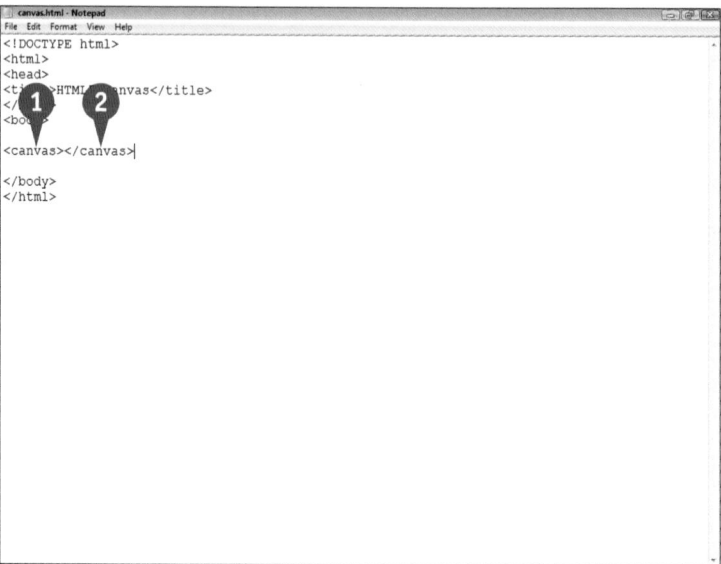

③ Type `id="?"`, replacing *?* with an identifier.

④ Within the `<canvas>` tag, type `width="?"` and `height="?"`, replacing *?* with the pixel dimensions.

⑤ In the style sheet for your page, type `canvas#?`, replacing *?* with the identifier defined in step 3.

⑥ In the declaration, type `border: solid gray 1px` to give the canvas a gray border to make it visible.

Note: For more about using the `id` attribute for identifying HTML5 elements, see Chapter 4.

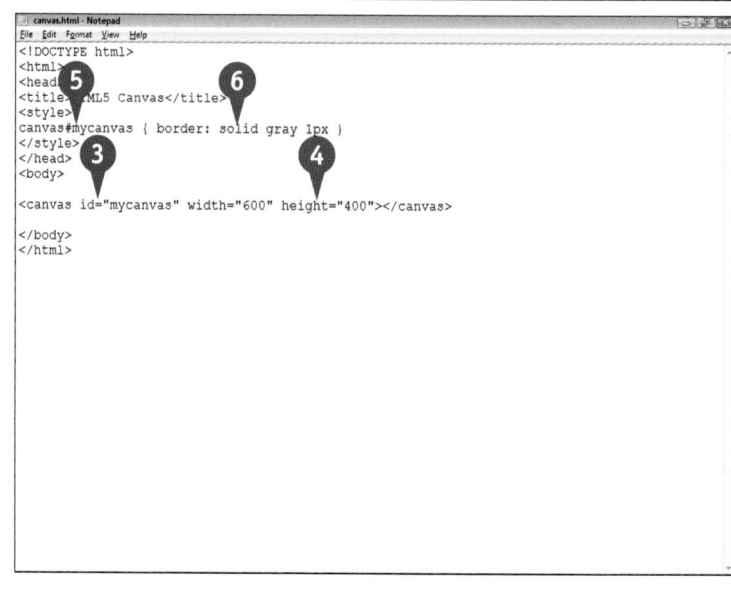

7 After the `<canvas>` tags in your document, type `<script>`.

8 Type `var canv = document.getElementById('?');`, replacing `?` with the `id` value of your canvas.

9 Type `var ctx = canv.getContext('2d');`.

Steps **8** and **9** set up your script so that you can access your canvas and draw on it.

10 Type `</script>`.

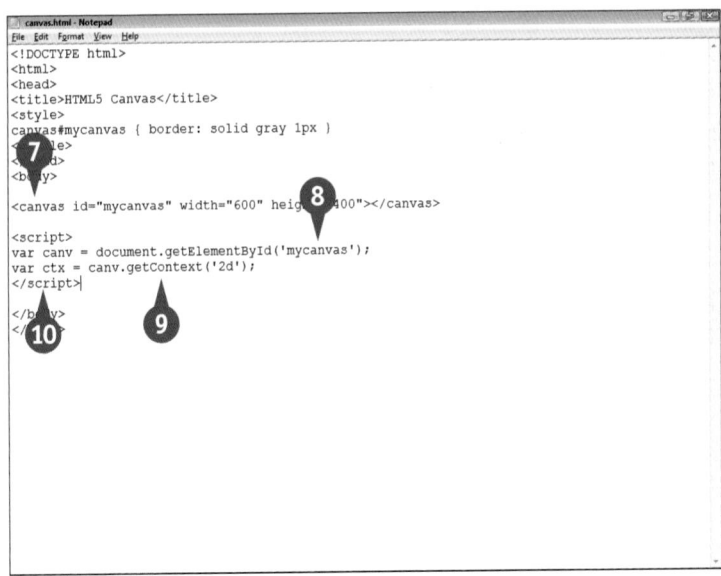

● The browser displays the canvas on the web page, surrounding it with a gray CSS border.

To draw on the canvas, see the sections that follow in this chapter.

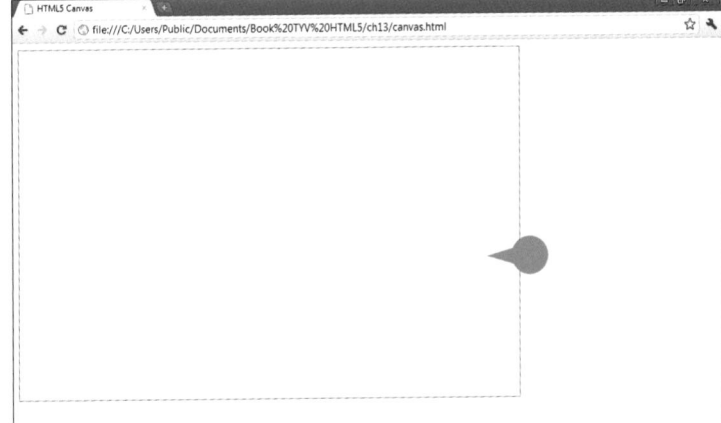

TIP

Do I have to place my script after my canvas?
To successfully draw on your canvas using JavaScript, your HTML5 canvas has to be loaded prior to your script code running. You can do this by placing your script after your canvas on your page, which is what is done in these examples.

An alternative is to place your drawing script in a JavaScript function (●), which can go anywhere on your page. You can then call that function using the `onload` attribute in the `<body>` tag (●). The page waits for all the page content to load before calling the function. For more about the `onload` attribute and other event handlers, see Chapter 12.

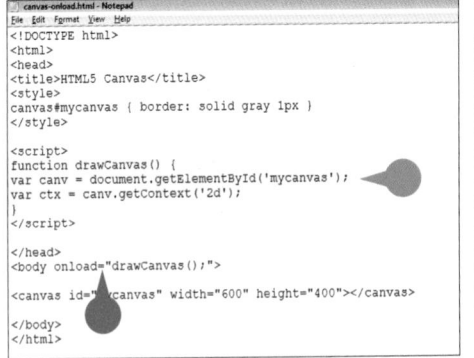

Draw Rectangles

You can draw rectangles on your canvas to create basic designs on your web page or as a starting point for more complex drawings. When creating a rectangle, you define a starting coordinate as well as lengths of each side. For the rectangle to appear within the canvas, your coordinates and lengths cannot extend outside of the canvas boundaries.

JavaScript has methods for creating a filled rectangle and for creating an outlined rectangle. By default, a black color is used to draw the rectangle. You can change the color with JavaScript.

Draw Rectangles

Prepare the Page

1 Set up the canvas and script on your page.

Note: For details, see "Set Up a Canvas."

```
canvas-rect.html - Notepad
File  Edit  Format  View  Help
<!DOCTYPE html>
<html>
<head>
<title>HTML5 Canvases</title>
<style>
canvas#mycanvas { border: solid gray 1px }
</style>
</head>
<body>

<canvas id="mycanvas" width="600" height="400"></canvas>

<script>
var cnv = document.getElementById('mycanvas');
var ctx = cnv.getContext('2d');|          ◀━ 1
</script>

</body>
</html>
```

Draw a Filled Rectangle

2 Type ctx.fillStyle = '?';, replacing ? with a color.

3 Type ctx.fillRect(?);, replacing ? with four numbers separated by commas.

The first two numbers define a starting coordinate on the canvas. The second two numbers define the length of the horizontal and vertical sides, respectively.

```
canvas-rect.html - Notepad
File  Edit  Format  View  Help
<!DOCTYPE html>
<html>
<head>
<title>HTML5 Canvases</title>
<style>
canvas#mycanvas { border: solid gray 1px }
</style>
</head>
<body>

<canvas id="mycanvas" width="600" height="400"></canvas>

<script>          2            3
var cnv = document.getElementById('mycanvas');
var ctx = cnv.getContext('2d');
ctx.fillStyle = 'red';
ctx.fillRect(25, 25, 300, 200);
</script>

</body>
</html>
```

Draw an Outlined Rectangle

④ Type ctx.strokeStyle = '?';, replacing ? with a color.

⑤ Type ctx.lineWidth = '?';, replacing ? with a width in pixels.

⑥ Type ctx.strokeRect(?);, replacing ? with four numbers separated by commas. The first two numbers define the starting coordinate and the second two numbers define the lengths of the sides.

● The web browser displays rectangles on the canvas in the styles that you defined.

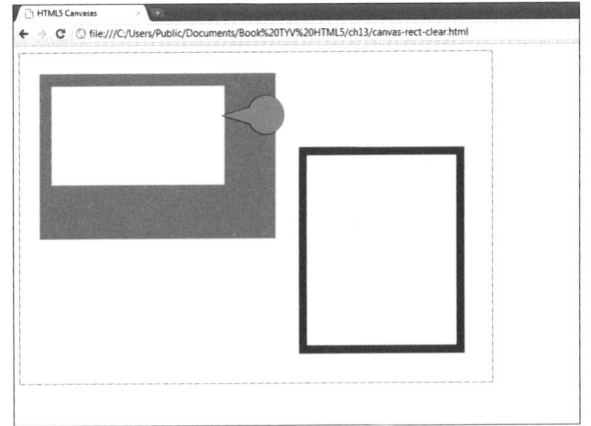

```
canvas-rect.html - Notepad
File  Edit  Format  View  Help
<!DOCTYPE html>
<html>
<head>
<title>HTML5 Canvases</title>
<style>
canvas#mycanvas { border: solid gray 1px }
</style>
</head>
<body>

<canvas id="mycanvas" width="600" height="400"></canvas>

<script>
var cnv = document.    lementById('mycanvas');
var ctx    v.getC    t('2d');
ctx.fil    e = 'red
ctx.fillR  ct(25, 25,  00, 200);
ctx.strok Style = 'blue';
ctx.lineWidth = '10';
ctx.strokeRect(360, 120, 200, 240);|
</script>

</body>
</html>
```

file:///C:/Users/Public/Documents/Book%20TYV%20HTML5/ch13/canvas-rect.html

---

TIP

How can I cut a hole in my rectangle?

You fill the inside of your rectangle with a clear rectangle so that it looks like a rectangular hole has been cut out of it. For example, you can add to the code in the example above:

① Type ctx.clearRect(40, 40, 220, 120);.

● A clear rectangle is placed inside the solid rectangle.

file:///C:/Users/Public/Documents/Book%20TYV%20HTML5/ch13/canvas-rect-clear.html

Draw Circles

You can draw circles on your canvas to add curved decorations to an otherwise block-based page. When creating a circle, you define a center coordinate as well as a radius, which determines the circle size. In your drawing instruction, you also define how far along the circumference of the circle to draw. You define this value in radians, and to draw a complete circle this value is two times the value of pi.

JavaScript has methods for drawing a filled circle and an outlined circle. By default, a black color is used to draw the circles. You can change the color with JavaScript.

Draw Circles

Prepare the Page

1. Set up the canvas and script on your page.

Note: For details, see "Set Up a Canvas."

```
canvas-circle.html - Notepad
File  Edit  Format  View  Help
<!DOCTYPE html>
<html>
<head>
<title>HTML5 Canvases</title>
<style>
canvas#mycanvas { border: solid gray 1px }
</style>
</head>
<body>

<canvas id="mycanvas" width="600" height="400"></canvas>

<script>
var cnv = document.getElementById('mycanvas');
var ctx = cnv.getContext('2d');          ◀ 1
</script>

</body>
</html>
```

Draw a Filled Circle

2. Type `ctx.fillStyle = '?';`, replacing ? with a color.

3. Type `ctx.arc(?,0,Math.PI*2,false);`, replacing ? with three numbers separated by commas. The first two numbers define the coordinates of the circle center and the last number defines the radius of the circle in pixels.

4. Type `ctx.fill();`.

```
canvas-circle.html - Notepad
File  Edit  Format  View  Help
<!DOCTYPE html>
<html>
<head>
<title>HTML5 Canvases</title>
<style>
canvas#mycanvas { border: solid gray 1px }
</style>
</head>
<body>

<canvas id="mycanvas" width="600" height="400"></canvas>

<script>                          2
var cnv = document.getElementById('mycanvas');
var ctx = cnv.getContext('2d');
ctx.fillStyle = 'green';
ctx.arc(380,240,120,0,Math.PI*2,false);   ◀ 3
ctx.fill();
</script>

</body>              4
</html>
```

Draw an Outlined Circle

5 Type `ctx.beginPath();`. This resets the script for drawing a new circle.

6 Type `ctx.strokeStyle = '?';`, replacing *?* with a color.

7 Type `ctx.lineWidth = '?';`, replacing *?* with a width in pixels.

8 Type `ctx.arc(?,0,Math.PI*2,true);`, replacing *?* with three numbers separated by commas. The first two numbers define the coordinates of the circle center and the last number defines the radius of the circle.

9 Type `ctx.stroke();`.

● The web browser displays circles on the canvas in the styles that you defined.

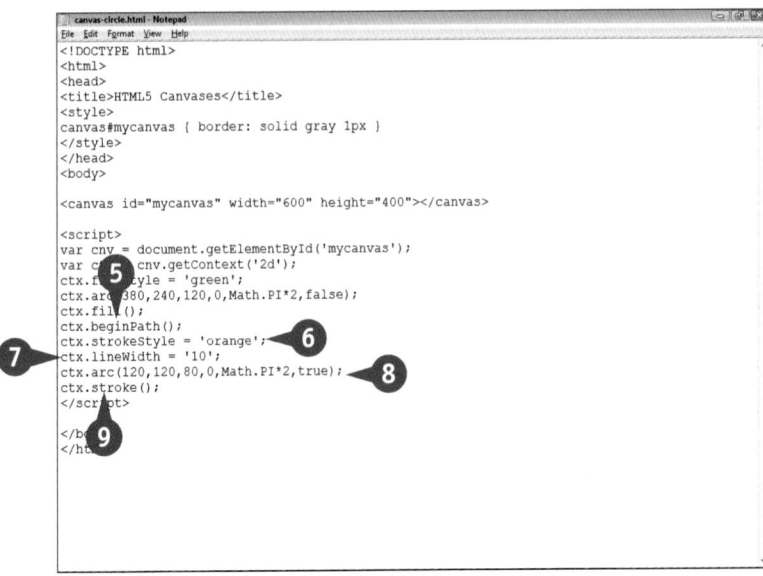

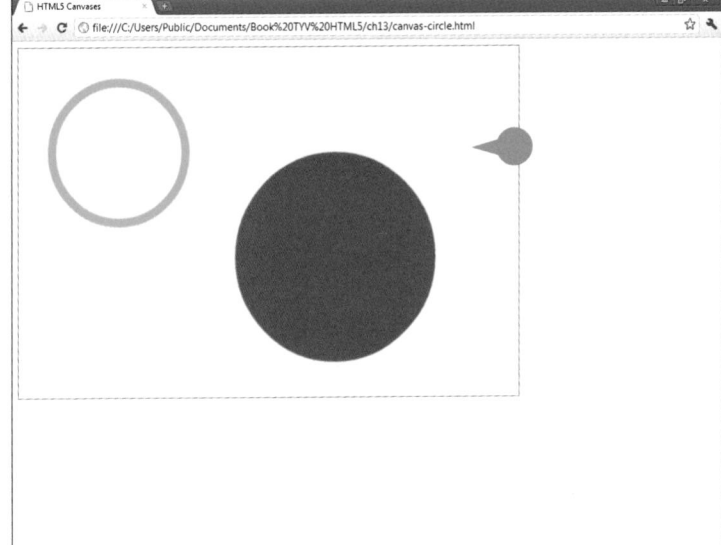

TIPS

How can I draw a half circle?
You can change the starting and ending angles in the `arc` method of your circle-drawing script. In the above example, the starting angle is 0 and the ending angle is `Math.PI*2`. To draw a half circle, you can change the ending angle to `Math.PI`. You can adjust these values to get different half-circle orientations.

How do I draw the circle in the opposite direction?
The last value in the `arc` method can be `true` or `false`. A `true` value draws the circle in a clockwise direction, and `false` draws it in a counterclockwise direction. If you are drawing a partial circle, the direction makes a difference.

Draw Lines

You can draw straight lines on your canvas that run horizontally, vertically, or diagonally. You create a line by specifying the coordinate at which to start the line using the `moveTo` method. Then you specify an ending point with the `lineTo` method. Calling the `stroke` method draws the line.

By repeating line commands you can create a grid or draw complex shapes. You can customize your lines by specifying different colors or different widths.

Draw Lines

① Set up the canvas and script on your page.

Note: For details, see "Set Up a Canvas."

② Type `ctx.strokeStyle = "?";`, replacing `?` with a line color.

③ Type `ctx.lineWidth = '?';`, replacing `?` with a line width in pixels.

```
canvas-lines.html - Notepad
File Edit Format View Help
<!DOCTYPE html>
<html>
<head>
<title>HTML5 Canvases</title>
<style>
canvas#mycanvas { border: solid gray 1px }
</style>
</head>
<body>

<canvas id="mycanvas" width="600" height="400"></canvas>

<script>
var cnv = document.getElementById('mycanvas');       ①
var ctx = cnv.getContext('2d');
ctx.strokeStyle = "purple";       ②
ctx.lineWidth = '4';|
</script>

</body>       ③
</html>
```

④ Type `ctx.moveTo(?);`, replacing `?` with a starting coordinate on the canvas.

⑤ Type `ctx.lineTo(?);`, replacing `?` with an ending coordinate.

⑥ Type `ctx.stroke();` to draw the line.

● To include comments in your JavaScript code, precede text with two slashes (//).

```
canvas-lines.html - Notepad
File Edit Format View Help
<!DOCTYPE html>
<html>
<head>
<title>HTML5 Canvases</title>
<style>
canvas#mycanvas { border: solid gray 1px }
</style>
</head>
<body>

<canvas id="mycanvas" width="600" height="400"></canvas>

<script>
    cnv = document.getElementById('mycanvas');
    ctx = cnv.getContext('2d');
  .strokeStyle = "purple";
c x.lineWidth = '4';
// Vertical
ctx.moveTo(50, 50);       ④
ctx.lineTo(50, 360);
ctx.stroke();
</script>

</body>       ⑥  ⑤
</html>
```

⑦ Repeat steps 4 to 6 to draw more lines on your canvas.

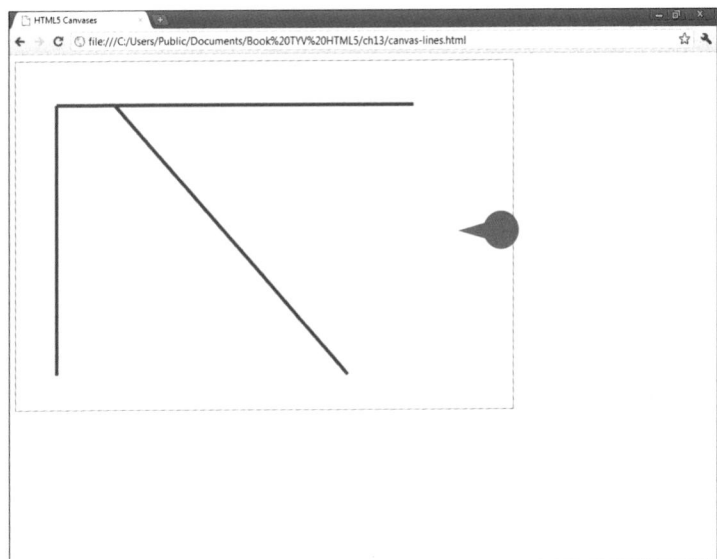

```
canvas-lines.html - Notepad
File  Edit  Format  View  Help
<!DOCTYPE html>
<html>
<head>
<title>HTML5 Canvases</title>
<style>
canvas#mycanvas { border: solid gray 1px }
</style>
</head>
<body>

<canvas id="mycanvas" width="600" height="400"></canvas>

<script>
var cnv = document.getElementById('mycanvas');
var ctx = cnv.getContext('2d');
ctx.strokeStyle = "purple";
ctx.lineWidth = '4';
// Vertical
ctx.moveTo(50, 50);
ctx.lineTo(50, 360);
ctx.stroke();
// Horizontal
ctx.moveTo(50, 50);
ctx.lineTo(480, 50);         ⑦
ctx.stroke();
// Diagonal
ctx.moveTo(120, 50);
ctx.lineTo(400, 360);
ctx.stroke();
</script>

</body>
</html>
```

● The web browser displays lines on the canvas in the styles that you defined.

How do I draw horizontal or vertical lines using the line-drawing methods?
Whether your lines are horizontal or vertical depends on the relationship of the starting and ending coordinates. To draw a horizontal line, keep the second coordinate value, which is the distance from the top of the canvas, constant. For example, specifying 10, 20 and 50, 20 draws a horizontal line. To draw a vertical line, keep the first value constant — for example, 60, 80 and 60, 10.

How do I draw an enclosed shape using the arc method?
To draw a shape, you can write multiple lineTo methods in a row, one for each side of the shape. You can enclose the shape by having the final lineTo coordinate be the same as the initial moveTo coordinate. When you execute the stroke command, a multisided shape is drawn.

Add Text

You can add words and sentences to your canvas just like you can to your web page with HTML text tags. You can set a font family and size using the `font` method in your script. Similar to drawing rectangles, you can create filled text using the `fillText` method or outlined text using the `strokeText` method. To add extra styling to your text you can rotate it. For details, see "Rotate Canvas Content."

Add Text

Prepare the Page

1 Set up the canvas and script on your page.

Note: For details, see "Set Up a Canvas."

```
canvas-text.html - Notepad
File  Edit  Format  View  Help
<!DOCTYPE html>
<html>
<head>
<title>HTML5 Canvases</title>
<style>
canvas#mycanvas { border: solid gray 1px }
</style>
</head>
<body>

<canvas id="mycanvas" width="600" height="400"></canvas>

<script>
var cnv = document.getElementById('mycanvas');
var ctx = cnv.getContext('2d');
</script>

</body>
</html>
```
1

Draw Filled Text

2 Type `ctx.fillStyle = '?';`, replacing *?* with a color.

3 Type `ctx.font = '?';`, replacing *?* with a size and font name separated by a space. If your font name has multiple words, surround them with double quotes.

4 Type `ctx.fillText(?);`, replacing *?* with the text to draw followed by the coordinates at which to start drawing. Enclose the text with quotes and separate the values with commas.

● To include comments in your JavaScript code, precede text with two slashes (//).

```
canvas-text.html - Notepad
File  Edit  Format  View  Help
<!DOCTYPE html>
<html>
<head>
<title>HTML5 Canvases</title>
<style>
canvas#mycanvas { border: solid gray 1px }
</style>
</head>
<body>

<canvas id="mycanvas" width="600" height="400"></canvas>

<script>
var cnv = document.getElementById('mycanvas');
var ctx = cnv.getContext('2d');
// Filled text
ctx.fillStyle = "purple";
ctx.font = '44px "times new roman"';
ctx.fillText('M and B Adventure Travel', 70, 150);
</script>

</body>
</html>
```
2 **3** **4**

Draw Outlined Text

5 Type ctx.strokeStyle = '?';, replacing *?* with a color.

6 Type ctx.lineWidth = '?';, replacing *?* with the outline width.

7 Type ctx.font = '?';, replacing *?* with a size and font name separated by a space.

8 Type ctx.strokeText(?);, replacing *?* with the text to draw followed by the coordinates at which to start drawing. The coordinates define the location of the base of the text.

View the Text

● The web browser displays text on the canvas in the styles that you defined.

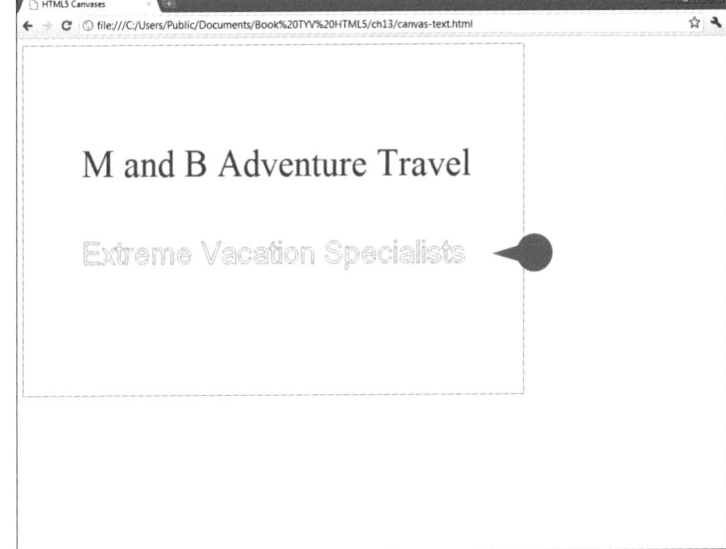

```
canvas-text.html - Notepad
File  Edit  Format  View  Help
<!DOCTYPE html>
<html>
<head>
<title>HTML5 Canvases</title>
<style>
canvas#mycanvas { border: solid gray 1px }
</style>
</head>
<body>

<canvas id="mycanvas" width="600" height="400"></canvas>

<script>
var cnv = document.getElementById('mycanvas');
var ctx = cnv.getContext('2d');
// Filled text
ctx.fillStyle = "purple";
ctx.font = '44px "        new roman"';
ctx.fillText('M and  Adventure Travel', 70, 150);
// Outlined text
ctx.strokeStyle = "gray"
ctx.lineWidth = '1';
ctx.font = '36px "arial"
ctx.strokeText('Extreme Vacation Specialists', 70, 250);
</script>

</body>
</html>
```

M and B Adventure Travel

Extreme Vacation Specialists

TIPS

How do I make my text italic or bold?
You can add extra information to the font property to define the style or weight of your text. For example, the following creates italic and bold text when drawn:

```
ctx.font = 'italic bold 44px "Times New Roman"';
```

How do I align text?
You can set an alignment for your canvas text by defining a textAlign property. You can set the property to left, which is the default, center, or right relative to the starting coordinates for drawing the text. The following example center-aligns text:

```
ctx.textAlign = 'center';
```

Add an Image

You can add an image to your canvas to display photos shot with a camera or graphics that you have created in an illustration program. You can place the image precisely on the canvas by specifying coordinates. You can combine images with other drawing elements using the other sections in this chapter.

In order for your script to place the image on the canvas, the image must first be loaded into the browser. If the script attempts to place it prior to it being loaded, nothing will appear. Script execution is delayed until after page loading using the `onload` property. For more about the `onload` property and other event handlers, see Chapter 12.

Add an Image

1 Set up the canvas and script on your page.

Note: For details, see "Set Up a Canvas."

2 Type `var pict = new Image();` to define a new image in your script.

3 Type `pict.src = "?";`, replacing *?* with the path to the image.

In this example, the image is stored in the same directory as the HTML, so you can reference it using the image name.

4 Type `pict.onload = function(){.`

This creates a function that runs after the image is loaded.

5 Type `ctx.drawImage(pict, ?);`, replacing *?* with the coordinates at which to place the image on the canvas.

6 Type `}` to end the function.

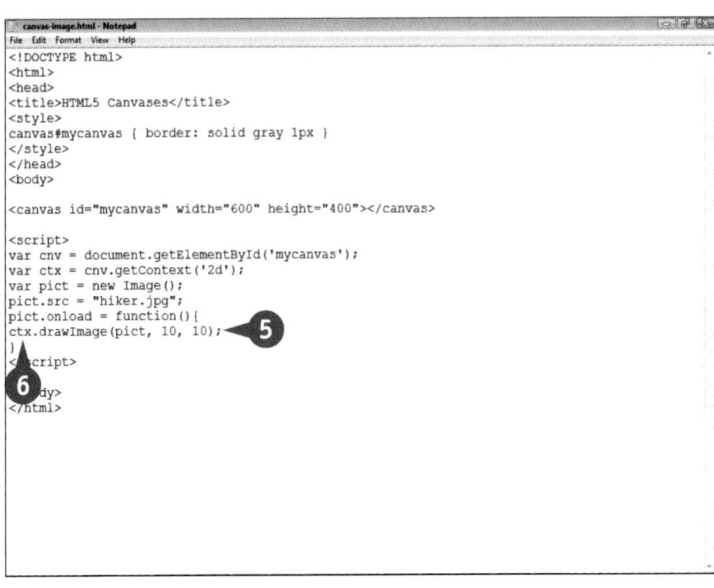

● The web browser displays the image on the canvas at the position that you defined.

How can I scale an image on my canvas?
For scaling, the `drawImage` method accepts two additional values separated by commas. The first value defines the width of the resulting image, and the second defines the height.

In most cases, you want to scale the image proportionally. In the example above, you can get the dimensions of the original image with `pict.width` and `pict.height`. To scale the image, use the original dimensions multiplied by the same value. For example, you can scale the image to half its size with the following code:

```
ctx.drawImage(pict, 10, 10, pict.width*0.5, pict.
height*0.5);
```

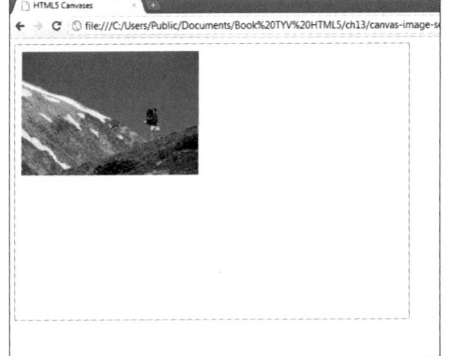

Slice an Image

You can define just a part of an image and then place that part on your canvas. This is known as image slicing. It enables you to place the part of the image that interests you, or place several parts of the same image by repeating the slicing.

You can slice an image at the same time you define where and how it is drawn using the `drawImage` method. You define the slice by defining the rectangular slice with a pair of coordinates. You order the values in the method differently than when you draw an entire image.

Slice an Image

① Set up the canvas and script on your page.

Note: For details, see "Set Up a Canvas."

② Type `var pict = new Image();` to define a new image in your script.

③ Type `pict.src = "?";`, replacing ? with the path to the image.

In this example, the image is stored in the same directory as the HTML, so you can reference it using the image name.

④ Type `pict.onload = function(){.`

This creates a function that runs after the image is loaded.

5 Type `ctx.drawImage(pict, ?);`, replacing *?* with four values pairs.

The first pair defines the starting coordinates of the rectangular slice in the original image.

The second pair defines the width and height of the slice.

The third pair defines the coordinates where the slice is placed on the canvas.

The fourth pair defines the dimensions of the slice on the canvas.

For no scaling, the second and fourth pairs of values are identical.

6 Type } to end the function.

● The web browser displays the sliced image on the canvas at the position that you defined.

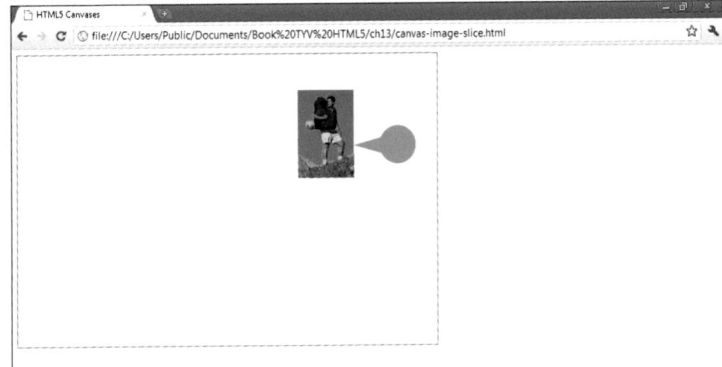

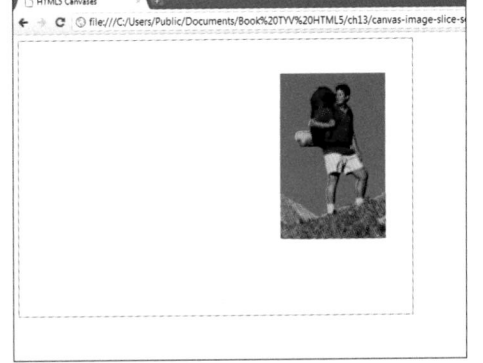

TIP

How can I scale a sliced image on my canvas?

You can scale a slice by adjusting the fourth pair of values in the `drawImage` method, described in step **5** above. This is similar to scaling an entire image as described in the tip for "Add an Image."

In most cases, you want to scale the slice proportionally. In step **5** above, you can multiply the second set of values, which are the width and height of the original slice, by a number to generate the fourth set of values, which are the dimensions of the inserted slice. For example, you can scale the image to twice its size with the following code:

```
ctx.drawImage(pict, 360, 160, 80, 120, 400, 50,
80*2, 120*2);
```

Add a Gradient

You can add a gradual transition from one color to another, known as a *gradient*, to your canvas. You can create a linear gradient, which is a shift in color that moves along a straight line. You can also create a radial gradient, which is a burst of color outward from a central point.

A simple gradient has two color stops, which define where the color transitions begin and end for a gradient. You can add additional color stops to create a rainbow of different colors. You can adjust stop settings to make transitions gradual or abrupt.

Add a Gradient

① Set up the canvas and script on your page.

Note: For details, see "Set Up a Canvas."

② Type `var grd = ctx.createLinearGradient(?);,` replacing ? with two coordinates.

The first defines where to start the gradient, and the second defines where to end the gradient.

Keeping the first and third values the same creates a vertical gradient. Keeping the second and fourth values the same creates a horizontal gradient.

③ Type `grd.addColorStop(?,,` replacing ? with a number from 0 to 1. This defines where along the line the color becomes solid, with values at 0 and 1 being at the ends of the gradient.

④ Type `"?");,` replacing ? with a color name.

⑤ Repeat steps 3 and 4 for other color stops in your gradient.

In this example, a three-color gradient is created from red to green to blue.

```
canvas-gradient.html - Notepad
File  Edit  Format  View  Help
<!DOCTYPE html>
<html>
<head>
<title>HTML5 Canvases</title>
<style>
canvas#mycanvas { border: solid gray 1px }
</style>
</head>
<body>

<canvas id="mycanvas" width="600" height="400"></canvas>

<script>
var cnv = document.getElementById('mycanvas');      ①
var ctx = cnv.getContext('2d');
var grd = ctx.createLinearGradient(0, 0, 600, 0);   ②
</script>

</body>
</html>
```

```
canvas-gradient.html - Notepad
File  Edit  Format  View  Help
<!DOCTYPE html>
<html>
<head>
<title>HTML5 Canvases</title>
<style>
canvas#mycanvas { border: solid gray 1px }
</style>
</head>
<body>

<canvas id="mycanvas" width="600" height="400"></canvas>

<script>
var cnv = document.getElementById('mycanvas');
var ctx = cnv.getContext('2d');
var grd = ctx.createLinearGradient(0, 0, 600, 0);
grd.addColorStop(0, "red");
grd.addColorStop(0.5, "green");
grd.addColorStop(1, "blue");      ⑤
</script>

</body>
</html>
```

6 Type `ctx.fillStyle = grd;` to load the gradient.

7 Type `ctx.fillRect(?);` to draw the gradient, replacing *?* with the starting coordinate of the gradient rectangle followed by the lengths of the sides.

```
canvas-gradient.html - Notepad
File  Edit  Format  View  Help
<!DOCTYPE html>
<html>
<head>
<title>HTML5 Canvases</title>
<style>
canvas#mycanvas { border: solid gray 1px }
</style>
</head>
<body>

<canvas id="mycanvas" width="600" height="400"></canvas>

<script>
var cnv = document.getElementById('mycanvas');
var ctx = cnv.getContext('2d');
var grd = ctx.createLinearGradient(0, 0, 600, 0);
grd.addColorStop(0, "red");
grd.addColorStop(.5, "green");
grd.addColorStop(1, "blue");
ctx.fillStyle = grd;
ctx.fillRect(0, 0, 600, 400);
</script>

</body>
</html>
```

● The web browser displays the gradient on the canvas at the position that you defined.

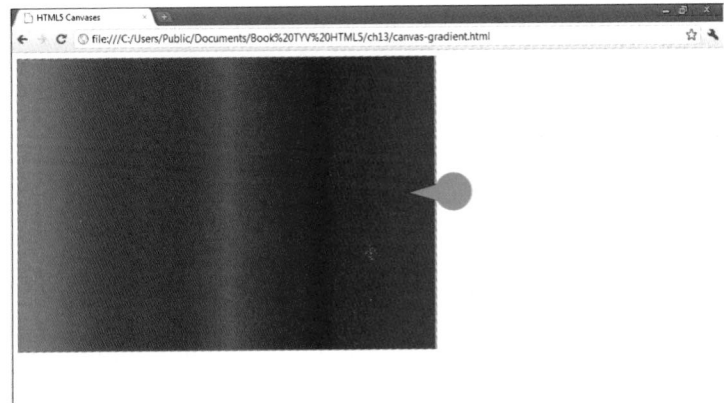

TIP

How can I create a radial gradient?

In the example above, for step 2, type `createRadialGradient(?);`, replacing *?* with the definition of an inner and an outer circle. To define each circle, specify a center coordinate followed by a radius. For example, to create two concentric circles from the coordinates 300, 200, type:

```
var grd = ctx.createRadialGradient(300, 200, 10,
300, 200, 360);
```

When opened in a browser, a radial gradient appears (●).

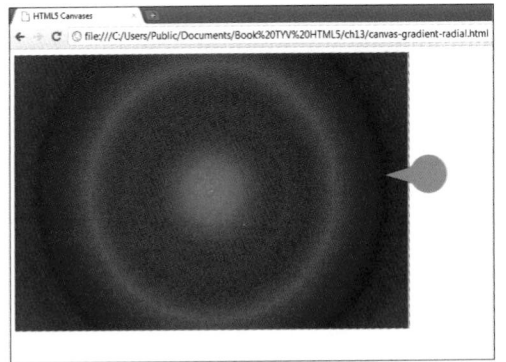

Rotate Canvas Content

You can rotate an item that you place on a canvas to give it an interesting or whimsical presentation. You can rotate shapes, images, text, and other elements on a canvas. Generally, the rotation occurs relative to the starting coordinate for an object.

The `rotate` method accepts the amount of rotation in radians. In radians, a full rotation is two times the value of pi. You can add an additional calculation to your script so that you can specify the rotation in degrees rather than radians, such as in the example below.

Rotate Canvas Content

① Set up the canvas and script on your page.

Note: For details, see "Set Up a Canvas."

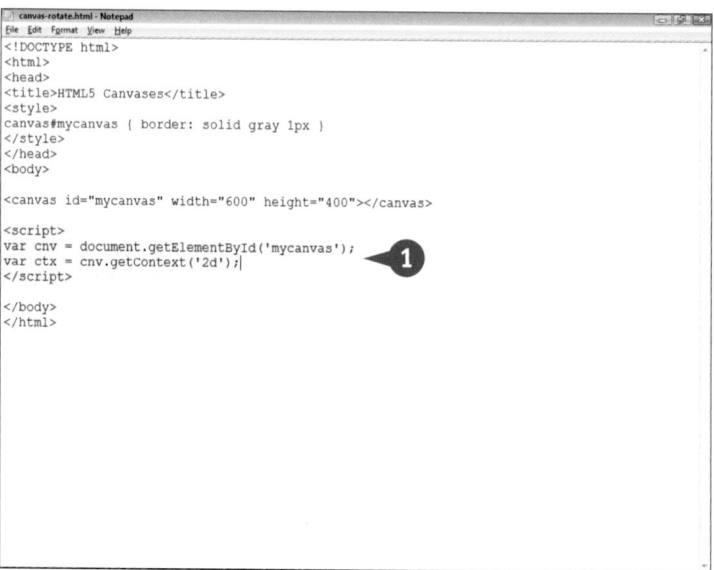

② Add the element you want to rotate to your canvas.

In this example, an image is added to the canvas. For more about adding images, see "Add an Image."

● When the image is rotated, the rotation occurs about this coordinate.

```
canvas-rotate.html - Notepad
File  Edit  Format  View  Help
<!DOCTYPE html>
<html>
<head>
<title>HTML5 Canvases</title>
<style>
canvas#mycanvas { border: solid gray 1px }
</style>
</head>
<body>

<canvas id="mycanvas" width="600" height="400"></canvas>

<script>
var cnv = document.getElementById('mycanvas');
var ctx = cnv.getContext('2d');
</script>

</body>
</html>
```
①

```
canvas-rotate.html - Notepad
File  Edit  Format  View  Help
<!DOCTYPE html>
<html>
<head>
<title>HTML5 Canvases</title>
<style>
canvas#mycanvas { border: solid gray 1px }
</style>
</head>
<body>

<canvas id="mycanvas" width="600" height="400"></canvas>

<script>
var cnv = document.getElementById('mycanvas');
var ctx = cnv.getContext('2d');
var pict = new Image();
pict.src = "hiker.jpg";
pict.onload = function(){
ctx.drawImage(pict, 20, 0);
}
</script>

</body>
</html>
```
②

③ Before the method that draws the element on the page, type `ctx.rotate(? * Math.PI/180);`, replacing *?* with the amount of rotation in degrees.

The amount of rotation can be a negative number.

● The web browser displays the element on the canvas in a rotated state.

Note: If you rotate an element too much on a small canvas, the element may appear outside the canvas area.

TIP

How can I rotate multiple elements on a canvas?
You can add a `rotate` method before each drawn element. However, rotations are additive when you perform more than one on a page. That means if you make a 30-degree rotation, draw an object, make a 40-degree rotation, and draw another object, the second object appears rotated 70 degrees, which is probably not what you want.

You can avoid this by saving the canvas context prior to performing any canvas methods. Then you perform the `restore` method after drawing the element, thereby resetting rotation. For example, the following rotates the "Teach Yourself" text 30 degrees and the "Visually" text 40 degrees:

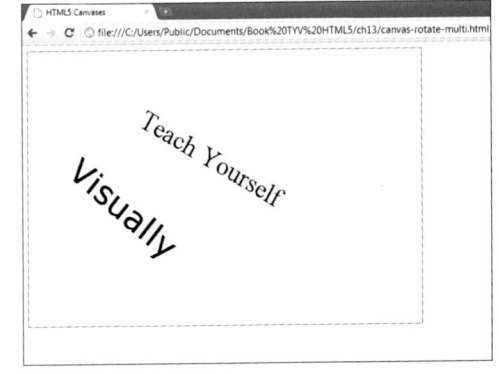

```
ctx.save();
ctx.font = '40px "Times New Roman"';
ctx.rotate(30 * Math.PI / 180);
ctx.fillText('Teach Yourself', 200, 10);
ctx.restore();
ctx.save();
ctx.font = '50px Verdana';
ctx.rotate(40 * Math.PI / 180);
ctx.fillText('Visually', 160, 100);
ctx.restore();
```

Animate Canvas Content

You can create an animation by drawing an object on a canvas repeatedly, each time changing the position of the object. Animations can be used to draw attention to part of a page or to create a game with which the user can interact. This example shows how to make a ball bounce back and forth between the sides of a canvas.

Before HTML5 and the `<canvas>` tag were available, web designers had to resort to animation technologies such as Flash to create this type of content on a web page. To add interactivity to such content, you can add event handlers that react to user behavior. See Chapter 12 for more about event handlers.

Animate Canvas Content

① Set up the canvas and script on your page.

Note: For details, see "Set Up a Canvas."

② Define variables for the animation.

The `x` and `y` variables determine the position of the animated ball.

The `change` variable determines how far the ball moves during a redraw and in which direction.

The `w` and `h` variables determine the dimensions of the box.

③ Type `function ?() {`, replacing `?` with the name of the animation function. Do not include spaces in the name.

The function is used to draw the background and animated ball.

④ Type `ctx.fillStyle = '?';`, replacing `?` with the color of the background.

⑤ Type `ctx.fillRect(0, 0, w, h);` to draw the rectangular background.

During a redraw, the background covers any existing content to clear the canvas.

6 Type `ctx.fillStyle = '?';`, replacing *?* with the color of the animated ball.

7 Type `ctx.beginPath();` to begin a new drawing path for drawing the ball.

```
canvas-animate.html - Notepad
File  Edit  Format  View  Help

<canvas id="mycanvas" width="600" height="400"></canvas>

<script>
var cnv = document.getElementById('mycanvas');
var ctx = cnv.getContext('2d');

x = 200;
y = 200;
change = 4;
w = 600;
h = 400;

function animate() {
  ctx.fillStyle = 'lightgray';
  ctx.fillRect(0, 0, w, h);
  ctx.fillStyle = 'red';   ⬅ 6
  ctx.beginPath();

</script>
                 7
</body>
</html>
```

8 Type `ctx.arc(x, y, ?,,` replacing *?* with the diameter of the ball in pixels.

9 Type `0, Math.PI*2, true);` to complete the ball path.

For more about drawing circles, see "Draw Circles."

10 Type `ctx.fill();` to fill the path and draw the ball.

```
canvas-animate.html - Notepad
File  Edit  Format  View  Help

<canvas id="mycanvas" width="600" height="400"></canvas>

<script>
var cnv = document.getElementById('mycanvas');
var ctx = cnv.getContext('2d');

x = 200;
y = 200;
change = 4;
w = 600;
h = 400;

function animate() {
  ctx.f   8  yle = 'lightg
  ctx.f      ct(0, 0, w, h    9
  ctx.fillStyle = 'red';
  ctx.beginPath();
  ctx.arc(x, y, 20, 0, Math.PI*2, true);
  ctx.fill();

</scr  t>
       10
</bo
</html>
```

TIP

What other animation can I make?

You can change the bouncing ball animation
to display an expanding and shrinking shape. Instead of redrawing a moving
ball in the animation function, you redraw a differently sized rectangle. You
use the `clearRect` command to reset the canvas each time you draw. To
create the animation, change the code in the `animate()` function to the
following:

```
ctx.clearRect(0, 0, w, h);
ctx.fillStyle = 'gray';
ctx.fillRect(0, 0, x, h);
if (x >= w || x <= 0) {
  change = -change;
}
x = x + change;
```

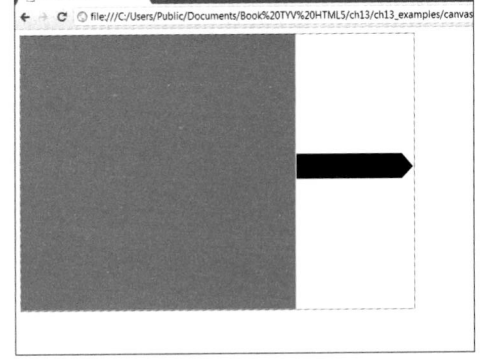

In the bouncing ball animation, you keep track of the position of the ball using JavaScript *variables*, which are placeholders that store data. Each time the ball is drawn, the variable that defines the horizontal position of the ball is updated. You also check if the position of the ball is at the edge of the canvas. If so, you change the direction of movement.

The `setInterval` command is used to repeat the animation function and helps make it easy to create animations on your canvas.

Animate Canvas Content (continued)

11 Type `if (x >= w || x <= 0) {` to check if the position of the ball is at the right or left edge of the canvas.

12 Type `change = -change;`. This code is executed if the result of step 11 is true. The value of the `change` variable is switched to reverse the direction of the animated ball.

13 Type `}`.

```
canvas-animate.html - Notepad
File  Edit  Format  View  Help

<canvas id="mycanvas" width="600" height="400"></canvas>

<script>
var cnv = document.getElementById('mycanvas');
var ctx = cnv.getContext('2d');

x = 200;
y = 200;
change = 4;
w = 600;
h = 400;

function animate() {
  ctx.fillStyle = 'lightgray';
  ctx.fillRect(0, 0, w, h);
  ctx.fillStyle = 'red';
  ctx.beginPath();
  ctx.arc(x, y, 20, 0, Math.PI*2, true);
  ctx.fill();
  if (x >= w || x <= 0) {       11
    change = -change;
  }                             12
</script>                  13
</html>
```

14 Type `x = x + change;` to update the horizontal position of the animated ball.

15 Type `}` to complete the drawing function.

```
canvas-animate.html - Notepad
File  Edit  Format  View  Help
<script>
var cnv = document.getElementById('mycanvas');
var ctx = cnv.getContext('2d');

x = 200;
y = 200;
change = 4;
w = 600;
h = 400;

function animate() {
  ctx.fillStyle = 'lightgray';
  ctx.fillRect(0, 0, w, h);
  ctx.fillStyle = 'red';
  ctx.beginPath();
  ctx.arc(x, y, 20, 0, Math.PI*2, true);
  ctx.fill();
  if (x >= w || x <= 0) {
    change = -change;
  }
  x = x + change;       14
}
</script>
15 body>
</html>
```

16 Type `setInterval(?,`, replacing *?* with the name of the function from step **3**. This causes the function to repeat.

17 Type `?);`, replacing *?* with a time, in milliseconds, to wait between each repetition. Adjusting this value changes the speed of the animation.

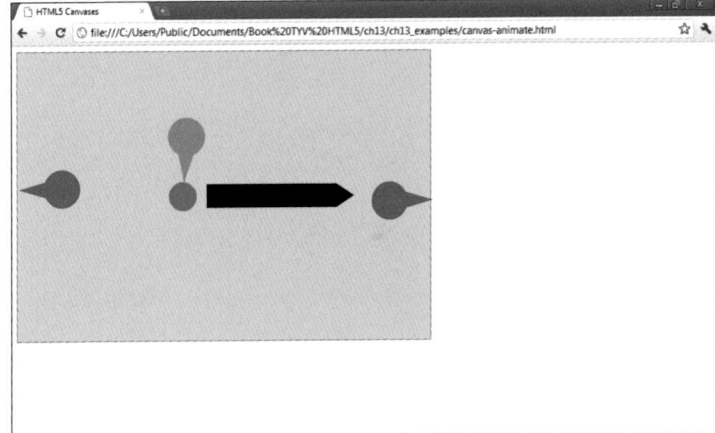

```
change = 4;
w = 600;
h = 400;

function animate() {
  ctx.fillStyle = 'lightgray';
  ctx.fillRect(0, 0, w, h);
  ctx.fillStyle = 'red';
  ctx.beginPath();
  ctx.arc(x, y, 20, 0, Math.PI*2, true);
  ctx.fill();
  if (x >= w || x <= 0) {
    change = -change;
  }
  x = x + change;
}

setInterval(animate, 10);

</script>

</body>
</html>
```

● The web browser displays the animation.

● When the animated ball reaches the right or left side of the canvas, the ball reverses direction.

TIP

How do I bounce a ball in both dimensions?
To bounce the ball up and down as well as left and right, change the y variable in the drawing step as well as the x variable. To do this, first add a new variable in step **2** above to control how the y variable changes:

`otherchange = 3;`

Also add the following code to the `animate()` function. Add it just *before* you add the ending parenthesis in step **13**:

```
if (y >= h || y <= 0) {
  otherchange = -otherchange;
}
y = y + otherchange;
```

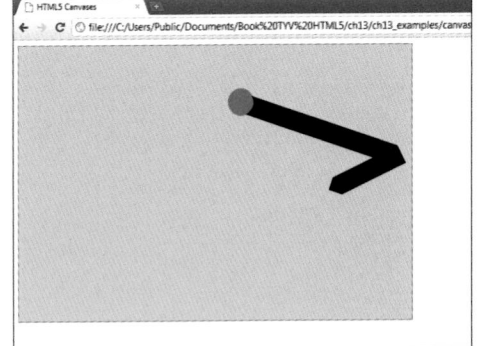

Adding Video and Audio

Do you want to add multimedia to your web pages? Adding video enables you to tell a story, feature a product, or provide interactivity to your viewers. Some concepts can be presented more effectively using moving pictures rather than static words and photos. By embedding audio, you can add background music to your pages to add ambiance.

HTML5 includes new tags for adding video and audio to your website. This chapter covers how to add multimedia with these tags, turn on player controls for audio and video, and provide alternative file formats to make the user experience as optimal as possible for all users.

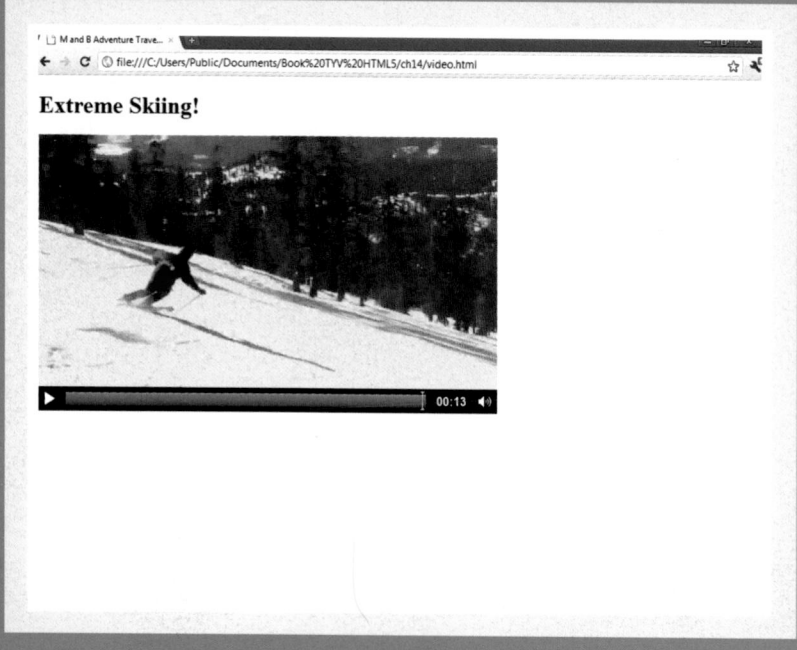

Understanding Video and Audio

Video and audio can create an ambiance for a site, enhance a site's message, illustrate a product or service, or simply entertain. You can incorporate your video and audio elements into your HTML5 pages in different ways, but you should first understand how such elements work on the web.

Video

With the increasing availability of broadband Internet connections and inexpensive tools for capturing video clips, web video has become more and more popular. Basic video on the web can be recorded with a camcorder, digital camera, or mobile phone, uploaded to a standard web server, and integrated into a page using HTML5. Working with video on the web is still more challenging than working with other content, given the larger size of video files and the fact that not all browsers support the same video formats. However, once you have your video file saved and ready to go, adding it to your page with HTML5 is as easy as adding an image.

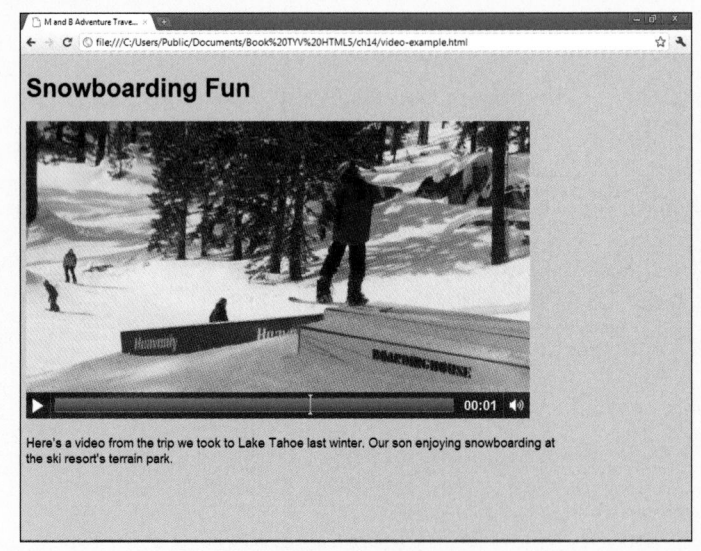

Audio

Audio files enable you to integrate songs, spoken word, and sound effects with your web page. You can also deliver audio-based episodes of content, known as *podcasts*, on your site. Podcasts can also involve video. Working with audio on your web page is similar to working with video. File sizes are generally smaller and the content typically takes up less real estate on your page. When you add audio, the file is typically represented by a small set of player controls that let users play, pause, and control the volume.

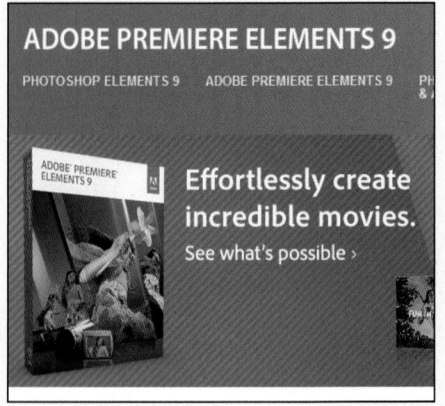

HTML5 Tags

HTML5 introduces two new tags, `<video>` and `<audio>`, for embedding multimedia into web pages. You embed a file by providing a `src` value along with the tag, similar to how you embed an image file with the `<img>` tag. Attributes for the `<video>` and `<audio>` tags enable you to show player controls, make clips repeat, preload content, and provide alternative formats and sources of the media. Prior to HTML5, web designers embedded video and audio using complicated combinations of `<embed>` and `<object>` tags. Those tags depended on web browsers having separate helper applications known as *plug-ins* installed to view the content. Browsers that support the HTML5 `<video>` and `<audio>` tags can play video and audio content *natively*, which means they do not need extra plug-ins.

Creating Your Media

Before you add video or audio to your page using HTML5, you need to create it. Mobile phones and low-end digital cameras offer an inexpensive way to record low-resolution video, which can be great for capturing spur-of-the-moment scenes. More expensive camcorders enable you to capture high-definition video that will look better when played on your site. Remember that the higher quality the video and audio, the greater the file size and the longer it takes for viewers to download. Before putting the clips online, you can download the files to your computer for editing. Most cameras come with basic video-editing software for trimming clips and adding titles and transitions. For a fancier final product, you can edit your video in applications such as Adobe Premiere Elements and Apple iMovie. For audio, you can edit files in applications such as Audacity and Apple GarageBand.

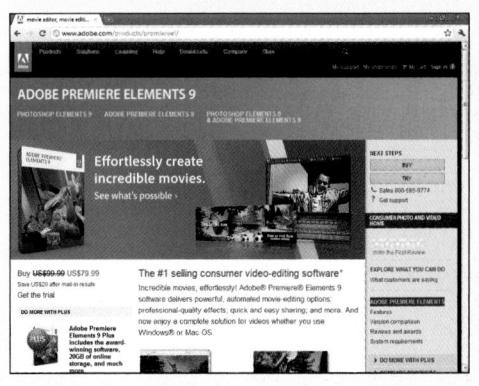

Saving and Converting Files

A key challenge in making video and audio available online is choosing from the many available file formats. To reach the widest audience, you can save your files in multiple formats and make several available at once. If you have your media in one format, you can convert it to other web-friendly formats with free and inexpensive converters. One handy tool for PCs and Macs is the MiroVideo Converter, which can convert video to formats such as WebM and Ogg Theora. It is available at www.mirovideoconverter.com. AVS Audio Converter is a free, downloadable program for converting sound, available at www.avs4you.com.

Different Browsers, Different Formats

Support for video and audio file formats varies across browsers. Below is a table listing which browsers play what file types. In parentheses are the common file extensions for those formats.

Browser	Video	Audio
Google Chrome 10	Ogg Theora (ogg, .ogv), H.264 (.m4v), WebM (.webm)	Vorbis (.ogg, .oga)
Mozilla Firefox 4	Theora (.ogg, .ogv), WebM (.webm)	Vorbis (.ogg, .oga)
Internet Explorer 9	H.264 (.m4v), WebM (.webm)	Vorbis (.ogg, .oga)
Apple Safari	H.264 (.m4v)	MP3 (.mp3)

To make sure as many users can see your content as possible, you can offer clips in multiple formats at once. For details, see "Offer Multiple Sources."

Insert a Video File

You can add a video file to your page to display a movie inside your page. You specify the location of the video file using the `src` attribute. You can add videos to explain concepts visually or simply to entertain. You can have your browser display controls so that viewers can play and pause the video, seek through the video, and adjust the volume. Controls may appear slightly different across different web browsers.

An alternative to hosting the video file yourself and adding it to your page is embedding a video from a video-sharing site such as YouTube. For more details, see "Embed a YouTube Video."

Insert a Video File

1 Type `<video src="?">` where you want to insert the video clip, replacing *?* with the relative path to the file you want to insert.

In this example, because the audio file was saved in the same folder as the HTML file, you reference it with just the filename.

Note: If you want to add a video that exists on an external site, you can type a URL instead of a filename.

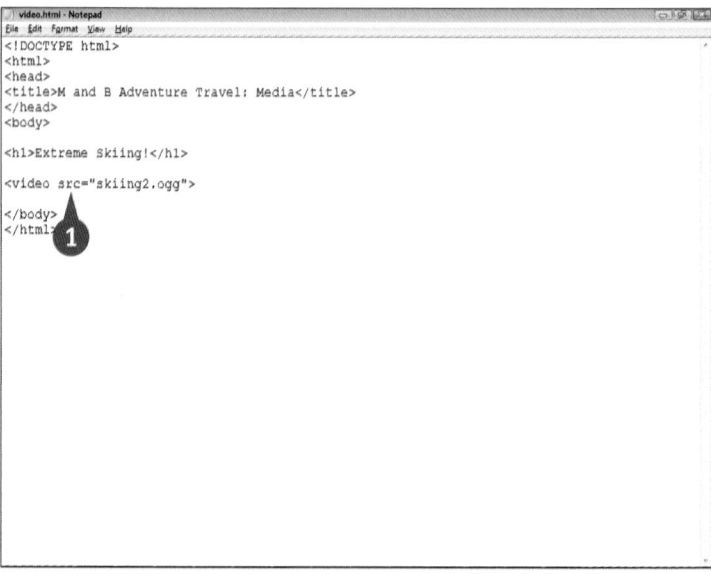

2 Inside the `<video>` tag, type a space and then type `controls`.

Without the `controls` attribute, the user cannot start and stop the video clip or control it in other ways.

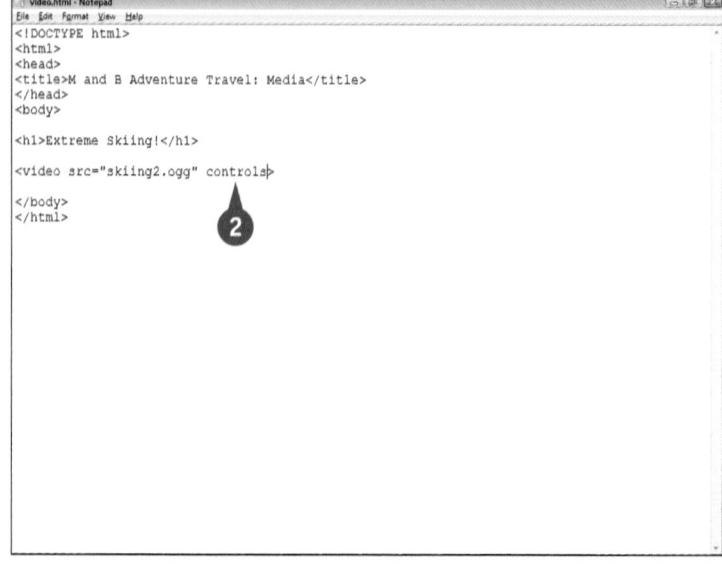

③ After the `<video>` tag, you can type alternative content that appears if the browser is unable to load the video file.

This example displays a link to the file. For more about creating links, see Chapter 7.

④ Type `</video>`.

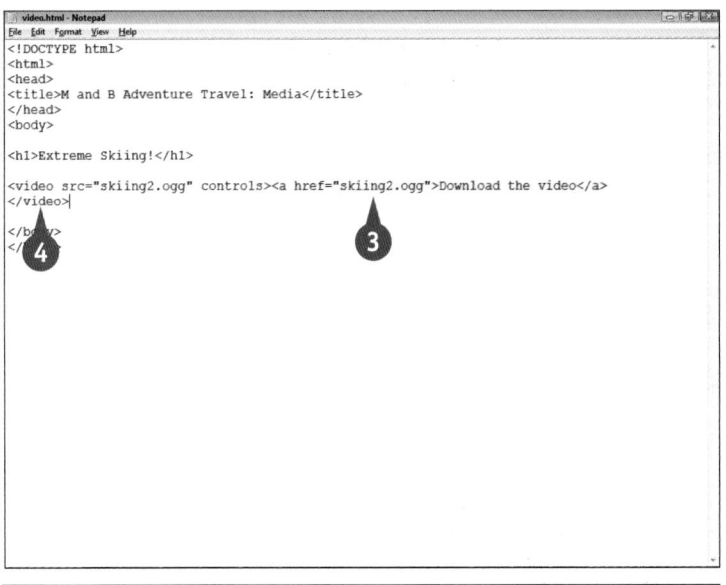

The web browser displays the video on the page.

● You can click the play button to play the video.

The video appears at the dimensions at which it was saved. To change the dimensions, see "Resize a Video."

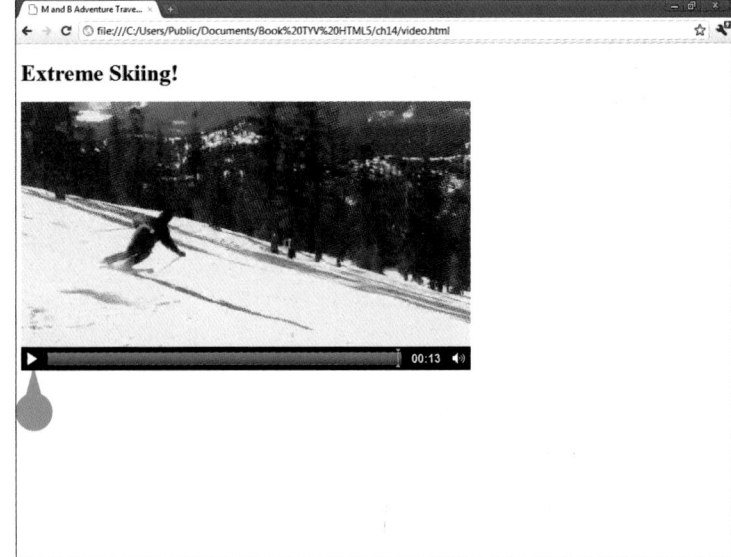

How do I make a video automatically start when my page loads?
You can add the `autoplay` attribute to the `<video>` tag. For example:

`<video src="myvid.ogg" autoplay></video>`

If you add `autoplay` and leave off controls, most browsers will play the video but not give you any way to stop it. The `autoplay` attribute also works with the `<audio>` tag. See "Insert an Audio File" for more details.

What video format should I use?
HTML5-capable browsers support different video formats, including Theora (.ogg, .ogv), H.268 (.m4v), and WebM (.webm). For more details, see "Understanding Video and Audio." To specify multiple formats for download, see "Offer Multiple Sources."

Insert an Audio File

You can add an audio file to your page to add background music or provide a song or spoken-word performance that users can play. You can have the browser display controls so that viewers can play and pause the audio, seek through the audio content, and adjust the volume. Controls may appear slightly different across different web browsers.

You can add alternative text inside your `<audio>` tag that appears if the browser is unable to play the audio file.

Insert an Audio File

① Type `<audio src="?">` where you want to insert the audio clip, replacing *?* with the relative path to the file you want to insert.

In this example, because the audio file was saved in the same folder as the HTML file, you reference it with just the filename.

Note: If you want to add an audio file that exists on an external site, you can type a URL instead of a filename.

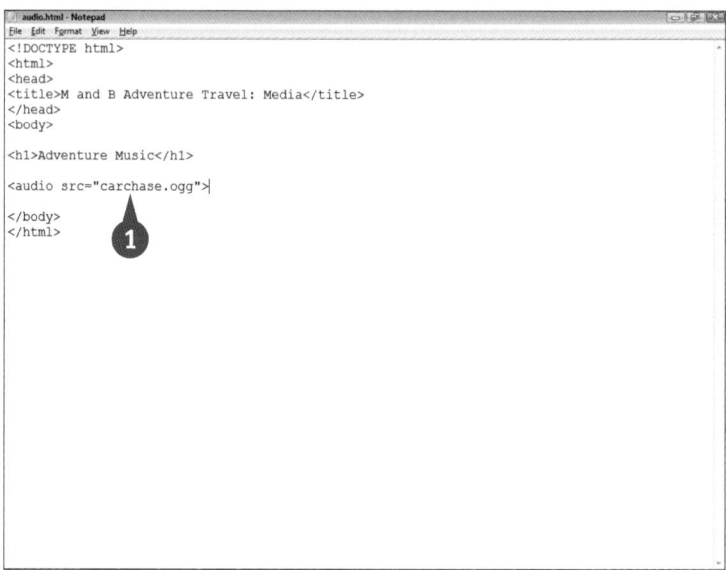

② Inside the `<audio>` tag, type a space and then type `controls`.

Without the `controls` attribute, the user cannot start and stop the audio clip or control it in other ways.

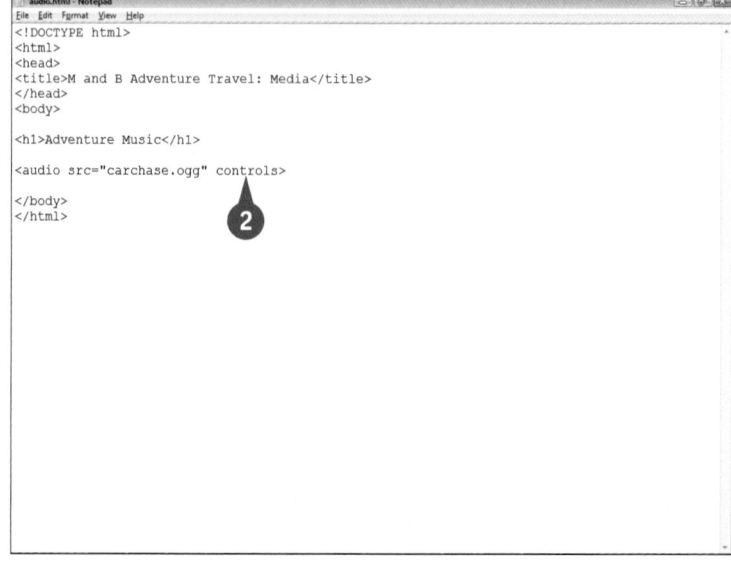

③ After the `<audio>` tag, you can add alternative content that appears if the browser is unable to load the audio file.

This example displays a link to the file. For more about creating links, see Chapter 7.

④ Type `</audio>`.

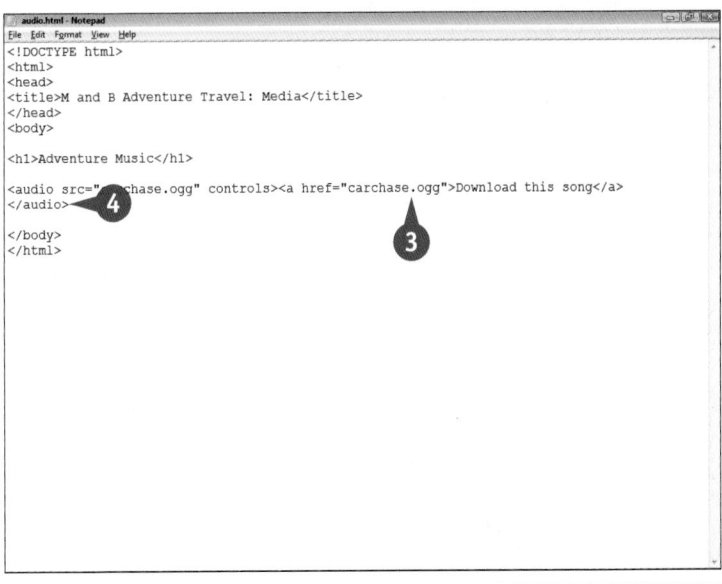

The web browser displays the audio on the page with controls.

● You can click the play button to play the audio.

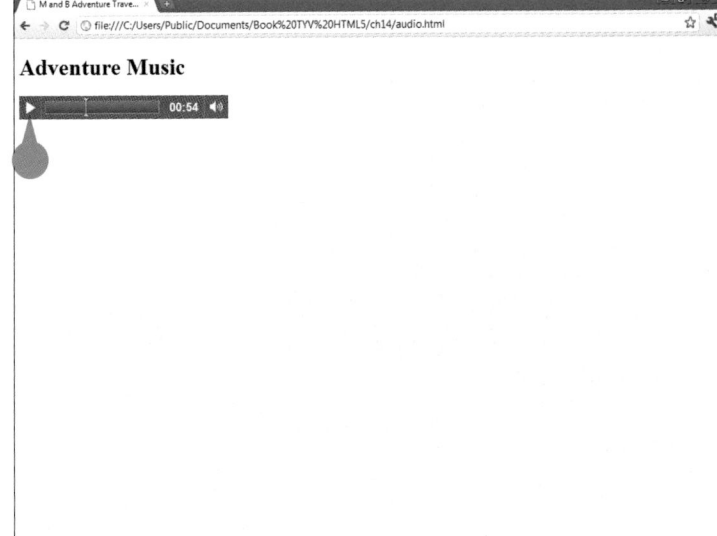

How do I add background music to a page without displaying controls?

In the `<audio>` tag, you can leave out the `controls` attribute to hide the controls and add the `autoplay` attribute to start the audio file automatically after it loads. The audio plays as background music. For example:

`<audio src="mysong.ogg" autoplay></audio>`

The downside to this is that it offers no way for the user to mute or pause the music.

What audio format should I use?

HTML5-capable browsers support different audio formats, including Vorbis (.ogg, .oga) and MP3 (.mp3). For more details, see "Understanding Video and Audio." To specify multiple formats for download, see "Offer Multiple Sources."

Resize a Video

You can resize a video on your web page to make it fit with the other content on your page. Within the <video> tag, you can add width and height attributes to change the dimensions of the video. If you do not specify dimensions, the browser plays the video at the size at which it was saved. Changing the video size can negatively affect the quality of the video, especially if you make the video much larger than the original size.

Resize a Video

Resize to the Same Aspect Ratio

1. Add a video file to your page using the <video> tag and the src attribute.

Note: See "Insert a Video File" for details.

2. Within the <video> tag, type a dimension attribute, either width or height.

3. Type ="?", replacing ? with a measurement in pixels.

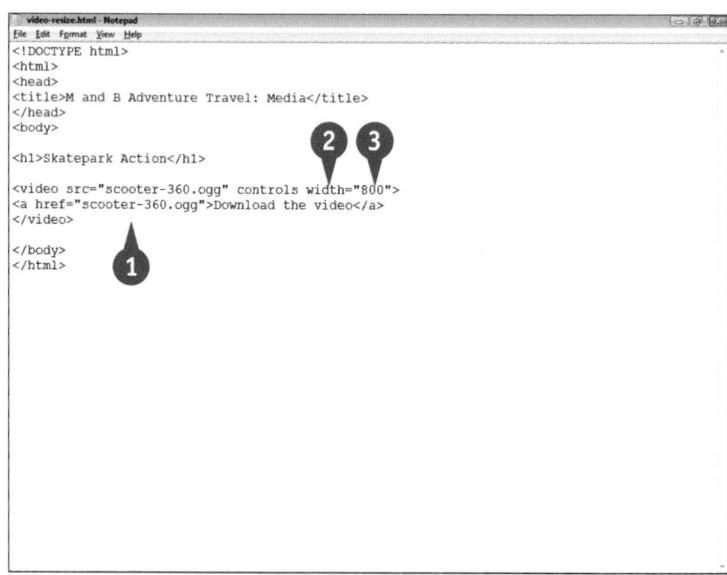

The web browser displays the video at the specified size.

● The other dimension is scaled so that the video retains the same aspect ratio.

Resize with Letterboxing

1 Add a video file to your page using the `<video>` tag and the `src` attribute.

2 Within the `<video>` tag, type `width="?"`, replacing *?* with the width in pixels.

3 Type `height="?"`, replacing *?* with the height in pixels.

For letterboxing to occur, the dimensions should differ in aspect ratio from the original aspect ratio of the video.

4 You set the `background-color` CSS property of the `<video>` tag to color the letterboxing space.

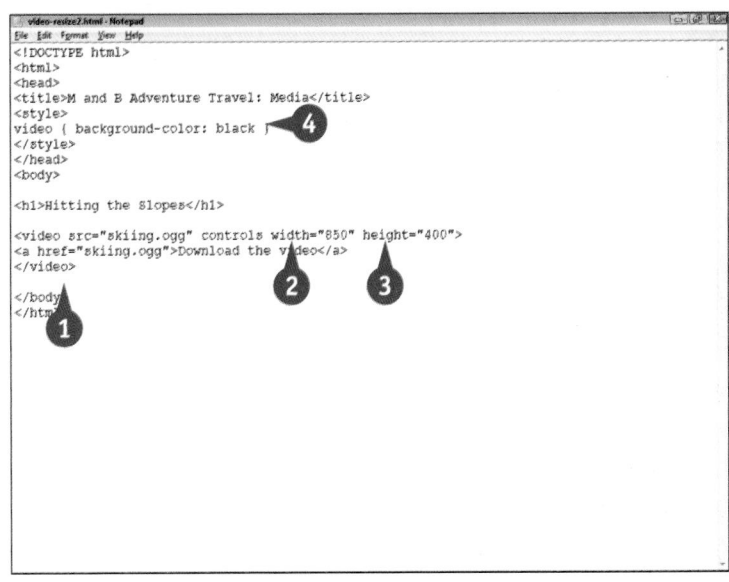

The web browser displays the video at the specified dimensions.

● Instead of stretching the video to fit the longer dimension, in this case the width, the browser adds letterboxing.

What if I add dimensions to my <audio> tag?
Most browsers will not resize the audio content. Dimensions apply to `<video>` tag content on web pages but not `<audio>` tag content. Note that you can keep controls from appearing with your audio by removing the `controls` attribute.

How do I align a video to the side of the page?
After you resize the video, you can align it to either side of your page using the `float` CSS property, similar to how you can align an image on your page. For example, to align videos on your page to the right:

```
video { float: right }
```

You can align individual videos by applying a CSS class. For more details about applying CSS, see Chapter 4.

Preload Multimedia

You can preload a multimedia file on your web page, which means the browser starts downloading it whether or not the user is actually playing it. This can give viewers a better experience when they play the video or audio clip because there is less chance the media must pause midstream if the download speed is not sufficient. If the video is the primary element on your page, preloading can be helpful to users. The downside is that it wastes network resources if the user never plays the file.

Preload Multimedia

1 Add a video file to your page using the `<video>` tag and the `src` and `controls` attributes.

Note: See "Insert a Video File" for details.

2 Inside the `<video>` tag, type `preload="auto"`.

Note: This example shows preloading a video file. You can similarly preload an audio file using the `<audio>` tag and the `preload` attribute.

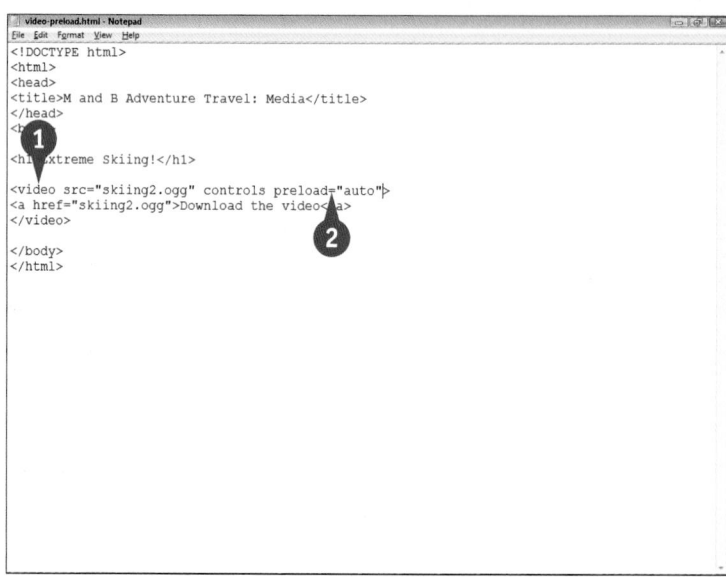

The web browser preloads the video when the page loads.

● Because the video is preloaded, you can click and drag the seek-bar slider on the video controls to skip ahead within the video.

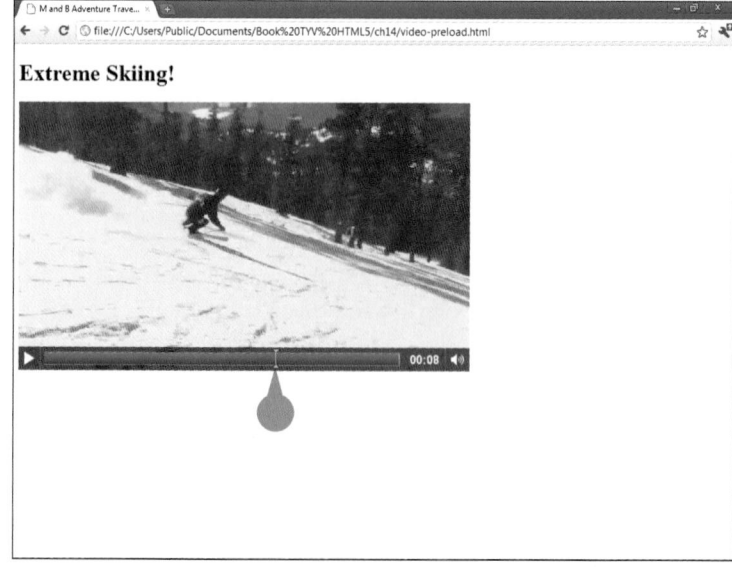

Loop Multimedia

You can use the `loop` attribute in the `<video>` or `<audio>` tags to cause your clips to repeat after they finish. This can be useful if you have a short clip that you want to play over and over again for an artistic effect on your page. You may also want to loop background music. To have the audio or video clip also automatically start when a page loads, you can add the `autoplay` attribute to your tag.

Loop Multimedia

① Add a video or audio file to your page using the `<video>` or `<audio>` tag and the `src` and `controls` attributes.

Note: See "Insert a Video File" or "Insert an Audio File" for details.

② Inside the tag, type `loop`.

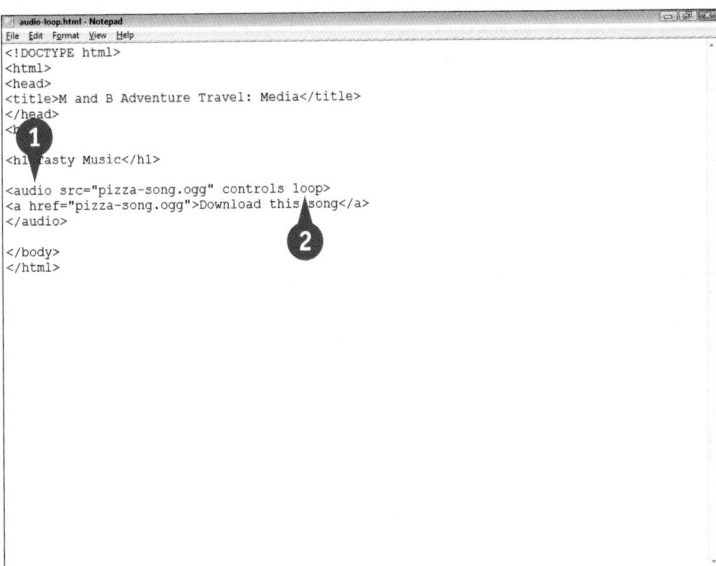

The web browser loops the multimedia when it reaches the end. In this example, an audio clip is looped.

● If the `controls` attribute is present, you can click the pause button to stop the clip from playing.

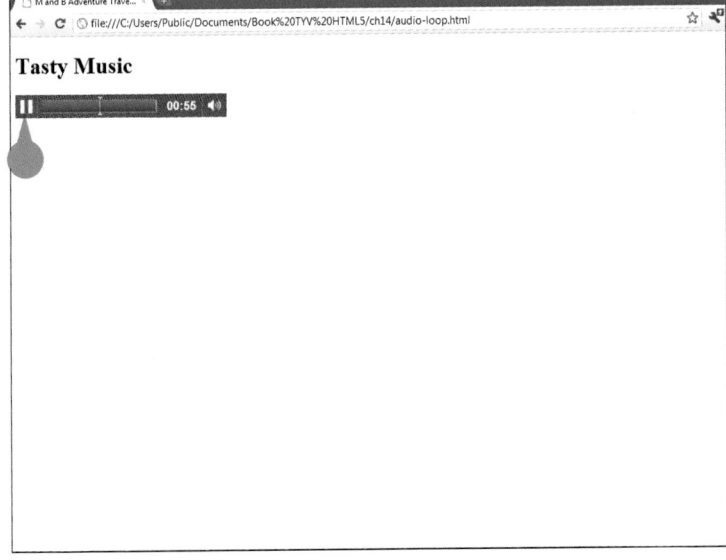

Offer Multiple Sources

When adding video or audio to your page, you can specify multiple file sources for your clips. For example, you can associate your `<video>` tag with both a WebM video file (.webm) as well as an Ogg Theora video file (.ogg, .ogv) at the same time. HTML5-capable browsers attempt to load one source and, if it is not recognized, can try loading the next source.

This is useful because not all HTML5-capable browsers support all possible media types. By saving your multimedia as different formats, then specifying multiple sources in your `<video>` or `<audio>` tag, you can improve the experience for people who visit your site. See "Understanding Video and Audio" for a list of supported file formats.

Offer Multiple Sources

① Type a `<video>` or `<audio>` tag, depending on the type of media you want to insert.

② Type a `controls` attribute to display player controls.

③ Do not include a `src` attribute to define the location of the media file as in previous examples.

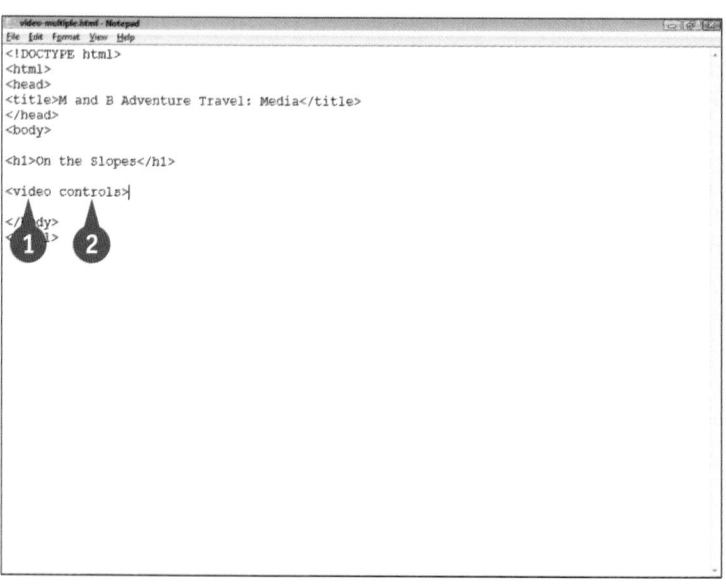

④ Type `<source src="?"`, replacing *?* with the path to the media file.

⑤ Type `type="?">`, replacing *?* with the MIME type of the source file you added in step **4**.

In this example, a WebM (.webm) file is added, so the `"video/webm"` MIME type is used.

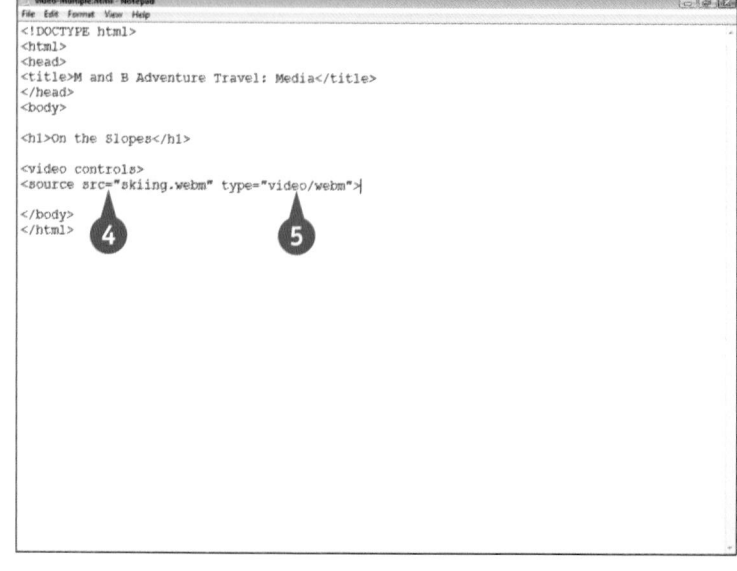

6 Repeat steps **4** and **5** for a second media file and any additional sources that you want to add.

In this example, an Ogg Theora (.ogg) file is added, so the `"video/ogg"` MIME type is used.

7 Type `</video>` or `</audio>`, depending on the tag added in step **1**.

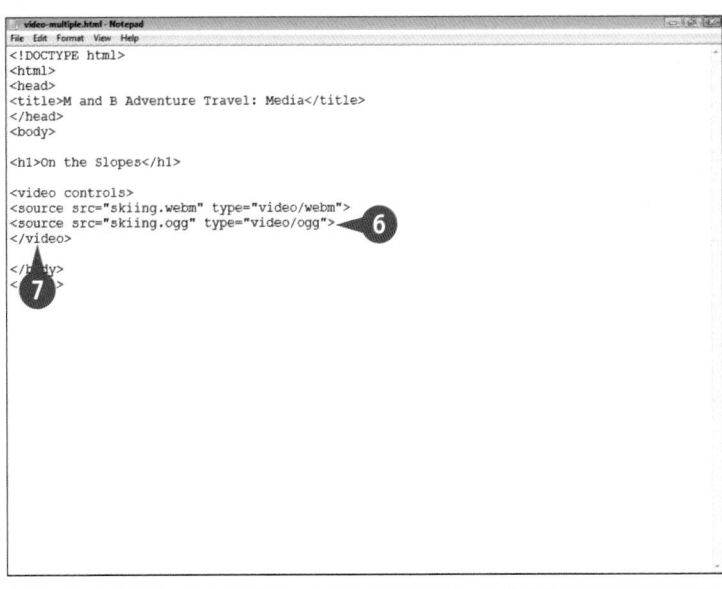

The web browser displays the video on the page.

This example shows the Firefox 3.6 browser, which cannot read the WebM video source file but can read the Ogg Theora video source file.

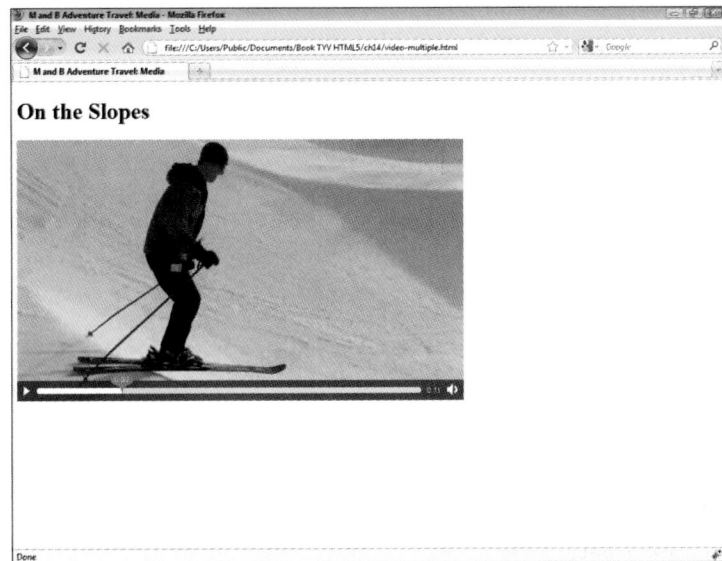

TIPS

What happens if the browser cannot load any of the sources?
The video or audio clip will not appear or play in the browser. This may happen with older browsers that do not support the new `<video>` or `<source>` tags. This may also occur if the browser does not support the file formats. You can add additional content inside the `<video>` or `<audio>` tag that the browser can fall back on, such as a download link to the content. See "Insert a Video File" and "Insert an Audio File" for details. You can also add multimedia tags that older browsers support. See "Support Older Browsers" for more information.

What is a MIME type?
Also known as an Internet Media Type, a MIME type is a two-part identifier for files on the Internet. In the `<source>` tag, the MIME type tells the browser what type of file it is loading. If the browser does not support the MIME type, it does not need to download the file, which can save bandwidth. MIME stands for *Multipurpose Internet Mail Extensions*, because MIME types were originally used in e-mail. For a list of MIME types, visit www.wooldridge.net/html5

Support Older Browsers

HTML5 is a new web standard, and not all web browsers support HTML5 tags. Fortunately, there are ways to offer fallback measures for browsers that do not support HTML5. For video, you can include additional HTML tags with your `<video>` tag to support older web browsers. By including both the `<embed>` tag and the `<object>` tag, you can support the majority of browsers in use today. You can use the same technique to support audio files. See the tip for details.

Support Older Browsers

① Add a video to your page using the `<video>` and `</video>` tags. You use a `src` attribute to specify the path to the video file.

Note: For more information, see "Insert a Video File."

② Between the `<video>` and `</video>` tags, type `<embed src="?">`, replacing *?* with the path to your video file.

③ Within the `<embed>` tag, type `width="?" height="?"`, replacing *?* in both attributes with width and height values for the video.

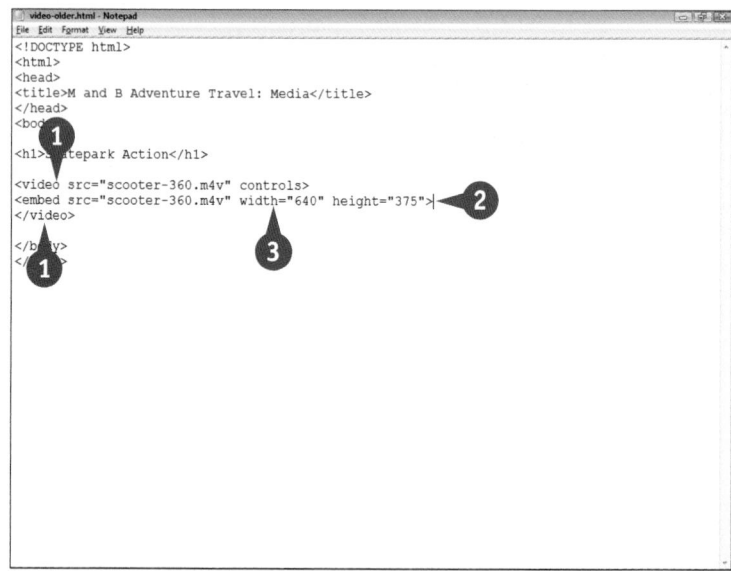

④ Between the `<video>` and `<embed>` tags, type `<object classid="clsid: ?">`, replacing *?* with the class ID for a multimedia plug-in.

In this example, the M4V plug-in is specified with a class ID of `02BF25D5-8C17-4B23-BC80-D3488ABDDC6B`.

For a list of common class ID values, visit: www.wooldridge.net/html5

⑤ Within the `<object>` tag, type `width="?" height="?"`, replacing *?* in both attributes with width and height values.

⑥ Type `<param name="src" value="?">`, replacing *?* with the path to the video file.

⑦ Type a closing `</object>` tag between the `<embed>` tag the `</video>` tag.

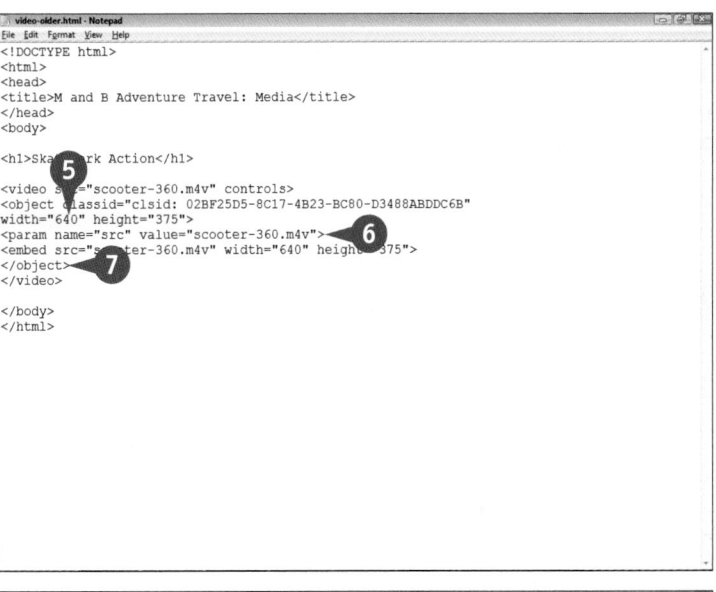

The code supports older browsers that do not support the HTML5 `<video>` tag for displaying multimedia.

In this example, a video is displayed in the Firefox 3.0 browser, which supports the `<embed>` tag but not the `<video>` tag.

TIPS

How do I add audio to my page in a way that supports older browsers?
Repeat the steps above, except use an `<audio>` tag instead of a `<video>` tag and reference your audio file with the `src` attributes. You must specify different `width` and `height` attributes to account for the smaller dimensions of the audio controls. You will also need to specify the appropriate class ID in the `<object>` tag. The class ID value depends on the type of audio file you are displaying.

How does an older browser process the <video>, <object>, and <embed> tags in the example?
Typically, browsers ignore HTML tags that they do not understand. If a browser loading the page does not recognize the newer `<video>` tag, it ignores the tag and reads the `<object>` tag that is inside. If the browser does not recognize the `<object>` tag either, it ignores that and reads the `<embed>` tag.

Embed a YouTube Video

You can embed a video stored on a hosting service such as YouTube by inserting HTML code into your web page. The video appears on the page the same way as a video stored locally with your HTML files. Hosting content on a separate server can be necessary if your web host does not offer sufficient server space or has strict bandwidth requirements.

To host videos at YouTube, you can sign up for a free account at www.youtube.com and use the service's uploading tool.

Embed a YouTube Video

1 Open your web browser to the YouTube video you want to add to your web page.

You can visit YouTube at www.youtube.com.

2 Click **Share**.

3 Click **Embed**.

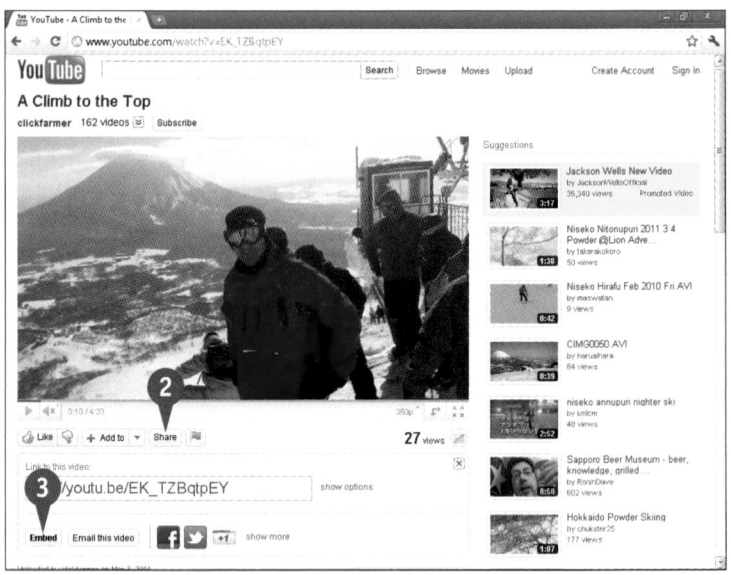

- The HTML appears.

4 Click here to select options for your embedded video.

5 Click and drag to select the HTML code.

6 In your web browser, right-click the selected text.

A contextual menu appears.

7 Click **Copy**.

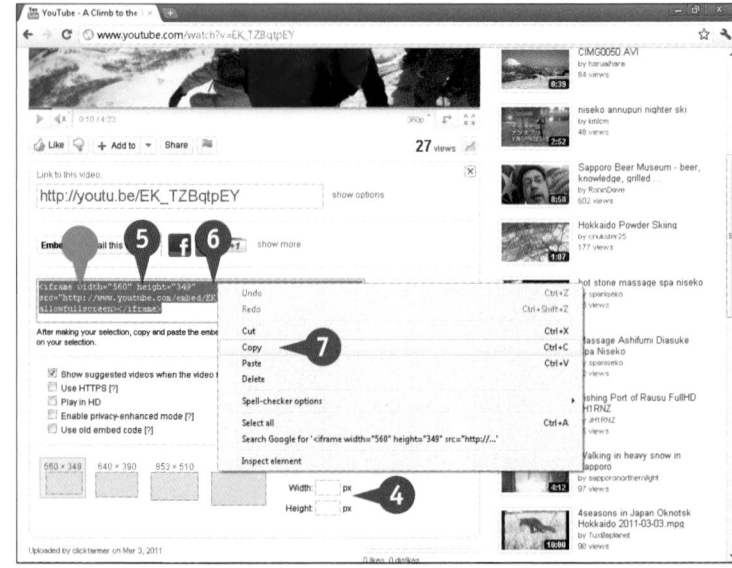

8 Open the HTML5 document in which you want to embed the video.

9 In your HTML5 code, click where you want to insert the video.

10 Click **Edit**.

11 Click **Paste**.

The video HTML is inserted.

12 Save your HTML document

13 Open the document in a browser.

● The video clip appears on the page with controls for playing the video.

TIPS

Can I embed any YouTube video in my page?
When you put a video on YouTube, you can control whether that video can be embedded on other pages. The embed feature works only for videos that have the embedded setting turned on. For YouTube videos, embedding is allowed unless you explicitly disallow it.

How do I change the dimensions of the video?
The YouTube code includes an `<iframe>` tag for embedding the video. You can change the dimensions of the video by changing the `width` and `height` attributes in the `<iframe>` tag. You can also choose from popular sizes or specify a custom size with the options on the YouTube page.

CHAPTER 15

Publishing Your Web Pages

Are you ready to place your HTML5 document on the web? This chapter shows you how to find a web host and transfer your files to a server using FTP client software. After the files are transferred, users can view your pages with a web browser. This chapter also explains how to register a domain name for your website and fix common problems on your pages.

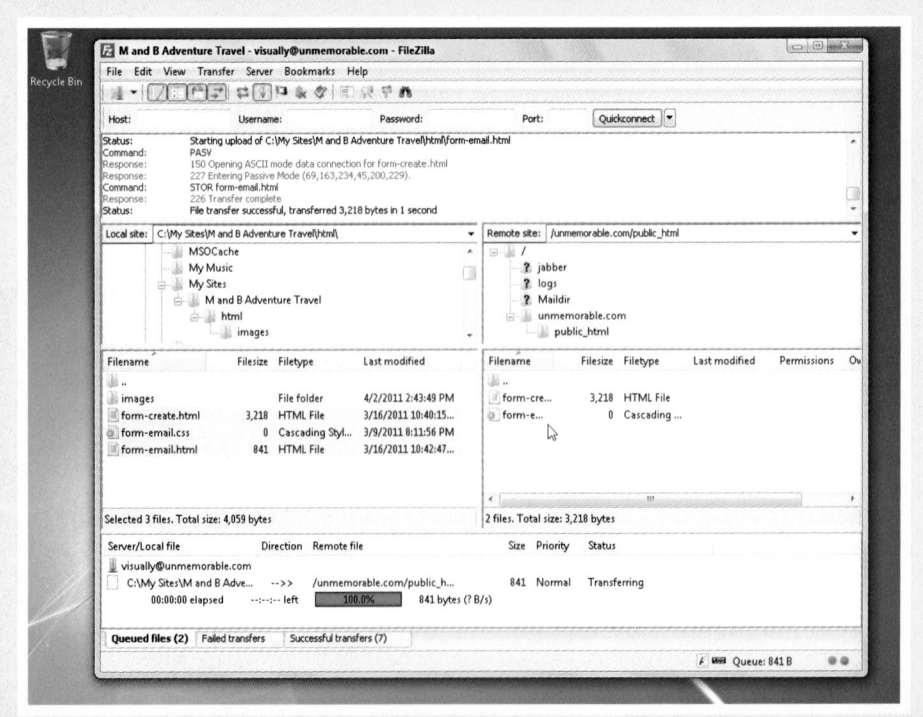

Understanding Web Page Publishing

The final phase of creating a website is publishing your pages. When it comes to building websites, the term *publishing* refers to all the necessary steps you must take to make your HTML5 documents, images, and other content available to others. This includes finding a service provider to host your pages and registering a domain name. The final step is to transfer the files for your pages from your local computer to a web server at your service provider.

Web Hosts

To place your pages on the web, you need a web server — an Internet-connected computer specifically set up to store and manage web pages. Unless you have your own web server, you need to find a service provider that will give you access to one. These companies are commonly called *web hosts* because they provide the computers that host your HTML documents and other files. Sometimes the same company that you receive Internet access from also includes hosting services as part of the package. Checking with them first could save you money.

Determining Your Needs

Before you start looking for a web host, first determine what features and services you need. For example, how much storage space do you anticipate using for your website? Although HTML documents are generally small in size, images and multimedia files included with web pages can consume large amounts of space. Does your site require e-commerce features such as an online shopping cart or a secure server for handling confidential information? How about advanced web technologies such CGI scripts, PHP, and database access? Do you need to keep track of web statistics, such as who visits your site and how often? Knowing your needs beforehand can help you find the right host.

Finding a Web Host

The best place to start looking for a host is with your existing Internet service provider. If it does not offer web hosting services, you can look for a web host on the Internet. For example, *Web Host Magazine & Buyer's Guide* (www.webhostmagazine.com) can help you compare offerings. Also consider asking friends and family for recommendations. When publishing your first website, technical support is often important, so you might consider paying extra for a host that has a good track record in that area.

Acquiring Your Own Domain Name

An Internet domain name, such as wiley.com, can give your website a personalized address that is easy for users to remember. You can register for a domain name through a domain name registrar, of which there are hundreds. Your web host may also offer domain registration services, sometimes for a reduced fee because you are already a customer. Once you acquire a domain name, you can associate the name with your website by setting up domain name service, or *DNS*, with your web host. This enables you to use your custom domain name rather than the host's in the web addresses for your pages. For more information, see "Look Up a Domain Name." After you register a domain name, you can also use it for e-mail.

Transferring Files

After you set up an account with a web host, you can transfer your HTML5 files, images, and other content to the server to set up your website. Transferring files from your computer to a web server is called *uploading*. Depending on your server, you can transfer files using FTP (File Transfer Protocol) or a web interface provided by your hosting service. More often than not, you use FTP to upload your files.

FTP Programs

FTP is a standard method for transferring files over the Internet. To transfer files with FTP, you need an FTP program, also called a *client*. You can find free and inexpensive FTP clients on the Internet. Popular

FTP programs include FileZilla (filezilla-project.org), WS_FTP (www.ipswitchft.com) and CuteFTP (www.globalscape.com/cuteftp). Also, check your web host to see what FTP clients or file-uploading tools it recommends. See the section "Transfer Files to a Web Server with FileZilla" for more information.

Maintaining Your Site

After you upload your pages, you can view and test your site. One of your chores as a web developer is to maintain your website. Keeping your information and links current is up to you. Regularly testing your site for broken links is good practice. See the section "Troubleshoot Your Web Pages" to learn more about fixing page problems. It is also good practice to update your content on a regular basis or give it a fresh look from time to time. Stale data can keep visitors from returning to your site.

Look Up a Domain Name

Registering a custom domain name gives viewers an easy-to-remember way to get to your website. You can look up the status of a domain name at a *domain name registrar*, which is a company that provides domain registration services. If the domain name is available, you can register it. If it is not available, you can check who owns it and when the registration expires via a WHOIS search. Domain names are classified by the characters that follow the dot in their names, also known as *extensions*. Although the .com, .net, and .org extensions are the most popular, you can also choose from dozens of other extensions.

Look Up a Domain Name

Check Availability

1. Visit the website of a domain name registrar.

   This example uses Network Solutions at www.networksolutions.com. Most registrars have a similar lookup process.

2. Type a name in the search box.

3. Click one or more extensions to check (☐ changes to ☑).

   A domain name can have up to 63 characters and can include letters, numbers, and hyphens.

4. Click **Search**.

The domain name registrar looks up the availability of the domain name and returns the results.

- Typically, a registrar offers multiple domain extensions and checks the availability of all of them.

5. Select one or more extensions to register (☐ changes to ☑).

6. Click **Add Selected to Cart** to begin the registration process.

   The registration process includes submitting contact information, paying for the registration, and possibly adding related services.

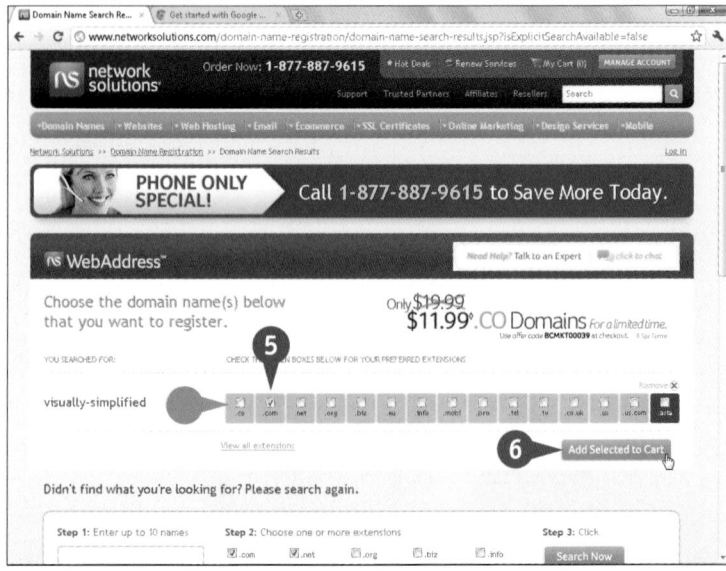

Check Registration Information

① Visit a website that offers WHOIS lookup services.

WHOIS is an Internet protocol for checking domain name information.

This example uses the Network Solutions WHOIS service at www.networksolutions.com/whois.

② Type a domain name.

③ Click **Domain Name** (○ changes to ●).

④ Click **Search**.

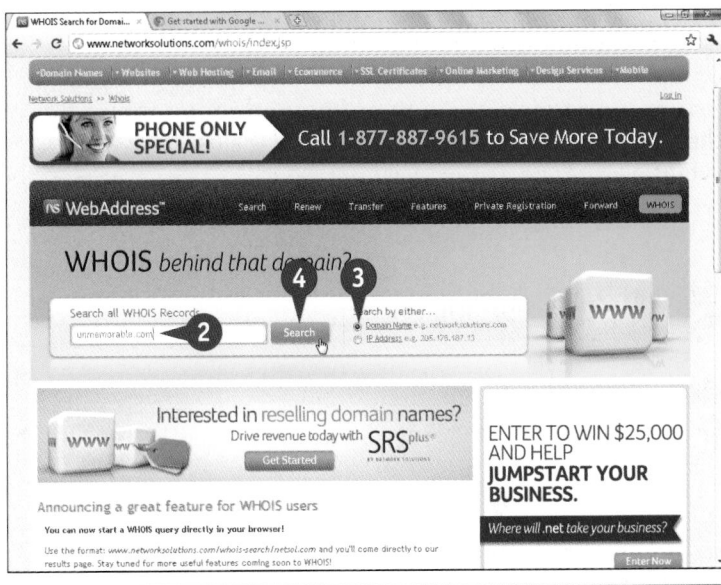

The service returns the registration information for the domain name.

⑤ Scroll down the page.

● The page displays the contact and website status.

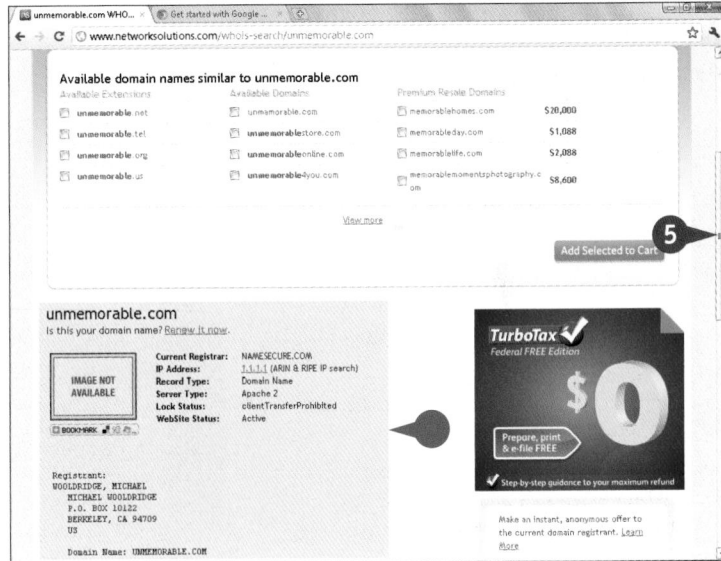

Transfer Files to a Web Server with FileZilla

You can transfer your web page files to a web server using FTP software. FTP stands for *File Transfer Protocol*, which is a method for moving files on the Internet. In this section, you learn how to transfer files using FileZilla, a popular free program for transferring web files. If you use another FTP program, your steps may differ. Once you transfer your HTML files, images, style sheets, and other supporting files to the web server, you can view your pages on the Internet using a web browser.

Transfer Files to a Web Server with FileZilla

Set Up Your Connection

1 Open the FileZilla program window. If you have not opened FileZilla before, you may need to click **OK** on the first screen.

Note: If you have not downloaded and installed the program, visit filezilla-project.org. Download the client version of FileZilla.

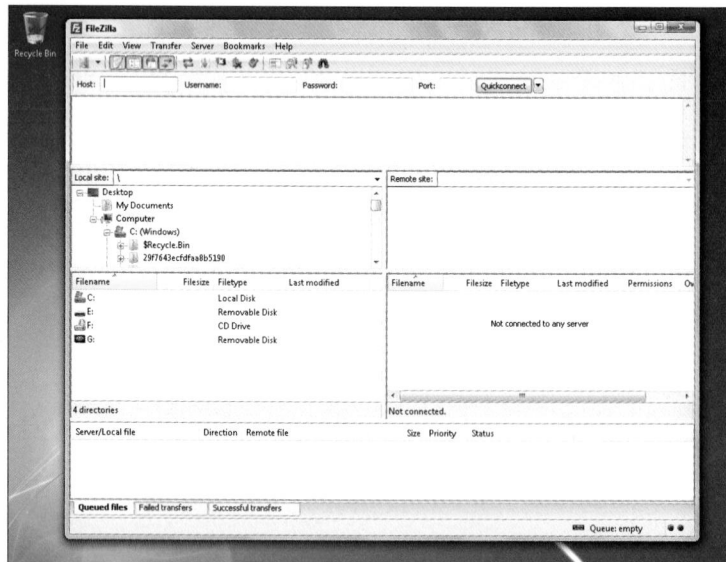

2 Click **File**.

3 Click **Site Manager**.

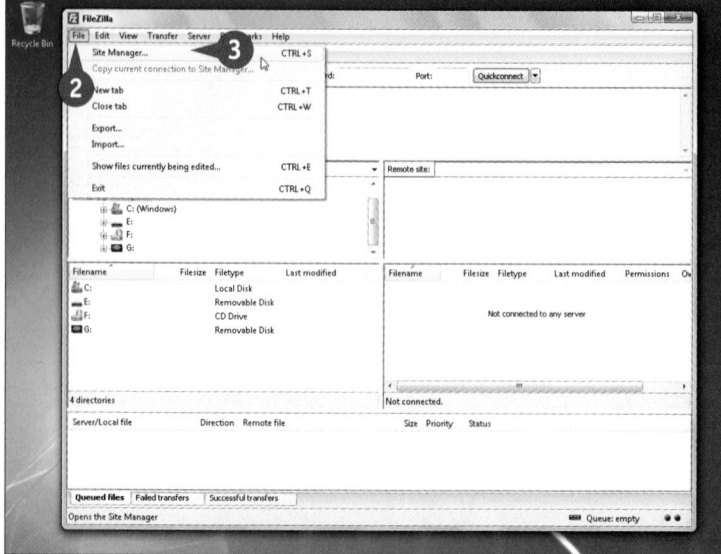

The Site Manager window opens.

④ Click **New Site** and type a name for your connection. This can be the name of your website.

⑤ Type your host name or IP address. This information will be several words or numbers separated by periods (.).

If you do not know the host name or IP address, contact your service provider for more information.

Typically, you receive this information when you sign up for an account.

⑥ Select a connection type, or protocol.

The default and most common type for transferring files is FTP.

⑦ To access an FTP server that requires a username and password, click here and select **Normal**.

⑧ Type your username.

⑨ Type your user password.

If you do not know your user ID or password, contact your service provider.

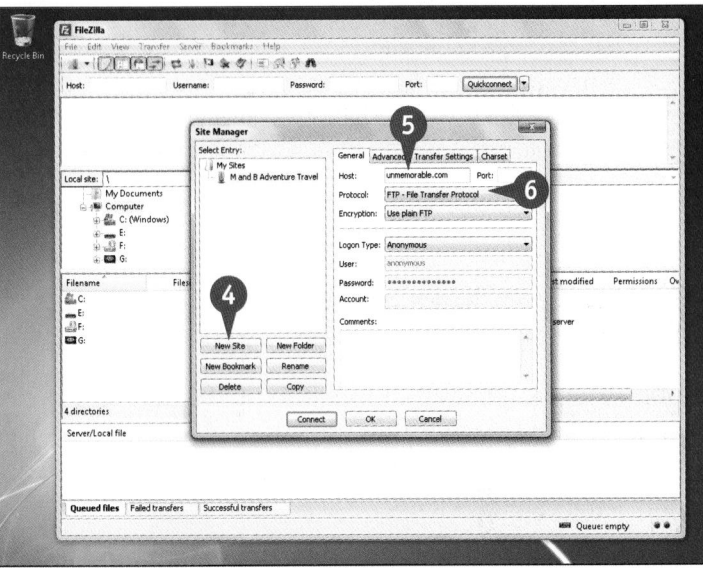

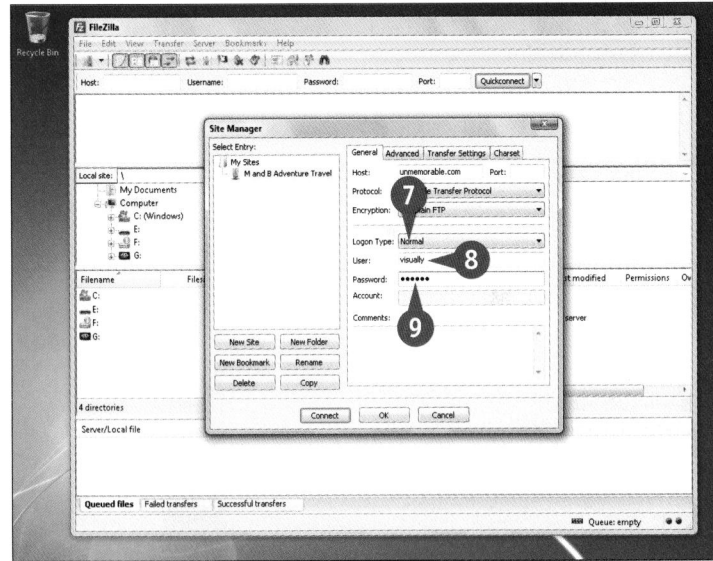

TIPS

Where can I find an FTP program?
You can find a variety of downloadable FTP programs on the Internet, including freeware and shareware programs. Download.com (www.download.com) is a popular site for obtaining such programs. Many programs offer a free trial version you can experiment with to see if you want to purchase the full version.

What information do I need to connect to my server with an FTP program?
Most servers ask you for a server address, a username, and a password. When you create an account with a web host provider, you are assigned this information, including a destination folder on the server's directory. You can use this folder to store your HTML files, along with any image and multimedia files you include with your web page.

continued ▶ **299**

After you establish your server connection, you can start transferring files. The top pane in the FileZilla program window shows the status of your connection. Below the top pane are four more panes. The left two panes display the folders and files on your computer, and the right two panes display the folders and files on the server. You can move files between your computer and the server by dragging and dropping files in the panes. The bottom pane shows the status of file transfers in progress.

You can upload a single file or multiple files. Any time you need to update your site, you can transfer more files from your computer to the server.

Transfer Files to a Web Server with FileZilla (continued)

- You can click **Connect** to immediately open your connection to the FTP server.

⑩ Click **OK** to save the site connection information and connect later.

Your connection information is saved and the program window remains open and ready for any file transfer activities you want to perform.

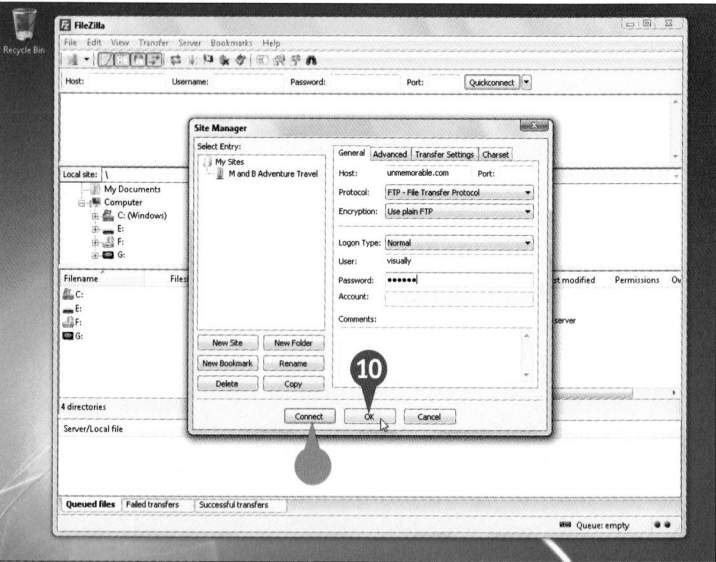

Transfer Files

① If you have not connected to your server, click **File** and then **Site Manager**.

The Site Manager window opens.

Note: You must connect to the Internet before transferring files.

② Click your connection name from the list.

③ Click **Connect**.

The Site Manager window closes.

FileZilla connects your computer to the server.

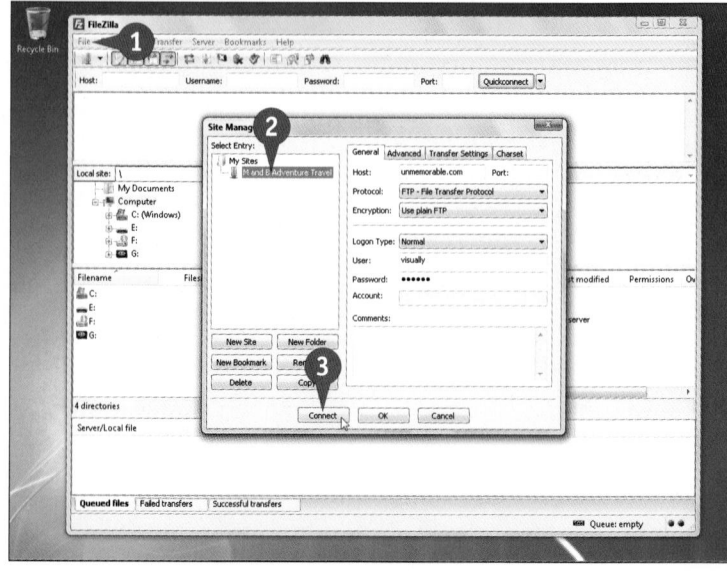

④ Navigate to the folder on your computer that contains your HTML and other site files.

● You may need to navigate to a special folder on the server where website files are stored. Check with your web host for details.

⑤ Click the files to transfer.

To select multiple files, press and hold **Ctrl** while clicking the filenames.

⑥ Click and drag the files to the destination folder.

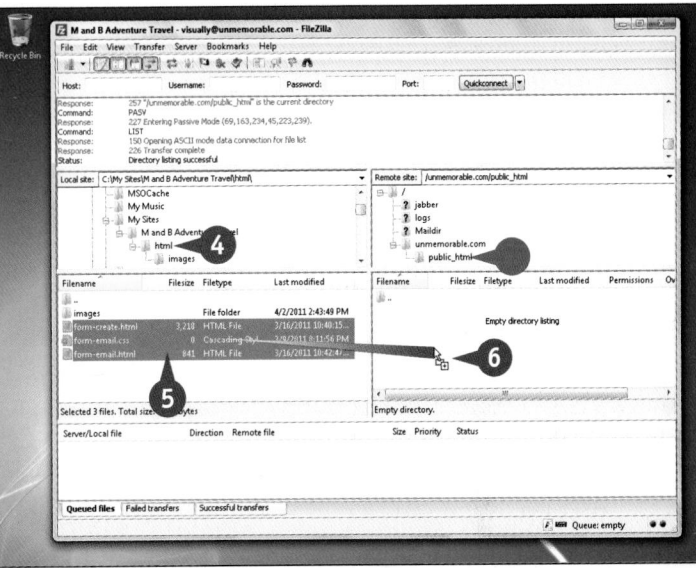

● FileZilla shows status messages as it transfers the files. The transfer may take several minutes.

● The transferred files appear in the list of server files.

⑦ Click **Close** (✕) to exit the program when you finish transferring files.

You can now use your browser to view the pages.

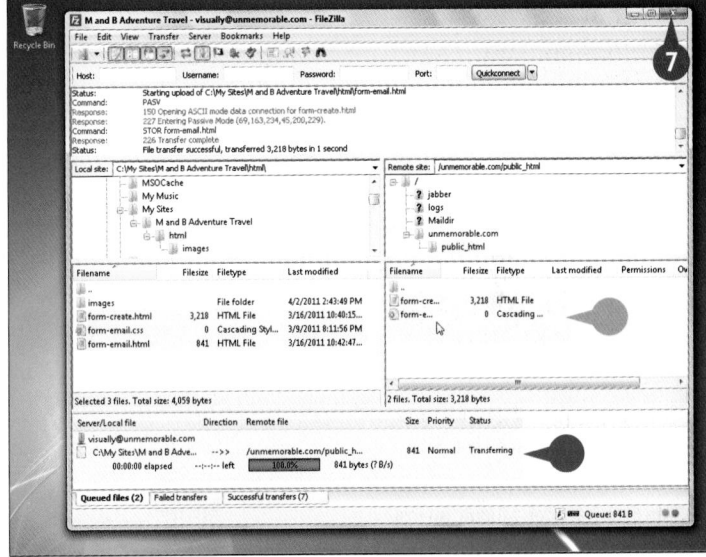

How do I remove a file from my website?
Open your connection to the server, select from the web server pane the file you want to delete, and press the delete button (**Del**). A prompt box appears asking if you really want to remove the file. Click **Yes** to remove the file from the server.

What address do I use to access my newly published page?
The address you type in your browser to access your page depends on the domain name for your site, the name of your HTML file, and the location of the file on the server. If your domain name is example.com, your HTML file is page.html, and you uploaded the file to the main HTML folder on the server, your address might be something like http://www.example.com/page.html. Contact your service provider for more details. For more about web addresses, see Chapter 7.

Troubleshoot Your Web Pages

No matter how carefully you create your pages, errors can creep in. If your web page does not appear properly in a browser, you must track down the problem. In most situations, you can track the problem to a common coding error. If you cannot find the error even after a thorough check, you can share your document with another web developer for feedback or submit your code to an HTML5 validator.

Typing Errors

Typing errors are the most common mistake in HTML5 documents. Web browsers ignore tags they do not recognize, so always start your troubleshooting process with a careful proofread of your document. Read each line in your document, paying close attention to tags and attributes. One mistyped character, quotation mark, or bracket can cause a browser to display a broken page. Many web editors color-code HTML to help you find such errors.

Invalid Paths and Extensions

Typing the wrong path to a file can cause an error on your pages. This can occur in hyperlinks, image and multimedia tags, and references to CSS and script files. If a server cannot locate a file on the web server, it cannot access or display the corresponding content. When page content does not appear as expected, double-check your text for the correct paths. Using the correct file extensions when specifying files, such as .css for style sheets, is also essential.

Broken Links

Even if the paths to your links are syntactically correct, that does not guarantee that the file on the corresponding server is still there. Nothing is more frustrating to web page visitors than clicking a nonfunctioning link, so test your links on a regular basis. Because pages come and go on the web, make it a regular practice to check your links.

404. That's an error.

The requested URL /doesnotexist.html was not found on this server. That's all we know.

Missing Image Files

If the web browser cannot display your images, you may have entered the wrong filename. Verify your image name, making sure you typed the correct upper- and lowercase letters for the filename. It is also common to type the wrong file extension for an image file, such as typing .gif instead of .jpg. Remember, not all browsers support all kinds of image files. Be sure to stick with formats commonly found on the web. See Chapter 6 to learn more.

HTML5 Tags Do Not Work

As this book is being written, the specifications for HTML5 are still being debated by the standards organizations, and no browser supports all of the HTML5 tags. Many older browsers do not support *any* HTML5 tags. If you open an HTML5 page and content is missing, it might be because your browser does not yet support the tags. For example, some browsers may not display multimedia inserted with the new `<video>` (●) and `<audio>` tags. Other browsers may not display the new form fields. To address this, you can provide alternative content for older browsers. See Chapter 14 for tips on offering multimedia alternatives. For additional tips, perform an online search for "HTML5 graceful degradation."

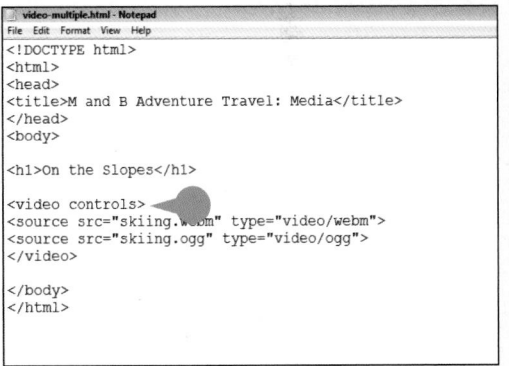

HTML Validators

After you upload your pages, you can access an HTML5 validator and have it automatically download and process your page content. Because most validators reference the official HTML5 specification, they can point out syntax errors and tell you if you are coding to the latest official standard. The W3C, which maintains HTML5 specifications, offers a validation service at http://validator.w3.org. To ensure that a validator checks your code correctly, make sure your HTML5 page includes a document declaration. See Chapter 2 for details.

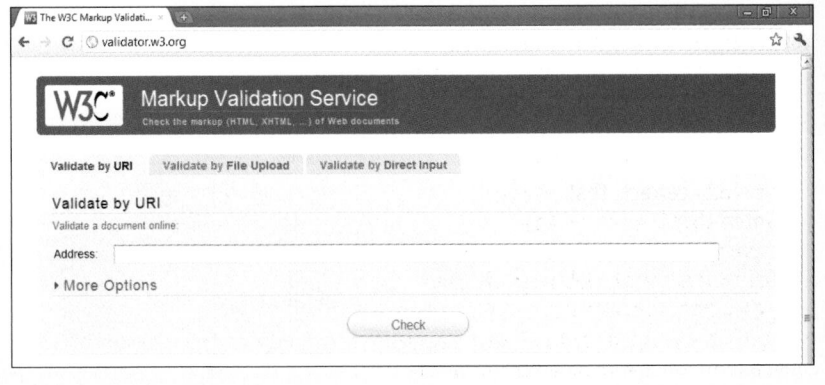

HTML Reference

Basic Tags/Attributes

Tag/Attribute	Description
<!-- -->	Defines a comment
<!DOCTYPE html>	Indicates that HTML5 is used on a page
<body>	Contains the content appearing on a page
 	Creates a line break
<h1>, <h2>, <h3>, <h4>, <h5>, <h6>	Creates heading levels
<head>	Contains the page title, style sheets, scripts, and metadata
<html>	Identifies an HTML document
<meta>	Defines extra information, or *metadata*, for a page
content	Defines the metadata content
name	Defines the type of metadata
<p>	Defines a paragraph
<title>	Creates a title for a Web page

Text Formatting Tags/Attributes

Tag/Attribute	Description
<abbr>	Defines abbreviated text
title	Defines the abbreviated term
<address>	Defines contact information for a page
<b>	Creates bold text
<base>	Defines the default target for links on a page
<target>	Defines the link target
<blockquote>	Sets text off from the main flow
<cite>	Defines a citation
<code>	Defines computer code
<del>	Defines deleted text
<dfn>	Defines a defined term
<em>	Emphasizes text
<hgroup>	Groups titles and subtitles on a page
<i>	Creates italic text
<ins>	Defines inserted text
<kbd>	Defines keyboard text
<mark>	Defines marked, or highlighted, text
<pre>	Retains preformatted spacing in text
<q>	Defines text as quoted

Tag/Attribute	Description
<small>	Distinguishes less important text on a page
<samp>	Defines sample computer code
<strong>	Defines important text
<sub>	Defines subscripted text
<sup>	Defines superscripted text
<time>	Marks text as a date or time

List Tags/Attributes

Tag/Attribute	Description
<dd>	Identifies a definition in a definition list
<dl>	Defines a definition list of terms
<dt>	Identifies a term in a definition list
<li>	Identifies an item in an ordered or unordered list
<ol>	Defines an ordered list
start	Defines a start number for an ordered list
type	Defines a number style for an ordered list
reversed	Reverses the numbering order for an ordered list
<ul>	Defines an unordered list

Image and Canvas Tags/Attributes

Tag/Attribute	Description
<canvas>	Defines a canvas area for drawing on a page
height	Defines the height of a canvas
width	Defines the width of a canvas
<figcaption>	Defines a caption for a figure
<figure>	Defines an image as a figure
<hr>	Creates a horizontal rule
<img>	Inserts an image on a page
alt	Displays alternative text when an image cannot be displayed
height	Defines the height of an image
src	Specifies the location of the image file
title	Defines a label for an image
width	Defines the width of an image
<meter>	Displays a graphic showing a value within a range
<progress>	Displays a graphic showing progress toward a goal

HTML Reference

Tag/Attribute	Description
<a>	Creates a link to another page or resource
href	Specifies the location of a linked page or other resource
target	Specifies where linked information appears
rel	Defines a relationship between a link and the current page
id	Defines the destination for a link on the same page

Tag/Attribute	Description
<caption>	Adds a caption to a table
<table>	Creates a table
<td>	Defines a data cell in a table
colspan	Combines two or more cells across columns
rowspan	Combines two or more cells down rows
<th>	Defines a header cell in a table
colspan	Combines two or more header cells across columns
rowspan	Combines two or more header cells down rows
<tr>	Defines a row in a table

Tag/Attribute	Description
<button>	Creates a clickable button
type	Defines the type of button
<form>	Creates a form
action	Specifies the location of a CGI script for a form
enctype	Specifies how form data is encoded for sending to a server
method	Specifies how form information is sent to a server
<input>	Creates an input item in a form
checked	Defines a radio button or check box as selected
max	Sets the maximum value for a form item
maxlength	Sets the maximum number of characters allowed in a form item

Tag/Attribute	Description
min	Sets the minimum value for a form item
name	Identifies a form item for the server
pattern	Defines a pattern for validating form content
required	Identifies a form item that must have a value
size	Defines the size of a form item
step	Sets the increment for a form item
type	Defines the type of form item
value	Identifies the value of a form item for the server
<label>	Labels a form element
for	Specifies the form item to which a label belongs
<option>	Creates an option in a selectable menu
selected	Defines a menu option as selected
value	Identifies the value of a menu option for a server
<select>	Creates a selectable menu in a form
name	Identifies a form menu for a server
size	Defines the number of options displayed in a list menu
<textarea>	Creates a large text area in a form
cols	Specifies the width of a text area
name	Identifies a form text area for a server
rows	Defines the height of a text area
wrap	Defines text wrapping behavior in a text area

JavaScript Tags/Attributes

Tag/Attribute	Description
id	Identifies an element for referencing by scripts
<noscript>	Defines alternative content for browsers that cannot run scripts
<output>	Defines the output of a script calculation
<script>	Adds a script to a Web page
src	Specifies the location of the script file
type	Identifies the type of script

HTML Reference

Multimedia Tags/Attributes

Tag/Attribute	Description
<audio>	Adds an audio clip to a page
autoplay	Causes an audio clip to automatically play when a page loads
controls	Displays controls with an audio clip
loop	Controls whether an audio clip repeats
preload	Causes an audio clip to automatically load when a page loads
src	Specifies the location of the audio file
<embed>	Provides an alternative way to add media to a page
height	Defines the height of embedded media
src	Specifies the location of the embedded media file
width	Defines the width of embedded media
<object>	Provides an alternative way to add media to a page
classid	Identifies the class ID of the object being embedded, and is used to add video and audio in the browsers that do not support HTML5
height	Defines the height of a media object
width	Defines the width of a media object
<param>	Defines a parameter for a media object
src	Specifies the location of the media object file, and is used to add video and audio in the browsers that do not support HTML5
<source>	Defines the source of audio or video content
src	Specifies the location of audio or video file
type	Defines the type of media file
<video>	Adds a video to a page
autoplay	Causes a video to automatically play when a page loads
controls	Displays controls with a video
height	Defines the height of a video
loop	Controls whether a video repeats
preload	Causes video to automatically load when the page loads
src	Specifies the location of the video file
width	Defines the width of a video

Tag/Attribute	Description
<article>	Defines a self-contained composition
<aside>	Defines tangential information on a page
<footer>	Defines boilerplate information at the end of a page or section
<header>	Defines title and introductory information
<nav>	Defines important navigation links
<section>	Defines related content on a page

Style Sheet Tags/Attributes

Tag/Attribute	Description
class	Applies style rules to page elements
id	Uniquely identifies a page element for adding style rules
style	Applies style rules to an element as an attribute value
<div>	Defines block-level content for adding style rules
<span>	Defines inline content for adding style rules
<link>	Links a page to an external style sheet
href	Defines the location of an external style sheet
rel	Defines the type of link
type	Specifies the type of style sheet
<style>	Defines an internal style sheet

Style Sheet Selectors

Selector	Description
.classname	Defines a style sheet class with the name classname.
#idname	Applies style rules to content having the ID idname.
a:active	Selects links that are actively being clicked
a:hover	Selects links that are being hovered over
a:link	Selects unvisited links on a page
a:visited	Selects links that were previously clicked

HTML Reference

Style Sheet Properties

Property	Description
background	Defines a background color or image
background-color	Defines a background color
border	Defines a border
border-color	Defines a border color
border-spacing	Controls the amount of space between borders in a table
border-style	Defines a border style
border-width	Defines a line thickness for a border
color	Defines the color of text
float	Aligns an element to the side and wraps content around it
font	Applies multiple styles at once to text
font-family	Defines a font
font-size	Defines the font size
font-style	Styles text as italic
font-weight	Styles text as bold
height	Defines the height of an element
left	Positions an element relative to the left side of its enclosure
letter-spacing	Defines the spacing between letters
line-height	Defines line spacing
list-style-image	Specifies an image to be used as list bullets
list-style-type	Defines a bullet style for lists
margin	Sets the spacing outside the borders of an element
overflow	Controls how to display text extending outside an element
padding	Sets the spacing between the content and borders of an element
position	Defines the type of positioning for an element
text-align	Aligns text
text-decoration	Adds underlining, overlining, line-through, or blinking to text
text-indent	Indents the first line of text
text-transform	Changes the text case
top	Positions an element relative to the top of its enclosure
width	Defines the width of an element
z-index	Defines the overlap index of a page element

HTML5 Colors

Color	Name
	Black (#000000)
	Silver (#c0c0c0)
	Gray (#808080)
	White (#ffffff)
	Maroon (#800000)
	Red (#ff0000)
	Purple (#800080)
	Fuchsia (#ff00ff)
	Green (#008000)
	Lime (#00ff00)
	Olive (#808000)
	Yellow (#ffff00)
	Navy (#000080)
	Blue (#0000ff)
	Teal (#008080)
	Aqua (#00ffff)

Index

Numbers

3-D table borders, 141

A

abbreviations, defining, 49

absolute links, 116

absolute positioning, 196, 202–203

absolute size, 198

alert message boxes, displaying with JavaScript, 237

alignment, 84, 154–155, 208–209, 283

alternative text, 95, 100

Android-specific style sheets, linking to, 73

animating content on canvases, 270–273

articles, defining, 218–219

asides, defining, 224–225

aspect ratio, resizing video to same, 282

attributes, 11. *See also* HTML tags/attributes

audio, 276, 280–281. *See also* multimedia

author names, adding, 28

authoring programs, specifying, 29

autocompletion, preventing, 181

B

backgrounds

color, adding, 88–89, 148, 149

images, adding, 110–111

music, adding, 281

for navigation links, 223

of tables, 137

blank spaces, inserting, 36

block quotes, adding, 41

block-level HTML5 tags, 196

body, 19

bold text, creating, 37

borders, table, 137, 140–141, 143, 159

box model, 196

broken links, troubleshooting, 302

browsers. *See* web browsers

bulleted lists, 46, 90–91

C

calculations, displaying with JavaScript, 246–247

canvases

accessing, 250

adding scripts, 250

animating content, 270–273

circles, drawing, 256–257

context, setting up, 250

defining, 250

drawing content on, 251

general discussion, 13

gradients, adding, 266–267

HTML tags/attributes, 305

images on, 262–263, 264–265

lines, drawing, 258–259

measuring with coordinates, 251

rectangles, drawing, 254–255

rotating content, 268–269

setting up, 252–253

styles, defining, 251

text, drawing, 260–261

captions, adding table, 147

Cascading Style Sheets (CSS). *See* CSS styles

case, changing text, 21, 85

cells, table

background color, adding, 148

extending, 156, 157

height, setting, 145

horizontal alignment, setting, 152

merging, 156

overview, 136

padding, 142

spanning, 136

vertical alignment, setting, 153

width, setting, 144

center alignment, table, 155

centering images, 104, 106, 209

CGI scripts, 162

check boxes, 164, 172–173

circles, drawing, 256–257

There's a Visual book
for every learning level...

Simplified®

The place to start if you're new to computers. Full color.

- Computers
- Creating Web Pages
- Digital Photography
- Excel
- Internet
- Laptops
- Mac OS
- Office
- PCs
- Windows
- Word

Teach Yourself VISUALLY™

Get beginning to intermediate-level training in a variety of topics. Full color.

- Access
- Algebra
- Astronomy
- Bass Guitar
- Beadwork
- Bridge
- Car Care and Maintenance
- Chess
- Circular Knitting
- Collage & Altered Art
- Computers
- Crafting with Kids
- Crocheting
- Digital Photography
- Digital Video
- Dog Training
- Drawing
- Dreamweaver
- Excel
- Flash
- Golf
- Guitar
- Hand Dyeing
- Handspinning
- HTML
- iLife
- iPad
- iPhone
- iPhoto
- Jewelry Making & Beading
- Knitting
- Lightroom
- Macs
- Mac OS
- Office
- Outlook
- Photoshop
- Photoshop Elements
- Piano
- Poker
- PowerPoint
- Quilting
- Scrapbooking
- Sewing
- Web Design
- Windows
- Wireless Networking
- Word
- WordPress

Top 100 Simplified® Tips & Tricks

Tips and techniques to take your skills beyond the basics. Full color.

- Digital Photography
- eBay
- Excel
- Google
- Office
- Photoshop
- Photoshop Elements
- PowerPoint
- Windows

...all designed for visual learners—just like you!

Master VISUALLY®

Your complete visual reference. Two-color interior.

- 3ds Max
- Creating Web Pages
- Dreamweaver and Flash
- Excel
- iPod and iTunes
- Mac OS
- Office
- Optimizing PC Performance
- Windows
- Windows Server

Visual Blueprint™

Where to go for professional-level programming instruction. Two-color interior.

- ActionScript
- Ajax
- ASP.NET 2.0
- Excel Data Analysis
- Excel Pivot Tables
- Excel Programming
- HTML
- JavaScript
- Mambo
- Mobile App Development
- Perl and Apache
- PHP & MySQL
- SEO
- Ubuntu Linux
- Vista Sidebar
- Visual Basic
- XML

Visual™ Quick Tips

Shortcuts, tricks, and techniques for getting more done in less time. Full color.

- Beading
- Crochet
- Digital Photography
- Excel
- Golf
- Internet
- iPhone
- iPod & iTunes
- Knitting
- Mac OS
- Office
- Paper Crafts
- PowerPoint
- Quilting
- Sewing
- Windows
- Wire Jewelry

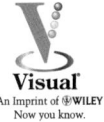

Visual®
An Imprint of ⊕**WILEY**
Now you know.

For a complete listing of Visual books, go to wiley.com/go/visual